Rebound 1985

Understanding
DEATH & DYING
An Interdisciplinary Approach

Alfred
PUBLISHING CO., INC

Understanding
DEATH & DYING
An Interdisciplinary Approach

SANDRA GALDIERI WILCOX and MARILYN SUTTON

California State College, Dominguez Hills

Published by Alfred Publishing Co., Inc.,
75 Channel Drive, Port Washington, N.Y. 11050

Copyright © 1977 by Alfred Publishing Co., Inc.
All rights reserved.

Printed in the United States of America

Library of Congress Cataloging in Publication Data
Main entry under title:

Understanding death and dying.

Includes bibliographies.
1. Death—Addresses, essays, lectures.
I. Wilcox, Sandra, 1943-   II. Sutton, Marilyn,
1944-
BD444.U47   128'.5   76-30406
ISBN 0-88284-052-5

for
Stephen, Paul, and Matthew

CONTENTS

TWO: THE EXPERIENCE OF DYING

THREE: GRIEF, MOURNING, AND SOCIAL FUNCTIONS

FOUR: DEATH AND THE CHILD

FIVE: CHOICES AND DECISIONS IN DEATH

EPILOGUE

APPENDICIES

INDEX

PREFACE

A class in thanatology is likely to appeal to diverse interests. The student of death and dying might be a curious but slightly scared twenty-year-old; the mother of teen-age children wanting to prepare herself and her family for future crises; the nurse or paramedic wanting to improve patient care; the social worker who regularly sees the impact of violent death on the family; the teacher whose small pupils are in the process of discovering death; the widow who is seeking answers for herself as well as skills for helping others; the clergyman who must console bereaved families; or the funeral director who wants to improve his services to the community. Several disciplines—particularly medicine and the social sciences—offer college courses in death and dying. Often, one- and two-day workshops sponsored by university extension divisions, churches or hospitals stimulate an interest in further study.

Understanding Death and Dying can be adapted to any of these interests and uses. The readings from many fields collected in this introductory survey include experience-based pieces that ground the discussion of death and dying to realistic situations, theoretical statements that develop cognitive skills and analyses that suggest guides for intervention. The chapters in the text have been arranged to lead the student through a studied progression from initial definition to active choice.

Chapter Organization

As the overall book leads the reader from self-study to ultimate reappraisal and action, each chapter proceeds through a somewhat analogous pattern, opening with an encounter followed by multi-disciplinary academic readings and closing with one or more structured exercises.

Encounter—The encounter, whether it is a brief set of questions as in Chapter One, a news account as in Chapter Five or short samples of children's writing as in Chapter Four, brings the dominant themes of the chapter into focus, to root theoretical concepts in actual experience and to provoke interest that will result in questions.

Readings—Each reading is introduced by a brief headline which places each piece within the structure of the chapter. The readings present key concepts in the social sciences (psychology, sociology) and medicine (psychiatry and nursing) as well as in gerontology and social welfare. They outline the germinal concepts in a study of death and dying and embed these concepts in a context provided by the history of ideas.

Questions and Projects—The questions and projects placed at the end of each chapter help the student to assimilate the ideas in the readings and to integrate information from several readings. Where the questions ask the students to synthesize ideas presented in the chapter, the projects lead the students beyond the readings to further research and independent study. They invite the student to apply the tools of research and patterns of investigation accepted in the social sciences. The projects have been selected to allow for a number of levels of sophistication; some can be used to introduce students to the ways a professional in the discipline investigates a topic; others can be expanded to provide a serious research problem for the more advanced student.

Structured Exercises—The structured exercises at the close of each chapter provide the instructor with a ready means to tie together the concepts introduced in the readings and the student with a means to apply those concepts to his own life through a structured personal growth experience.

For Further Reading—In a relatively new field where the instructor may not feel prepared to select the most appropriate support material, the five or six most useful resources for each chapter are listed. The bibliographies taken as a whole provide an introductory survey of the field of thanatology.

Appendices—The three appendices provide additional teaching aids that instructors might not otherwise have readily at hand. They include materials necessary for the structured exercises, examples of forms and tables which present statistical and legal aspects of death, suggestions for specific topics the individual instructor might select to expand the coverage of his course as well as an annotated list of multi-media resources and ordering information.

ACKNOWLEDGEMENTS

We wish to thank Bill Knowles for his early encouragement and Emmett Dingley together with his colleagues at Alfred Publishing Company for their continued enthusiasm and professional counsel. We also warmly acknowledge the contributions of children at St. Toribius, Annunciation, and St. Emydius Schools in Los Angeles for their writings represented in the Chapter Four Encounter.

NOTE TO THE INSTRUCTOR
The Use of Structured Exercises in the Classroom

The structured exercises have been arranged topically at the end of each chapter throughout the course. Most exercises can be adapted to fit topics in other chapters. The kidney machine exercise in Chapter One, for example, could be equally effective as a closing activity for Chapter Five if the instructor led the class to focus on a different aspect of the exercise or modified the discussion questions. The students could be asked, for instance, to role-play the patients rather than the hospital committee and the decision under study might be "Who will accept the treatment?" and "Why?" rather than "Who will be given the opportunity of the treatment?"

The instructor should note that some of the exercises are constructed to pull latent attitudes, and for that reason potentially volatile terms are included. The instructor who has had little experience in conducting such experiences might wish to schedule a separate "experience" group where a staff member of the campus Counseling Center or an interested and qualified colleague from the Psychology Department could assist. The "experience" group should be limited to students enrolled in the course. The relationship of the group to the regular class can be determined by the individual instructor: the group could be optional or required, or offer additional units of credit; it may meet during regularly scheduled class time, or at another time and location.

Some instructors prefer to limit the use of group experiences to an intense day-long or weekend session at the end of the course. An intense encounter of this kind should be conducted only with the participation of a qualified group leader and participation by students should be contingent upon appropriate screening methods. The American Psychological Association (1973) has provided "Guidelines for Conducting Growth Groups,"* which lists responsibilities of group leaders.

The use of group exercises in any classroom requires responsible planning and constant attention from the instructor. At the beginning of each exercise, students should be reminded that they may choose not to participate without penalty, and that they may, at any time, withdraw from parts of the exercise that they find uncomfortable or anxiety-evoking. Before the exercise begins, the class as a whole should discuss the obligation to respect each participant's needs. Even an exercise which appears emotionally innocuous may elicit anxiety in a psychologically vulnerable individual. Students often choose their courses for personal as well as for scholarly or professional reasons. In a "death and dying" class these personal reasons may involve unresolved grief, anticipatory grief, or occasionally, suicidal preoccupations. In addition, adolescents as a group tend to be "mourning at a distance" for developmental losses of their own childhood and former parental relationships as they struggle toward the independence of adulthood.

A difficult moment for one or all students may occur from time to time. In such cases the students themselves can

---

*A P A Guidelines for Psychologists Conducting Growth Groups, *American Psychologist*, 1973, *38*, 933.

usually be trusted to respond supportively and constructively. When tensions in the group seem to be running high, it may be helpful to stop and go around the room, allowing each student to express his opinions and feelings in turn. Other students should not interrupt or argue until everyone has had a chance to speak, though the instructor may want to sum up and reflect back to the group the thrust of a series of related comments.

Understanding
DEATH & DYING
An interdisciplinary Approach

1

The Definition and Meaning of Death

INTRODUCTION

At what moment is a human organ to be removed for transplant?

At death, our instinctive reply.

But when does death occur? And, how do we know when death occurs?

More perplexing, what is the responsibility of the living towards the dead and the dying?

A single technological development can throw us back to ancient dilemmas. For instance, social custom of centuries may dictate that disposal of the body follows on death but, given the medical resources to transplant human organs, the dictates of social custom undergo reassessment. And as they do, we as a society are forced to examine our attitudes and to seek out the assumptions that underlie those attitudes: in short, to redefine the meaning of death.

The work of this chapter will be an exploratory study, an effort to determine the meaning of the term *death* at the present time in Western culture. Efforts to discover meaning are always grand designs, but a survey of the definitions that various disciplines give to death will reveal the existing boundaries of meaning.

Historical Perspective

The scientific tradition has, in some senses, bequeathed us an adversary relationship with death. Scientific research, motivated often by an effort to conquer death and prolong life, has encouraged us to see the relationship between life and death as one of polar opposition. And though science assumes that we have biological immortality, in the sense that every creature alive today represents an "unbroken line of life that stretches back to the first primitive organism," that immortality is a continuance of the germ plasm rather than of the body. The scientist today is more likely to think of life in the same terms as Xavier Bichat, an eighteenth-century physiologist who described life as the "totality of all those functions that resist death."

Where the scientific heritage weighs death against life, the tradition of mythopoetic thought (including art, literature, philosophy and folklore) denies the polarity by employing a third category; placing death within the continuum of life, death, after-life. Death, for the philosopher, has most often suggested a transition to a different state of being: eternal sleep, a world of shades or heavenly reward. But in any case, it was a continuance.

Contemporary Situation

The concept of immortality, once accepted quite literally, has come to be interpreted symbolically by many today. Consequently, a man may see his children as his immortality in biologic terms, his life work as his social immortality and his memorialization in the arts (whether architecture, literature

4

or painting) as a form of cultural immortality. Unlike the medieval, whose guiding concern was his preparation for afterlife, the contemporary has, in the words of Nathan A. Scott, "relocated the ultimate problem of human existence from the dimension of Eternity to the dimension of time." The interest in death no longer centers on *what follows* but on the more immediate issues of *how* and *when*.

We now have the technological ability to alter the time of death, within certain limitations. In the near future we are likely to expand that control. As the power to extend life increases, the question may arise as to whether we should ever accept death. But we must remember that together with the power to extend life, we have the equally potent capacity to dilute the quality of life beyond recognition. Clinical death is no longer synonymous with *death*: it is only the most extreme of many kinds of death including the social death of the forgotten widower living in isolation and the mental death of the mongoloid child. Now the issue has become, *"What constitutes an appropriate death?"*

Appropriate Death

Though the term "appropriate death" was introduced into the study of death quite recently, notions of appropriate death can be found in most cultures. To discover how firmly entrenched present notions of appropriate death are, one need only witness the almost universal outrage at the accidental death of a child or at the violent slaying of a leader in his prime. Whether it be the Biblical "threescore and ten," the expectation of a task fulfilled or the life expectancy from a statistician's mortality table, assumptions about appropriate death *do operate* in our society.

Attitudinal research is always of interest to the social scientist, but it is of primary value in the study of death. For death must always remain unknowable, at least from personal experience. Thus, the meaning of death will depend on the meaning a particular culture gives it. To discover the meaning our own time and place give to death, we will conduct a review both of the definitions that various fields of inquiry employ and of the assessments that philosophers, poets and social scientists have offered. But before we begin that review of the thoughts of others, we might well reflect upon the personal attitudes and assumptions that we as individuals bring to the study. For that purpose, a brief set of questions is presented in the following Encounter.

ENCOUNTER

CONFRONTING YOUR DEATH

1. Who died in your first personal involvement with death?

   a. Grandparent or great-grandparent
   b. Parent
   c. Brother or sister
   d. Other family member
   e. Friend or acquaintance
   f. Stranger
   g. Public figure
   h. Animal

2. What aspect of your own death is the most distasteful to you?

   a. I could no longer have any experiences
   b. I am afraid of what might happen to my body after death
   c. I am uncertain as to what might happen to me if there is a life after death
   d. I could no longer provide for my dependents

       e.   It would cause grief to my relatives and friends
       f.   All my plans and projects would come to an end
       g.   The process of dying might be painful
       h.   Other (Specify) _____

3.   What does death mean to you?

       a.   The end, the final process of life
       b.   The beginning of a life after death; a transition, a new beginning
       c.   A joining of the spirit with a universal cosmic consciousness
       d.   A kind of endless sleep; rest and peace
       e.   Termination of this life but with survival of the spirit
       f.   Don't know
       g.   Other (Specify) _____

4.   If you had a choice, what kind of death would you prefer?

       a.   Tragic, violent death
       b.   Sudden, but not violent death
       c.   Quiet, dignified death
       d.   Death in line of duty
       e.   Death after a great achievement
       f.   Suicide
       g.   Homicidal victim
       h.   There is no "appropriate" kind of death
       i.   Other (Specify) _____

5.   If you could choose, when would you die?

       a.   In youth
       b.   In the middle prime of life
       c.   Just after the prime of life
       d.   In old age

6.   For whom or what might you be willing to sacrifice your life?

       a.   For a loved one
       b.   For an idea or a moral principle
       c.   In combat or a grave emergency where a life could be saved
       d.   Not for any reason

7. If you were told that you had a terminal disease and a limited time to live, how would you want to spend your time until you died?

    a. I would make a marked change in my life style; satisfy hedonistic needs (travel, sex, drugs, other)
    b. I would become more withdrawn; reading, contemplating or praying
    c. I would shift from a concern for my own needs to a concern for others (family, friends)
    d. I would attempt to complete projects; tie up loose ends
    e. I would make little or no change in my life-style
    f. I would try to do one very important thing
    g. I might consider committing suicide
    h. I would do none of these

8. If or when you are married, would you prefer to outlive your spouse?

    a. Yes; I would prefer to die second and outlive my spouse
    b. No; I would rather die first and have my spouse outlive me
    c. Undecided or don't know

The questions in the opening encounter are inherent in the condition of morality, but often we avoid them until a crisis. In the Phaedo, as Socrates awaits his death, his friends are compelled to face the issues of death, dying and afterlife. Their comments suggest that they have much in common with our contemporaries; typically they see death as unnatural and just as typically assume life is the natural condition. In the following selection, Socrates has worked through his reactions to dying and is ready to contemplate death as he counsels his companions.

PHAEDO: The Death Scene

Plato

CHARACTERS[1]

Socrates   Phaedo
Crito   Echecrates
Apollodorus
The Servant of the Eleven
The Executioner
Scene—The Prison of Socrates

When he had finished speaking, Crito said, "Well, Socrates, have you any instructions for your friends or for me about your children or about anything else? How can we best serve you?"

"Simply by doing what I always tell you, Crito. Take care of your own selves, and you will serve me and mine and yourselves in all that you do, even though you make no promises now. But if you are careless of your own selves, and will not follow the path of life which we have pointed out in our conversations both today and at other times, all your promises now, however profuse and earnest they are, will be of no avail."

"We will do our best," said Crito. "But how shall we bury you?"

"As you please," he answered, "only you must catch me first, and not let me escape you." And then he looked at us

From Plato: *Euthyphro, Apology, Crito,* translated by F. J. Church and revised by Robert D. Cumming, copyright ©1948, 1956, by the Liberal Arts Press, Inc., reprinted by permission of The Bobbs-Merrill Company, Inc.

with a smile and said, "My friends, I cannot convince Crito that I am the Socrates who has been conversing with you, and putting his arguments in order. He thinks that I am the body which he will presently see a corpse, and he asks how he is to bury me. All the arguments which I have used to prove that I shall not remain with you after I have drunk the poison, but that I shall go away to the happiness of the blessed—all the arguments with which I tried to comfort you and myself, have been thrown away on him. Do you therefore offer security for me to him, as he offered security for me at the trial, but in a different way. He offered security for me then that I would remain; but you must offer security to him that I shall go away when I am dead, and not remain with you. Then he will feel my death less; and when he sees my body being burnt or buried, he will not be sad because he thinks that I am suffering something terrible; and at my funeral he will not say that it is Socrates whom he is laying out, or bearing to the grave, or burying. For, dear Crito, you must know that to use words wrongly is not only a fault in itself; it also corrupts the soul. You must be of good cheer, and say that you are burying my body; and you may bury it as you please, and as you think right."

With these words he rose and went into another room to bathe. Crito went with him and told us to wait. So we waited, talking of the argument and discussing it, and then again dwelling on the greatness of the calamity which had fallen upon us; it seemed as if we were going to lose a father, and to be orphans for the rest of our life. When he had bathed, and his children had been brought to him—he had two sons quite little, and one grown up—and the women of his family were come, he spoke with them in Crito's presence, and gave them his last instructions. Then he sent the women and children away and returned to us. By that time it was near the hour of sunset, for he had been a long while within. When he came back to us from the bath he sat down, but not much was said after that. Presently the servant of The Eleven came and stood before him and said, "I know that I shall not find you unreasonable like other men, Socrates. They are angry with me and curse me when I tell them to drink the poison because the authorities order me to do it. But I have found you all along the noblest and gentlest and best man that has ever come here; and now I am sure that you will not be angry with me, but with those who you know are responsible. And so farewell, and try to bear what must be as easily as you can; you know why I have come." With that he turned away weeping, and went out.

Socrates looked up at him and replied, "Farewell, I will do as you say." Then he turned to us and said, "How courteous the man is! And the whole time that I have been here, he has constantly come in to see me, and sometimes he has talked to me, and has been the kindest of men; and now, how generously he weeps for me! Come, Crito, let us obey him; let the poison be brought if it is ready, and if it is not ready, let it be prepared."

Crito replied, "But, Socrates, I think that the sun is still upon the hills; it has not set. Besides, I know that other men take the poison quite late, and eat and drink heartily, and even enjoy the company of their chosen friends, after the announcement has been made. So do not hurry; there is still time."

Socrates replied, "And those whom you speak of, Crito, naturally do so; for they think that they will be the gainers by so doing. And I naturally shall not do so; for I think that I should gain nothing by drinking the poison a little later but my own contempt for so greedily saving up a life which is already spent. So do not refuse to do as I say."

Then Crito made a sign to his slave who was standing by; and the slave went out, and after some delay returned with the man who was to give the poison, carrying it prepared in a cup. When Socrates saw him, he asked, "You understand these things, my good man, what have I to do?"

"You have only to drink this," he replied, "and to walk about until your legs feel heavy, and then lie down; and it will act of itself." With that he handed the cup to Socrates, who took it quite cheerfully, Echecrates, without trembling, and without any change of color or of feature, and looked up at the man with that fixed glance of his, and asked, "What say you to making a libation from this draught? May I, or not?" "We only prepare so much as we think sufficient, Socrates," he answered. "I understand," said Socrates. "But I suppose that

I may, and must, pray to the gods that my journey hence may be prosperous. That is my prayer; may it be granted." With these words he put the cup to his lips and drank the poison quite calmly and cheerfully. Till then most of us had been able to control our grief fairly well; but when we saw him drinking, and then finish drinking, we could do so no longer; my tears came fast in spite of myself, and I covered my face and wept for myself; it was not for him, but at my own misfortune in losing such a friend. Even before that Crito had been unable to restrain his tears, and had turned away; and Apollodorus, who had never once ceased weeping the whole time, burst into a loud wail and made us one and all break down by his sobbing, except Socrates himself. "What are you doing, my friends?" he exclaimed. "I have sent away the women chiefly in order that they might not behave in this way; for I have heard that a man should die peacefully. So calm yourselves and bear up." When we heard that, we were ashamed, and we stopped weeping. But he walked about, until he said that his legs were getting heavy, and then he lay down on his back, as he was told. And the man who had given the poison after a while began to examine his feet and legs. Then he pressed his foot hard, and asked if there were any feeling in it, and Socrates said, "No"; and then his legs, and in this way moved upwards, showing us that he was cold and stiff. And again he felt him, and said that when it reached his heart, he would be gone. He was already growing cold about the groin, when he uncovered his face, which had been covered, and spoke for the last time. "Crito," he said, "I owe a cock to Asclepius,[2] do not forget it." "It shall be done," replied Crito. "Is there anything else that you wish?" He made no reply to this question; but after a moment he stirred, and the man uncovered him. His eyes were fixed. Then Crito closed his mouth and his eyes.

Such was the end, Echecrates, of our friend, who was, I think, of all the men of our time, the best, the wisest, and the most just.

NOTES

1. The dialogue, of which this selection is the conclusion, is presented as Phaedo's eyewitness report to Echecrates of the last day in Socrates' life. The Eleven were the police commissioners who had charge of the Athenian prison.

2. It was customary on recovering from sickness to offer a cock to Asclepius, the god of healing.

ocrates was sentenced to death in midlife so it is not surprising that his friends found his
'eath untimely. But any death raises the question of whether or not there can be a timely
'eath. Although Americans have often been accused of denying death, sociologist Talcott
'arsons and psychiatrist Victor Lidz claim that American society demonstrates an atti-
ude of acceptance limited only by an understanding of appropriate timing. Using a
istorical model, Parsons and Lidz demonstrate that the study of the meaning of death
1 America has been concentrated either on the completion of a normal life cycle or a
echnological control over death._

selection from
DEATH IN AMERICAN SOCIETY
Talcott Parsons and Victor Lidz

The present paper will examine the basic patterns of
orientation toward death in American society, their cultural
roots, and their relations to the social structure. We hope also to
suggest problems for further research, as social science clearly
lacks crucial knowledge about the subject, as well as to shed
light upon some related aspects of American society and
e.g., attitudes toward life purposes or strivings and toward
aging, problems occasioned by the increasing proportion of
older people in our population and by the high incidence of
suicide, and the nature of current funeral practices.

We shall begin with a foil—the widespread view that the
realities of death are characteristically met with "denial" in
contemporary American society,[1] an opinion that seems dubi-
ous to us. Usually cited as evidence of this opinion are practices
such as embalming, the elaborate dressing of corpses, and the
use of cosmetics upon them, as well as more extreme ones such
as concern with coffins' impermeability to decay and the
seeming apathy of many terminal patients about their diseases.

Such practices are commonly interpreted as indications
that Americans are "going soft," becoming progressively less

Talcott Parsons and Victor Lidz, "Death in American Society," _Essays in
Self-Destruction._ Edited by Edwin S. Shneidman. New York: Science
House, Inc., 1967, 133-140. Copyright © by Jason Aronson, Inc., New
York, New York. Reprinted by permission.

capable of facing the harsh reality of the actual world. In such interpretations, reality and harshness are often equated, whereas the pleasant things of life are considered not very "real." Americans are said, then, to live in a world of illusion, constructing elaborate defenses against intrusions of reality. Our handling of death is considered only one striking manifestation of a general deplorable tendency.[2]

This paper will present an alternative view, namely that American society has institutionalized a broadly stable, though flexible and changing, orientation to death that is fundamentally not a "denial" but a mode of acceptance appropriate to our primary cultural patterns of activism. We cannot develop our argument until we have reviewed some of the salient characteristics of American society and have discussed some aspects of death and dying. However, it seems appropriate to register immediately a basic difficulty of the denial hypothesis: it would be very anomalous for a society that has no thoroughly institutionalized scientific values to adopt an attitude so drastically discrepant with the realism of science in an area so close to biology and medicine.

Death is a "natural" phenomenon rooted in the conditions of the biological existence of man and all the higher organisms. Moreover, modern biological science has established that death is not only inevitable among higher organisms but is also a positive factor in species' adaptations within the broader physical and organic system.

The differentiation between germ plasm and somatoplasm, which is the crux of the mortality of the higher organisms, enhances both stability and variability of genetic materials in adaptational terms. Bisexual reproduction favors controlled genetic variation by combining two independent genetic lines to produce a new, unique genetic constitution in practically every individual of the offspring generation. However, if the resulting adaptive changes are to accumulate with much efficiency, the parental generation must die off so that its genetic materials can be replaced by those of the offspring. Hence death is positively functional for biological adaptation.[3]

The death of the individual human personality seems to be

similarly functional for the sociocultural system to which it belongs. Human kinship systems tend to ascribe reproduction and its correlate in the sociocultural system, the socialization process, to each other, though there is certainly some independent "play" between the two. Through its structuring of marital selection and family maintenance, a kinship system determines both what organic-social components in the society are combined for perpetuation and how the resultant offspring are submitted to the primary learning processes that introduce them to members within the continuing society. In maturing through the life cycle, a new generation comes to internalize the cultural patterns of the society as communicated by the parental generation.[4] It then becomes important that the older generation be "on the way out" so that its offspring can "take over" the controlling positions of the society, perhaps especially those of reproduction and socialization, and can be free to innovate, both socially and culturally.[5] Like genetic patterns, the cultural patterns communicated to specific offspring seem to vary with both generation and the particular "lines" in the kinship system which the parents represent. Clearly, death plays an important part in the genesis and utilization of new variations in the cultural patterns that will have adaptive significance for the society.

Thus death must be regarded as a fundamental aspect of the human condition, not only by us in our roles as social scientists but by all men as members of their various social groups. All who attain even a moderate longevity must undergo the strains of losing at least some persons to whom they have been closely attached. And, by virtue of being human and being oriented in action by long-accumulating, complex symbol systems, all will have anticipatory knowledge of, and must contemplate, their own deaths. Furthermore, it seems that mortality must always be a particularly important example and trenchant symbol of the finitude of the concrete human being. It is the barrier to omnipotence and the limit to capacities that simply cannot be overcome but must be adjusted to and accepted.

Because death inherently has such critical meaning for humans, it must be given an important position in the "constitutive symbolism" of all viable religious systems. In terms of its own fundamental patterns of orientation, each culture must attribute some "ultimate" meaning or reference to death. If a religion is to remain a workable, institutionalized complex, it can *never* simply deny the ultimate relevance of such a basic condition, although it can (and must) select among the many possibilities which are viable within the human condition, including some rather extreme ones.[6] It must provide a framework for interpreting death that is meaningful and appropriate, in relation to other elements of the culture, for defining attitudes regarding both the deaths of others and the prospect of one's own death. Closely associated with such a framework, of course, are the conventions for occasions of death, particularly the complex of funeral practices.[7]

Some massive facts indicate that modern Western society stands very far along in a major evolutionary development in the biological-demographic sphere. It is well known that "nature" is generally prodigal with the potentials of reproduction at the lower levels of evolution. Among the lower species, the ratio of ova produced to ova fertilized is exceedingly high, as is the ratio of fertilized ova to those which develop into mature organisms. The general evolutionary trend is toward reducing these ratios and increasing the species' "investment" in the probability that particular organisms will perpetuate its patterns.[8] For example, the long periods of gestation and postnatal care that characterize mammals are evidence of this trend. Man has a particularly prolonged gestation period and a relatively extreme postnatal dependency, but he also has a generally high rate of successful maturation (and reproduction). Modern societies seem to accentuate this development within the broad range of possibilities that comprises the biologic basis of the human condition.

Most striking is the recent prolongation of the individual life and concomitant reduction in the ratio of, first, conceptions and, then, live births to completions of a relatively maximum life cycle. The dramatic demographic fact is that in modern societies life expectancy at birth has approximately doubled in the last century, from in the thirties to about seventy years. However, this has occurred without a marked change in the typical maximum life span—the proportion of centenarians has increased little, if at all. The essential fact, then, is that a substantially larger proportion of a birth cohort, or cohort of young adults, lives to approximate completion of the life cycle. Premature death, relative to a normality of attaining "old age," has been enormously reduced.

This broad development comprises a gain in control over the effects of death in that we need not fear its caprices so acutely now that we have fair (statistical) assurance of living out our most active days. Nevertheless, in some other senses the problem of death has concomitantly come to be posed even more massively and trenchantly.

Modern societies contain a rapidly increasing class of persons who have attained old age. Over 9 percent of the American population is now over 65 years of age, as opposed to only 4 percent only 60 years ago.[9] A very large proportion of these people have completed their more obvious and important life tasks, as valued by the ordinary criteria of our society. In general, they have retired from their occupational jobs, and their children have matured and become independent and have families of their own. By the nature of their social positions, they are "on the way out" and are living "in the shadow of death," having entered what is—by most *institutional* criteria— a terminal period of their lives. Thus, there is a relatively large group institutionally placed so that, in some sense, it must rather directly confront the problem of inevitable death. Moreover, this situation affects a much wider group, as those associated with the aging, particularly their children, must prepare to lose them in the relatively near future.

Both for the individual as he faces death and for the social groups intimately attached to him, the problem of the *meaning* of death is coming in a new sense to be concentrated about death occurring as the completion of a normal life cycle. This central, irreducible problem is becoming disentangled from the problem of adjusting to deaths that occur earlier in the life cycle, particularly in infancy and early childhood, which was much more general in the premodern period.

This development may be regarded as differentiating two aspects of the historic problem of death: that stemming from the inevitability of death and that pertaining to deaths which are potentially subject to some kind of human control. We generally value very highly efforts to minimize deaths of the latter type and are particularly upset by such deaths when they do occur. This seems to be the underlying reason why we feel deaths in automobile accidents to be so shocking and their rates to warrant so much public concern. Similarly, lapses in control over avoidable deaths that we now take for granted are experienced as especially disturbing—e.g., the great international concern over the Zermatt typhoid epidemic. Similarly, a major rise in deaths due to smallpox or plague would be highly traumatic, very largely because it is now so completely unexpected and considered to be unnecessary.

This basic differentiation within the complex of orientations toward death has some important correlates. We have come to expect that death will occur primarily among the old and only rarely in other groups. Parents no longer frequently experience the deaths of young children, nor do they ordinarily expect that they will. Similarly, the death of young adults, once so closely associated with tuberculosis, is now relatively uncommon—Violetta and Mimi, though characters still as tragic as when *La Traviata* and *La Boheme* were composed, no longer represent a common fate. The fact that people killed in automobile accidents are often the young probably contributes greatly to our concern over such deaths.

With the prevention of premature death being so heavily and broadly emphasized, difficult problems of meaning are raised by instances in which death either is deliberately imposed or could be avoided through greater care. Significantly, the imposition of capital punishment has been declining, even in proportion to convictions for capital crimes, and is being opposed by widespread movements to abolish the death penalty altogether. Similarly, the contemporary world has newly developed general and intense convictions about the ethical unacceptability and irrationality of war.

Death also has a very broad, if complex, association with suffering and violence. On the one hand, it is an ultimate severity on the scales of punishment, violence, and suffering. On the other hand, it is just as ultimate a release from them. Our modern concerns with control clearly bear upon these scales, and the minimization of suffering in general has certainly become highly valued. The deliberate imposition of physical suffering through torture has generated very great humanitarian opposition, so much so that torture is now almost considered basically unacceptable in the main Western tradition, no matter how "good" its cause may be. Throughout our era, torture has been a major focus of the moral objection to totalitarian regimes. Increasingly, the aggressive employment of violence for overt political ends seems to be attracting opposition of a similar moral generality, except in the cases of certain extreme situations. The most massive developments in the control of suffering, however, have been those in modern medicine. These are salient, not only in the prevention and cure of disabling diseases but also in the reduction of the physical suffering that is involved in illness, including mortal illness. Anesthetics and narcotics have been the most important means for this accomplishment (note that even those who are alarmed by contemporary American attitudes toward death object very little to such "denial" of pain) and have enabled modern man almost to exclude physical suffering from the problems which death inevitably presents.

Thus, modern institutions differentiate three components of the more diffuse problem of death from the core phenomenon of "inevitable death": "premature" death that can be avoided by human measures; deliberately imposed death; and the physical suffering that dying may entail. The modern tendency has been to mobilize control measures to minimize the undesirable impact of each of these three components. In a sense, all three comprise the "uncertainty" of death, as distinguished from its inevitability, and it is this adventitious uncertainty that we strive to control. Although it is unlikely that any of the three components will ever be completely eliminated, all have already been sufficiently reduced to be distinguished clearly from the category of the inevitable "natural" death of all individuals. They need be involved in only a small and varying minority of deaths—they are no longer constitutive components of "man's fate." Moreover, when they occur, they may be seen as "irrational" relative to the "normal," natural aspects of death.

Here we may note how radically these ideas contrast with most pre-modern orientations toward death. Many primitive societies evidently regard *all* deaths as a result of the adventitious play of human or magical factors and lack a clear conception of "natural death." Deaths can then be warded off or adapted to on some combination of political and religio-magical grounds, but they cannot be the foci of distinct cultural complexes that discriminate between their "ultimately" and scientifically meaningful aspects. Most of the classical civilizations adopted a rather fatalistic attitude toward death and illness, when early in life as well as in old age.[10] They regarded the loss of a large proportion of a population cohort before maturity as quite normal. Furthermore, they would have considered any very elaborate efforts to save the dying and to mitigate suffering as interference with Divine provision. Thus, the modern development of both a pattern for valuing the prolongation of life and a highly rationalized schema for identifying the controllable components of the death complex must not be taken for granted.

The comparative evidence suggests that the concomitant emergence in modern societies of the two general developments we have noted, the prolongation of actual life expectancy and the orientation toward controlling the "adventitious" components of the death complex, can hardly be fortuitous. It suggests that we should view the modern, differentiated orientation toward death as a component of a much broader orientation system which emphasizes dedication to activity that can be expected on rational grounds to maximize human control over the *conditional* elements of the life situation. A major tradition of sociological research, stemming largely from Max Weber's comparative studies in religion, has shown that such a general orientational system, which may be conveniently called instrumental activism, characterizes modern Western civilization, particularly American society,[11] and underlies much of the modern day's rather spectacular reconstruction of the human condition.[12] A major theme in our analysis as it develops will be that American attitudes and practices regarding death can be interpreted very generally as elements of that reconstruction.

This bears directly on our rejection of the view we have set as a foil, that American attitudes tend to "deny" death. Instrumental activism is a rational orientation in that, when specified to a particular sphere of action, it can develop the type of control that it values only by accurately recognizing the facts and conditions of the relevant situation. Here, the development of science that it has fostered is evidently prototypical—surely science is not grounded primarily in fantasies that deny basic realities of the empirical world, no matter how problematic is any sense in which it simply reflects these realities. It would seem that the modern orientation toward controlling the adventitious aspects of death must involve a very similar realism, both because of its interpenetration with science (e.g., medicine) and because of its need for highly rationalized means for meeting human strains. However, it is evident that the orientation of control cannot apply to the "inevitable" aspect of death, which is its core phenomenon, in quite the same sense. Rather, the differentiation between the adventitious and inevitable aspects of death has rendered the latter still more irreducible—something that must be faced still more squarely than ever before. The sense in which such facing of death has been incorporated in the value pattern of instrumental activism is extremely complex; it can be treated only after we have considered the "ultimate" meaning that Western tradition has given to the fact of death.

NOTES

1. Herman Feifel states that "denial and avoidance of the countenance of death characterize much of the American outlook," by way of summarizing a predominating theme in the book he edited, *The Meaning of Death* (New York: McGraw-Hill Book Co., 1959), which contains contributions by many distinguished people in a variety of disciplines. Quotation is from p. xvii.
2. Perhaps the most sociological discussion of funeral practices and such a hypothetical general trend is Peter Berger and Richard Lieb-

an, "Kulturelle Wertstruktur und Bestattungspraktiken in den Vereinigten Staaten," *Kolner Zeitschrift fur Soziologie und Sozialpsychologie*, No. 2, 1960.

3. Simpson, George Gaylord, *The Meaning of Evolution* (New Haven, Conn.: Yale University Press, 1949).

4. Parsons, Talcott, *Social Structure and Personality* (New York: The Free Press, 1964), especially chap. 4.

5. S. N. Eisenstadt has probably made the most important contribution to the understanding of problems in this field. See his *From Generation to Generation* (New York: The Free Press, 1956).

6. Max Weber's *Sociology of Religion* (English ed.; Boston: Beacon Press, 1963) is probably still the best single statement of the broad analytical position we are taking toward religion.

7. These last paragraphs are intended to give death its due in terms of its general implications for action systems. We wish to note, however, that our account is quite distinct from that of much current existentialism, which seems to claim that, very generally, life purposes and a great many life activities gain their meaning *only* from being contrasted with and opposed to death. Analytically, this seems extreme and perhaps hinges upon a rather pejorative use of the term "meaning."

8. See Simpson, *op. cit.*

9. Gendell, M., and Zetterberg, H. L., *A Sociological Almanac for the United States*, (2nd ed.; New York: Scribner's, 1961), p. 42.

10. Buddha, we may recall, viewed sickness, old age, and death, with their attendant suffering, as the aspects of this world that led him to recognize the need for adopting a radical other-worldly orientation.

11. The best statement on the characteristics of the pattern of instrumental activism that is yet in print is given in Talcott Parsons and Winston White, "The Link Between Character and Society," chap. 8 in *Social Structure and Personality*. It should be clear that we are referring to a general orientational pattern that can be specified, in principle, to all contexts of social action. We are not simply talking about the "scientific" orientation.

12. Parsons, Talcott, *The System of Modern Society*. Englewood Cliffs, N.J.: Prentice-Hall, 1971.

One might expect that death would be readily accepted in the case of the aged. But British poet, Dylan Thomas on the death of his father writes that, "Old age should burn and rage at the close of day."

DO NOT GO GENTLE INTO THAT GOOD NIGHT

Dylan Thomas

Do not go gentle into that good night
Old age should burn and rave at close of day;
Rage, rage against the dying of the light.

Though wise men at their end know dark is right,
Because their words have forked no lightning they
Do not go gentle into that good night.

Good men, the last wave by, crying how bright
Their frail deeds might have danced in a green bay,
Rage, rage against the dying of the light.

Wild men who caught and sang the sun in flight,
And learn, too late, they grieved it on its way,
Do not go gentle into that good night.

Grave men, near death, who see with blinding sight
Blind eyes could blaze like meteors and be gay,
Rage, rage against the dying of the light.

And you, my father, there on the sad height,
Curse, bless, me now with your fierce tears, I pray.
Do not go gentle into that good night.
Rage, rage against the dying of the light.

In the following lyric on age, William Carlos Williams mingles opposing themes of loss and fruition, strength and frailty, death and rebirth.

TO WAKEN AN OLD LADY

William Carlos Williams

Old age is
a flight of small
cheeping birds
skimming
bare trees
above a snow glaze.
Gaining and failing
they are buffeted
by a dark wind—
But what?
On harsh weedstalks
the flock has rested,
the snow
is covered with broken
seedhusks
and the wind tempered
by a shrill
piping of plenty.

William Carlos Williams, *Collected Earlier Poems.* Copyright © 1938 by New Directions Publishing Corporation. Reprinted by permission of publisher.

The impetus to study death alternately throws one back to a reexamination of life and hurtles him forward into an exploration of the nature of immortality. Throughout cultural history, myths have promoted belief in the solidarity of life and insulated man from an overwhelming fear of death. Robert Jay Lifton, a psychoanalyst, explores the reconstruction of myth in general, and the modes of symbolic immortality in particular, during times of severe historical dislocation such as our own.

Lifton conducts his exploration of immortality on a number of levels simultaneously: biological, theological, creative, natural and transcendental. He ends by reaffirming the timeless pattern of death and rebirth with the statement that "every significant step in human existence involves some inner sense of death."

THE STRUGGLE FOR CULTURAL REBIRTH

Robert J. Lifton

In times of relative equilibrium, the symbols and institutions of a society provide comforting guidelines, a prescribed life cycle, for our internal experience as well as our external behavior. But in times of severe historical dislocation, these institutions and symbols—whether having to do with worship, work, learning, punishment, or pleasure—lose their power and psychological legitimacy. We still live in them, but they no longer live in us. Or rather we live a half-life with one another.

The quest for images and symbols in new combination, for what might be called communal resymbolization, is precarious and threatening—so much so that it can itself be viewed as the cause for the cultural breakdown everyone senses.

Whether we acknowledge it or not, feelings of disintegration and loss permeate contemporary life. Consider, for instance, the widespread inclination to name and interpret man in our present situation not in terms of what he might actually be but rather in terms of what he has been, that is, what he has survived. We speak of man as post-modern, post-industrial, post-historic, post-identity, post-materialist, post-technocratic, and so forth. There are pitfalls in this way of naming the present (or the future) after what no longer is (or will be), but the terms have an authentic source in the sense of survivorship, present or anticipated, that so pervades our deepest image of ourselves.

In other writings I have emphasized the importance of holocaust in our symbolic vocabulary—of the recent past (Nazi death camps, Hiroshima and Nagasaki), the present (Vietnam), and the future (imagery of ultimate destruction by nuclear weapons, environmental pollution, or other means). Now we see the imagery of holocaust coming together with the experience of post-modern cultural breakdown: our loss of faith not so much in this symbol or that but in the entire intricate web of images, rituals, institutions, and material objects that make up any culture. The urgency of contemporary innovation stems from this sense of survival and loss at the most profound experiential level. I keep thinking of a (more or less) rhetorical question put to me recently by a thoughtful student: "Are four thousand years of human experience merely adding up to the capacity to repair a deficiency in a space ship several million light-years from home?"

In recent years we have witnessed the emergence of a "Protean" psychological style of flux and flow of the self, or self-process—of what the young call "goin' through the changes" in an interminable series of experiments and explorations of varying depth, each of which may be readily abandoned in favor of still another psychological quest. The Protean style is that of a survivor of the kinds of technological and cultural holocausts, real and anticipated, that swirl around us.

The Protean process is a product of a convergence of history and evolution. The two have always intertwined: Darwin's message was that man emerged from other species in a historical process; and there has been no lack of evolutionary interpretations of history. But we tend to view evolution as prehistorical, and history as post-evolutionary. The separation has been based upon our assumption of radically differing time scales in their impact upon man: during a historical unit of a decade or century, man was rarely changed in a fundamental way—an evolutionary unit of a millennium or more was required for that to be accomplished. But our present revolutionary technology and unprecedented historical velocity cast doubt upon that distinction. We sense, uneasily, our capacity to eliminate man in evolution no less than in history, and short of that to alter man—whether genetically or through organ exchange or mind influence—as never before.

Like so many of our boundaries, that between history and evolution is obscured rather than eradicated. As history and evolution converge, innovators embrace our new access (made possible by technology) to all forms ever known to human culture. Poised at a confusing and liberating psychic brink, ready to plunge wildly ahead in an unknowable process devoid of clear destination, man suddenly finds, swirling about him, the total array of images created over the full course of his historical and evolutionary past. These images become an elusive form of psychic nutriment, to be ingested, metabolized, excreted, and, above all, built upon and recombined in a process of organic growth.

Richard Sennett has observed that when a machine's parts wear down, the machine cannot operate. "But," Sennett continues, "the essence of human development is that growth occurs when old routines break down, when old parts are no longer enough for the needs of the new organism. This same kind of change, in a larger sphere, creates the phenomenon of history in a culture." Death and loss can occasion profound research, recreation, and renewal. But for such transformation to occur, the relationship of man to machine and of man to work must be altered in the direction of organic growth.

This is Lewis Mumford's principle of transition from mechanism to organism. But something more is involved as well: social arrangements that permit and encourage technology to become part of a larger principle of imaginative transcendence.

MODES OF SYMBOLIC IMMORTALITY

Everywhere, men and women band together to confront the pervasive sense of "living deadness" emanating from holocaust, undigested change, large techno-bureaucracy, and above all the image of the machine. They seek new forms of connection, movement, and integrity around which to build new communities for living and working. One way to probe some of the fundamental dimensions of this process of communal resymbolization is to view it within a framework of shifting modes of symbolic immortality.

Symbolic immortality is an expression of man's need for an inner sense of continuity with what has gone on before and what will go on after his own limited biological existence. The *sense* of immortality is thus more than mere denial of death, and grows out of compelling, life-enhancing imagery of one's involvement in the historical process. This sense of immortality may be expressed *biologically*, by living on through one's sons and daughters and their sons and daughters, extending out into social dimensions (of tribe, organization, people, nation, or even species); *theologically*, in the idea of a life after death or of other forms of spiritual conquest of death; *creatively*, through "works" and influences persisting beyond biological death; *naturally*, through identification with nature, with its infinite extension into time and space; or *transcendentally*, through a feeling-state so intense that time and death disappear.

Historical change itself can be understood in terms of shifts in these modes, or in combinations of these modes. Darwinism, for instance, became the center of a shift (always gradual and partial) from the theological to the biological and natural modes. Or the Chinese Revolution of the twentieth century can be understood as a shift from the biological mode (the socio-religious principles of family continuity and filial piety) to a form of "revolutionary immortality" that embodies aspects of all the modes. I believe that the significance of contemporary social experiments can best be grasped within this larger quest not just for change but for a change in enduring connectedness and commitment, in relationship to contemporary paths to immortality.

The biological-biosocial mode is at issue in the new kinds of families and family-like structures now taking shape. A wide variety of experimental communal arrangements press toward new forms of biosocial continuity—toward new "tribes," a new "people," or at least new forms of community. These groups (sometimes but not always called communes) concern themselves with root psychobiological matters—organic food, greater sexual freedom, collective child-rearing, and spontaneity of mental and physical expression.

Observe the altered definitions of manhood and womanhood taking shape not only in such experimental enclaves but throughout much of society. Within a single generation we have seen the virtually exclusive American male ideal of the tough (even brutal), tight-lipped, fist-ready, physically powerful, hard, anti-artistic, no-nonsense, highly competitive sexual conqueror give way to the gentle, open, noncombative, physically unimpressive, soft, aesthetic-minded, indirect and associative, noncompetitive, sexually casual self-explorer— with a variety of types in between. Similarly, the feminine ideal of the soft, compliant, self-sacrificing, family-oriented helpmate has given way to that of the aggressive, physically and psychically strong, self-expanding, liberation-oriented feminist. Much of the original hippie and Women's Liberation movements can be understood as explorations in broadened definitions of sex roles, so that one can be soft and tentative while still manly, hard and assertive while still womanly. This kind of experiment on the part of any of these groups must inevitably include excesses and absurdities. But in reaching for both the center and periphery of maleness and femaleness there is a groping toward fundamental alteration of the bio-social mode of immortality.

There is, in other words, a biological base to Protean experimentation. And the theme of community—of quest for bio-social continuity—becomes fundamental to all contemporary transformation. The struggle for "community control" is often a struggle for community formation. It is an effort to reassert authority over the most fundamental aspects of life, to combine autonomy with lasting human connection.

31

Protean efforts at transformation are very active in the theological—or, more accurately, religious or spiritual—mode, as is evident in experiments with both social-activist and experiential-meditative forms of Christianity and Judaism, as well as with Buddhist, Hindu, and other Eastern religions. One can also point to revived interest in various premodern religious-like rituals and superstitions—Eastern and Western astrological charts, the Chinese Book of Changes (*I Ching*), and tarot cards and other forms of fortune-telling.

Most commentary emphasizes the antirational nature of this embrace of seemingly primitive spirituality, which can indeed be present, especially for those who develop a preoccupation with charts and cards or feelings and vibes that excludes ideas, growth, and change. More characteristic, I believe, are the people who make forays in and out of these varied spiritual alternatives, as experiments in both knowing and feeling, in which one absorbs a fragment here, an image there, and maintains a sense of flow that is more consistent (more "stable") than the involvement with any one of them.

John S. Dunne, the distinguished Catholic theologian, posits as the new religion of our time "a phenomenon we might call 'passing over' . . . a going over to the standpoint of another culture, another way of life, another religion . . . followed by an equal and opposite process we might call 'coming back,' coming back with new insight to one's own culture, one's own way of life, one's own religion." The process, and the new religion itself, are epitomized not by Jesus or any other founder of a world religion but by Gandhi, who followed such a trajectory from Hinduism to Christianity (and even to some extent to Islam) and then back to Hinduism. But even Gandhi, in the very focus of his faith, has a certain nostalgic ring for us. Could it be that the holy man of our time has only just begun to invent himself, that he will not merely "pass over" and "come back" in that relatively orderly sequence but will do so in a sustained, repeated, perhaps even endless process, in which spiritual depth no longer depends upon exclusive doctrine of any kind and realization combines "the principle of permanence"with that of continuing open search?

32

Whatever form our next prophet may take, we can be certain that we will be witnessing great waves of religious feeling. For what we call religion directs itself, at least at its best, to precisely the kinds of altered relationships to death and the continuity of life that occur during any historical turning point. But lest contemporary priests misunderstand the stirrings within their churches and temples (and the much stronger religious expressions outside of them), this kind of renewed religious feeling presses not toward the stability of denominations and orders but toward their overthrow, not towards orderly worship within existing social arrangements but towards forms of worship—of celebration and immortalization—that subvert the numbing pseudoritual of "normal religion" in favor of newly immortalizing visions.

The third mode of symbolic immortality, that of immortality via man's works, has been a crucial area of social preoccupation. Involved here is the disorganized but powerful critique now under way of all major social institutions: those within which one learns, is governed, judged, or punished, and, above all, finds significance. In the fundamental questions now being raised about universities and schools, political and judicial arrangements, intellectual disciplines and professional practices, there is a common overriding theme: the quest for significant work experience, both in immediate involvement and in a sense of the work's contribution to the continuing human enterprise. For what we call work is a uniquely important boundary between self-process and social vision. Perhaps for the first time in history very large numbers of men and women are beginning to demand harmony and meaning at that boundary; to demand a reasonable equation between work and "works."

This fundamental relationship between work and symbolic immortality is typified in the passions of the "work commune" movement—the creation of small communities that permit poolings of professional, political, and psychobiological experiments. In these and such related groups as radical institutes and radical caucuses in all the professional disciplines, there is not only a powerful transformative element but a conservative one as well: a determination to confront and thereby preserve a particular social or intellectual tradition—rather than dismiss or ignore it—in a spirit critical both of the tradition itself and of its conventional applications.

This task of resymbolization, traditionally the mission of great innovators, has now become something close to a mass experience. Large numbers of people, in one way or another, move (in Daniel Berrigan's phrase) "toward the edge"of their profession or craft, not necessarily because they originally plan to but because their situation evokes altered relationships and judgments—involving the lost ethical and hypertrophied technical components of work and profession, the separation of work and life, and the nature of the society and culture in and for which one works. All this is part of a largely inchoate yet profound quest for newly immortalizing combinations of human influence. We may suspect that the structures and institutions that emerge will have to build into their own evolving tradition the expectation of the unexpected, the capacity to engender a stability in equilibrium with periodic transformation—which may, indeed, be the only form of true stability possible.

The natural mode of immortality has obvious relationship to ecological passions and to general fears about destruction of the environment, fears all too appropriate. But there is also a more positive impulse toward nature among many innovators as exemplified by the rural commune movement. Many have ridiculed this movement and have looked upon it as nothing more than a pathetic form of pastoral romanticism, a regression to a discredited myth that is particularly misdirected in our present urban-technological society. There is no doubt that many of these communal efforts *have* been romantically envisioned and poorly planned. Moreover there is pathos and error in the claim, occasionally made, that they are *the* answer to our urban-technological dilemmas. But what is often missed in these exchanges is the psychological significance of reclaiming a relationship to nature as part of a more general psychic renewal. When young Americans create a rural commune in New Mexico or New Hampshire, they approach nature with contemporary sensibilities. They seek to bring nature back into the human imagination. They embrace nature in an experiment with the self. The ramifications of that experiment may yet make their way into the most urban minds.

The final mode, that of experiential transcendence, differs from the others in being a psychic state per se. It includes various forms of ecstasy and rapture associated with the Dionysian principle of excess, and with the mystical sense of oneness with the universe Freud referred to as the "oceanic feeling." Mystics speak of a state of awareness where, totally unencumbered by any particuar idea or image, one is able to perceive the entirety of the larger universe and of one's own being within it.

This is the "high" one can get from drugs or from various forms of intense encounter; the "trip"; the state of being "stoned." The terms are interesting. "High" implies elevation of psychic state in the direction of transcendence. "Trip" implies being in motion but something briefer and more temporary than, say, a "journey," and having the implicit suggestion of return. "Stoned" implies an absolute intensity (the smoothness, hardness, solidity, and finality of stone), in this case intensity of feeling, ecstasy—but also the numbness, insensitivity, or deadness of a stone (stone blind, stone deaf, stone dumb, stone cold, stone dead). The duality may be appropriate; one undergoes a "small death" (of more or less ordinary feeling) in order to open oneself up to a "new life" (to feeling on a different plane of intensity), to a sense of transcendence. One becomes impervious to the prosaic idea of mortality and feels oneself so exquisitely attuned to—indeed merged with—the universe as a whole that the issue of life versus death is no longer of consequence. Should the process fail, whether because of depending too much upon the technology of becoming "stoned" (the drugs themselves) or for other reasons, one is left in a state of perpetual numbing (stone dumb, stone cold, etc.).

In a wide variety of experiments—sexual, political, aesthetic—there is a powerful insistence upon making the quality of "awareness" or transcendence basic to the act. Indeed, there is a very real sense in which experiential transcendence is the key, the baseline, for the other four modes. That is, one requires some form of ecstasy and oneness—whether all-consuming or of a more gentle variety—in order to experience oneself as living on in one's children, works, spirituality, or relationship to nature. And that level of experience is also required for the inner psychological reordering necessary to individual transformation.

TRANSFORMATION AS RECREATION

Transformation is achieved only by touching a mythic or formative zone, very close to that Mircea Eliade speaks of as "the zone of the sacred, the zone of absolute reality." For the seeker, it is "the road to the self, the road to the 'center' of his being." The principle is one of *psychic action*, by which I mean the genuine inner contact leading to confrontation, reordering, and renewal. As Eliade expressed in reference to ancient rituals surrounding the new year, one experiences "the presence of the dead," the ceremonial depiction of "a 'death' and a 'resurrection,' a 'new birth,' a 'new man,'" and the overall principle that "life cannot be restored but only recreated." This, too, is the principle of genuine Protean transformation.

Consider just a few of the psychological difficulties of individual and social transformation. For those moving into adulthood, the newness and instability of the contemporary situations is such that there can be few "formative fathers" available for them to emulate. Those who do exist are likely to be approached with a tenuous ambivalence or equally tenuous romanticism.

Apart from models or leaders, there are very few existing social institutions within which fundamental transformations can be explored or developed. The result is a form of floating confusion that is in turn related to profound difficulties in connecting innovation with a sense of actuality. The innovator is thus likely to fluctuate between extreme self-doubt and a seemingly opposite but psychologically related self-righteous moralism that claims dominion over truth. Issues of betrayal and self-betrayal confront him at every point: his effort to innovate "betrays" his family and his past; his failure to take a particular leap or his tendency to remain associated with existing society "betrays" his new associates in innovation. More generally, he experiences what I have called the guilt of social breakdown, the self-condemnation of the man without anything to be loyal to.

Most of all the Protean experimenter must call forth dark areas of the psyche, demonic imagery of destruction and suffering as threatening to himself as to society. These "death sources" both reflect his dislocation and energize his renewal. While the ordinary person erects protective devices to avoid confronting them, the innovator moves toward them, sensing that his innovation depends upon them. And today that confrontation must take place within the precarious diversity of the Protean pattern. No wonder young innovators ask the question, as one did of me: "In order to make revolution do you have to destroy yourself?"

To grasp some of the complex relationship between would-be innovators and their society, one must consider the theme of the "underground." One thinks of underground movements, especially in the political realm, as those relegated to a secret, invisible place by their very illegitimacy—by their unacceptability to those in control of society. For some groups such a definition undoubtedly still holds. But in broader present usage the theme of the underground may have greater importance as a psychic and social realm sought out by innovators in order to experiment with the work of transformation. Hence the word becomes almost interchangeable with "free" or "alternative"—and we have the underground church, the underground press, underground films, free or alternative schools, the free university, etc.

One should not be misled by the short life of most underground institutions or their confused and precarious relationship to, and frequent absorption by, the "overground" of proper society. We will continue to need underground themes in our society—imagery of a subterranean realm of both exquisite mysteries and terrible demons—a realm signifying the unconscious mind in Freud's sense and a land of death and continuous life in the paradigm I am suggesting. However often our social critics announce the death of the avant-garde, the counterculture, or the underground, we can expect continuous psychic experimentation in that realm, with individuals and groups periodically emerging from it renewed by insight and vision with which to confront the formative zone of the larger society.

The ultimate task of transformation is the recreation of the adult self. In significant degree, an adult is one who has ceased to play and begun to work. Of course adults play too, but their play tends to be in the service of maintaining the social order, as opposed to the spontaneous subversiveness of the play of children. Adult work is the work of culture: everyday tasks are conducted under the guiding principles of the culture's assumptions about transcendence and are subservient to the prevailing modes of immortality. Each steel girder installed, each mile driven in a taxi, each product order typed and approved contributes to a culture's collective effort to cope with individual mortality through lasting enterprises, structures, and sequences. Adult work is always tied in with a larger spiritual principle—whether that principle is the Protestant ethic, the deification of capital, or the revolutionary vision. Indeed, one way of defining adulthood is as a state of maximum absorption in everyday tasks subsumed to transcendent cultural principles, permitting minimal awareness of the threat of individual death. This is in contrast to both old age and youth: in old age one is impinged upon by the imminence of death and becomes preoccupied with immediate evidence of continuity and integrity, while in youth one requires more intense and direct modes of transcendence rather than the more indirect workaday kind.

Therefore when many of the young are accused of refusing to grow up and become adults, there is a sense in which the accusation is true—and, indeed, must be true for innovators during any period of radical dislocation and change. What they reject is the existing version of adult existence—their sense of adulthood as a locked-in, desensitized state; one of unquestioned assumptions about work and productivity, family and other human relationships; and of fuzzy, nonviable, half-religious images about death, life, and "ultimate meaning."

Contemporary innovators are clear about their quest for a form of adulthood with more play in it. Play and playfulness are central—for the kind of adulthood sought, and for the process of change itself on the way to that state. Great innovators have always been able to play and, in many cases, have come to their innovations via elaborate and disciplined forms of play. While this play is in some ways more characteristic of the child than of the average adult, it is nonetheless the play of adults, playfulness seasoned by form and accessible to insight. The innovator has always lived in exquisite equilibrium between his refusal to be an adult as ordinarily defined and his burdensome assumption of responsibility for a large segment of adult action and imagination. We sense now a demand that all, whatever their innovative talents, share in this playfulness and Proteanism until "adulthood" either disappears entirely or is renewed and transformed.

Ultimately, genuine transformation requires that we "experience" our annihilation in order to prevent it, that we confront and conceptualize both our immediate crises and our long-range possibilities for renewal. Joseph Campbell reminds us: ". . . the idea of death and rebirth . . . is an extremely ancient one in the history of culture," frequently in the form of a "shock treatment for no longer wanted personality structure." In our present Protean environment the principle still holds: *every significant step in human existence involves some inner sense of death*. As Francis Huxley puts the matter, "Where there is anxiety—as there is in every human culture—the imagination is called upon to destroy it by an act of reconstruction."[11] Destruction and reconstruction—death and rebirth in the quest for immortalizing connectedness—is at the center of man's creation of culture. From this process alone can the urgently needed transformation of our own culture ensue. Heinrich Boll tells us that "an artist always carries death within him like a good priest his breviary." The priest, the artist, the human being within us requires that we do no less.

At the time of Socrates' death, the issue of when life ceased and death began seemed clear. Socrates would be dead, his friends knew, when the poison reached his heart. For centuries the definition of death was based on the operation of the heart. Functional as such definitions were, they did not preclude speculation on the distinction between death and life.

In the nineteenth century, Mary Shelley describes frequent conversations with English Romantic poets Lord Byron and Percy Bysshe Shelley on "the nature of the principle of life." In fact, it was as the result of one such conversation that she accepted the challenge to create a tale of terror and for that tale she latched on to the idea of having a young medical student, Victor Frankenstein, "create" human life by assembling multiple transplants.

selections from
FRANKENSTEIN

Mary Shelley

In the Preface to the 1831 edition of Frankenstein, Mary Shelley set out to answer the much-asked question, "How I, then a young girl, came to think of, and to dilate upon, so very hideous an idea?"

Many and long were the conversations between Lord Byron and Shelley, to which I was a devout but nearly silent listener. During one of these, various philosophical doctrines were discussed and among others the nature of the principle of life, and whether there was any probability of its ever being discovered and communicated. They talked of the experiments of Dr. Darwin (I speak not of what the Doctor really did, or said that he did, but, as more to my purpose, of what was then spoken of as having been done by him) who preserved a piece of vermicelli in a glass case, till by some extraordinary means it began to move with voluntary motion. Not thus, after all, would life be given.

Mary W. Shelley. *Frankenstein, or The Modern Prometheus.* Edited by M. K. Joseph. London: Oxford University Press, 1969.

Perhaps a corpse would be re-animated; galvanism had given token of such things: perhaps the component parts of a creature might be manufactured, brought together, and endued with vital warmth.

Night waned upon this talk, and even the witching hour had gone by, before we retired to rest. When I placed my head on my pillow, I did not sleep, nor could I be said to think. My imagination, unbidden, possessed and guided me, gifting the successive images that arose in my mind with a vividness far beyond the usual bounds of reverie. I saw — with shut eyes, but acute mental vision — I saw the pale student of unhallowed arts kneeling beside the thing he had put together. I saw the hideous phantasm of a man stretched out, and then, on the working of some powerful engine, show signs of life, and stir with an uneasy, half vital motion. Frightful must it be; for supremely frightful would be the effect of any human endeavour to mock the stupendous mechanism of the Creator of the world. His success would terrify the artist; he would rush away from his odious handywork, horror-stricken. He would hope that, left to itself, the slight spark of life which he had communicated would fade; that this thing, which had received such imperfect animation, would subside into dead matter; and he might sleep in the belief that the silence of the grave would quench forever the transient existence of the hideous corpse which he had looked upon as the cradle of life. He sleeps; but he is awakened; he opens his eyes; behold the horrid thing stands at his bedside, opening his curtains, and looking on him with yellow, watery, but speculative eyes.

I opened mine in terror. The idea so possessed my mind, that a thrill of fear ran through me, and I wished to exchange the ghastly image of my fancy for the realities around. I see them still; the very room, the dark *parquet,* the closed shutters, with the moonlight struggling through, and the sense I had that the glassy lake and white high Alps were beyond. I could not so easily get rid of my hideous phantom; still it haunted me. I must try to think of something else. I recurred to my ghost story — my tiresome unlucky ghost story! O! if I could only contrive one which would frighten my reader as I myself had been frightened that night!

Swift as light and as cheering was the idea that broke in upon me. 'I have found it! What terrified me will terrify others; and I need only describe the spectre which had haunted my midnight pillow.' On the morrow I announced that I had *thought of a story.* I began that day with the words, *It was on a dreary night of November,* making only a transcript of the grim terrors of my waking dream.

Once into the story, Victor Frankenstein, the young medical student, takes over the telling of the tale, describing the moment of his creation of life in the laboratory. In the following selection, notice the difference in Frankenstein's reaction to his creation, before and after he has infused it with life.

It was on a dreary night of Novemeber, that I beheld the accomplishment of my toils. With an anxiety that almost amounted to agony, I collected the instruments of life around me, that I might infuse a spark of being into the lifeless thing that lay at my feet. It was already one in the morning; the rain pattered dismally against the panes, and my candle was nearly burnt out, when, by the glimmer of the half-extinguished light, I saw the dull yellow eye of the creature open; it breathed hard, and a convulsive motion agitated its limbs.

How can I describe my emotions at this catastrophe, or how delineate the wretch whom with such infinite pains and care I had endeavoured to form? His limbs were in proportion, and I had selected his features as beautiful. Beautiful! –Great God! His yellow skin scarcely covered the work of muscles and arteries beneath; his hair was of a lustrous black and flowing; his teeth of a pearly whiteness; but these luxuriances only formed a more horrid contrast with his watery eyes, that seemed almost of the same colour as the dun white sockets in which they were set, his shrivelled complexion and straight black lips.

The different accidents of life are not so changeable as the feelings of human nature. I had worked for nearly two years, for the sole purpose of infusing life into an inanimate body. For this I had deprived myself of rest and health. I had desired it with an ardour that far exceeded moderation; but now that I had finished, the beauty of the dream vanished, and breathless horror and disgust filled my heart. Unable to endure the aspect of the being I had created, I rushed out of the room, and continued a long time traversing my bedchamber, unable to compose my mind to sleep. At length lassitude succeeded to the tumult I had before endured; and I threw myself on the bed in my clothes, endeavouring to seek a few moments of forgetfulness. But it was in vain: I slept indeed, but I was disturbed by the wildest dreams. I thought I saw Elizabeth, in the bloom of health, walking in the streets of Ingolstadt. Delighted and surprised, I embraced her; but as I imprinted the first kiss on her lips, they became livid with the hue of death; her features appeared to change, and I thought that I held the corpse of my dead mother in my arms; a shroud enveloped her form, and I saw the grave-worms crawling in the folds of the flannel. I started from my sleep with horror; a cold dew covered my forehead, my teeth chattered, and every limb became convulsed: when, by the dim and yellow light of the moon, as it forced its way through the window shutters, I beheld the wretch — the miserable monster whom I had created. He held up the curtain of the bed; and his eyes, if eyes they may be called, were fixed on me. His jaws opened, and he muttered some inarticulate sounds, while a grin wrinkled his cheeks. He might have spoken, but I did not hear; one hand was stretched out, seemingly to detain me, but I escaped, and rushed down stairs. I took refuge in the courtyard belonging to the house which I inhabited; where I remained during the rest of the night, walking up and down in the greatest agitation, listening attentively, catching and fearing each sound as if it were to announce the approach of the demoniacal corpse to which I had so miserably given life.

Oh! no mortal could support the horror of that countenance. A mummy again endued with animation could not be so hideous as that wretch. I had gazed on him while unfinished; he was ugly then; but when those muscles and joints were rendered capable of motion, it became a thing such as even Dante could not have conceived.

Statements on death tell as much about the meaning a society places on life as they do about death. As technological control over death increases, medical and legal efforts are directed toward determining a boundary between life and death. But to know where to place the boundary requires that the meaning of "alive" and "dead" be understood.

Now, the medical profession is faced with the dilemma of determining when death occurs. The report stresses that the criteria for the determination of death are not the same as the definition of death. Nor does changing the criteria alter the fact of death itself.

REFINEMENTS IN CRITERIA
FOR THE DETERMINATION OF DEATH

Task Force on Death and Dying
of the Institute of Society, Ethics
and the Life Science

The growing powers of medicine to combat disease and to prolong life have brought longer, healthier lives to many people. They have also brought new and difficult problems, including some which are not only medical but also fundamentally moral and political. An important example is the problem of determining whether and when a person has died — a determination that is sometimes made difficult as a direct result of new technological powers to sustain the signs of life in the severely ill and injured.

Death was (and in the vast majority of cases still is) a phenomenon known to the ordinary observer through visible and palpable manifestations, such as the cessation of respiration and heartbeat. However, in a small but growing number of cases, technological intervention has rendered insufficient these traditional signs as signs of continuing life. The heartbeat can be

Institute of Society, Ethics and the Life Sciences, Task Force on Death and Dying, "Refinements in Criteria for the Determination of Death: An Appraisal." *Journal of the American Medical Association,* CCI (July 3, 1972), 48-53. (Vol. 221). Copyright © 1972, American Medical Association.

stimulated electrically; the heart itself may soon be replaceable by a mechanical pump. Respiration can be sustained entirely artificially with a mechanical respirator. If the patient requiring these artificial supports of vital functions is also comatose (as is often the case), there is likely to be confusion about his status and about his proper disposition.

Such confusion and uncertainty can have far-reaching and distressing consequences. Many social institutions, arrangements, and practices depend upon a clear notion of whether a person is still alive or not. At stake are matters pertaining to homicide, burial, family relations, inheritance, and indeed, all the legal and moral rights possessed by and the duties owed to a living human being. Also at stake is the role of the physician as the agent of the community empowered to determine, pronounce, and certify death. Thus, the establishment of criteria and procedures to help the physician answer the question "Is the patient dead?" would seem to be both necessary and desirable, and in the interests of everyone — patients, physicians, families, and the community.

In an effort to clear up the confusion and to provide the necessary guidelines, various individuals and groups have set forth proposals offering specific procedures, criteria, and tests to help the physician determine whether his patient has died. These proposals have been widely discussed, both by physicians and by the public. While they have gained acceptance in some quarters, they have stimulated considerable controversy and criticism, and have given rise to some public disquiet. In an effort to clarify this state of affairs, an interdisciplinary task force of the Institute of Society, Ethics and the Life Sciences has undertaken an appraisal of the proposed new criteria for determining death and of the sources of public disquiet. This article reports the results of our deliberations.

SOME BASIC QUESTIONS AND DISTINCTIONS

An exploration of the meaning and definition of death unavoidably entails an exploration of some profound and enduring questions. To ask "What is death?" is to ask simultaneously "What makes living things alive?" To understand death as the transition between something alive and that "same" something dead presupposes that one understands the difference between "alive" and "dead," that one understands what it is that dies. Some people point out that it is possible to speak of life and death on many levels: the life and death of civilizations, families, individuals, organs, cells. Both clinical medicine and the community (and hence, also our task force) are concerned primarily with the life and death of individual human beings. The boundary between living and dead that we are seeking is the boundary that marks the death of a human organism.

Yet, even with this clarification, difficulties persist. First, the terms "human" and "organism" are ambiguous. Their meaning has been and remains the subject of intense controversy among and within many disciplines. Second, in addition to the ambiguity of each of the terms taken separately, it may make a considerable difference which of the two terms — "human" or "organism" — is given priority. Emphasis on the former might mean that the concepts of life and death would be most linked to the higher human functions, and hence, to the functioning of the central nervous system (CNS), and ultimately, of the cerebral cortex. Emphasis on the latter might mean that the concepts of life and death would be most linked to mere vegetative existence, and hence, to the functioning of the circulatory system and the heart. Finally, the concept of a "boundary" itself invites questions. How "wide" is the line between living and dead? Is there any line at all, or are "living" and "dead" parts of a continuum? Is death a process or an event? The various answers to these last questions very much depend upon the various understandings of the more fundamental ideas of "living," "dead," "human," and "organism."

We have considered some of these philosophical questions about the concept of death. (For a preliminary refinement of some of these issues, see references[1] and [2].) Not surprisingly, we have been unable to resolve many of the fundamental issues. We are convinced that some controversy concerning proper procedures for determining death is likely to persist so long as there is controversy concerning the proper concept of death. However, the present and persisting practical problems facing physicians, families, and the community need to be and can be addressed at a more practical level — by means of refinements in the criteria for determining whether death has already occurred. Hopefully, criteria can be developed that will be acceptable to persons holding various concepts of death. The rest of this report concerns itself with efforts to provide such refined criteria.

SOME CRITERIA FOR GOOD CRITERIA OF DEATH

When approaching the problem of setting down or evaluating criteria and procedures for determining death, it is worthwhile to keep in mind some formal characteristics that a set of criteria or procedures should share. We suggest that at least the following characteristics be considered.

1. The criteria should be clear and distinct, and the operational tests that are performed to see if the criteria are met should be expected to yield vivid and unambiguous results. Tests for presence or absence are to be preferred to tests for gradations of function.

2. The tests themselves should be simple, both easily and conveniently performed and interpreted by an ordinary physician (or nurse), and should depend as little as possible on the use of elaborate equipment and machinery. The determination of death should not require special consultation with specialized practitioners.

3. The procedure should include an evaluation of the permanence and irreversibility of the absence of functions and a determination of the absence of other conditions that may be mistaken for death (e.g. hypothermia, drug intoxication).

4. The determination of death should not rely exclusively on a single criterion or on the assessment of a single function. The more comprehensive the criteria, the less likely will be the occurrence of alleged or actual errors in the final determination.

5. The criteria should not undermine but should be compatible with the continued use of the traditional criteria (cessation of spontaneous heartbeat and respiration) in the vast majority of cases where artifical maintenance of vital functions has not been in use. The revised criteria should be seen as providing an alternative means for recognizing the *same* phenomenon

of death.

6. The alternative criteria, when they are used, should determine the physician's actions in the same way as the traditional criteria; that is, all individuals who fulfill either set of criteria should be declared dead by the physician as soon as he discerns that they have been fulfilled.

7. The criteria and procedures should be easily communicable, both to relatives and other laymen as well as to physicians. They should be acceptable by the medical profession as a basis for uniform practice, so that a man determined to be dead in one clinic, hospital, or jurisdiction would not be held to be alive in a different clinic, hospital, or jurisdiction, and so that all individuals who equally meet the same criteria would be treated equally, that is, declared dead. The criteria and procedures should be acceptable as appropriate by the general public so as to provide the operational basis for handling the numerous social matters which depend upon whether a person is dead or alive, and so as to preserve the public trust in the ability of the medical profession to determine that death has occurred.

8. The reasonableness and adequacy of the criteria and procedures should be vindicated by experience in their use and by autopsy findings.

APPRAISING A SPECIFIC PROPOSAL

The most prominent proposal of new criteria and procedures for determining, in the difficult cases, that death has occurred has been offered in a Report of the Ad Hoc Committee of the Harvard Medical School to Examine the Definition of Brain Death.[3] The following criteria were presented, and described in some detail: (1) unreceptivity and unresponsivity to externally applied stimuli and inner need; (2) no spontaneous muscular movements or spontaneous respiration; (3) no elicitable brain reflexes; and (4) flat electroencephalogram. (The complete description of these criteria as given in the Harvard report is presented in the Box.) In addition, the report suggests that the above findings again be verified on a repeat testing at least 24 hours later, and that the existence of hypothermia and CNS de-

Criteria of the Ad Hoc Committee of the Harvard Medical School

1. *Unreceptivity and Unresponsivity.* — There is a total unawareness to externally applied stimuli and inner need and complete unresponsiveness — our definition of irreversible coma. Even the most intensely painful stimuli evoke no vocal or other response, not even a groan, withdrawl of a limb, or quickening of respiration.

2. *No Movements or Breathing.* — Observations covering a period of at least one hour by physicians is adequate to satisfy the criteria of no spontaneous muscular movements or spontaneous respiration or response to stimuli such as pain, touch, sound, or light. After the patient is on a mechanical respirator, the total absence of spontaneous breathing may be established by turning off the respirator for three minutes and observing whether there is any effort on the part of the subject to breathe spontaneously. (The respirator may be turned off for this time provided that at the start of the trial period the patient's carbon dioxide tension is within the normal range, and provided also that the patient had been breathing room air for at least 10 minutes prior to the trial.)

3. *No Reflexes.* — Irreversible coma with abolition of central nervous system activity is evidenced in part by the absence of elicitable reflexes. The pupil will be fixed and dilated and will not respond to a direct source of bright light. Since the establishment of a fixed, dilated pupil is clear-cut in clinical practice, there should be no uncertainty as to its presence. Ocular movement (to head turning and to irrigation of the ears with ice water) and blinking are absent. There is no evidence of postural activity (decerebrate or other). Swallowing, yawning, vocalization are in abeyance. Corneal and pharyngeal reflexes are absent.

As a rule the stretch of tendon reflexes cannot be elicited; i.e. tapping the tendons of the biceps, triceps and pronator muscles, quadriceps and gastrocnemius muscles with the reflex hammer elicits no contraction of the respective muscles. Plantar or noxious stimulation gives no response.

4. *Flat Electroencephalogram.* — Of great confirmatory value is the flat or isoelectric EEG. We must assume that the electrodes have been properly applied, that the apparatus is functioning normally, and that the personnel in charge is competent. We consider it prudent to have one channel of the apparatus used, for an electrocardiogram. This channel will monitor the ECG so that, if it appears in the electroencephalographic leads because of high resistance, it can be readily identified. It also establishes the presence of the active heart in the absence of EEG. We recommend that another channel be used for a noncephalic lead. This will pick up space-borne or vibration-borne artifacts and identify them. The simplest form of such a monitoring noncephalic electrode has two leads over the dorsum of the hand, preferably the right hand, so the ECG will be minimal or absent. Since one of the requirements of this state is that there be no muscle activity, these two dorsal hand electrodes will not be bothered by muscle artifact. The apparatus should be run at standard gains $10\mu v/mm$. $50\mu v/mm$. Also it should be isoelectric at double this standard gain which is $5\mu v/mm$ or $25\mu v/5$ mm. At least ten full minutes of recording are desirable, but twice that would be better.

It is also suggested that the gains at some point be opened to their full amplitude for a brief period (5 to 100 seconds) to see what is going on. Usually in an intensive care unit artifacts will dominate the picture, but these are readily identifiable. There shall be no electroencephalographic response to noise or to pinch.

All of the above tests shall be repeated at least 24 hours later with no change.

The validity of such data as indications of irreversible cerebral damage depends on the exclusion of two conditions: hypothermia (temperature below 90 F [32.2 C]) or center nervous system depressants, such as barbiturates.

pressants be excluded. It is also recommended that, if the criteria are fulfilled, the patient be declared dead before any effort is made to disconnect a respirator. (The reasoning given for this recommendation was that this procedure would "provide a greater degree of legal protection to those involved. Otherwise," the report continues, "the physicians would be turning off a respirator on a person who is, under the present strict, technical application of the law, still alive.")

The criteria of the Harvard Committee Report meet the formal characteristics of "good" criteria, as outlined in this communication. The criteria are clear and distinct, the tests easily performed and interpreted by an ordinary physician, and the results of the tests generally unambiguous. Some question has been raised about the ease of obtaining an adequate electroencephalographic assessment, but the report does not consider the electroencephalographic examination mandatory. It holds that the EEG provides only confirmatory data for what is, in fact, a clinical diagnosis. Recognizing that electroencephalographic monitoring may be unavailable, the report states "when available it should be utilized."

On the score of comprehensiveness, the tests go beyond an assessment of higher brain function to include a measure of various lower brain-stem (vegetative) functions, and go beyond an assessment just of brain activity by including the vital function of spontaneous respiration. It is true that the circulatory system is not explicitly evaluated. However, because of the close link between circulation and respiration, a heartbeat in a patient on a mechanical respirator (i.e., in a patient who has permanently lost his spontaneous capacity to breathe) should not be regarded as a sign of continued life. The continued beating of the heart in such cases may be regarded as an "artifact," as sustained only by continued artificial respiration.

The new criteria are meant to be necessary for only that small percentage of cases where there is irreversible coma with permanent brain damage, and where the traditional signs of death are obscured because of the intervention of resuscitation machinery. The proposal is meant to complement, not to replace, the traditional criteria of determining death. Where the latter can be clearly established, they are still determinative.

The Harvard Committee Report does not explicitly require that the physician declare the patient dead when the criteria are fulfilled; because it was a novel and exploratory proposal, it was more concerned to permit, rather than to oblige him to do so. However, once the criteria are accepted as valid by the medical profession and the community, nothing in the report would oppose making the declaration of death mandatory on fulfillment of the criteria. Thus, the alternative criteria and the traditional criteria could be — and should be — used identically in determining the physician's actions.

Experience to date in the use of these criteria and procedures for determining death suggest them to be reasonable and appropriate. Support for their validity has come from post-mortem studies of 128 individuals who fulfilled the Harvard criteria. On autopsy, the brains of all 128 subjects were found to be obviously destroyed (E. Richardson, unpublished results). The electroencephalographic criterion has received an independent evaluation. The largest single study,[4] done with 2,642 comatose patients with isoelectric (i.e., flat) EEGs of 24-hours' duration, revealed that not one patient recovered (excepting three who had received anesthetic doses of CNS depressants, and who were, therefore, outside the class of patients covered by the report); Although further evidence is desirable and is now being accumulated (in studies by the American EEG Society and by the National Institute of Neurological Diseases and Stroke, among others), the criteria seem well-suited to the detection of whether the patient has indeed died.

We are not prepared to comment on the precise technical aspects of each of the criteria and procedures. Medical groups, and especially neurologists and neurosurgeons, may have some corrections and refinements to offer. Nevertheless, we can see no medical, logical, or moral objection to the criteria as set forth in the Harvard Committee Report. The criteria and procedures seem to provide the needed guidelines for the physicians. If adopted, they will greatly diminish the present perplexity about the status of some "patients," and will thus put an end to needless, useless, costly, time-consuming, and upsetting ministrations on the part of physicians and relatives.

CAUSES OF CONCERN

Despite the obvious utility and advantages of the proposed criteria and procedures, the Report of the Ad Hoc Committee of the Harvard Medical School has met with opposition, both within and outside the medical profession.[5-8] Some public disquiet is to be expected when matters of life and death are at stake. In fact, little concern has been generated by the criteria themselves. Rather, the concern which has been expressed is largely due to the ways in which some people have spoken about the reasons why they are needed. Four causes of concern have been identified: (1) problems with concepts and language; (2) reasons behind the new criteria and the relationship of organ transplantation; (3) problems concerning the role of the physician and the procedures for establishing the new criteria; and (4) fears concerning possible further updatings of the criteria.

Problems With Concepts and Lanugage. — Some of the difficulties go back to the unresolved ambiguities surrounding the concept of death. The proliferation and indiscriminate use of terms such as clinical death, physiological death, biological death, spiritual death, mind death, brain death, cerebral death, neocortical death, body death, heart death, irreversible coma, irreversible loss of consciousness, and virtual death only add to the confusion. The multiplicity of these terms and the difficulties encountered in defining them and in relating them to one another and to the idea of death of a person testify to the need for greater clarity in our understanding of the concept of death. Pending the advent of such clarity, it should be remembered that what is needed are criteria and procedures for determining that a man has died. The various abstract terms listed above do not contribute to the devising of such criteria. They are, perhaps, best avoided. Even more to be avoided is the notion that the new criteria constitute a new or an alternative *definition* of death, rather than a refined and alternative means for detecting the same "old" phenomenon of death.

A second confusion concerns the relation of the "medical" and "legal" definitions of death. Some commentators have drawn a sharp distinction between these two definitions, and have gone so far as to say that a given individual died medically on one day and legally on another. This is loose, misleading, and probably incorrect usage. It is true that the law offers its own various "definitions" of "death" to serve its own various purposes — for example, in deciding about inheritance or survivorship. But these so-called "definitions" of "death" are in fact only definitions of "who shall inherit." With regard to the actual biological phenomenon of death, the law generally treats the matter as a medical question of fact, to be determined according to criteria established by physicians. No statutory change in the law will be necessary once the medical profession itself adopts the new criteria — provided, of course, that the public does not object.

A third confusion concerns the use of the term "arbitrary" to describe the new criteria. It is the arbitrary (in the sense of "capricious," "without justification") conduct of physicians that the public fears in regard to the definition of death. To be sure, the criteria are man-made, the result of human decision and arbitrament, but they are in no sense capricious. The selection of 24 hours as the waiting period between examinations is, it is true, arbitrary in the sense that it could just as well have been 20 hours or 30 hours. But the selection of 24 hours was considered reasonable, i.e., sufficient to check for any reversibility in the signs of death. The criteria themselves, far from being arbitrary, have been selected as best suited to reveal the phenomenon of death.

A fourth confusion is especially serious, since it goes to the very heart of what is being done and how. Some have spoken of the criteria enunciated by the Harvard Committe Report as criteria for stopping the use of extraordinary means to keep a patient alive. (Actually, the report itself invokes the statement of Pope Pius XII to the effect that there is no obligation on the part of the physician to employ extraordinary means to prolong life.) This language serves to confuse the question of the determination of death with a second important question facing the physician, namely, "When is it desirable or permissible to withdraw or withhold treatment so that a patient (unquestionably still alive) may be allowed to die?" The only question being considered in this communication, and by the Ad Hoc Committee, is "When does the physician pronounce the (ex)patient

53

dead?" The two questions need to be kept apart.

Reasons Behind the New Criteria: The Relation of Transplantation. — Following the first heart transplantation, there appeared in the medical literature and in the popular press a series of articles calling for clarification of the criteria for determining death. Some called for an "up-dating" of the criteria to facilitate the work of the transplant surgeons and the taking of organs. Others asked for the establishment of agreed-upon guidelines to protect the integrity of the donor against possible premature organ removal or to protect the physician against possible charges of malpractice, or even of homicide. The frequent mention of organ transplantation in connection with proposals offering new criteria of death has created an uneasiness on the part of many people — including some physicians.[5,8] and also a few members of this task force[6,9] — that the need for organs for transplant has influenced, or might sometime in the future influence, the criteria and procedures actually proposed for determining that death has occurred.

While we cannot deny the fact that the growth of the practice of transplantation with cadaveric organs provided a powerful stimulus to reassess the criteria for determining death, the members of this task force are in full agreement that the need for organs is not and should not be a reason for changing these criteria, and especially for selecting any given criterion or procedure. Choice of the criteria for pronouncing a man dead ought to be completely independent of whether or not he is a potential donor of organs. The procedures, criteria, and the actual judgment in determining the death of one human being must not be contaminated with the needs of others, no matter how legitimate those needs may be. The medical profession cannot retain trust if it does otherwise, or if the public suspects (even wrongly) that it does otherwise.

There are ample reasons, both necessary and sufficient, and independent of the needs of potential transplant recipients, of the patient's family and of society, for clarifying and refining the criteria and procedures for pronouncing a man dead. It is the opinion of the task force that the widespread adoption and use of the Harvard Committee's (or similar) clearly defined criteria will, in fact, allay public fears of possible arbitrary or mischievous practices on the part of some physicians. We also be-

lieve that if the criteria for determining death are set wholly independently of the need for organs, there need be no reticence
or embarrassment in making use of any organs which may actually become more readily available if the criteria are clarified
(provided, of course, that other requirements of ethical medical
practice are met).

*Problems Concerning the Role of the Physician and the
Procedures for Establishing the New Criteria.* — Even if it has
been agreed that there is a need for a revision of the traditional
definition or criteria of death, there remain questions of who is
to make the revision, and how (i.e. according to what procedure) that revision is to be made. There are at least five levels
where decisions are made with respect to the death of a human
being: (1) establishing a concept of death; (2) selecting general
criteria and procedures for determining that a patient has died;
(3) determining in the particular case that the patient meets the
criteria; (4) pronouncing him dead; and (5) certifying the death
on a certificate of record. Until recently, because there was tacit
agreement on the concept of death, our society was content to
leave the last four matters solely in the hands of physicians. At
the present time, opinion is divided on the proper role and authority of the physician, especially with respect to the first two
decisions. Some have questioned the status and authority of the
various groups who have proposed new criteria. Some have questioned the status and authority of the various groups who have
proposed new criteria. Some have questioned whether the decision to move to a "brain centered" concept of life and death is
a decision to be left to the medical profession, whereas others
have questioned whether any other profession or group may be
any more qualified. Some have called for the establishment of a
definition of death by legal statute.

The state of Kansas has recently enacted a statute which
establishes two alternative concepts of death (it refers to them as
"definitions of death"): permanent absence of spontaneous respiratory and cardiac function, and permanent absence of spontaneous brain activity.[10] The specific criteria are left to "ordinary standards of medical practice." Both the desirability of this law and
its specific language have recently been attacked.[11] and defended[12,13] The controversy over the Kansas statute has illuminated
some of the advantages and disadvantages of legislation in this

area. We are sympathetic to the value of having any changes in the concept of death, or even major changes in criteria for determining death, ratified by the community, as a sign of public acceptance and for the legal protection of physicians. On the other hand, we are concerned about the possibility of confused, imprecisely drafted, or overly rigid statutes. Moreover, we do not believe that legislation is absolutely necessary in order to permit physicians to use the new criteria, once these receive the endorsement and support of the medical profession. Clearly, these matters of decision-making and the role of law need further and widespread discussion. The acceptability of any new concept or criteria of death will depend at least as much on the acceptability of the procedure by which they are adopted as on their actual content. The precedents now established are likely to be very important, given the likelihood that the increase of organ transplantation or the rising costs of caring for the terminally ill will produce renewed pressures to alter again concepts and criteria of death.

Fears Concerning Possible Further Updatings of the Criteria. — The fear of being pronounced dead prematurely is an understandable human fear, and, in some earlier ages, a justifiable fear based upon actual premature burials. A similar fear may be behind the concern that current revisions in criteria for determining death will serve as precedents for future updatings, with the result that persons who would be considered alive by today's criteria will be declared dead by tomorrow's criteria. In protest against this prospect, one commentary has put the matter succinctly and well: "A living body turns into a corpse by biological reasons only — not by declarations, or the signing of certificates."[8]

Recent proposals to place exclusive reliance on electroencephalography for the determination of death may be said to represent a current example of efforts to further update the criteria. In accord with other commentators,[7] we view this prospect with some concern. Leaving aside technical questions having to do with the reliability of the electroencephalographic evaluations, we wish to comment on some of the assumptions underlying the proposed shift away from the recommendation that the EEG be used as a *confirmatory* adjunct to the clinical

56

determination of death, and not as a definitive criterion.

Most such proposals appear to rest on three assumptions: (1) that the existence of human life, no less than its essence, is defined in terms of activities normally associated with higher brain function; (2) that such activities are exclusively centered in the anatomical locus known as the neocortex; and (3) that the EEG provides a full and complete measure of neocortical function. From these assumptions, the following conclusion is drawn: In the absence of a functioning neocortex, as determined by an isoelectric EEG, human life has ceased.

These assumptions appear to be sufficiently questionable to rule out exclusive reliance on the EEG for determinations of death: the first on purely philosophical grounds, and the second and third on the strength of preliminary experimental findings. For example, the second assumption that activities like instrumental learning and cognition reside entirely in the neocortex has now been called into question by a recent report describing evidence for instrumental learning in neodecorticate rabbits.[14]

The overall conclusion that an isoelectric EEG signifies the end of human life must be questioned in the light of a recent article reporting that patients with isoelectric EEGs (and subsequently verified anatomical death of their neocortices) continued to breathe spontaneously for up to six months. [15] The authors of this study express uncertainty as to whether or not such decorticate patients should be declared dead. While they agree that the Harvard criteria pointed clearly to a diagnosis of "alive," they imply that they have some difficulty with this conclusion. While an isoelectric EEG may be grounds for interrupting all forms of treatment and allowing these patients to die, it cannot itself be the basis for declaring dead someone who is still spontaneously breathing and who still has intact cerebral reflexes. It is inconceivable that society or the medical profession would allow the preparation of such persons for burial. To prevent such confusion and the possible dangerous practices that might result from a shift to exclusive reliance on the EEG, we urge that the clinical and more comprehensive criteria of the Harvard Report be adopted. We are supported in this conclusion by the report that a majority of neurologists have rejected the proposition that EEG determinations are sufficient as the sole basis for a determination of death.[16]

Members of the Task Force on Death and Dying include: Eric Cassell, MD, and Leon R. Kass, MD, PhD (*co-chairmen*); Marc Lappe, PhD (staff associate); Henry K. Beecher, MD; Daniel Callahan, PhD; Renee C. Fox, PhD; Michael Horowitz, LLB; Irving Ladimer, SJD; Robert Jay Lifton, MD; William F. May, PhD; Joseph A. Mazzeo, PhD; Robert S. Morison, MD; Paul Ramsey, PhD; Alfred Salder, MD; Blair Sadler, LLB; Jane Schick, MD; Robert Stevenson, PhD; and Robert Veatch, PhD.

This study was supported in part by a grant from The New York Foundation.

NOTES

1. Morison, R.S., "Death: Process or event?" *Science,* 173:694-698, 1970.
2. Kass, I.R., "Death as an event: A commentrary on Robert Morison." *Science,* 173:698-702, 1970.
3. A definition of irreversible coma: Report of the Ad Hoc Committee of the Harvard Medical School to examine the definition of brain death. *JAMA,* 205:337-340, 1968.
4. Silverman, D., Masland, R. Saunders M., *et. al.,* "Irreversible coma associated with electrocerebral silence." *Neurology,* 20:525-533, 1970.
5. Rutstein, D.D., "The ethical design of human experiments." *Daedalus,* 98:523-541, 1969.
6. Jonas, H., "Philosophical reflections on human experimentation." *Daedalus,* 98:219-247, 1969.
7. Toole, J.F., "The neurologist and the concept of brain death." *Perspect Biol. Med.,* 14:599-607, 1971.
8. Rot, A., and VanTill, H.A.H., "Neocortical death after cardiac arrest." *Lancet,* 2:1099-1100, 1971.
9. Ramsey, P., *The Patient as Person: Explorations in Medical Ethics.* (New Haven: Yale University Press, 1970), pp. 101-112.
10. Kansas Statutes, ch 77, sect 202.
11. Kennedy, I.M., "The Kansas statute on death." *New Eng J Med,* 285:946-950, 1971.
12. Curran, W.J., "Legal and medical death: Kansas takes the first step." *New Eng J Med,* 284:260-261, 1971.
13. Mills, D.H., "The Kansas death statute: Bold and innovative." *New Eng J Med,* 285:968-969, 1971.
14. Oakley, D.A., "Instrumental learning in neodecorticate rabbits." *Nature,* 233;185-187, 1971.

15. Brierly, J.B., Adams, J.H., Graham, D.I., *et. al.*, "Neocortical death after cardiac arrest." *Lancet,* 2:560-565, 1971.

16. Silverman, D., Masland, R., Saunders, M.G., *et. al.*, "EEG and cerebral death: The neurologist's view." *Electroenceph Clin Neurophysiol,* 27:549, 1969.

As the Report on Death and Dying noted, controversy over proper procedures for determining death will continue as long as the debate over the proper concept of death ensues. Definitions are often regarded as authoritative statements, yet, by nature, a definition is a reflection of cultural attitudes, not a source of knowledge.

Three definitions of life and death follow: the first are definitions for daily discourse, the latter two are definitions found in legal and medical dictionaries. A reading of the definitions for life and death quickly becomes cyclic, as the reader is thrown back to his original terminology. Given the current exploratory work in medicine and social science on the nature of death and dying, you might speculate upon what changes will be reflected in future definitions.

LIFE AND DEATH: DEFINITIONS

COMMON USAGE*

Death –
(1) The act or fact of dying; the final cessation of the vital functions of an animal or plant. Often personified. (2) The state of being dead. (3) The loss or cessation of life in a part (1800).

Life –
(1a) Primarily, the condition, quality, or fact of being a living person or animal, (b) More widely: the property which differentiates a living animal or plant, or a living portion of organic tissue, from dead or non-living matter. (2) The period from birth to death. (3) The series of actions and occurrences constituting the history of an individual from birth to death.

---

*"Life," "Death." *Shorter Oxford English Dictionary*, 3rd Edition, 1964. Prepared by Wm. Little, H. W. Fowler, J. Coulson. Revised and edited by C.T. Onions.

LEGAL[†]

Death –
The cessation of life; the ceasing to exist; defined by physicians as a total stoppage of the circulation of the blood, and a cessation of the animal and vital functions consequent thereon, such as respiration, pulsation, etc.

This is "natural death," in contradistinction to "civil death," and also, to "violent death."

Life –
That state of animals and plants or of an organized being, in which its natural functions and motions are performed, or in which its organs are capable of performing their functions. Webster. The sum of forces by which death is resisted. Bichat.

MEDICAL[††]

Death –
Permanent cessation of all vital functions. The following definitions of death have also been considered: (1) Total irreversible cessation of cerebral function, spontaneous function of the circulatory system. (2) The final and irreversible cessation of perceptible heart beat and respiration. Conversely, as long as any heart beat or respiration can be perceived, either with or without mechanical or electrical aids, and

Life –
(1) State of being alive; quality manifested by metabolism, growth, reproduction, and adaptation to environment; state in which the organs of an animal or plant are capable of performing all or any of their functions. (2) Time between birth or inception and death of an organism. Biologically, unitary life begins at the moment of conception and ends at death. However, for legal and other reasons the defi-

---

† Reprinted with permission from *Black's Law Dictionary*, Revised Fourth Edition, Copyright © 1968 by West Publishing Co.
†† Courtesy of F. A. Davis Co., *Taber's Cyclopedic Medical Dictionary*, 12th ed. (1973). Clayton L. Thomas, M.D., editor.

61

regardless of how the heart beat and respiration were maintained, death has not occurred.

Defining death is complicated. Conditions such as cardiac standstill or complete lack of renal function would have meant certain death at one time. The use of cardiac pacemakers, artificial hearts and kidneys, heart transplants, and kidney transplants have made delaying death possible.

nition of when life begins has been subject to a variety of interpretations. Nevertheless, it is undeniable that life is a continuum which can be arbitrarily but not logically indicated as having begun at some point in time or development past the moment of conception. (3) The sum total of those properties which distinguish living things (animals or plants) from non-living inorganic chemical matter or dead organic matter.

Definitions of life and death establish an endless cycle. When R.A. Kalish tackles the problem of "dividing the indivisible," he expands the life-death dichotomy to a study of a series of states of being: pre-life, life, death and immortality. Kalish then proceeds to delineate the characteristics of each of these states in terms of a particular perspective: physical (biological and clinical), psychological, social (self and other perceived) and sociological. In suggesting these perspectives as an overlay of meaning, Kalish demonstrates that there are many kinds of death; for instance, a patient who has given up on life and who is neglected by both family and nursing staff may be "alive" from a biological or clinical point of view, but "dead" from a social or sociological standpoint.

As Kalish establishes his categories he recalls for the reader Mary Shelley's treatment of the biological death/life boundary and the treatment of the clinical definitions of death and life in the medical dictionary. Robert Jay Lifton's psychological perspectives and concepts of after-life are reflected in Kalish's distinctions among definitions of immortality, while the sociological research reported by Parsons and Lidz, which focuses on technological issues of physical death, also touches on various social definitions of death and immortality.

LIFE AND DEATH: DIVIDING THE INDIVISIBLE

R.A. Kalish

	Pre-life	Life	Death	Immortality
Physical Biological	None	Organs begin to function. At conception? In utero, perhaps 2-3 months.	Organs cease to function; presently irreversible; at varying rates; not all-or-none.	Through natural children; freezing process.
Clinical	None	Organism begins to function. Point of viability or else at birth.	Organism ceases to function; presumably irreversible; closest to legal definition of death.	Folklore and superstition; ghosts. Embalming.
Psychological	None in Western thought; exists in Eastern theology, but without continuity of awareness. Bridey Murphy type assumption.	Aware of self. Slow process developing during infancy.	Loses awareness of self. Comatose, drugged, hopelessly senile. Often irreversible; perhaps accelerated by isolation and feelings of hopelessness.	Christian form of after-life; also Islam. Exists in Eastern theology, but without continuity of awareness.

	Pre-life	Life	Death	Immortality
Social **Self-perceived**	None	Awareness of self as alive. Follows psychological life, perhaps around 2-3 years.	Considers self as not alive, "as good as dead." Produced by isolation and feelings of hopelessness, but assumes self-awareness continues. Reversible.	Impossible by definition, except in *Twilight Zone*.
Other-perceived	May occur before birth or even before conception. As soon as an individual, perhaps still in planning stage, has a role in eyes of someone.	Definitely begun by birth, almost always to parents.	Occurs when individual has been isolated and is considered a non-person or "as good as dead." May accelerate psychological and physical forms of death. Reversible.	To those who continue to think of him "as though he were still alive." Parenthood with natural or adopted children is frequent approach. Perhaps ancestor worship.
Sociological	Similar to other-perceived social pre-life, but in reference to social status in community rather than to role in the eyes of individual.	Normally around time of clinical life.	Normally around time of clinical death. Reversible.	Many years or even centuries for famous people and for those who have made a contribution to posterity which will be identified with them. Perhaps ancestor worship.

QUESTIONS

1. Define each of the following terms by referring to the papers in this chapter and consulting a dictionary:

   denial   constitutive symbolism
   adaptive changes   premature death
   germ plasm   protean man
   somatoplasm   electroencephalogram
   socialization   autopsy
   identity   comatose
   symbolic immortality

2. Acceptance of death often depends on a person's readiness to begin the grief work before the death occurs, whether it is his own death or that of another person. In the *Phaedo* Socrates demonstrates that he has cut his ties, but his friends are convinced that his death will rend their world. Contrast the final concerns expressed by Socrates with those of a typical contemporary.

3. Great literature contains meaning for all time, but it also reflects the culture of its own time. How does the *Phaedo* reveal the social patterns of its age? Consider social structure, the administration of civil justice, medical knowledge and sex roles.

4. The ability to "make sense of" death depends in large measure on the degree to which we find it appropriate. The following statements suggest different ways of justifying death. What factors make death acceptable to the speakers? Compare each attitude to your own idea of appropriate death.

    a. Mother, 42, speaking of her son who died suddenly at age 19 as a result of a previously undetected congenital heart defect:

        "He died at the right time. He had decided on his major, made the track team, and had just fallen in love. Life had never been better for him. He seemed to have found himself. In another year, things might have fallen apart."

    b. Woman, 55, at a study group discussion of funeral practices:

        "My family will not have to fight about my funeral. I have worked hard and I have got it all paid for. I have always made do with second best, but this I am going to do right."

    c. Male student, 28, in seminar on Death and Dying:

        "What's all this talk about appropriate death? If I have lived my life well, why should the circumstances of my death matter to me?"

5. Victor Frankenstein is the name of the medical student who created a monster, yet today we have the expression "to create a Frankenstein." What attitude does the expression suggest? What responsibility does Victor have as creator? Does he, for instance have the right to destroy the creature?

6. Lifton explains that every step in life involves an inner

sense of death. Many rituals celebrate the beginning of a new life and the "death" of a former existence. How is the death/life progression evident in the following: baptism, bar mitzvah, graduation, marriage, divorce, birth of a child, job promotion?

7. It has been said that there is no difficulty in the human condition that immortality wouldn't solve. Would Socrates agree? Lifton?

    a. Would you choose the possibility of extending your life indefinitely through multiple transplants? Why or why not? At what point in organ replacement would your original identity change?

8. Refer to the categories offered by R.A. Kalish in the table, "Life and Death: Dividing the Indivisible." How many of the different categories are illustrated by each of the following?

    a. Socrates
    b. Frankenstein's monster
    c. The father in "Do Not Go Gentle Into That Good Night"
    d. Protean man
    e. Patient who breathes spontaneously, has cerebral reflexes intact, yet has an isoelectric EEG.

9. Kalish suggests that life and death be considered two points on a continuum rather than polar states. Where would each of the following fit on such a continuum?

    a. An anecephalic baby whose parents must decide whether to continue heroic measures to maintain life.
    b. A chronically ill 80-year-old woman who lives in a nursing home totally ignored by her family.

67

PROJECTS FOR FURTHER STUDY

1. Terminal illness has become a popular subject for movies and television. Watch three different medical series on television during a one-week period and observe both the portrayal of death and its effects on the participants: patient, family, nurse, and doctor. Profile the dying patient in terms of age, sex, occupation, personal and social attractiveness and social status. What is the cause of death? Where do they die? Note the attitudes of each person toward death. Based upon your analysis, what do you feel television presents as appropriate death? As inappropriate death?

2. Cultural attitudes determine what one does to "put his house in order" before death. Our society has very different expectations, for instance, from a community in medieval times or more recent Eskimo culture. Research the types of arrangements that are expected and available in our society. Include psychological, financial, legal and religious factors in your research.

3. To explore society's attitude to aging collect samples (pictures or tape recordings) of advertisements portraying people over sixty-five years of age. Observe your materials carefully for indicators of the subject's degree of engrossment in society, physical condition and advertised need. You might want to make a comparison with similar materials portraying younger adults. Speculate on how each

subject would allocate his time on a daily basis, and what other people he would see frequently.

4. As Lifton indicated, there are many vehicles of symbolic immortality; one of the most frequent is social immortality. Observe your environment, campus and community, for physical memorials, dedications, memorial events, donations, endowed programs and awards. List as many as you encounter within one week. Compare your list with others and discuss the degree to which social immortality is valued in our culture.

STRUCTURED EXERCISES

1.   *Kidney Machine Decision.* To help a class experience how their own attitudes, values and past experiences with death would influence their decision making, the class can be divided into groups of five to seven. Copies of the *Kidney Machine Description Sheet* can be distributed to each group. An additional piece of information, the *Kidney Machine Psychological Reports Sheet* is included in Appendix A. Its use is optional. If it is to be used in this exercise, the student should not turn to the additional material until the middle of the decision-making process. The groups will need time to read through the materials and about 30 minutes to arrive at a solution. Each group can list the criteria the participants used in decision making. At the end of the allotted time, the groups can evaluate their work in terms of the following:

   a.   Who did they choose? Why?
   b.   Did they feel they had enough information about each candidate to make a decision?
   c.   What effect did the psychological data have on their decision?
   d.   To what extent were they motivated to *avoid* making a decision (e.g., leaving the decision to chance in some way)?
   e.   Were any novel or unusual solutions proposed?

f.   To what extent did their group try to "objectify" their decision i.e., by rating candidates or devising a formula? Were such efforts helpful?

The decisions of all the groups can then be shared for a discussion of criteria. If time allows, the class can then discuss what factors in subject's profiles would change on their decision.

KIDNEY MACHINE DESCRIPTION SHEET

Located at Swedish Hospital in Seattle, Washington, is the famous kidney machine. A marvel of technological ingenuity, it is the only hope of life for people with a rare kidney disease.

In actuality, the machine functions as a kidney for people who have lost the use of their own. By connecting themselves to the machine for twenty-four hours each week, people with renal failure can remain alive indefinitely — or until they are killed by some other ailment not connected with their kidneys.

There are several problems associated with using this machine, for there are many more people who need it than there is time available on the machine. In fact, only about five people can be placed on it at any one time. Doctors examine all potential patients and determine those who could profit most from connection to the machine. They screen out those with other diseases, for whom the machine would be only a temporary expedient, and they turn their list of recommended patients over to the hospital administration. At present, the doctors have submitted the names of five persons for *one* place on the machine.

The committee assembled to make the decision has been given a brief biography of each person appearing on the list. It is assumed that each person has an equal chance of remaining alive if allowed to use the machine. Thus, the committee is asked to decide which *one* of these may have access to the machine.

You are asked to act as if you were a member of this committee. Remember, there is only one vacancy, and you must fill it with one of these five people. You must agree, *unanimously*, on the single person who is permitted to remain alive, and you must decide your own criteria for making this choice.

The only medical information you have is that people over forty seem to do more poorly on the machine than those under forty (although they do not necessarily find it useless). It is up to you.

71

KIDNEY MACHINE BIOGRAPHICAL SHEET

Alfred: White, male, American, age 42. Married for 21 years. Two children (boy 18, girl 15), both high school students. Research physicist at University medical school, working on cancer immunization project. Current publications indicate that he is on the verge of a significant medical discovery.

On the health service staff of local university, member of county medical society, member of Rotary International, and Boy Scout Leader for 10 years.

Bill: Black, male, American, age 27. Married for five years. One child (girl, 3), wife six months pregnant. Currently employed as an auto mechanic in local car dealership.

Attending night school and taking courses in automatic-transmission rebuilding. No community service activities listed. Plans to open auto-transmission repair shop upon completion of trade school course.

Cora: White, female, American, age 30. Married for eleven years. Five children (boy 10, boy 8, girl 7, girl 5, girl 4 months). Husband self-employed (owns and operates tavern and short-order restaurant). High school graduate. Never employed.

Couple has just purchased home in local suburbs, and Cora is planning the interior to determine whether she has the talent to return to school for courses in interior decoration. Member of several religious organizations.

David: White, male, American, age 19. Single, but recently announced engagement and plans to marry this summer. Presently a sophomore at large eastern university, majoring in philosophy and literature. Eventually hopes to earn Ph.D. and become a college professor.

Member of several campus political organizations, an outspoken critic of the college "administration," was once suspended briefly for "agitation." Has had poetry published in various literary magazines around the New York area. Father is self-employed (owns men's haberdashery store), mother is deceased. Has two younger sisters (15, 11).

Edna: White, female, American, age 34. Single, presently employed as an executive secretary in large manufacturing company, where she has worked since graduation from business college. Member of local choral society; was alto soloist in Christmas production of Handel's *Messiah*. Has been very active in several church and charitable groups.

© Gerald M. Phillips. "Kidney Machine." *1974 Annual Handbook for Group Facilitators.* Edited by J. William Pfeiffer and John E. Jones. La Jolla, California: University Associates Publishers, Inc., 1974, 78-83. Used by permission of Gerald M. Phillips.

2. *Attitude Survey.* A good way to stimulate thought and to begin discussion of personal attitudes toward death is to fill out an attitude scale. A comprehensive attitude scale compiled by E.S. Shneidman from various sources can be found in the magazine *Psychology Today*, August, 1970. This survey was filled out and voluntarily sent back by readers of the magazine, and a summary of the results was published in the June, 1971 issue. The results have also been reprinted in one of Shneidman's books (Shneidman, E.S. *Deaths of Man.* New York: Quadrangle, 1973). The result for the class could be tabulated and then compared with the magazine data, if the class is a large one. In a small class the response to individual items could be discussed in class in several ways. Students could be asked to comment on the areas which stimulated or interested them most. They could be asked to administer all or part of the questionnaire to parents, grandparents or research groups.

FOR FURTHER READING

The following books and papers provide in-depth coverage of the topics introduced in this chapter.

Aries, P. *Western Attitudes Toward Death*. Baltimore: Johns-Hopkins University Press, 1974.

Becker, E. *The Denial of Death*. New York: Free Press, 1973.

Blauner, R. Death and Social Structure. *Psychiatry*, 1966, *29:* 378-394.

Camus, A. *Myth of Sisyphus and Other Essays*. New York: Knopf, 1955.

Choron, J. *Death and Western Thought*. New York: Collier Books, 1963.

Feifel, H. (ed.). *The Meaning of Death*. New York: McGraw-Hill, 1959.

Fulton, R. (ed.). *Death and Identity*, rev. ed. Bowie, Md.: Charles Press, 1976.

Hendin, D. *Death as a Fact of Life*. New York: Warner, 1972.

Shneidman, E.S. *Deaths of Man*. New York: Quadrangle, 1973.

Stannard, D.S. (ed.) *Death in America*. University of Pennsylvania Press, 1975.

Steinfels, P. and Veatch, R.M. (eds.). *Death Inside Out.* New York: Harper and Row, 1974.

Toynbee, A. (ed.). *Man's Concern with Death.* New York: McGraw-Hill, 1969.

Vernon, G.M. *Sociology of Death: An Analysis of Death-Related Behavior.* New York: Ronald Press, 1970.

2

The Experience
of Dying

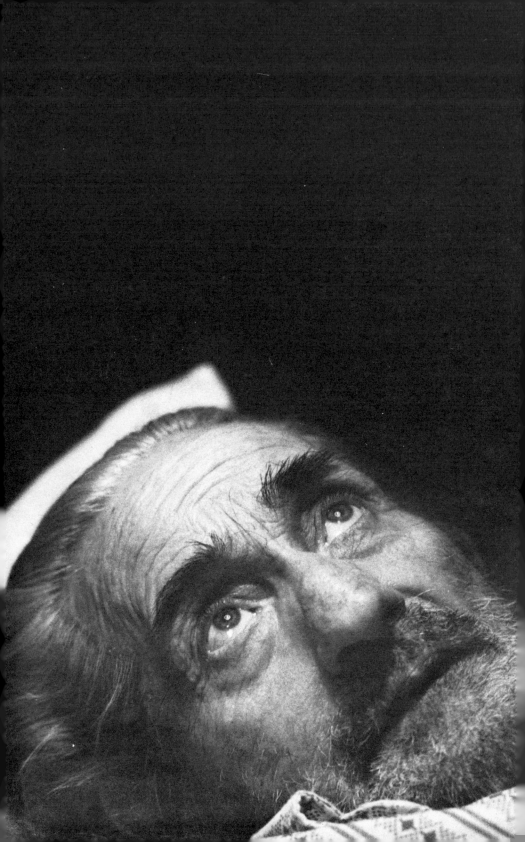

INTRODUCTION

The person who is dying passes through a social transition from being alive to being dead. Yet all too often, as soon as the dying person enters that transition, he is treated as if he were already dead: left alone and forced to conspire in the fiction that "nothing is wrong." More and more, we are coming to recognize the interval of dying as a time for the resolution of conflicts, achievement of personal closure and even a time for continued psychological growth. Clearly if a person is to make his dying a time for growth he must be informed and allowed to assume a more active role than has been customary in recent decades.

Early Voices

When social scientists began the study of death, they did so "at a distance," focusing more on organizational structures in the hospital than on the dying patient himself. Individual humanists like the early-twentieth-century physician, Sir William Osler and, more recently, psychotherapists such as Kurt Eissler and Lawrence and Eda LeShan had recognized the needs of the dying and urged their peers in medicine, psychiatry and psychology to remain with dying patients even when nothing more than palliative care was possible. But the advice of these perceptive individuals was directed to a professional audience that was limited and often skeptical about the patient's willingness or his ability to confront death.

Dialogue with the Terminally Ill

When Elizabeth Kubler-Ross first attempted to involve terminally ill patients in a seminar for hospital staff in 1966, she repeatedly heard, "We have no dying patients." Yet, encouraged to discuss their feelings about impending death, the patients were grateful for the opportunity and spoke freely and honestly. Faced with the openness of the patients, the hospital staff realized that they would have to confront their own feelings about death and dying before they could face death directly with their patients. The resulting demand for seminars, classes and special training has moved thanatology, the study of death, into the health curriculum, and significant changes in health care have resulted. For example, there is strong interest in the Hospice movement, begun in England, which emphasizes innovative methods of pain control and programs for home care; both are concerns the dying patient typically communicates to the receptive listener.

Popular Response

The public interest in studies of the terminally ill has been so great that shortly after the publication of *On Death and Dying* (1968), Kubler-Ross came to be regarded as a spokesperson for the "death and dying movement." Her work created a widened audience for earlier research that had seldom been noticed beyond professional circles. The one-time public silence on the subject of death has been shattered. For now, the media frequently treat such themes as the unique and complex character of the dying person, the value of the terminal patient discussing death with his family and the rewards (as well as the costs) of sharing another person's dying.

Dying: Transition vs Institution

Indeed the current interest in death and dying is so great as to threaten saturation. Given the machinery to prolong dying and the rapidly developing study of the dying patient, there is a danger that the experience of dying will not only be recognized but be institutionalized, much the same way as society has institutionalized death. Dying, like mourning, could become a ritualized action with an expected role and scripts for behavior. The words of Montaigne recall the essentially transitional nature of the experience of dying: "If we have not known how to live, it is wrong to teach us how to die, and to give the end a different shape from the whole."

ENCOUNTER

RETURN FROM CLINICAL DEATH

I had a heart attack, and I found myself in a black void, and I knew I had left my physical body behind. I knew I was dying, and I thought, 'God, I did the best I knew how at the time I did it. Please help me.' Immediately, I was moved out of that blackness, through a pale grey, and I just went on, gliding and moving swiftly, and in front of me, in the distance, I could see a grey mist, and I was rushing toward it. It seemed that I just could not get to it fast enough to satisfy me, and as I got closer to it I could see through it. Beyond the mist, I could see people, and their forms were just like they are on earth, and I could also see something which one could take to be buildings. The whole thing was permeated with the most gorgeous light, a living, golden yellow glow, a pale color, not like the harsh gold color we know on earth.

As I approached more closely, I felt certain that I was going through that mist. It was such a wonderful, joyous feeling: there are just no words in human language to describe it. Yet, it wasn't my time to go through the mist, because instantly from the other side appeared my Uncle Carl, who had died many years earlier. He blocked my path, saying 'Go back. Your work on earth has not been completed. Go back now.' I did not want to go back, but I had no choice, and immediately I was back in my body. I felt that horrible pain in my chest, and I heard my little boy crying, 'God, bring my mommy back to me.'

Reported in R. A. Moody, Jr., *Life After Life*. Covington, Georgia: Mocking Bird Press, 1975.

1. Have you ever had a close brush with death? Describe the experience. What effect did it have on you at the time? Later?

2. What is your immediate reaction to the account given above? If you had heard the same account from a close friend would your reaction have been any different? If so, how?

3. Stop. Close your eyes. Imagine your heart has stopped on the operating table. What do you imagine happens next?

The young woman's account of her experience with clinical death reprinted above is reassuring to many. Psychiatric research is beginning to identify common elements contained in reports of such interactions with death. For example, Raymond Moody lists fifteen such elements, including out-of-the-body experience, awareness of light as a guide, debate about whether the person should return to life, the subject's resistance to returning, and the conviction on return that one's life has taken a different course. In the following article, "Help in the Dying Process," psychiatrist E. Mansell Pattison distinguishes between the fact of death and the process of dying. Pattison views the living-dying interval as a psychological crisis period which reactivates anxieties and conflicts central to the organization of the individual's personality. His framework, which differentiates among the fears that are normally encountered in the dying process, enables him to describe criteria for appropriate death and to make specific recommendations for psychological support during this time.

HELP IN THE DYING PROCESS

E. Mansell Pattison

"There's nothing more I can do for you, you're going to die." Having failed to preserve life, the physician leaves, for what has he to do with death?

And what has the psychotherapist to do with death? It has been suggested that physicians have failed to provide assistance to the dying because of unresolved conflicts towards death that lie buried in the unconscious of the medical profession. There is ample experimental and clinical evidence to support that assertion.[1,2] Yet little comment has been made on

E. Mansell Pattison. "Help in the Dying Process." *Voices*, V (Spring, 1969), 6-14.

the attitudes of psychotherapists toward death, particularly as it affects clinical practice. Thus Wahl[3] observed:

> It is interesting to note that anxiety about death, when it is noted in the psychiatric literature, is usually described solely as a derivative and secondary phenomenon, often as a more easily endurable form of the "castration fear." . . . it is important to consider if these formulations also subserve a defensive need on the part of psychiatrists themselves.

The problem was inadvertently stated by a psychiatrist reporting on his research on aging.[4]

> I myself tend to adhere to the concept of death as an accident, and therefore find it difficult to reconcile myself for myself or for others . . . people do not forgive themselves easily for having failed to save their own or others' lives.

One can observe the failure to face death in many psychotherapeutic situations. Consider how often a patient's threat of suicide cows the therapist. Or the therapist who puts himself in physical danger with a dangerous patient without noting the real danger. Or the reluctance to allow a patient to expose his deepest threatening and psychotic thoughts which intimate the annihilation of personality. I recall the long discussions I had as a young psychiatrist working in a prison. How could we work therapeutically with men serving life sentences? To what purposes? They seemed dead in contrast to our bright anticipatory lives.

I am struck by the fact that most psychotherapists feel sorely prepared to deal with death. This was brought home to me in a very personal way. Shortly after I published an article on dying,[5] I received the following letter from a well-known psychotherapist:

> Dear Dr. P.: I noticed your article on dying, I read it, enjoyed it and 'forgot' about it, until last month when my wife developed acute cancer to which she succumbed in three weeks. I would like you to know how immeasurably your article helped me (and her, indirectly), during that trying period. It is impossible to put into words—all I can say is that I had comfort during and after her dying in the knowledge that I could and did contribute some psychic comfort to her. Not only does your article have obvious personal

significance to me, but I feel the wisdom in it should be reaching others in the profession.

I was deeply moved by this, but I know that my wisdom was borrowed from others. Yet how to deal with death has not been part of the curriculum of "training for life." Every psychotherapist ought to read Allen Wheelis' parable,[6] "The League of Death," for Wheelis says to his fellow psychotherapists (as I read him) that we cannot face life until we can face death.

But we must move on, for our psychotherapeutic concern is not with death (that we can only assimilate) but rather with the process of dying. Indeed our preoccupation with death often precludes our looking at the process of dying—the period of life between knowledge of death and the point of death. How do we help people during this period of "dying life?"

A Seattle physician, Dr. Merrill Shaw, had a rectal cancer which had slowly gnawed away until death was only a few weeks away. Yet at that point he addressed the American Academy of General Practice with words of relevance:

> The period of inactivity after a patient learns there is no hope for his condition can be a period of great productivity. I regard myself as fortunate to have had this opportunity for a 'planned exit.' Patients who have been told there is no hope need help with their apprehension. Any doctor forfeits his priesthood of medicine, if, when he knows his patient is beyond help, he discharges the patient to his own services. Then the patient needs his physician more than anybody else does. The doctor who says merely, 'I'll drop in to see you once in a while, though there's nothing more I can do,' is of no use to the patient. For the patient goes through a period of unnecessary apprehension and anxiety.

The problem is that we do not perceive the healing task in existential terms, but rather in death-defensive terms. If we cannot pretend that we defeat death (and all treatment is in a sense a delaying-action), then we give in to ennui. But was it not Oliver Wendell Holmes who reminded us that "the physician's task is to cure rarely, relieve sometimes, and comfort always?"

The real help that can be given in the "living-dying" process of dying was brought home to me personally by another letter:

Dear Dr. P.: Quite by accident I read your treatise on dying. Because I am so grateful for your guidance I am writing not only to thank you but to suggest that the article be made available to relatives who care for patients . . . My husband has been treated for chronic glomeruli nephritis for nine years. For the past five years he has had biweekly dialysis which equates to a living-dying stage of long duration. In these times when there is no doctor-patient relationship in this type of indirect care the entire burden of sharing the responsibility of death falls to the member of the family caring for the nephritic. Your listing of the fears was so apparent when I read your paper, yet when my husband experienced them I was unprepared to see them or even acknowledge them. Whenever a patient is accepted on a kidney program he knows he is dying. Would it not be a kindness to the person caring for him to have access to your fine article?

Again, I was touched by a person and learned from her. It is not death that is so much the problem, but how to handle the process of dying. This can be seen in the following diagram. Note that the knowledge of death often precedes the point

THE PROCESS OF DYING SUBSEQUENT
TO THE CRISIS OF KNOWLEDGE OF DEATH

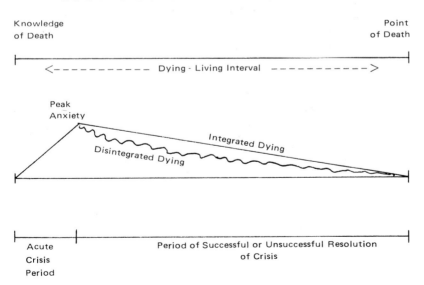

87

of death by many days, weeks, months, years. The *knowledge of death* produces a crisis in the life of the person. Will the crisis lead to a disintegrating process of dying? Or can we help the person to deal with the crisis of knowledge of death and help the person to attain an integrated process dying?[7]

The concepts of crisis intervention can be applied here to the *knowledge of death*.[8] This crisis can be seen as having five characteristics:

1. This stressful event poses a problem which by definition is insoluble in the immediate future. Dying in this sense is most stressful because it is ultimately insoluble and one to which we have to bow rather than solve.

2. The problem taxes one's psychologic resources since it is beyond one's traditional problem-solving methods. One is faced with a new experience with no prior experience to fall back on, for although one lives amidst death, that is far different from one's own death.

3. The situation is perceived as a threat or danger to the life goals of the person. Dying interrupts a person in the midst of life and even in old age it abruptly confronts one with the goals that one had set for one's own life.

4. The crisis period is characterized by a tension which mounts to a peak, then falls. As one faces the crisis of death, anxiety begins to mount, rises to a peak during which the person either mobilizes his coping mechanisms to deal with this anxiety or experiences disorganization and capitulation to his anxiety. In either event, one then passes to a state of diminishing anxiety as one approaches death. Hence, the peak of acute anxiety usually occurs considerably before death.

5.   The crisis situation awakens unresolved key problems from both the near and distant past. Problems of dependency, passivity, narcissism, inadequacy, identity, and more, are all reactivated by the process of dying. Hence, one is faced not only with the problem of death per se, but a host of unresolved feelings from one's own lifetime and its inevitable conflicts.

The importance of dying as a crisis is that the crisis is experienced as an overwhelming insuperable feeling of personal inadequacy in dealing with the dying process. There is bewilderment, confusion, indefinable anxiety, and unspecified fear. The person is faced with a total problem that he does not have resources to deal with, and the ensuing anxiety makes it impossible to deal with any of the part-aspects. *Here lies our opportunity to intervene, for although we cannot deal with the ultimate problem of death, we can help the person to deal with the various parts of the process of dying.* By focusing on these part-problems, the dying person can cope with himself and with his dying in some measure to resolve the crisis in a rewarding fashion that enhances his self-esteem, dignity, and integrity. The dying person can take pride then in having faced his crisis of dying with hope and courage and come away having dealt successfully with the crisis. One might call this healthy dying! Now let us turn to each of these part-aspects of the experience of dying:

The Fear of the Unknown

That which is strange and which we cannot anticipate strikes a deep fear within ourselves. This fundamental anxiety might be termed a *basic death anxiety*. A case report by Janice Norton illustrated this well.[9]

> Three days before a patient's death and a few hours before she became terminally comatose, we had a long conversation about her dying. She told me her only remaining fear was that dying was strange and unknown to her, that she had never done it before. Like birth, it was something that only happened once to any individual, and that similarly one might not remember what it was

really like, only know that it had once happened. She no longer worried about what was to happen to her after death, any more than an infant being born might worry about what his future life might be; she felt that she might be unnecessarily concerned with the actual process of death itself. She then asked me if I had been with other patients when they died and seemed relieved by my affirmative answer. One very comforting recurring thought to her was that throughout the centuries many people had died before her; more importantly, it had occurred to her that I would share this experience with her, although not at this time. I agreed that this was certainly so and added that I hoped I might equal her courage. She was pleased by this and then she reminisced about our relationship.

The Fear of Loneliness

Sickness of itself isolates one from the rest of humanity and the more so when one is dying. It is a commonplace observation that as death approaches others literally depart. This detachment is not only a psychologic phenomenon, but is also a reflection of our urban technology where the process of dying has become dehumanized and mechanized. There is inevitable separation in death, and yet our culture is perhaps one of the first in the history of humanity to reinforce the isolation of dying.

Now as John Donne said, "No man is an island," and our spirits feed on the food of human companionship. As experiments in sensory deprivation have vividly shown us, the human deprived of contact with other humans quickly disintegrates and loses his ego integrity. For the dying person, the mere fact of institutionalization has already set the stage for human deprivation that leads to a type of anaclitic depression. It is not the depression of the loss of a loved one, but depression resulting from the loss of necessary nurturing persons. Without this support, one rapidly falls into a confusional syndrome of human deprivation which we term loneliness. Indeed, it appears that this fear of loneliness is most paramount and immediate when a person first faces the prospect of death.

Fear of Loss of Family and Friends

Related to the actual separation that begins to occur is the real event of losing one's family and friends through one's own death just as much as if they themselves were dying. Hence, there is a real grief for this loss which must be mourned and worked through. Being able to resolve this separation can lead to a sense of attainment for both the patient and the family before death actually occurs. Failure to recognize this loss or being blocked in the grief process may make it difficult for the dying person to distinguish between his own problem of death and the natural and necessary process of grief which can be resolved before death.

Fear of Loss of Body

Our bodies are very much part of our self-image so that when illness distorts our body image there is not only a loss of function but a loss of self. This narcissistic blow to the integrity of oneself results in shame, and feelings of disgrace and inadequacy, for vital parts of the integral self-image are lost. Here again, one comes to genuine grief for the loss of part of oneself. In addition, the loss of body leads to the perception of self as disfigured and unlovely, hence unlovable. So the physically ill fear that they will no longer be loved by their families, will be rejected, and left alone. It bears comment that patients seem better able to tolerate external disfigurement than internal disease. Although external disfigurement may be difficult to bear, it seems to pose less threat than unknown and unspecified processes that the person cannot see and thereby keep track of. Hence, the hidden cancer or the failing heart may provoke more anxiety than the external symptoms of disease.

Fear of Loss of Self-Control

Debilitating disease makes one less capable of control of one's self, particularly when mental capacity is also affected.

This is particularly relevant in our society. We are a hyper-rational culture in which the ideal man is one who has full conscious willful rational control of himself. A tremendous fancy! As a result, we become anxious and feel threatened by anything that poses loss of consciousness or control. This is one of the reasons that our society is so ambivalent about the use of psychedelic drugs, tranquilizing, or energizing drugs, or even alcohol—they diminish our rationalistic self-control. So, too, our culture is skeptical and wary of any type of mystical experiences. Loss of self-control that might be quite acceptable among Eastern mystics is quite foreign to our Western human experience. It is rare that Americans experience any sort of self-acceptable loss of control. So when they come to the loss of control and rationality in the process of dying they have nothing in their past by which to measure or deal with this internal experience.

In studies by Goldstein 25 years ago it was shown that patients with brain disease often were troubled more by their own reaction to their mental deficits than by the deficit itself. Likewise, for the dying it is a giving up of total conscious willful control of the self that poses a threat to the ego. One is placed in a position of dependency as well as inadequacy so that in a sense the ego is no longer master of its own fate nor the captain of the self. So it is important to encourage and allow the dying person to retain whatever decisions and authorty he can, to sustain him in retaining control of small daily tasks and decisions, and to let him find reward and meaning in whatever self-control is available to him.

Fear of Loss of Identity

The loss of human contact, the loss of family and friends, the loss of one's body and control are all tied in with the sense of one's identity. Human contacts affirm who we are, family contacts affirm what we have been, and the control of our bodies affirms one's own self. There is a threat to the ego by losing the feelings for one's own body just as there is a threat to the ego by losing contact with family and cultural tradition.

In the dying process, one is faced with the crisis of maintaining an integrity of ego in the face of forces toward dissolution and annihilation of the person. Erikson sums it up as the crisis between *integrity versus despair*:[10]

> It is the acceptance of one's own and only life cycle and of the people who have become significant to it as something that had to be and that, by necessity, permitted of no substitutions. It thus means a new different love of one's parents, free of the wish that they should have been different, and an acceptance of the fact that one's life is one's own responsibility. It is a sense of comradeship with men and women of distant times and of different pursuits, that have created orders and objects and sayings conveying human dignity and love. Although aware of the relativity of all the various life styles which have given meaning to human striving, the possessor of integrity is ready to defend the dignity of his own life style against all physical and economic threats. For he knows that an individual life is the accidental coincidence of but one life cycle with but one segment of history; and that for him all human integrity stands and falls with the one style of integrity of which he partakes.

Despair, in contrast, is the consequence of the loss of self-esteem—the failure to maintain respect for oneself, for what one has been. Erikson's apt phrase is: "To be—through having been." Speaking of his own death, Willie Loman, the salesman, says: "A man must not be allowed to fall into his grave as a dead dog." It is not that you die, but how you die—and hope and courage contribute to maintaining a respect for self until death.

Allied with the idea of integrity then is the desire for both a reunion and a continuity. The reunion has to do with fantasies of return to a primal maternal figure as well as reunion with specific loved ones. And perhaps in some sense the fantasies of the reunion with one's parentage and one's race is a reaffirmation of the fact that one is part of a continuing line of human existence.

With our emphasis on individualism and cultural discontinuity, this sense of affinity is perhaps less available to us in American culture than it is to other peoples. Man as part of the enduring community, as part of the extended and continuing family of man is reflected in the following lines by an African poet, Birago Diop:

Listen more often
To things than to beings;
The fire's voice is heard
Hear the voice of water.
Hear in the wind
The bush sob
It is the ancestor's breath.
Those who have died have never left,
They are in the woman's breast
They are in the wailing child
And in the kindling firebrand
The dead are not under the earth,
They are in the forest, they are in the home
The dead are not dead.

Likewise, there is the desire for the maintenance and the continuity of one's life via one's family and the human race by bequeathing parts of oneself and one's possessions to those who will stay behind. This is most obvious in the tradition of leaving a will. But more personal is the fact that the dying person often finds meaning and significance in the maintenance of his own integrity by sharing of his belongings with those who are most immediately close to him. The most concrete example is the bequest of parts of one's body. We make good cultural use of this through eye banks, bone banks, and so on. As an example, some years ago as an intern I took care of a man with undiagnosed cancer of the neck. He was obviously debilitated and rapidly progressing toward death. We talked many times of the meaning of death and of his life and what he had done and what he would like to have done. He was interested in my plans and my future and hoped that I would learn from his case things that would be of value to me as I continued in my life in medicine. He was discharged and returned to the hospital several months later near the point of death. The surgeons wished to obtain a neck biopsy but the patient refused until he had talked with his doctor, namely me. So I shortly got a call from the professor of surgery asking if I would please see the patient as their consultant! The patient was much relieved when he saw me and wanted my professional opinion as to whether I thought that the surgery professors were right in their management of his case. When I explained to him that biopsy would probably not change the course of his disease nor prevent him from dying in the immediate future, but that it would help us in our understanding of the disease process and would help me in my training and education, he was very happy to comply, feeling that he had something that he could give and share with me, namely his disease process and his body. In this sense he had given to me part of himself that would remain with me after his death.

Fear of Regression

Finally, there is a fear of those internal instincts within oneself that always push us to retreat from the outer world of reality to a primal world of fantasy and bliss. Throughout life, our ego fights against this internal pull to an eternal primordial existence. Freud called it Thanatos—instinct to death. Whatever the theoretical grounds, it does appear that the dying person begins to return to a state of being at one with the world where there is a helpless and timeless existence, where I (the ego) and you (outer world) no longer are differentiated. At this point, one is rapidly approaching the state of surrender to the process of renunciation of life and return to union with the earth out of which we have sprung. Indeed, psychic death is now acceptable, desirable and now at hand.

The Sequence of Dying

What I have sketched out here is a rough and tentative outline of the sequence of dying. First is facing a seemingly impossible crisis that threatens to overwhelm the self. Mankind seems to have always recognized that no one has the capability to face this crisis alone, and so we have cultural customs whereby we actually and literally help people to die! Given our inter-

95

est, support, and guidance, the dying person may turn to use his available capacities to deal with the several distinct part-processes of dying. He can face death as unknown with the realization that he cannot know, and instead consider the process of dying that he can know and deal with. He can learn to endure the inevitable degrees of separation that begin to occur if he is not actually deprived of human contact. He can face the loss of relatives, friends, and activities and actively mourn their loss and become reconciled to it if this grief is defined and accepted. He can tolerate the loss of self-control if it is not perceived by himself and others as a shameful experience, and if he can gain control of himself to the degree that he is able. He can retain dignity and self-respect in the face of the completion of his life cycle, gradually relinquish the unattainable and respect himself for what he has been. Then one can place one's life in a perspective of both reunion and continuity with one's personal history and human tradition. If this is accomplished, then one can move toward an acceptable regression where the self gradually returns to a state of nonself.

The Appropriate Death

If the dying person is provided the opportunity and assistance, then the experience of dying can be a part of living. Weisman and Hackett[11] speak of appropriate death whose criteria closely approximate the clinical sequence outlined above.

1. Conflict is reduced.
2. Compatibility with the ego ideal is obtained.
3. Continuity of important relationships is preserved or restored.
4. Consummation of basic instincts and wishes of fantasy re-emerge and are fulfilled.

The importance of an appropriate death is that dying is not an extraneous foreign process but rather it is a process integrated into the style, meaning and sequence of that which has gone before. The concrete nature of each man's appropriate death will be different, but can be appropriate for him.

Philosophy has always concerned itself with death, and great literature speaks of the enduring conflicts common to all men in all ages. Only recently, as death has been pushed further and further away from everyday life, has it become a subject of study for the social sciences. Sociologists have compiled bodies of data on the organization of death and of dying; more recently, psychiatrist Elizabeth Kubler-Ross has done much to establish dying as a discipline of its own within psychiatry and psychology. In the article below, "What Is It Like to Be Dying?" she summarizes her best known work with the dying. Although she readily admits that all patients do not follow "a classical pattern," and that a patient may well remain in one "stage" or another, by outlining a psychological process of dying she provides a structure for understanding the reactions and needs of the dying person. Kubler-Ross also emphasizes how those close to the dying patient must work to understand their own attitudes toward death in order to be able to help the patient.

WHAT IS IT LIKE TO BE DYING?

Elisabeth Kubler Ross

What is it like to be dying? Not from the nurse's point of view, nor from the doctor's, nor the family's, but from the patient's point of view: what is it like? Because, if we have some idea of what the answer might be, then we're going to be in a better position to help.

At the University of Chicago Billings Hospital, some of us have made it our business to find out a little more about what it is like to be dying. Before sharing this information with you, though, let me first raise another question: why—at this time, in this society—must we have so many books on death and dying, so many lectures and seminars on the subject? After all, we should be experts on dying. It is the one thing that has been with mankind as long as man himself. So why has it suddenly become such a big issue?

Death has always been a fearful thing to men. We have a hard time conceiving of our own death. We believe with the psalmist who says, "A thousand shall fall at thy side, and ten thousand at thy right hand; *but* it shall not come nigh thee." Deep down, we believe, or would like to believe, that we are immortal. We cannot conceive of dying a natural death at the end of our lives, just falling asleep one night and not waking up. Instead, when we have to conceive death, we see it as something malignant and catastrophic: a destructive intervention from the outside that hits us suddenly and finds us unprepared.

Death in the old days came in the form of epidemics: produced by nature, not by man. Man tried to master epidemics, he mastered illness, he developed antibiotics and vaccinations, he learned to prolong life, he was able to master many, many causes of death. But in his fear of death and his need to master things, he has also developed weapons. If he has the choice to kill or be killed, he chooses to kill.

In the old days, an enemy in the battlefield could be seen. You had a chance to defend your family, your tribe, or your honor; you could choose a good weapon or a good hill. You had a chance to survive.

But today, out of man's need to be stronger, to defy death, he has developed bigger and more horrible weapons. One reason for our present death-denying society, I believe, is that man has now created weapons of mass destruction— man-made, mind you, not like nature's epidemics. He has developed weapons which, in a very concrete way, represent our fear of death, the catastrophic death that hits us from the outside when we are not prepared. You can't see, you can't smell, and you can't hear this enemy, whether it be chemical or bacteriological warfare, atom bombs, or even pollution.

What do we do when we have created such weapons of mass destruction? We cannot defend ourselves physically against them, we have to defend ourselves psychologically. We can pretend that nobody will push the wrong button. We can build ourselves bomb shelters in the garden, or we can build anti-missiles and have the illusion that we are safe.

But none of these defenses really works. What works partially is that we can deny that we are finite. That it shall happen to thee and thee but not come nigh to me. We can pretend that we are not finite by developing "deep freeze societies," where we freeze those who die and put them into some sort of mausoleum and promise the next of kin to defrost them in 50 or 100 years from now. These societies really exist; they serve the need to deny that people actually die.

We see this same need and tendency in the hospital. When we are assigned to dying patients, we feel very, very uncomfortable. In fact, even when we know that a patient is dying, we have a hard time facing that fact and acknowledging it—not in the head but in the gut. And our patients very often die with more difficulty than they used to.

In the old days, people were more likely to die at home rather than in the hospital. When a person is at home, he's in his own familiar environment, with his family and his children around him. Dying, under these circumstances, is not only easier and more comfortable for the patient, but it also does something for his family—especially the children, who can share in the preparatory grief for a person who is dying in the house. Such a child will grow up and know that death is part of life.

But if the sick person is shipped off to the hospital, with visits limited to perhaps five minutes every hour in the intensive treatment unit, it is not the same experience. And children are not allowed to see those patients, those parents. In Europe, even now, there is no embalming, no make-believe sleep, no slumber rooms, no euphemisms. All this, I think, helps us to face death as part of life. But today, in the United States, we have a long way to go before we can accept death as part of life. Dying, as many patients have expressed to us, has become not only more lonely and more isolated, but very often more impersonalized, dehumanized, and mechanized.

Some five years ago, four theology students asked me if I couldn't help them in a project. They had to write a paper on crisis in human life, and they had chosen dying. That's the biggest crisis people have to face, they said, and they asked,

"How do you go about it? How do you do research on dying? You can't experience it. You can't experiment with it, you can't verify it, you can't do all the things that one ought to do with a good research project."

So I suggested to them that it would be very simple to ask dying patients, "What is it like? How does it feel? What fears, needs, fantasies do you have? What kind of things are we doing that are helpful? What kind of things do we do that are detrimental?" The students agreed, and I volunteered to work with them and to find a seriously ill patient for our first interview.

How naive I was: I discovered that there was not a single dying patient in a 600-bed hospital! I went from ward to ward and told the nurses and the doctors that I would like to talk to a terminally ill patient.

"What about?"

"About dying."

"Oh, we have nobody dying."

If I pushed, they said, "He's too weak" or "too sick" or "too tired" or "he doesn't feel like talking." A lot of not only denial and rationalization but also hostility and some very aggressive behavior emerged. One nurse asked me, "Do you enjoy playing God?" and another: "Do you get a kick out of telling a 20-year-old that he has one week to live?" And, of course, there was much well-meant protectiveness for the patients.

I had had the same experience a few years earlier in another hospital. There, the only way I was able to find a dying patient was to go through the wards and look at the patients and guess that somebody was very sick. That way I saw an old man who looked very sick and who was reading a paper with a headline, "Old Soldiers Never Die." I asked him if he wasn't afraid to read that, and he said, "Are you one of those doctors who can't talk about it when you can't help us no more?" So I gave him a pat on the back and said, "You're the right kind of man and I want to talk with you."

Eventually, though, we started to receive an ever-increasing number of referrals. Our first patient was perhaps the most troubling one—to me, anyway. I went to see this old man the day before I was to see him with the students. He put his arms out and with pleading eyes said, "Please sit down *now*." With the emphasis on *now*. But I did what we always do. I could only hear my own needs, I was frustrated and tired of running around, and tomorrow was the day I was supposed to see him with the students. So I told him "No, I can't stay now, I'll be back tomorrow," and I left.

When I came back with the students the next day, it was too late. He was in oxygen, he could hardly breathe, and the only thing he was able to say was, "Thank you for trying, anyway." And he died a short time later. He helped us a lot, however, although not in any verbal way. What he told us was that when a terminally ill patient says, "Sit down *now*," you have to sit down *now*. Because somehow these patients sense that *now* is the time that they can talk about it. There may not be such a time again, so even if you can sit down only two or three minutes, you will feel better, and so will the patient.

The students and I had so many feelings when we left that man's room that we did something that we have continued to do for almost five years now: we went to my office and shared our gut reactions. Not nice things. Not the kinds of things that one ought to say and feel: those come from your head. But how does it feel in the gut? That's what we talk about. We try to get to know each other's feelings—to understand them, not to judge them. We try to help each other express them so that we can learn to listen to our gut reaction and to differentiate between the patient's needs and our own.

So far, we have interviewed over 400 terminally ill patients. By "terminally ill," I mean patients with a serious illness which may end fatally. They don't necessarily die the next day or the next week. Many of them have gone home or have had a remission. Some have lived only 12 hours, and others have lived for a year or two.

What have we learned from them? We have learned that our patients all know when they are dying, and I think that's consoling for us to know. Half of them have never been told that they have a serious illness. We are often asked what or whether a patient should be told. Actually, I don't think any patient should be told that he is dying. He will tell *you* that when you dare to listen, when you are able to hear it.

But patients should, I think, with very few exceptions, be told when they have a serious illness. Our patients say that they would like to be told this under two conditions: one is that the person telling them allows for some hope, and the second is that "you are going to stick it out with me—not desert me—not leave me alone." If we can, indeed, "stick it out" with them, then I think that we can help them the most.

We have learned, too, that dying patients generally go through a series of stages. The stages don't always follow one another; they overlap sometimes and sometimes they go back and forth.

Most patients, when told they have a serious illness, react with shock and denial. "No, it can't be me. It's not possible." Only three of our 400, however, maintained this denial to the very end, although many have maintained denial in the presence of other people—usually family or staff members—who need denial themselves. If a family needs denial, the patient will not talk to them about the seriousness of his illness or how he feels. But if they, or we, can tell him that we are ready to talk about it, that we are willing to listen, he will drop the denial quite quickly and will talk about his situation.

Our patients usually drop part of their denial when they have to take care of unfinished business or financial matters, especially when they begin to worry about their children. But they also drop their denial if they know that the person with them will help them to express the multitude of feelings that emerge when they face the given reality.

Perhaps the second most important and common response is anger. When a person can no longer say, "No, not me," the next question is usually "Why me?" The patient should be allowed to express this, and you don't have to have an answer because none of us will ever have an answer to that question. Just listen.

At this stage these patients will be very difficult: not only with the family (they visit too early or too late or with too many people or not enough people), but also with the nurses. You come in and shake a pillow and the patient complains, "Why are you bothering me now? I just want to take a nap." When you leave him alone, he protests that you don't straighten out his bed. The physician doesn't have the right prescriptions or the right diet or the right tests. In short, these are extremely "difficult and ungrateful" patients.

What do you do when you have a patient like that? What is your gut reaction? Remember, the harder you try, the harder the time he gives you. What do you do? You withdraw, you get angry at him, maybe you wait twice as long until you answer his light.

In one study, they measured the time it took nurses to answer patients' lights. And they discovered that patients who were beyond medical help—terminally ill patients—had to wait twice as long as the others.

That, too, you have to try to understand and not judge. It is very hard to be around patients like this for very long, especially if you try to do your best and all you get is criticism and abuse. What we have found to be most helpful to the patients and ourselves is not to get angry back at them or take their abuse personally (which we normally do) but to try to find out what they are so angry about.

We asked our patients about this. What came out was that the peppier, the more energetic, the more functioning you are when you come into that room, the more anger you often provoke. And the patient says angrily to you, *"You* can walk out of here again, you know. *You* can go home again at five and see your kids. *You* can go to work." They're not angry at you as a person, but at what you represent—life, functioning, pep, energy, all the things they are in the process of losing or have already partially lost.

We tried to see if it would help if we poured fuel on the fire, if we let them ventilate, let them express their anger. If we can say to them, "You know, I would be angry, too. Get it off your chest. Scream if you feel like screaming," then they will express their rage and anger, but it never comes out as loud and frightening as you might think.

The best example is the mother of a small child who died. She looked very numb, so I said to her. "You look as though you need to scream." And she said, "Do you have a screaming room at the hospital?" She was serious. I said, "No, but we have a chapel," which was a silly answer because she immediately replied, "I need just the opposite. I need to scream and rage and curse. I've just been sitting in the parking lot and cursing and screaming at God. 'God, why do you let this happen to my child? Why do you let this happen to me?' " And I said, "Do it here. It's better to do it *with* somebody than out in a parking lot all alone."

And that's what I mean by the stage of anger, of rage, of a sense of impotence, of helplessness. You can help not only the patient to express this rage and anger, but the family, too, because they go through the same stages. And, from a practical point of view, the nursing staff will be saved many, many steps. The nurse will be called less, the patient will be more comfortable.

Sometimes the patient gets to this point—loses his anger—without any external help, and you wonder what happened. Very often it is because he has entered the state of bargaining. Most bargaining is done with God. "If you give me one more year to live, I will be a good Christian or I will donate my kidney or this or that." Most of the time it is a promise, in exchange for some prolongation of life.

We had one patient who depended on injections around the clock to control her terrible pain. She was one of our most difficult patients, and it became very hard to keep on visiting her. Then one day she was very friendly and she said, "You know, if you help me get out of this hospital for one single day, I will be a good patient." She wanted that one day to get up and get dressed and attend her son's wedding. This was finally possible, and she left, looking like a million dollars.

And we began to wonder, "What is it like? How must it feel to ask only for one single day? It must be terribly difficult to come back to the hospital."

When she returned, she wasn't happy to see me. Before I could ask a single question she said, "Dr. Ross, don't forget I have another son." That's the briefest, quickest example of the bargaining stage I know.

In the denial stage it's "No, not me!" In the anger, "Why me?" In the bargaining, "Yes, me, but. . . ." When the patient finally drops the "but," then it's "Yes, me." And "Yes, me" means that he has the courage to acknowledge that it has indeed "come nigh" to him, and he is naturally very depressed.

After a while, these patients become silent. It's a kind of grief which is difficult for us to accept—where they don't talk much any more, where they don't want any more visitors. How do we react to them when we come into their rooms and find them crying or silently mourning? What do we do? Can we tolerate this?

This is sometimes even more difficult to bear than the angry patients. As long as they complain about all the things they have lost, it's something we can grasp. But when they become quiet and the tears are running down—and especially if it's a man—then it's very hard. We have a tendency to say, "What a beautiful day outside. Look at those lovely flowers. Cheer up. It's not so bad."

It *is* bad. If I were to lose one beloved person, everybody would allow—even expect—me to grieve. It would be perfectly normal because I would have lost one person I loved. But the dying patient is about to lose not just one beloved person but everyone he has ever loved and everything that has been meaningful to him. That is a thousand times sadder. If the patient has the courage to face this, then he should be allowed to grieve; he has a right to it.

We call this the preparatory grief. If he can prepare himself slowly, if he is allowed to grieve and, if necessary, to cry, then he becomes able to decathect, to separate himself. He will have the courage to ask for no more relatives to come after a while, no more children. And at the very end he will want perhaps only one loved person—someone who can sit silently and comfortably by his side, without words, but just touching his hand or perhaps stroking his hair or just being there.

That's when a patient has reached the stage of acceptance. And acceptance is not resignation! Resignation is a bitter kind of giving up ("What's the use?"), almost a defeat. But acceptance is a good feeling. "I have now finished all of my unfinished business. I have said all of the words that have to be said. I am ready to go."

These patients are not happy, but they are not terribly sad. They usually have very little physical pain and discomfort, and they slip into a stage which very often reminds us of the beginning of life: when a person has physical needs and needs only one person to give him some tender, loving care and compassion—who can be with him but doesn't have to talk all the time. It's the comfort of being together that counts.

"Do you have to be a psychiatrist to work with these people?" I am often asked. No. Many of our patients are angry when a psychiatric consultation is called because they have dared to become depressed. What I have talked about so far is the normal behavior of a dying patient, and it doesn't take a psychiatrist to help him. It doesn't take much time, either— only a very few minutes.

Last fall, we saw a young man who was the father of three small children. He had never been sick, never been in the hospital before, and now he was admitted with acute leukemia. Every day when I saw him, he was on the verge of talking. He wanted to talk but he couldn't. So he would say, "Come back tomorrow." And I would come back the next day, but he would say again, "Come back tomorrow."

Finally, I said to him, "If you don't want to talk about it, that's alright." He quickly responded: "No, if I don't do it now, I'll never be able to do it. Why don't you come back tomorrow morning very early, before rounds, before anybody else comes? I have to get it out." (We never talked, by the way, about what "it" meant, but both of us knew.)

The next day I came very early and the nurses told me that this patient had been dying during the night, that he had put up a physical fight for about three and a half hours, that he was really not in a condition to talk. But when I promise a patient I will see him, I keep that promise even if he is comatose or not in a position to communicate. So I went to his room and, to my surprise, he almost sat up in his bed. "Come on in," he said; "close the door and sit down." And he talked as he had never talked before.

He said, "I have to tell you what happened last night, you will never believe it." (I'm using his own words because I want to show you what we mean about talking about dying. Patients do not always use the word "dying" but you can talk about dying in many languages.)

"Last night," he continued, "I put up a fight for several hours. There was a big train going rapidly down the hill towards the end, and I had a big fight with the train master. I argued and fought with him. And I ordered him to stop this train one tenth of an inch short."

Then he paused and asked me, "Do you know what I am talking about?" I said, "I guess the train that goes rapidly down toward the end is your life. And you had a big fight with the train master—for just a little bit more time." Then I smiled and added, "You made it." (That's bargaining. He bargained for one tenth of an inch.)

At that moment his mother came in and I said, "How can I help you with the tenth of an inch?" using his language since I didn't know on what level this mother and son communicated. And he said, "Try to help me convince my mother that she should go home now and bake a loaf of bread and make my favorite vegetable soup; I want to eat that once more." And the mother did go home and he did get his bread and soup—his last solid food. He died about three days later.

I think this man went through all the stages of dying in this overnight struggle. He tried to maintain his denial as long as possible—and then he dropped it in that one night. The anger, the bargaining and the depression, preceded the final stage of acceptance.

My last example is a woman whose story illustrates what hope means and how the nature of hope changes from the healthy to the sick to the dying. If we can elicit the patient's hope and support *his* hope, then we can help him the most.

This woman came to our hospital feeling very sick and weak, and her doctor said that she should go to a specialist in another hospital. So she hoped at that time that it was nothing serious, that it could be treated, that she would get well. After a while she was told that she had a serious kidney disease; then she hoped for treatment that would cure it. Next, she was told her life could be prolonged if she were accepted on a dialysis program for indigent people. This, too, was something for her to hope for—but she was rejected.

The social worker and the nurses, who were really fond of this woman, could not accept this. It was hard for them to visit her after dialysis had been denied, so they asked us to see her in our death and dying seminar.

The patient was very relieved when we were frank and told her why we wanted to see her. Many little but unfortunate things had happened to her at the hospital to which she was sent—hurriedly and unprepared—to be considered for dialysis. Confusion and misunderstanding grew until finally, when all the doctors stopped at her bedside on rounds, she realized that this was the moment of truth.

"A big cloud came over me," she said, "and I had the idea that I had a kidney operation and didn't need those doctors. When I woke up they were gone." In other words, she had a fantasy that she didn't need the doctors to save her life. Considered to be psychotic and hallucinating, she was rejected for dialysis.

We explored a lot of feelings about that, and then we discussed with her what kinds of things we could do now to make whatever time she had left more meaningful or more bearable.

She said, "Don't be so upset. When I die, it will be just like going from this garden to God's garden." But something was really bothering her, she added. She didn't know quite what it was and it was hard to talk about it.

Two days later, I said to her, "You know, there was something that bothered you, and that's what we call unfinished business. What is it?" And she kept saying, "I'm bad, I'm bad, I'm bad. Because what she was really saying was that she had to confess something that she felt guilty about, but she didn't know the origin of this guilt. And we searched like two children who are looking in the dark for something they have lost.

Finally, I gave up and I said, "God only knows why you should be bad," which was a genuine gut reaction on my part. And she looked up and said, "That's it: 'God. I called on God for help for the last few days. 'God help me. God help me.' And I heard Him say in the back of my mind, 'Why are you calling me now, why didn't you call me when things were all right?' What do you say to that, Dr. Ross?" And my gut reaction was to take off. Why couldn't a priest be here? Or a minister? Or somebody? But not me.

But you can't give a patient like this a phony answer. You have to be you and you have to be honest. So I struggled, and finally I said, "Just imagine that the children are playing outside and the mother is in the house and the little boy falls and hurts his knee. What happens?" And she said, "The mother goes out and helps him back on his feet and consoles him." I said, "OK, and he is all right now. What happens next?" And she said, "The boy goes back to his play and the mother goes back in the house." "He has no use for her now?" I asked, and she said "No," and I said, "Does the mother resent this terribly?" She looked at me almost angrily and said, "A mother? A mother wouldn't resent that." And I said, "If a mother wouldn't resent that, do you think that our Father would?"

Then the happiest, most beautiful smile came over her face, and she asked me something I'll never forget: "What is your concept of death?" (I felt like saying, "How dare you ask me!" It shall not "come nigh" to me, even after seeing so many dying patients.) So I said something about liking her idea about the garden, but she just shook her head and asked again, "What is your concept of death?" Then I looked at her face and said, "Peace." That was a genuine answer. And she said, "I'm going very peacefully, now, from this garden into the next one."

This patient taught us how hope can change: from hoping it's nothing serious, then hoping for treatment, then hoping for a prolongation of life. And finally hoping that "If I'm not accepted in this garden, I hope I'll be accepted in the next garden."

It is the patient's hope that we should support. I had known this woman less than an hour, yet I learned from her. And I think I helped her.

It didn't take much time. But what it did take, and will always take, is a sense of comfort in the face of death. What all of us have to learn is to accept death as part of life. When we have learned this, then maybe we can help our patients learn it, too.

The threat posed by a terminal illness is an obvious motivation for contemplation of death and dying. But in earlier centuries individuals lived more closely with their deaths than they do today. This intimacy with death is expressed by Emily Dickinson, nineteenth-century American poet, who displays a fascination with exploring the experience of death.

In her poetry she moves to the brink of death only to be saved and return again. In "Exultation Is the Going" she romanticizes death as a peak experience. But does her work represent acceptance of death?

I HEARD A FLY BUZZ WHEN I DIED

Emily Dickinson

I heard a Fly buzz—when I died—
The Stillness in the Room
Was like the Stillness in the Air—
Between the Heaves of Storm—

The Eyes around—had wrung them dry—
And Breaths were gathering firm
For that last Onset—when the King
Be witnessed—in the Room—

I willed my Keepsakes- Signed away
What portion of me be
Assignable—and then it was
There interposed a Fly—

With Blue—uncertain stumbling Buzz—
Between the light—and me—
And then the Windows failed—and then
I could not see to see—

Reprinted by permission of the publishers and the Trustees of Amherst College from *The Poems of Emily Dickinson,* edited by Thomas H. Johnson, Cambridge, Mass.: The Belknap Press of Harvard University Press, © 1951, 1955 by the President and Fellows of Harvard College.

EXULTATION IS THE GOING

Emily Dickinson

Exultation is the going
Of an inland soul to sea,
Past the houses—past the headlands—
Into deep Eternity—

Bred as we, among the mountains,
Can the sailor understand
The divine intoxication
Of the first league out from land?

There are many ways to die, and there are many ways of facing death. Terminal illness is not the only condition in which one knows that one's death is imminent. Capital punishment sets the individual the same task of preparing to die, but in an ignominious way. Unlike the case of the patient, there is no question of keeping the fact of impending death from the prisoner, and little or no social support to help him rationalize the fact of death. In a series of brief case histories, psychiatrists Harvey Bluestone and Carl L. McGahee describe the development of characteristic coping mechanisms which serve to protect the prisoners from experiencing overwhelming anxiety or depression. Denial, projection and obsessional concerns may have a specific content here, but the process of adjustment to stress is a familiar one.

REACTION TO EXTREME STRESS: IMPENDING DEATH BY EXECUTION

Harvey Bluestone and Carl L. McGahee

We conventionally think of death as "the worst thing" that can happen to us. Knowing, as we all do, that we will die in some vague future does not impose any great stress. The man in the grip of a relentlessly fatal disease has to cope with much more severe stress. But mercifully, his death date is not fixed and he can always hope to see tomorrow's sun rise. Presumably, the greatest of stresses would be imposed on the man who knows he is going to be put to death—and knows just when that will be.

We have studied 18 men and one woman in the Sing Sing death house. Because of the inmate utilizing opportunities for appeals for clemency or commutation there is adequate time for repeated psychiatric interviews and psychologic examinations.

These men are housed in an area detached from the rest of the prison. They have few visitors, though the authorities impose no restrictions on visiting. One might expect them to

Bluestone, H. and McGahee, C.L. Reaction to Extreme Stress: Impending Death by Execution. *American Journal of Psychiatry*, vol. 119, pp. 393-396, 1962. Copyright © 1962, the American Psychiatric Association. Reprinted by permission.

show severe depression and devastating anxiety, yet neither symptom was conspicuous among these 19 doomed persons. By what mechanisms did they avoid these expected reactions to such overwhelming stress? Do their emotional patterns change during a year or two in a death cell? And, do these defenses function to the moment of execution—or do they crumble toward the end?

The 19 histories had certain features in common. All had come from deprived backgrounds. All but one came from homes where the father was missing (deserted, dead, unknown, or separated) during the childhood or adolescence. Practically all had been brought up (during their growing years) in institutions or foster homes. Not one had an education better than that of tenth grade. Some were illiterate. Their intelligence varied from an IQ of 60 to one with an IQ of 140. All had been convicted of murder. None of the murders was long planned: they were impulsive. Many were committed in connection with a felony. The world appeared as a hostile, dangerous, and menacing place, and they had reacted in their way—by aggression, suspiciousness and cynicism.

The following are brief summaries of the reaction of some of these men to their imprisonment in the death house. (For collective data, see chart to follow.)

---

1. **Age range of death house prisoners**
   - 18 or younger. 1
   - 19 or 20 2
   - 21 through 25. 5
   - 26 through 30. 3
   - 30 to 35 5
   - over 35 3

2. **Family background**
   - Parents together during most of childhood 1
   - Father unknown or deserted 7
   - Father divorced or separated 10
   - Father and mother unknown 1

3. **Highest school grade reached**
   - Fourth or lower 4
   - Fifth or sixth 8
   - Seventh or eighth 2
   - Ninth or tenth 5

4. **Intelligence quotient**

    60 through 69. 2

    70 through 79. 5

    80 through 89. 7

    90 through 119. 4

    120 through 140 1

5. **Family status of prisoner as adult**

    Never married, but had common-law

       spouse. 5

    Never married, no regular consortium 11

    Married, but separated 2

    Living with wife 1

6. **Psychological defense mechanisms used**

    Totals more than 19; some used more

    than one)

    Denial by isolation of affect 7

    Denial by minimizing the predica-

       ment. 4

    Denial by delusion formation. 1

    Denial by living only in the present. 4

    Projection 7

    Obsessive rumination in connection with

       appeals 3

    Obsessive preoccupation with religion 2

    Obsessive preoccupation with intellectu-

       al or philosophical matters 5

---

1. This man has the longest residence in the death house of those in this study, approximately two years. An overt confirmed homosexual, he maintained a calm conviction that he would be ultimately pardoned. This belief remained bolstered throughout by an unchanging contention that he had been framed by the legal and medical authorities involved in his prosecution. Psychological testing showed a man of average intelligence with considerable withdrawal from real emotional interaction with others. Defense mechanisms of denial and projection were effective in warding off anxiety and depression despite prolonged incarceration in the death house.

2. This inmate is the only woman in this series. She is of dull intelligence, acts in a playful and flirtatious manner. She was usually euphoric, but became transiently depressed when she thought her case was going badly. She frequently complained of insomnia and restlessness. These symptoms quickly disappeared when she was visited by a psychiatrist

whom she enjoyed seeing and talking to in a self-justifying and self-pitying manner. Psychological tests showed pervasive feelings of insecurity, repressive defenses, and an inability to handle angry and aggressive feelings in an effectual manner.

3. This inmate is a withdrawn, sullen, uncommunicative individual. When visited in the death house he would elaborately and slowly wash his clothes ignoring examiners. He spends much of his time reading proound philosophical works which are beyond his comprehension. His intelligence is dull-normal. He has become progressively more suspicious and grandiose during his death house stay.

4. This man gives a long history of delinquent behavior. He is a litigiously minded individual who states that he can appeal his case for years. He is obsessed with his own power and is convinced that a law suit against the district attorney for lost automobile tools kept that official from being reelected. He has become progressively more angry and abusive ultimately necessitating his physical isolation from other inmates. His IQ is 134. Projective tests show a chronically cold, withdrawn, narcissistically invested personality. Withdrawal, projection and denial are prominent defense mechanisms.

5. This man is at all times euphoric. He has shown little anxiety during the full year he has spent in the death house. He has led a hedonistic life and has never been able to make future plans. His inability to see beyond the day seems quite effective in enabling him to avoid anxiety and depression.

6. This inmate showed during his early months of incarceration a contemptuous indifference toward the authorities and his own plight. Gradually, however, depression appeared and became progressively more intense. This was rather dramatically reversed when the inmate presented an apparent religious conversion, which seemed to both occupy his mind and also elevate him above the authorities and his situation. However, this defense was only partially successful for this individual who had a life-long history of discharging all tensions by immediate impulsive acting-out. Psychological testing showed dull-normal intelligence and a primitive, self-absorbed, hostility-ridden personality.

8. This inmate related to examiners in an open and direct manner. He is mentally dull and preoccupied with thoughts of voodoo spells. His primary defense mechanism is denial of the possibility of being executed. This works poorly and he is chronically anxious and periodically depressed. His anger at his accomplice, who he is convinced is the cause of his difficulties, seems to relieve him of some of his unpleasant feelings. He amuses himself in working on a taunting poem which he proposes to recite when his accomplice is executed. This mechanism, too, is ineffectual and he reverts from these thoughts of revenge to a contemplation of his own plight.

117

9. This man is a moody individual who feels he is the victim of a Jewish plot since the judge, district attorney, and his own court appointed lawyer are Jewish. He denied his guilt repeatedly during his early days in the death house, but became progressively more confused and a few days before his scheduled execution asked the examiner for truth serum so that he would know whether or not he committed the crime. He showed alternating use of introjection and projection. He would become depressed when news of his appeal was bad, and when a stay of execution was granted he became paranoid and grandiose. He managed in some obscure way to identify his impending death with that of Lumumba, who had recently been killed in the Congo, and felt that his own execution would make him a martyr in the cause of anti-imperialism.

10. This man stands out in the series as being the one who most successfully employed intellectualization as a means of defending against anxiety and depression. He elaborated a philosophy of life and values in which his own criminal career became not only justifiable, but even respectable. He rationalized his crimes by emphasizing the hypocrisy and perfidy of society on the one hand and by comparing himself with policemen and soldiers and others who live honorably "by the gun" on the other. This system was so effective for him that even when execution appeared imminent he maintained his hero's martyr role and disdained to request executive clemency.

11. This inmate is an illiterate, inadequate individual who was convicted as an accomplice to a robbery-murder. He had an overall IQ of 51. He showed primarily depression, withdrawal, and obsessive rumination over the details of his crime and conviction. He eventually evolved a poorly elaborated paranoid system whereby he supposedly was betrayed and framed by his girlfriend and one of the co-defendants. Despite the looseness of his persecutory thinking, it was accompanied by a clear-cut elevation in his mood and reduction of anxiety.

12. This inmate, also an accomplice to a robbery-murder, showed one of the most florid pictures of any in this series. Both grandiose and persecutory themes were prominent, but the latter predominated. He maintained that his arrest and conviction were malicious frauds, and he meticulously and obsessively combed through the court record to substantiate his contentions. His arguments were labored and illogical, hinging on such points as the use of words like "who" and "whom." The paranoid mechanisms seemed to mitigate, but not completely defend him against depression.

13. He is one of the two inmates in this series who uses religious preoccupation as his major defense mechanism. He repeatedly, in an almost word for word way, stated his situation as follows. "No one can understand how I feel unless it happened to you. Christ came to me and I know He died for my sins. It doesn't matter if I am electrocuted or not. I am going to another world after this and I am prepared for it." As his stay

progresses he becomes increasingly more hostile and antagonistic, and his behavior progressively out of keeping with his professed religious ideas. In addition to obsessive rumination, projection and withdrawal are employed to ward off feelings of anxiety and depression.

DISCUSSION

Faced with certain and ignominious death, a person would presumably be overwhelmed with anxiety or plunge into the depths of depression. Yet this does not happen. What defense does the human mind set up against intense anxiety or a paralyzing depression? We suggest, on the basis of our 19 case studies, that the defenses are of mainly three types—denial, projection and obsessive rumination. The commonest form of *denial* is isolation of affect. "So, they'll kill me; and that's that"—this said with a shrug of the shoulders suggests that the affect appropriate to the thought has somehow been isolated. A second common form of denial is to minimize the gravity of the present situation and to take for granted that an appeal will be successful. The third and most extreme manifestation of denial, used by only one individual, was to delusionally believe that a pardon had been granted. Denial is also commonly used by persons dying of disease.

There is another phenomenon which deserves further explanation, since it may easily be confused with denial. Several cases impressed the examiners as being so immersed in the present moment as to virtually be insulated from any significant emotional relatedness with their own past or future. Thus, they do not have to deny anxiety since they do not experience it. This, incidentally, is the traditional profile of the "psychopath" who reacts only to present stimuli.

Projection is an obvious and not uncommon, mechanism. Typically, it takes the form of persecutory delusions. At least three of our prisoners considered themselves persecuted by specific groups in the community. This mechanism converts dissolute criminals into martyrs. It is a comforting delusion. While it does not deny that death is just around the corner, it tries to

119

lend it dignity and meaning. In some men there seems to be an almost quantitative reciprocal relationship between the use of projection and introjection so that they are either overly paranoid or depressed.

A third way of coping with painful affects is to *think furiously* about something else. Thus, the depressing thought is elbowed out of consciousness by the crowd of other ideas. We see this in a morbid obsessional concern about the preparing of appeals or pleas for clemency. One prisoner spoke to us for an hour about whether a pronoun in the appeal transcript should be "who" or "whom." To be sure, a meticulous concern with the appeal brief is rational; in these cases, however, the concern is obsessional, ruminative and ineffective. Another type of obsession (two of the men showed this) is preoccupation with religion to the exclusion of everything else. The prisoners who developed this syndrome had involved their confederates in death sentences too, though neither accomplice had killed anyone. Presumably, this religious conversion served to blunt guilt feelings about involving the accomplices. This activity served two other purposes: it distracted them from anxiety, and it offered a route to a happy life in the hereafter. The third type of obsessive rumination is the intellectual: a dipping into philosophical thought by a man whose life had hitherto been devoted to hedonistic pursuits.

Some try desperately to mould a respectable image of themselves. This is certainly one sluiceway for draining out anxiety—as illustrated, for example, in the way in which one of the prisoners identified himself with Lumumba and the world-shaking events in the Congo.

The group support these men receive from fellow inmates is variable. Some are quite appealing and receive considerable emotional and even material support in terms of cigarettes and help with their correspondence. Others manage quickly to antagonize their fellows and are in turn ridiculed and tormented by them in a direct and sadistic manner. This is often true when a man gets the reputation of being a malingerer. The inmates are quite antagonistic to anyone they feel is falsifying religious beliefs or feigning mental symptoms.

CONCLUSION

Traditional ego defense mechanisms alleviate distress. They also mitigate anxiety and depression which would otherwise overwhelm the prisoner in a death cell. Some psychiatrists allege that the death fear (whether on the battlefield or in the death house) serves as an irrational surrogate for some other fear—such as castration. This over-simplified explanation does scant justice to the inescapable certainty shared by all, but anticipated only by man.

Poetry provides further expressions of enduring attitudes toward death. "Carpe Diem," a Greek ode by Horace, gives verse to a traditional form of denial: live life's pleasures today because there may be no tomorrow.

CARPE DIEM

Horace

Odes I, II

Pray not in forbidden lore,
Ask no more, Leuconoë,
How many years—to you?—to me?—
The gods will send us
Before they end us;
Nor, questing, fix your hopes
On Babylonian horoscopes.

Learn to accept whatever is to be;
Whether Jove grant us many winters,
Or make of this the last, which splinters
Now on opposing cliffs the Tuscan sea.

Be wise; decant your wine; condense
Large aims to fit life's cramped circumference.
We talk, time flies—you've said it!
Make hay today,
Tomorrow rates no credit.

Horace. "Carpe Diem." *Selected Poems of Horace*. Translated by George F. Whicher. Oxford: Oxford University Press, 1947. Reprinted with permission.

John Donne, the seventeenth-century English poet, had a strong personal interest in the study of death. He had his portrait painted in his burial shroud while he was Dean of St. Paul's Cathedral in London; a stone effigy carved from the portrait is displayed there today. In the poem "Death Be Not Proud, Though Some Have Called Thee," Donne gives poetic expression to the tensions of denial and anger as he attempts to defeat death with wit by proving that death cannot be omnipotent since it is itself subject to external forces.

DEATH BE NOT PROUD

John Donne

Death be not proud, though some have called thee
Mighty and dreadfull, for, thou art not soe,
For, those, whom thou think'st, thou dost overthrow,
Die not, poore death, nor yet canst thou kill mee;
From rest and sleep, which but thy pictures bee,
Much pleasure, then from thee, much more must
        flow,
And soonest our best men with thee doe goe,
Rest of their bones, and soules deliverie.
Thou art slave to Fate, chance, kings, and
        desperate men,
And dost with poyson, warre, and sicknesse dwell,
And poppie, or charmes can make us sleepe as well,
And better then thy stroake; why swell'st thou then?
One short sleepe past, wee wake eternally,
And death shall be no more, Death thou shalt die.

John Donne. "Death Be Not Proud." *The Divine Poems*. Edited by Helen Gardner. Oxford: Clarendon Press, 1952.

In medieval times each dying person had a nuntius mortis, *an announcer of death, whose obligation it was to warn of impending death. Thus the dying person might prepare himself and his family. Today the person is more likely to be spared the preparatory period in an attempt to help him maintain hope throughout the dying process. When the dying occurs in a hospital, as it usually does in the United States, not only the family but also the hospital staff enter into complex interaction with the dying person in order to maintain the fiction of non-terminal illness. In "Awareness of Dying," sociologists Anselm Strauss and Barney Glaser describe the problems the nursing staff must face in maintaining denial and the organization strategies they use to avoid confrontation with the patient and his death.*

AWARENESS OF DYING

Anselm L. Strauss and Barney G. Glaser

Americans are characteristically unwilling to talk openly about the process of dying and death and are prone to avoid telling a dying person his prognosis. This is, in part, a moral attitude: life is preferable to whatever may follow it, and one should not look forward to death unless in great pain.

This moral attitude appears to be shared by the professional people who work with or near the patients who die in our hospitals. Although trained to give specialized medical or nursing care to terminal patients, much of their behavior toward the dying resembles the layman's. The training that physicians and nurses receive equips them principally for the technical aspects of patient care; their teachers deal only briefly or not at all with

Anselm L. Strauss and Barney G. Glaser, "Awareness of Dying," in *Loss and Grief: Psychological Management in Medical Practice.* Edited by Bernard Schoenberg, Arthur C. Carr, David Peretz, and Austin H. Kutscher, New York: Columbia University Press, 1970, 298-309.

the management of the emotional response of patients to illness and death.

Similarly, students at schools of nursing are taught how to give nursing care to terminal patients, as well as how to give "post-mortem care," but only recently have the psychological aspects of nursing care been included in the nurses' training. Few teachers talk about such matters, and they generally confine themselves to a lecture or two near the end of the course, sometimes calling in a psychiatrist to give a kind of "expert testimony."[1]

Beyond the medical education experience, management of the dying patient in the hospital setting is quite naturally only in strictly technical medical and nursing terms. Staff members are not required to report to each other or to their superiors what they have talked about with dying patients; they are "accountable" only for the technical aspects of their work with the dying.[2]

Medical and nursing personnel commonly recognize that working with dying patients is upsetting and sometimes traumatic. Consequently, some physicians purposely specialize in branches of medicine that will minimize their chances of encountering dying patients; many nurses frankly admit a preference for those wards or fields of nursing in which death is infrequently encountered. Those who bear the brunt of caring for terminal patients understandably develop both standardized and idiosyncratic modes of coping with the inherent threats. The most standard mode is a tendency to avoid contact with those patients who, as yet unaware of impending death, are inclined to question staff members about their increasing debilitation. Also avoided are those patients who have not "accepted" their approaching deaths, and those whose deaths are accompanied by great pain. Staff members' efforts to cope with death often have undesirable effects on both the social and psychological aspects of patient care and their own comfort. Personnel in contact with terminal patients are always somewhat disturbed by their own ineptness in handling the dying.

The social and psychological problems involved in dying are perhaps most acute when the dying person knows that he is dying. For this reason, among others, American physicians are quite reluctant to disclose impending death to their patients, and nurses are expected not to disclose it without the consent of the responsible physicians. At the same time, personnel generally agree that a patient will usually discover the truth without being told explicitly. Some physicians maneuver conversations with patients so that disclosure is made indirectly. In any event, the demeanor and actions of a patient who knows or suspects that he is dying differ from those of a patient who is not aware of dying. The problem of "awareness" is crucial to what happens both to the dying patient and to the people who give him medical and nursing care.

From one point of view the problem of awareness is a technical one: Should the patient be told he is dying, and what exactly is to be said if he knows, does not know, or only suspects? But the problem is also a moral one. Is it really proper to deny a dying person the opportunity to make his peace with his conscience and with his God, to settle his affairs and provide for the future of his family, and to determine his style of dying, much as he determined his style of living? Does anyone, the physician included, have the right to withhold such information? And on whose shoulders should this responsibility of disclosure fall — the physician, the family, or the patient?

Both the human and the technical aspects of the awareness problem are becoming increasingly momentous. One reason for this is that most Americans no longer die at home. Fifty-three per cent of all deaths in the United States in 1967 occurred in hospitals, and many more in nursing homes.[3] These people, then, pass through the dying process surrounded for the most part by strangers. Dying away from home is compounded by a noticeable and important medical trend — because medical technology has vastly improved, fewer people are dying from acute diseases and more from chronic diseases. Moreover, the usual duration of most chronic diseases has increased.

The public has become increasingly sophisticated regarding the implications of physical signs and symptoms and will not be put off by evasive or over-simplified answers to their questions. Inevitably, they will understand the truth. Therefore, it is predictable that the problem of awareness will become more and more central to what happens as people pass from life to death in American hospitals.

AWARENESS CONTEXTS

There are specific "awareness contexts" revolving around the confrontation of patient and hospital personnel: for example, a patient may not recognize his impending death even though everyone else does, or he may also suspect what everyone else knows for certain. On the other hand, both patient and others may know that death is imminent yet pretend this is not so. Or they may all act on such awareness relatively openly. We shall refer to these situations as the following types of awareness: *closed awareness, suspected awareness, mutual pretense awareness,* and *open awareness.* The impact of each type of awareness context upon the interplay between patients and personnel is profound, for people guide their talk and actions according to who knows what and with what certainty. As talk, action, and the accompanying cues unfold, certain awareness contexts tend to evolve into other contexts.

Closed Awareness and Suspected Awareness

There are at least five important structural conditions which contribute to the existence and maintenance of the closed awareness context:

First, most patients have had little or no experience in recognizing the signs of impending death.

A second structural condition is that American physicians ordinarily do not tell patients outright that death is probable or inevitable. As a number of studies have shown, physicians proffer medical justifications for not disclosing the fatal prognosis to their patients.[4] For instance, one investigator[5] found that many physicians maintain that when one announces terminality to a patient, he is likely to "go to pieces"; one must therefore carefully judge whether or not to tell after sizing up the individual patient. In actual fact, this investigator notes, the "clinical experience" is not genuinely grounded experience but a species of personal mythology. The judgment was found to be based on one or two unfortunate incidents or even incidents recounted

127

by colleagues.

Many physicians believe that patients really do not wish to know whether they are dying; if they did, then they would find out anyhow, so there is no sense telling them directly. Presumably some patients do not wish to know their fates, but there is no really good evidence that all wish to remain in blissful ignorance. There is, in fact, good evidence that they do wish to know.[6]

A third structural condition is that families tend to guard the secret, thereby confirming what the physician has announced. An interesting contrast is the practice in Asian countries, where the extended kin gather around the hospital death bed two or more days before death is expected, openly indicating to the patient that they are there to keep him company during his passage to death.

A fourth structural condition is that of the organization of hospitals and the commitments of personnel who work within them by which medical information is concealed from patients. Records are kept out of reach. Staff is skilled at withholding information. Medical talk about patients generally occurs in far-removed places, and if it occurs nearby it is couched in medical jargon. Staff members are trained to discuss with patients only the surface aspects of their illnesses, and, as we shall see, they are accustomed to acting collusively around patients so as not to disclose medical secrets.

A fifth structural condition, perhaps somewhat less apparent, is that ordinarily the patient has no allies who reveal or help him discover the fact of his impending death. Not only his family but other patients (if they know) withhold that information.

In her book, *Experiment Perilous,* Renée Fox has described a small research hospital whose patients recognized their own inevitable terminality.[7] Death was an open and everyday occurrence. Patients could talk familiarly to each other as well as to the staff members about their respective fatal conditions. Various consequences flowed from this *open* situation: patients could give each other support, and the staff could support the patients. Patients could even raise the flagging spirits of the staff! From their deathbeds, patients could thank the physicians for their unstinting efforts and wish them luck in solving their research problems in time to save other patients. They could close their lives with rituals such as letter writing and praying. They could review their lives and plan realistically for their families' futures. These consequences are, of course, not available to patients in the closed awareness situation. Instead, other consequences emerge. Since the unaware patient believes he will recover, he acts on that supposition. Thus he may convert his sick room into a temporary work-place, writing his unfinished book, telephoning his business partners, and in other ways carrying on his work somewhat "as usual." He carries on his family life and friendships with only the interruption necessitated by temporary illness. He plans as if life stretched before him. On the other hand, he may work less feverishly on his unfinished book than if he knew time was short and so fail to finish it. He may set plans into operation that in reality are useless and the plans will have to be undone after his death. The unaware patient may unwittingly shorten his life because he does not realize that special care is necessary to extend it, he may not understand the necessity for certain treatments and refuse them.

It is in some ways easier for the family to face a patient who does not know of his terminality, especially if he is the kind of person who is likely to die "gracelessly." And if an unaware person is suddenly stricken and dies, sometimes his family is grateful that "he died without knowing." On the other hand, when the kin must participate in a lengthy nondisclosure drama, they shoulder a tremendous burden. They suffer because they cannot express their grief openly to the dying person; this is especially true of husbands and wives who have always shared fully with each other.

A dying man's wife had been informed of the prognosis by the doctor and had shared this information with friends, whose daughter told the patient's young son. The son developed a strong distrust for the doctor, and felt disinherited by his father since they had not (nor could they have) discussed the responsibilities that would fall to him in the future.

The closed context instituted by the physician permits him to avoid the potentially distressing scene that may follow an announcement to his patient, but such a closed context only subjects nurses to strain, for it is they who must spend the most time with the unaware patient, guarding constantly against disclosure. Nurses may sometimes actually be relieved when the patient talks openly abut his demise and they no longer have to guard against disclosure. On the other hand, under certain conditions nurses prefer the closed context. Some do not care to talk about death with a patient, especially a patient who does not accept it with fortitude. An unaware person is sometimes easier to handle because he has not "given up." The closed awareness situation prevents staff members from enjoying certain advantages that accompany a patient's resigned – or joyous – meeting with death.

Important consequences of closed awareness also hold for the staff as a whole. Unaware patients who die quickly represent simply routine work for the staff. In contrast, the patient who moves explosively and resentfully from an unaware to a highly suspicious or fully aware state is disruptive.

The most crucial institutional consequence has already been mentioned: because American physicians generally choose not to tell patients of their terminal status, this burden falls squarely and persistently upon the nursing personnel. This considerable burden is built into the organization of the hospital services that deal with terminal patients. Another social structure condition intrinsic to the functioning of American hospitals also increases the nurse's burden, namely, the nurse's commitment to work relatively closely with and around patients. This structural condition can be better appreciated when seen in contrast to conditions in Asian hospitals, where the family clusters thickly and persistently around the dying patient, thus permitting the nursing personnel to remain at a relatively greater emotional distance from, and spend relatively little time with the patient. In addition, the enormously high patient-to-personnel ratio increases the probability of great distance and little contact.

Mutual Pretense Awareness and Open Awareness

The mutual pretense awareness context is perhaps less visible, even to its participants, than the closed, open, and suspicion

130

contexts. A prime structural condition of this context is that unless the patient initiates conversation about his impending death, no staff member is required to talk about it with him. The patient may wish to initiate such conversation, but surely neither hospital rules nor common convention urges it upon him. Consequently, unless either the aware patient or a staff member breaks the silence by words or gestures, a mutual pretense rather than an open awareness context will exist.

The patient, of course, is more likely than the staff members to refer openly to his death, thereby inviting them, explicitly or implicitly to respond in kind. If they seem unwilling, he may decide they do not wish to confront openly the fact of his death, and then he may, out of tact or genuine empathy for their embarrassment or distress, keep his silence.

Staff members, in turn, may give him opportunities to speak of his death without a direct or obvious reference. But if he does not care to act or talk as if he were dying, then they will support his pretense. In doing so, they have, in effect, accepted a complementary assignment of status — they will act with pretense toward his pretense.

Staff members may rationalize pretense by maintaining that if the patient wishes to pretend, it may well be best for his health. A second rationale is that perhaps they can give him better medical and nursing care if they do not have to face him so openly. A third rationale is that this sort of action is most tactful.

During the pretense episodes both sides naturally assume certain implicit rules of behavior. One rule is that dangerous topics should generally be avoided — the most obvious being the patient's death; another, the events that will happen afterward.

Talk about dangerous topics is permissible as long as neither party breaks down. The patient and the nurses may discuss daily events — such as treatments — as if they had implications for a real future, when the patient will have recovered from his illness. Some of the patient's brave, or foolhardy activities (as when he bathes himself or insists on tottering to the toilet by himself) may signify a brave show of pretense. The staff, in turn, permits his activity.

131

It is customary, then, that patient and staff focus determinedly on appropriately safe topics — daily routines of eating and sleeping; complaints and their management; minor personal confidences; events on the ward, and news events. Talk about the fatal illness is safe enough if confined to the symptoms themselves.

When something happens or is said that threatens to expose the fiction that both parties are attempting to sustain, then each must pretend that nothing has gone awry. Thus, a nurse may take special pains to announce herself before entering a patient's room so as not to surprise him at his crying. If she finds him crying, she may ignore it or convert it into an innocuous event with a skillful comment or gesture. A patient who cannot control a sudden expression of great pain will verbally discount its significance, while the nurse in turn goes along with his pretense. Clearly then, each party to the ritual pretense shares responsibility for maintaining it.

A mutual pretense context that is not sustained can only change to an open awareness context. The change may be sudden, temporary, or permanent. Or the change may be gradual: nurses, and relatives, too, are familiar with patients who admit to terminality more openly on some days than they do on other days, when pretense is dominant, until finally pretense vanishes altogether. Sometimes the physician skillfully paces his interaction with a patient, leading the patient finally to refer openly to his terminality and to leave behind the earlier phase of pretense.

Pretense generally collapses when certain conditions make its maintenance increasingly difficult, for example, when the patient cannot keep from expressing his increasing pain, or his suffering grows to the point that he must be kept under heavy sedation.

The pretense context can provide the patient with a measure of dignity and considerable privacy, although it may deny him the close relationship with his family that is created when he allows them to participate in his open acceptance of death. For the family — especially more distant kin — the pretense context can minimize embarrassment and other interactional strains; but for closer kin, openness may have many advantages. Oscillation between contexts of open awareness and mutual pretense is in itself a source of stress.

But whether staff or patient initiates the ritual of pretense, maintaining it creates a characteristic mood of cautious serenity throughout the ward. Even one such patient can set such an atmosphere. Denial in the patients of a cancer hospital (buttressed by staff silence), all of whom know the nature of the hospital, can be so strong that few patients talk openly about anyone's condition.

A persistent context of pretense profoundly affects the more permanent aspects of hospital organization as well. When closed awareness generally prevails, the personnel must guard against disclosure, but they need not organize themselves as a team to handle continued pretense and its sometimes stressful breakdown. Also a chief organizational consequence of the mutual pretense context is that it eliminates any possibility that staff members might "work with" patients psychologically on a professional basis. It is also entirely possible that a ward mood of tension can be set when a number of elderly dying patients continually communicate to each other their willingness to die, but the staff members persistently insist on the pretense that the patients are going to recover. On the other hand, the prevailing ward mood accompanying mutual pretense tends to be more serene — or at least less obviously tense — than when suspected awareness is dominant.

The context of open awareness does not eliminate complexity, and, in fact, certain ambiguities associated with two properties of the open awareness context are inevitable. Even when he recognizes and acknowledges the fact of terminality, the patient's awareness is frequently qualified by his ignorance or suspicion about other aspects of his dying. Thus, a patient who knows that he is dying may be convinced that death is still some months away. Staff members may then conceal their own knowledge of the time that death is expected to occur, even though they may refer openly to the fact that it is expected. Similarly, they may keep secret their expectation that the patient is going to deteriorate badly, so long as he is unaware of this contingency.

Of course, certain patients (such as physicians) may, as a matter of course, be aware of these subsidiary aspects of impending death. Patients who have the same disease are often kept together, so that each may observe a kind of rehearsal of

133

his own fate by watching others who are closer to death.

The second ambiguous element of the open awareness context is the divergence in expectations about "appropriate" ways of dying which reflects in part the common tendency for staff and patients to come from different class and ethnic backgrounds. It also reflects deeply inculcated professional and institutional norms which differ from those of patients.

Once a patient has indicated his awareness of dying, he becomes responsible for his acts as a *dying* person. He knows now that he is not merely sick but dying. He must face that fact. Sociologically, facing an impending death means that the patient will be judged, and will judge himself, according to certain standards of proper conduct concerning his behavior during his final days and hours. At the same time, hospital personnel will be judged and will judge themselves in their responses to dying patients.

At first glance, the medical personnel's obligation to a dying patient seems obvious enough. If possible, they must save him; if not, then they must give proper medical and nursing care until he dies. But ethical and social, in addition to medical, judgments enter into questions such as when to try to save a patient and when to cease trying, whether to prolong life when death is certain or the patient is already comatose, and so on. These judgments, as well as less dramatic ones such as administering "better" care, depend in many instances, not on objective, but subjective criteria such as the "deserving" character of the patient.

Patients defined as less deserving risk the additional judgment that they are acting with purpose. If they know that they are dying, their improper behavior cannot be interpreted as a consequence of ignorance. Patients known to be aware of death have two kinds of obligation: first, they should not act to bring about their own death; second, there are certain positive obligations one has as a dying patient. There are no clear rules of behavior provided for the dying nor are there clear expectations on the part of the staff regarding his behavior.

Nevertheless, staff members do judge the conduct of dying patients by certain implicit standards. These standards are related to the work that hospital personnel do, as well as to some rather general American notions about courageous and decent behavior. A partial list of implicit canons includes the following: the patient should maintain relative composure and cheerfulness; at the very least, he should face death with dignity; he should not cut himself off from the world, turning his back upon the living, but should continue to be a good family member, and be "nice" to other patients; if he can, he should participate in the ward social life; he should cooperate with the staff members who care for him, and if possible he should avoid distressing or embarrassing them. A patient who does most of these things will be respected.

What the staff defines as unacceptable behavior in aware dying patients is readily illustrated. For instance, physicians usually honor requests for confirmatory consultations with other physicians but object to "shopping around" for impossible cures. Some patients do not face dying with fortitude but become noisy or hysterical. Other patients make excessive demands. Some patients wail, cry out in terror, complain, accuse the staff of doing nothing, or refuse to cooperate in their medical or nursing care. Perhaps the most unnerving are the patients who become apathetic or hostile and reproachful.

In general, then, the staff appreciates patients who exit with courage and grace, not merely because they create fewer scenes and and cause less emotional stress, but because they evoke genuine admiration and sympathy, as well as feelings of professional usefulness. It is difficult to admire a patient who behaves improperly even though one can sympathize with his terrible situation. People cannot help judging him, even if by diverse and not altogether explicit standards. Occasionally a patient provides such a model of courage and fortitude that the staff remembers him with admiration long after his death. The reactions of staff members include not only respect for a great human being but also gratitude for being allowed to participate in the near-perfect drama of his dying.

A few points about the consequences of open awareness are worth emphasizing here. Awareness of impending death gives the patient an opportunity to close his life in the manner he chooses. He may finish important work, establish reconciliations, make satisfying farewells, give gifts to his friends, and leave detailed plans for his family and estate.

But open awareness has disadvantages for the patient, too. Other people may not approve of the patient's way of managing his death, and may attempt to change or subvert his management. A patient may not be able to close his life usefully and with dignity because he cannot face the dying process and death. An aware patient, therefore, may be unable to face death with equanimity, dying with more anguish and less dignity than he might if he were unaware of his terminality. For some patients there is the added stress of deciding whether to accept imminent death or to perhaps prolong life through surgery.

A patient who meets death with equanimity at the same time also makes this possible for his family. They will be able to share his satisfaction and they will treasure their experience for the remainder of their lives.

NOTES

1. J. C. Quint and A. L. Strauss, "Nursing Students, Assignments, and Dying Patients," *Nursing Outlook,* 12:24, January 1964.
2. A. L. Strauss, B.G. Glaser, and J. C. Quint, "The Nonaccountability of Terminal Care," *Hospitals,* 38:73, January 16, 1964.
3. R. Fulton, "Death and Self," *Journal of Religion and Health,* 3:364, July 1964.
4. H. Feifel, "Death," in *Taboo Topics,* edited by N.L. Farberow (New York: Atherton Press, 1963).
5. D. Oken, "What to Tell Cancer Patients: A Study of Medical Attitudes," *Journal of the American Medical Association,* 175:1120, April 1, 1961.
6. Eighty-two per cent of Feifel's sample of sixty patients wanted to be informed about their condition.
7. Renée Fox, *Experiment Perilous* (New York: Free Press of Glencoe, 1959.)

Acceptance appears as a desirable goal in many of the preceding pieces. But it is not always easy to distinguish between accepting death and being resigned to it. If one believes that the main developmental task of the aged is preparing to die, then it is easy to mistake resignation for acceptance. Robert Kastenbaum, a developmental psychologist, looks at the changing life perspective in order to summarize personal development over the entire life-span. While gerontologists have argued that gradual and mutual withdrawal of the aged from society is natural and inevitable, Kastenbaum suggests that we can assist in finding new forms of participation. He considers it a needless waste to wait for death to terminate an existence that has lost its social meaning.

THE FORESHORTENED LIFE PERSPECTIVE

Robert Kastenbaum

The elderly person is marked in more ways than one. His face, hands, and all those body parts which are significant in social communication have become unmistakably engraved with age. Before he speaks, he has already identified himself to others as a person who occupies an extreme position in the spectrum of life. Should his words and actions also betray those features we associate with advanced age, then we are further encouraged to mark him down as one who is strikingly different from ourselves. selves.

He is also marked by numbers, of course. In the case of the elderly person, the statistics relentlessly intersect and pursue. Begin any place. Begin by tracing the declining function of this organ system or that one. Begin by measuring changes in the musculoskeletal system or the speed of central nervous system activity. Begin by locating the elderly person within the actuarial charts. Wherever we begin, it is clear that the numbers have a common bias; they are all against him.

Reprinted with permission of the author from *Geriatrics*, Volume 24, Number 8, Pages 126-133, Copyright © The New York Times Media Company, Inc.

These markings, however, do not tell the whole story. As a matter of fact, they provide only the background and props. It is true enough that any of us might contrive the story of any elderly person's life, based upon these externals. We could manufacture suppositions about what he is experiencing within these biological and statistical markings—how he regards the past, how he views the future, and all the rest. The pity of it is—we do this sort of thing much of the time, without realizing that what we are hearing is not his story, but merely the sound of our own voices. It is so easy to suppose that he feels the way we think we would feel if we were in his situation, or simply that he must feel the way we think it proper for an elderly person to feel. Any time we begin with such a misstep we are likely to accumulate even further distortions. We are likely to generalize without correctives. We are likely to develop set ways of dealing with the way we think he is.

How does the elderly person actually view his own life? What is his perspective and how did he happen to develop it? What functions does it perform for him? In what ways might his perspective affect the course of his own life and the lives of others? Of his total life experiences—past, present, and potentially future—what has he included? What has he excluded? Has he settled upon this perspective as a fixed, permanent vantage point, or are other orientations to come? Most basically, has he managed to create a symbolic structure that comes to terms with his total existence at the very time that this existence itself has become so vulnerable?

To gain perspective on the life perspective of aged people, it might be helpful to back up all the way to infancy. Does the infant have a life perspective? Quite on the contrary—he is almost totally engrossed in life. He experiences the moment. He does not reexperience the past or preexperience the future, at least not in that sense which depends upon the development of symbolic structures. One of the most profound differences between infant and adult is the raw experiencing of the moment, an experiencing that lacks the protection afforded by perspective. Although this point may be an obvious one, it should be emphasized because it is important in a different light in the phenomenological world of the aged.

Very quickly, the infant comes to appreciate the difference between a presence and an absence. At first, this awareness does not distinguish between temporal and spatial dimensions. Either something (for example, smiling-mother-presenting-lunch) is both here-and-now or it is absent/totally absent. By contrast, the adult differentiates "absence" into several alternatives that have differential meanings to him: something exists now, but not here, in this space; or, something will be in this space at a later time, or something has been in this space, but at a previous time, or, again, something is neither here nor there, now, then, or ever.

Such distinctions, and many others that are crucial to the development of a life perspective, come later in life, but the first gropings toward a perspective begin in infancy. There is a clear directional movement. The infant becomes increasingly liberated from its biology, on the one side, and its immediate environment, on the other. The directional thrust is a general process that must be distinguished from what might be called the solidified achievements of human development. This is perhaps the most fundamental basis for challenging the notion that the aged person and the child have a great deal in common. Although certain similarities do exist, the fact remains that it is only the child who is being carried forward on the tide of psychobiological development. All of his behavior and experience is marked by the directional thrust.

The surge of general development continues with great vigor throughout the childhood years and is manifested in physical, social, and psychological changes. Although all of these developments contribute to the emergence of life perspectives, two of the most salient psychological discoveries that children make follow.

1. *The discovery of futurity.* This discovery has several components. First, there is the discovery of future time in the sense that "when this moment is over, there will be some more time coming." Second, there is the discovery of future time as qualitatively different from any other kind of time—it is fresh, unused time that can bring forth new experiences and events. This discovery implies a dawning appreciation of possibility and uncertainty. Third, there is the discovery of world or objective

future time. Implied in the discovery is the realization that one does not really possess magical control over the universe and cannot really "take time out." Additionally, this is one of the insights that prepares the child to appreciate that, for all his precious and self-evident individuality, he is simply one of many fellow creatures, all of whom dance (or drag) to the music of time.

2. *The discovery of mortality.* some rudimentary appreciation of nonexistence may be achieved in early childhood, perhaps even before the conquest of language, but many additional years of development are required before the child can frame the concept of personal mortality. The proposition "I will die" is intimately related to the sense of futurity. It will be the continuing task of the adolescent and the adult to define the nature of this relationship for himself, to integrate the concepts of more time—fresh, new time—possibility, hope, trust, and uncertainty with the concepts of certain death.

The available evidence suggests that adolescence is usually the time during which the developing person begins seriously to create his life perspective. He has had many of the elements previously but now, for the first time, he also has the intellectual equipment to forge these elements into a perspective—and the psychosocial readiness to venture forth as his own self. Children have their notions—but it is adolescents who have ideologies. It is the transformation in thought that underlies the adolescent's changes in social behavior. He now can think about thought, compare ideal with reality, shatter the world as it is presented to him with his new tools of intellectual analysis, and at least try to put the pieces together again in a new and more satisfying manner.

Adolescence, then, is the time of life in which the act of trying to develop perspectives is dominant.

Other characteristics of adolescence are: First, the adolescent has a strong sense of moving into the future. This is not at all the same thing as planning for or visualizing the future; rather, it is a restless experiencing of the developmental current running within oneself.

Second, the adolescent typically projects his thought and feeling intensively into a fairly narrow sector of the future. It is the proximate future that counts, that decisive and eventful time which is just around the corner. Old age is so remote and unappealing a prospect that it hardly can be located at all on his projective charts.

Third, the adolescent often neglects the past, especially his personal past. Neglect may be too passive a word to describe this phenomenon. I have the impression that many adolescents are waging an active battle against the past, trying to put psychological distance between who-I-used-to-be and who-I'm-going-to-be.

Finally, there is the adolescent's way of coming to terms with finality. The prospect of death, like the prospect of aging, often is regarded as a notion that is so remote as to have no relevance to one's own life. Death is avoided, glossed over, kidded about, neutralized, and controlled by a cool, spectator type of orientation. This is on the level of what might be called self-conscious, socially communicated thought. However, more probing and indirect methods of assessment suggest that many adolescents are extremely concerned about death—both in the sense of attempting to fathom its nature and meaning and in the sense of confronting the actual prospect of their own demise. We are no longer surprised when we come across an adolescent whose behavior is influenced by the expectation that he may die at an early age. Indeed, a foreshortened life perspective is by no means the special prerogative of the aged person.

What happens to life perspective during the adult years? We know less about mature perspectives than any other sort, but I think the life perspective of a mature adult has the following characteristics:

It is, first of all, a genuine perspective. This means that the individual has been able to subdivide his life-space into multiple points which stretch away in both directions from the present moment. He is able to locate himself at any one of these points and utilize the other points to achieve the effect of perspective. He might, for example, evaluate the immediate situation in terms of its possible future consequences. A more complex perspective consists of evaluating the immediate situation in terms of both past and future circumstances. More complex still is the perspective in which the individual flexibly shifts the emphasis among past, present, and future standpoints, with all three orientations always involved but varying in relationship to each other. At one moment his pivotal concern may be with past events; thus he calls upon his immediate observations and future projections to provide a context of meaning around the past. At another moment he locates himelf in the future and scans his past and present for what clues they can yield that would help him to comprehend his future self.

Upon closer inspection, his perspective will prove to be a structure that includes a variety of subperspectives. These might be visualized as operating in an umbrella type of arrangement. Opened slightly, the perspective system permits the individual to gain coverage of his proximate past and future. This could be called the yesterday-and-tomorrow framework. Opened more broadly, he now has perspective on a larger period of time, but this is still only a small range within his total lifespan, where he has been and where he is going, relative to where he is now.

A mature use of the life perspective involves good judgment in deciding when it is appropriate to use a particular subperspective. It involves the ability to scan time in two distinctly different ways—the axiological and the probabilistic. In projecting the future, for example, the individual identifies his hopes, fears, and values. This is the axiological orientation. But he also is capable of reading the future in a more objective style, trying to establish the most likely pattern of expectancies. The ability to sweep through time in both axiological and probabilistic styles seems to be one of the hallmarks of a mature life perspective that is maturely employed. Furthermore, there will be an optimal balance between perspectives-already-established and fresh perspective-seeking activities. A flexible life perspective makes it possible to identify and integrate the novel or unexpected event without scuttling the more enduring perspectivistic structure.

Just as important as the life perspective itself, however, is the ability to let go, to know when it is in one's best interests to become totally engrossed in a situation. All perspective and no engrossment makes for a barren, abstracted sort of life.

A mature life perspective is the type that permits a person to make constructive use of his past experiences without becoming enslaved to them and to confront his future, including the prospect of death, without capitulating in that direction either. Many people fail to develop a functional and versatile life perspective, however. In some cases we see a distorted or dysfunctional perspective; in other cases we are struck by the absence of perspective. These different psychological orientations cannot be expected to lead to the same situation when the individuals involved reach advanced age.

In exploring what has been learned and what has yet to be learned about life perspectives in the aged, we should examine the disengagement theory. This is not just a courtesy call to respect the contributions of Elaine Cumming and William E. Henry*—it happens that the disengagement theory is one of the few conceptual orientations to make something of life perspectives in later adulthood. Everybody knows by now that the hypothetical process of disengagement involves a gradual and mutual withdrawal of the aging individual and his society. It is said to be an inevitable and normal developmental process. to occur universally, or at least to occur universally under favorable conditions. Obviously, this is an important proposition. Is it also a true proposition? That is another question and one which would take us beyond the scope of this discussion.

But there is a relevant question here. How does the disengagement process itself get started? Cumming and Henry have suggested that disengagement begins with an event that takes place within ourselves, or more specifically, within our life perspectives. As we approach the later years of our lives we come to realize that our future is limited. There is not enough time left to do everything we had hoped and planned. Eventually we also realize that time is not only limited, but it is running out. Death comes into view as a salient prospect.

---

*Editor's Note: The original statement of disengagement theory can be found in Cumming, E. and Henry, W. *Growing Old*. New York: Basic Books, 1961.

Do Cumming and Henry mean that without this altered life perspective there would be no disengagement? They say: "It seems probable that disengagement would be resisted forever if there were no problem of the allocation of time and thus no anticipation of death. Questions of choice among alternative uses of time lead to curtailment of some activities. Questions of the inevitability of death lead to introspective reflections on the meaning of life."

Although this formulation emphasizes the importance of the individual's inner framework for organizing his experience and, in particular, the role of death anticipations, the formulation appears to be at variance with the facts. Although our knowledge of life perspectives is far from adequate, I believe that enough has been learned to indicate that the disengagement hypothesis has only limited application.

The disengagement hypothesis assumes that everybody has just about the same kind of perspective as they approach the later years of life. This generalization is not tenable. It is already clear that there are significant individual variations, even within particular subgroups in our own society. Some people, for example, never develop the complete umbrella of perspectives described earlier. They move through their life-span within a narrow shell of time, almost day-by-day. This kind of person does not wake up one morning and gasp, "My God, I have only a finite number of years ahead; I had best reallocate my time." The sound of distant drums never had much influence over him, and it may not get to him now, either. Many people in their seventh, eighth, and ninth decades maintain a well-entrenched narrow perspective.

By contrast, there are other people who have been brandishing a wide-open perspective umbrella ever since their youth. The use of time and the prospect of death are factors which have influenced their lives every step of the way. Such people confront different challenges than do those who may be first awakening to intimations of mortality, or those whose limited perspectives have been little influenced by the passing years.

Many people do not experience the altered outlook on time and death that Cummings and Henry proposed as the psychological trigger for disengagement, but even among those who do confront this prospect within their life perspectives, there are important variations. The disengagement theorists have stated that "The anticipation of death frees us from the obligation to participate in the ongoing stream of life. If there is only a little time left, there is no point in planning for a future and no point in putting off today's gratification."

On the contrary, many people intensify their participation in life in order to obtain the greatest possible yield from the time remaining to them. This orientation can persist well beyond the sixth and seventh decades. In studying the psychology of dying and death within a population of very aged patients in a geriatric hospital, we have encountered many who came to terms with approaching death by investing themselves solidly in the network of interpersonal life.

Furthermore, there is reason to believe that the aged person who does clamber out of "the ongoing stream of life" may be doing so for a different reason. Our research interviews suggest that in many cases the individual is not gracefully disengaging to enjoy today's gratification because the future is too short to support long-range plans. Rather, he is more likely to feel that he is no longer capable of making good use even of the limited time that is available to him. It is a sense of inner depletion, impotence, and frustration coupled with the appraisal that his environment offers very little that is inspiring or rewarding.

Perhaps Cumming and Henry have projected into the minds of elderly people the sort of outlook on time and death that they themselves believe to be reasonable and appropriate. This is one of the pitfalls of those who deal with the aged, but most aged people are not theoreticians and simply do not develop the kind of perspective that comes naturally to a theoretician's mind.

Also, we have learned from a number of aged people that they are likely to experience a double-bind regarding time— there is an awareness that future time is scarce but also a heavy sense of oppression at the hands of the clock, too much time that they cannot put to satisfying use. Even a heartfelt lament about the uselessness of future time is not identical with a will-to-die.

Finally, for at least some aged people, the qualitative nature of the future has changed radically. It is no longer the time in which exciting, fresh, novel events are to be expected. The future, in a sense, may be regarded as "used up" before it occurs. The past wends its way forward into the future.

Other points that have emerged from research and clinical experience include:

1. A foreshortened perspective at any age is likely to increase the probability of premature death. The specific pathway of lethality may be through suicide or accident, but particular attention should be given to what might be called psychosomatic or subintentional suicides, in which the individual's physical vulnerabilities are self-exploited to hasten his death.

2. The balance between perspective and engrossment becomes increasingly difficult to maintain with advanced age. An environment that truly shelters the aged person, that truly protects him during his periods of special vulnerability, would make it possible for him to enjoy the spirit-replenishing experience of engrossment more frequently. We become more vulnerable when we are engrossed. We could help our elders if we developed ways of enabling them to drop the burden of their perspectives from time to time without excessive physical or social danger.

3. The perspective of the aged person may become more diffuse or even collapse. Changes in the direction of simplification may be appropriate and beneficial to some people. But there is the danger that the entire perspective may become dysfunctional and contribute to an unnecessarily steep decline in social integration and behavioral competency. There are things we can do that are likely to have a bolstering effect on the aged person's perspectivistic system. For example, we could enter his past as an active force, a sort of participant-observer. Too often, the aged person's preoccupation with his past chases us away— he is snubbing us by focusing upon a scene in which we had no role. We can develop a sort of semirole in his past and, through this, help him to link his past with the pres-

ent that all of us share and the future that most of us expect. We are also likely to gain something ourselves through this interpenetration of life perspectives.

4. Both our formal and informal socialization processes emphasize personal growth and expansion during the early years of life. "The System" ill prepares us for living within limits, living with losses, and living with the prospect of death. When the achievement-oriented socialization system gets to work on a person who is growing up in a deprived or ruptured environment, he is alerted to the incongruity between the ideal and the reality. His reaction may take the form of a refusal to accept the socially-sponsored perspective, in the first place, or a rapid aging of the perspective if he does try it out. The person who is growing up in an environment that makes the goals of "The System" appear attractive and feasible is, of course, more likely to develop a life perspective that is centered around individual achievement in the usual sense of the term. Both kinds of people would be better served if our socialization processes—including the classroom—offered a broader, more versatile, and more humane model from which the individual could fashion his own life perspective.

QUESTIONS

1. Define the following terms and give examples of each where possible. The starred items are psychological, sociological or medical terms the authors of the papers expect readers to know. If you are not familiar with their meanings, consult a dictionary, a medical dictionary or an abnormal psychology textbook (e.g., J. C. Coleman's *Abnormal Psychology in Modern Life, 5th edition*, 1975).

*defense mechanism
*psychological crisis
*denial
*bargaining
 depression
 preparatory grief
 acceptance
 resignation
 living-dying interval
*crisis
*anxiety
*coping mechanism
 integrity *vs* despair
*regression
*ego function
*hemodialysis

*diagnosis
*prognosis
 awareness context
 closed awareness
 mutual pretense
  awareness
 open awareness
*structural conditions
 ritual pretense
 life perspective
 futurity
 engrossment
 axiological orientation
 probabilistic orientation
 disengagement
*projection

2. Pattison defines the period between *knowledge of death* and *actual death* as the "living-dying period." What support does he suggest that the patient needs during this time? Review the various kinds of "death" described by Kalish in Chapter 1. How would they apply to this period?

3. a. What is a "developmental stage"? How does Kubler-Ross use the term? Many critics have observed that patients display such reactions, but not necessarily in sequence, and that many exhibit denial, for example, periodically right up to death itself. Does such criticism seem to apply to Kubler-Ross formulation? Does it invalidate a "stage" conception?

    b. Do you think that the same stages of dying discussed by Kubler-Ross would be found in a non-western society with a different family structure and different set of religious beliefs?

4. Most of the research presented in this chapter is based on the study of relatively long-term illnesses with a terminal prognosis. How well do Pattison's "crisis model" and Kubler-Ross "stages" fit the death row prisoners described by Bluestone and McGahee? To what extent do you think the concepts would apply to patients with a "suspended sentence," i.e., chronic hemodialysis, chronic cardiac disease or emphysema?

5. Denial is a complex concept, perhaps more so than this chapter indicates. Kubler-Ross has described denial as a result of interpersonal dynamics but Glaser and Strauss have shown that it may be part of the social interaction process as well. What would you, as a helper, look for in deciding whether a patient's "denial" represented a serious inability to deal with significant facts of his illness, or an attempt to cope with what the patient perceived as others' inability to do so? What might you want to take into account in deciding whether, and how, to intervene?

149

6. Suppose the father in "Do Not Go Gentle into That Good Night" was admitted to a nursing home. What psychological supports would Pattison and Kubler-Ross recommend for the father? For the speaker in the poem?

7. In the seventeenth century, men prepared themselves for death through the contemplation of mortality and its relationship to their creator, as in Donne's "Death Be Not Proud." However, processes studies by contemporary psychologists can be observed in works of this period. Identify the expressions of anger and denial in this poem. Do you feel the poet reaches a point of resolution in "And death shall be no more; death, thou shalt die."

8. "Carpe Diem" is an early example of a familiar theme— enjoy life while you can. Why is it considered an example of denial since it explicitly states the possibility of sudden death? List other poems or contemporary song lyrics that express the "Carpe Diem" theme.

9. Does final acceptance require that a patient work through all of the other attitudes? What is the difference between the acceptance of death and the resignation to death? Contrast the attitudes expressed in "Carpe Diem" and "Death Be Not Proud" with the patients' statements reported by Kubler-Ross and Pattison. Do you agree that acceptance as described by Kubler-Ross is a natural and desirable goal for all dying patients? Why or why not? How does age or "engrossment" in life as described by Kastenbaum affect potential acceptance?

10. Kubler-Ross, Pattison, and to some extent, Kastenbaum, are writing about processes that occur in a person who is aware that he is dying. Having read these papers, would you recommend withholding terminal diagnosis from a dying person? Under what circumstances? Survey the class on the following two questions:

1. If you had a terminal illness, would you want to be told?

2. If your mother (or father) had a terminal illness, would you want her (or him) to be told?

Discuss your reasons for your answers. Consider both advantages and disadvantages of a closed awareness context from the point of view of the patient, the hospital staff and the family.

11. Considering only the United States and Canada, is it possible for death by execution to be considered an appropriate death today? Under what conditions? Compare Socrates' preparation for his death with the reactions of the contemporary prisoners described by Bluestone and McGahee? What accounts for the difference?

12. In a way, the death row prisoners and the terminal cancer patient are both awaiting the execution of a death sentence. Compare and contrast the two situations, considering the origin of the death sentence, the amount of control over it held by various individuals in the setting, the psychological and social meaning of the "sentence," the determinancy or indeterminancy of the "sentence" and the rationalizations of the death that are available to the individual.

13. a. List as many people as you can whom you consider to be "aged." What criteria did you use in choosing them? To how many does the concept of "disengagement" seem to apply? "Engrossment?" What do you think makes the difference?

    b. Contrast your own life perspective with that of an aged relative. Can you do the same for a mother of teenage children, who is dying of cancer?

151

PROJECTS FOR FURTHER STUDY

1. Psychiatrists, psychologists, and sociologists, among others, have investigated so-called "return-from-the-dead" stories in the past, but only recently have such reports been given wide distribution. Research some of these accounts (See for instance Noyes, R., Jr. "The Experience of Dying," *Psychiatry*, 1972, *35*, 174-184, which also contains an extensive bibliography). Consider the following questions:

   1. What features do the accounts have in common?

   2. What discrepancies are there in the "typical" features reported by the authors?

   3. Do you believe that such reports are evidence for "life after death," as some have claimed? If not, what do they tell us about phenomena of clinical death?

   4. What role do cultural factors play in the content of the reports?

   5. How do cultural variations in content affect the apparent validity of the reports in your mind?

2. Leo Tolstoy's novella, *The Death of Ivan Ilych,* is often used by contemporary humanists to illustrate the needs of the dying and the failures of family, friends and society to meet them. Read the novella and identify situations that seem to fit the ideas presented in this chapter:

    The fears of the dying patient (Pattison)

    The stages/reactions of dying (Kubler-Ross)

    The awareness context (Glaser and Strauss)

    The developmental perspective (Kastenbaum)

    In addition, it would be interesting to compare Ivan's transcendental experience with those reported by survivors of clinical death and those undergoing LSD psychotherapy for pain reduction and conflict resolution.

3. There is a growing movement in England and the United States to provide humane palliative care through home care or a specially designed "hospice," rather than an acute care facility. Hospice is a program which provides palliative and supportive care for terminally ill patients and their families either directly or on a consulting basis.

    Research the Hospice movement. A paper by Cecily Saunders in the Pearson volume listed at the end of this chapter provides an introduction to the principles and goals of the Hospice movement, including its approach to pain control. You can also write to the original United States Hospice for more information at the following address: Hospice, 765 Prospect Street, New Haven, Connecticut, 06511.

STRUCTURED EXERCISES

1. List six problems that you think would be most likely to trouble you if everything in your life was as it is now, except that yesterday you were told that you have an inoperable advanced cancer. Then, on a separate sheet of paper, rank order the six problems from one (most important to you) to six (least important to you). Show your original (unranked) list to someone else (this can be done pairwise, or by randomly redistributing the lists among the class) and have that person rank the list of problems according to their importance to him. Then compare the rankings together, discussing your reasons for agreeing or disagreeing with each other.

    As a further attempt to understand others' perspectives on terminal illness, you could consider how the original list would change if:

    a. you were 20 years older or younger

    b. you were the other sex

    c. you were on welfare

    d. you had just learned that your two-year old son was mentally retarded.

e.   your same-sexed parent had died of the same disease.

f.   you were recently married.

Adapted from R. Koenig "Counseling in Catastrophic Illness: A Self-Instructional Unit," *Omega*, 1975, *6*, 227-241.

2.   Try to look ahead to the time when you will actually die. Envision the ideal scene or your dying in some detail. Consider the following questions about how you would like your dying to be.

a.   How old would you be?

b.   Where would you be?

c.   What time of day would it be?

d.   What special objects would you see as you looked around you?

e.   What music would be playing in the background?

f.   What would you have been doing with your life just prior to this time?

g.   Who would be with you?

h.   What would you want to tell them?

In order to share the experience, the class could:

a.   Write the answers to these questions on a sheet of paper numbered from one to eight, and then, holding the sheet of paper in front of them, chest high, the students could walk around the room reading each other's comments. The reading should take place without conversation—involving only eye contact or other non-verbal communication. Once everyone has finished reading, class discussion of reactions can take place.

b. Each person can draw what he has imagined instead of writing it down. The drawings can be signed or left anonymous. They can be taped up around the room, the class can browse among them, and the group can discuss them.

FOR FURTHER READING

The following books and papers provide in-depth coverage of the topics introduced in this chapter.

Brim, O.G., Jr., Freeman, H. E., Levine, S. and Scotch, N. A. (eds.) *The Dying Patient.* New York: Russell Sage Foundation, 1970.

Glaser, B. G. and Strauss, A. L. *Awareness of Dying.* Chicago: Aldine, 1965.

——————. *Time for Dying.* Chicago: Aldine, 1968.

Hinton, J. *Dying.* Baltimore: Penguin Books, 1967.

Kastenbaum, R., and Aisenberg, R. *The Psychology of Death.* New York: Springer Publishing Co., 1972.

Kubler-Ross, E. *On Death and Dying.* New York: Macmillan Publishing Co., 1969.

——————. *Questions and Answers on Death and Dying.* New York: Macmillan, 1974.

Moody, R. A., Jr. *Life After Life.* Covington, Georgia: Mockingbird, 1975.

Pearson, L. (ed.) *Death and Dying:Current Issues in the Treatment of the Dying Person*. Cleveland: The Press of Case Western Reserve University, 1969.

Quint, J. *The Nurse and the Dying Patient*. New York: Macmillan, 1967.

Sudnow, D. *Passing on: The Social Organization of Dying*. Englewood Cliffs, N.J.: Prentice Hall, 1967.

Tolstoy, L. *The Death of Ivan Ilych and Other Stories*. New York: New American Library, 1960.

Weisman, A.D. *On Dying and Denying: A Psychiatric Study of Terminality*. New York: Behavioral Publications, 1973.

3

Grief, Mourning, and Social Functions

INTRODUCTION

Grief and Mourning

At the same time as modern man has been deprived of his own death, he has been similarly deprived of the right to mourn his dead. Historian Phillipe Ariès, surveying the reversal in social obligations attending death and mourning, charges that, ". . . modern society deprives man of his own death, and. . . it lows him this privilege only if he does not use it to upset the living. In a reciprocal way, society forbids the living to appear moved by the death of others; it does not allow them either to weep for the deceased or to seem to miss them."

Partially as a result of his own bereavement experiences, British anthropologist Geoffrey Gorer forcefully attacks the social prohibitions against mourning. Gorer claims death is "the new pornography," and mourning has become an "analogue of masturbation." Experiencing grief is a sign of weakness, thus any display of grief becomes a shameful act to be conducted in private.

A Necessary Process

Psychiatry, however, has long recognized that grief is a natural and necessary, albeit complex, reaction, accompanied by a range of contradictory emotions and apparently aberrant behaviors.

Unpleasant and irrational as it may appear to many, the grief process cannot be safely by-passed. As early as 1914, in his key paper, "Mourning and Melancholia," Sigmund Freud wrote, ". . . although mourning involves grave departures from the normal attitude to life, it never occurs to us to regard it as a pathological condition and to refer it to medical treatment . . . we look upon any interference with it as useless or even harmful." Freud's theoretical framework for understanding reactions to loss still underlies our conceptions of mourning.

The Freudian model has lead to the study of both the normal "symptomatology" of grief reactions and the pathological consequences of distorted grief. The condition of bereavement itself has been related not only to depression, suicide and psychosomatic disorders but even to death from "natural" causes.

Styles of Grief

The understanding and consequent acceptance of grief results in the recognition of varied styles of mourning: the dynamics of grief will vary with the nature of the death. One mourns differently for a child than for an aged parent; the aftermath of a loved one's suicide is different from the aftermath of death in wartime. As the state of extended dying becomes a common end to life, anticipatory grief must be given more prominence. Preparatory mourning shared by the dying person with his family in a state of open awareness can attenuate the experience of grief by providing mutual support and an opportunity for gradual separation during dying rather than after it.

Community

The shift from *intervention* to *prevention* in mental health care has been greatly influenced by the study of grief and bereavement. Now, informal grief counseling, educational seminars on psychological and practical aspects of bereavement and crisis intervention programs are often sponsored by churches, hospitals and schools. Model programs, such as "Widow to Widow," begun by Phyllis Silverman, Laboratory of Community Psychiatry and its West Coast counterpart, "Journey's End" at the University of Southern California have given rise to community support groups throughout the country. Such groups seek to provide not only emotional support during the crisis of bereavement, but also to offer practical information to aid the bereaved in the social readjustment to life as a single person.

Appropriate Grief

The development of "preventive" psychiatry emphasizes the relationship between personal pathology and pathological social structures that have failed to meet the individual's needs. If it is society's prohibition of mourning that has caused repression of grief, then it is society that must now develop new cultural forms to handle grief adequately. Ariès has emphasized the role that ritual has played in guiding mourning through the ages, both supporting the individual and maintaining the identity of the group when death occurs. Ritual makes sense of death by placing it in the context of a world view; by requiring individuals to return to their group identity, ritual publicly reminds them of their shared beliefs. As the distance from one's own death increases and the right to mourn is taken away, the ability to "make sense" of death breaks down and there is growing dissatisfaction with the ritual that supports that rationalization. Criticism is often directed at the funeral industry and religious liturgies for being "exploitative," and "insensitive," or simply "irrelevant." This dissatisfaction is symptomatic of dissatisfaction with the social prescriptions for mourning, but, at the same time, the dissatisfaction is also creative, reflecting a new awareness of mourning and of the benefits to both the mourner and society when grief is publicly recognized and accepted. The spawning of new professional roles reflects the search for functional new funerals in such innovations as "grief therapy" and "open-ended funerals." Some cultures provide a shaman who acts in the role of death-controller. Who are our new shamans?

163

ENCOUNTER

THE EXPERIENCE OF GRIEF

I knew Martin was dead, but somehow it took a long time for the reality to seep in, become part of me. I would go to the supermarket and think, "Oh, they have endive today. I'd better get some. Martin likes it so much." I would pick out an avocado for him, a fruit I've never really liked. Then I would realize, "My God! He is dead!" and put the avocado back as if it were burning me.

When something funny happened, I'd say to myself "Oh, wait until I tell Martin about this tonight! He'll never believe it." There were times in my office when I would stretch out my hand to the telephone to call him, to chat. Reality always intervened before I dialed that disconnected number. . . .

One day when I was on the Fifth Avenue bus I spotted a man who looked like Martin. I pulled the cord and plunged after him. I knew it wasn't Martin, but I tried desperately to catch up with him. I couldn't. I lost sight of him and it made me very depressed, as if Martin had rejected me.

And I had dreams. I would dream that I heard the door open while I was in the kitchen getting the ice for our evening drink. It was Martin, home from work. I would be so happy to hear him come in. But I always woke up before I saw him.

I had a sense of Martin, of some quality of Martin that had filtered into me. A very real feeling that part of me was Martin.

Lynn Caine, *Widow*. New York: Morrow, 1974.

1. Lynn Caine reports a disturbing but frequent, common and very natural reaction to a recent death. Can you recall similar experiences following a loss in your life such as divorce or separation? Describe three similar reactions to that loss.

2. Caine viewed the episodes in which Martin's presence continued to influence her behavior as part of her "crazy period." How do you account for similar experiences in your own life?

The work of mourning is more complex and requires more time than most people expect or can easily accept. In his key paper, "The Symptomatology and Management of Acute Grief," psychiatrist Erich Lindemann defines grief as a "definite syndrome with psychological and somatic symptomatology." Presenting the sometimes distressing responses to recent death as natural and necessary, Lindemann emphasizes the need to mourn: denial of grief is a predisposing factor in both psychopathology and physical illness. Lindemann's model of bereavement as a crisis period of increased vulnerability is one of the classic works in the preventive Community Psychiatry movement.

SYMPTOMATOLOGY AND MANAGEMENT OF ACUTE GRIEF

Erich Lindemann

INTRODUCTION

At first glance, acute grief would not seem to be a medical or psychiatric disorder in the strict sense of the word but rather a normal reaction to a distressing situation. However, the understanding of reactions to traumatic experiences whether or not they represent clear-cut neuroses has become of ever-increasing importance to the psychiatrist. Bereavement or the sudden cessation of social interaction seems to be of special interest because it is often cited among the alleged psychosomatic disorders. The enormous increase in grief reactions due to war casualties, furthermore, demands an evaluation of their probable effect on the mental and physical health of our population.

The points to be made in this paper are as follows:

1. Acute grief is a definite syndrome with psycho-

Erich Lindemann. "Symptomatology and Management of Acute Grief." *American Journal of Psychiatry,* CI (1944), 141-148. (Vo. 101)

logical and somatic symptomatology.

2. This syndrome may appear immediately after a crisis; it may be delayed; it may be exaggerated or apparently absent.

3. In place of the typical syndrome there may appear distorted pictures, each of which represents one special aspect of the grief syndrome.

4. By appropriate techniques these distorted pictures can be successfully transformed into a normal grief reaction with resolution.

Our observations comprise 101 patients. Included are psychoneurotic patients who lost a relative during the course of treatment, relatives of patients who died in the hospital, bereaved disaster victims (Cocoanut Grove Fire) and their close relatives, and relatives of members of the armed forces.

The investigation consisted of a series of psychiatric interviews. Both the timing and the content of the discussions were recorded. These records were subsequently analysed in terms of the symptoms reported and of the changes in mental status observed progressively through a series of interviews. The psychiatrist avoided all suggestions and interpretations until the picture of symptomatology and spontaneous reaction tendencies of the patients had become clear from the records. The somatic complaints offered important leads for objective study. Careful laboratory work on spirograms, g.-i. functions, and metabolic studies is in progress and will be reported separately. At present we wish to present only our psychobiological observations.

SYMPTOMATOLOGY OF NORMAL GRIEF

The picture shown by persons in acute grief is remarkably uniform. Common to all is the following syndrome: sensations of somatic distress occurring in waves lasting from twenty minutes to an hour at a time, a feeling of tightness in the throat, choking with shortness of breath, need for sighing, and an empty feeling in the abdomen, lack of muscular power, and an intense subjective distress described as tension or mental pain. The patient soon learns that these waves of discomfort can be precipitated by visits, by mentioning the deceased, and by receiving sympathy. There is a tendency to avoid the syndrome at any cost, to refuse visits lest they should precipitate the reaction, and to keep deliberately from thought all references to the deceased.

The striking features are the marked tendency to sighing respiration; this respiratory disturbance was most conspicuous when the patient was made to discuss his grief. The complaint about lack of strength and exhaustion is universal and is described as follows: "It is almost impossible to climb up a stairway." "Everything I lift seems so heavy." "The slightest effort makes me feel exhausted." "I can't walk to the corner without feeling exhausted." Digestive symptoms are described as follows: "The food tastes like sand." "I have no appetite at all." "I stuff the food down because I have to eat." "My saliva won't flow." "My abdomen feels hollow." "Everything seems slowed up in my stomach."

The sensorium is generally somewhat altered. There is commonly a slight sense of unreality, a feeling of increased emotional distance from other people (sometimes they appear shadowy or small), and there is intense preoccupation with the image of the deceased. A patient who lost his daughter in the Cocoanut Grove disaster visualized his girl in the telephone booth calling for him and was much troubled by the loudness with which his name was called by her and was so vividly preoccupied with the scene that he became oblivious of his surroundings. A young navy pilot lost a close friend; he remained a vivid part of his imagery, not in terms of a religious survival but in terms of an imaginary companion. He ate with him and talked over problems with him, for instance, discussing with him his plan of joining the Air Corps. Up to the time of the study, six months later, he denied the fact that the boy was no longer with him. Some patients are much concerned about this aspect of their grief reaction because they feel it indicates approaching insanity.

Another strong preoccupation is with feelings of guilt. The bereaved searches the time before the death for evidence of failure to do right by the lost one. He accuses himself of negligence and exaggerates minor omissions. After the fire disaster the central topic of discussion for a young married woman was the fact that her husband died after he left her following a quarrel, and of a young man whose wife died that he fainted too soon to save her.

In addition, there is often disconcerting loss of warmth in relationship to other people, a tendency to respond with irritability and anger, a wish not to be bothered by others at a time when friends and relatives make a special effort to keep up friendly relationships.

These feelings of hostility, surprising and quite inexplicable to the patients, disturbed them and again were often taken as signs of approaching insanity. Great efforts are made to handle them, and the result is often a formalized, stiff manner of social interaction.

The activity throughout the day of the severely bereaved person shows remarkable changes. There is no retardation of action and speech; quite to the contrary, there is a push of speech, especially when talking about the deceased. There is restlessness, inability to sit still, moving about in an aimless fashion, continually searching for something to do. There is, however, at the same time, a painful lack of capacity to initiate and maintain organized patterns of activity. What is done is done with lack of zest, as though one were going through the motions. The bereaved clings to the daily routine of prescribed activities; but these activities do not proceed in the automatic, self-sustaining fashion which characterizes normal work but have to be carried on with effort, as though each fragment of the activity became a special task. The bereaved is surprised to find how large a part of his customary activity was done in some meaningful relationship to the deceased and has now lost its significance. Especially the habits of social interaction— meeting friends, making conversation, sharing enterprises with others—seem to have been lost. This loss leads to a strong dependency on anyone who will stimulate the bereaved to activity and serve as the initiating agent.

These five points—(1) somatic distress, (2) preoccupation with the image of the deceased, (3) guilt, (4) hostile reactions, and (5) loss of patterns of conduct—seem to be pathognomonic for grief. There may be added a sixth characteristic, shown by patients who border on pathological reactions, which is not so conspicuous as the others but nevertheless often striking enough to color the whole picture. This is the appearance of traits of the deceased in the behavior of the bereaved, especially symptoms shown during the last illness, or behavior which may have been shown at the time of the tragedy. A bereaved person is observed or finds himself walking in the manner of his deceased father. He looks in the mirror and believes that his face appears just like that of the deceased. He may show a change of interests in the direction of the former activities of the deceased and may start enterprises entirely different from his former pursuits. A wife who lost her husband, an insurance agent, found herself writing to many insurance companies offering her services with somewhat exaggerated schemes. It seemed a regular observation in these patients that the painful preoccupation with the image of the deceased described above was transformed into preoccupation with symptoms or personality traits of the lost person, but now displaced to their own bodies and activities by identification.

COURSE OF NORMAL GRIEF REACTIONS

The duration of a grief reaction seems to depend upon the success with which a person does the *grief work*, namely, emancipation from the bondage to the deceased, readjustment to the environment in which the deceased is missing, and the formation of new relationships. One of the big obstacles to this work seems to be the fact that many patients try to avoid the intense distress connected with the grief experience and to avoid the expression of emotion necessary for it. The men victims after the Cocoanut Grove fire appeared in the early psychiatric interviews to be in a state of tension with tightened facial musculature, unable to relax for fear they might "break down." It required considerable persuasion to yield to the grief process before they were willing to accept the discomfort of bereavement. One assumed a hostile attitude toward the psychiatrist, refusing to allow any references to the deceased and rather rudely asking him to leave. This attitude remained throughout his stay on the ward, and the prognosis for his condition is not good in the light of other observations. Hostility of this sort was encountered on only occasional visits with the other patients. They became willing to accept the grief process and to embark on a program of dealing in memory with the deceased person. As soon as this became possible there seemed to be a rapid relief of tension and the subsequent interviews were rather animated conversations in which the deceased was idealized and in which misgivings about the future adjustment were worked through.

Examples of the psychiatrist's role in assisting patients in their readjustment after bereavement are contained in the following case histories. The first shows a very successful readjustment.

A woman, aged 40, lost her husband in the fire. She had a history of good adjustment previously. One child, ten years old. When she heard about her husband's death she was extremely depressed, cried bitterly, did not want to live, and for three days showed a state of utter dejection.

When seen by the psychiatrist, she was glad to have assistance and described her painful preoccupation with memories of her husband and her fear that she might lose her mind. She had a vivid visual image of his presence, picturing him as going to work in the morning and herself as wondering whether he would return in the evening, whether she could stand his not returning, then, describing to herself how he does return, plays with the dog, receives his child, and gradually tried to accept the fact that he is not there any more. It was only after ten days that she succeeded in accepting his loss and then only after having described in detail the remarkable qualities of her husband, the tragedy of his having to stop his activities at the pinnacle of his success, and his deep devotion to her.

In the subsequent interviews she explained with some distress that she had become very much attached to the examiner and that she waited for the hour of his coming. This reaction she considered disloyal to her husband but at the same time she could accept the fact that it was a hopeful sign of her ability to fill the gap he had left in her life. She then showed a marked drive for activity, making plans for supporting herself and her little girl, mapping out the preliminary steps for resuming her old profession as secretary, and making efforts to secure help from the occupational therapy department in reviewing her knowledge of French.

Her convalescence, both emotional and somatic, progressed smoothly, and she made a good adjustment immediately on her return home.

A man of 52, successful in business, lost his wife, with whom he had lived in happy marriage. The information given him about his wife's death confirmed his suspicions of several days. He responded with a severe grief reaction, with which he was unable to cope. He did not want to see visitors, was ashamed of breaking down, and asked to be permitted to stay in the hospital on the psychiatric service, when his physical condition would have permitted his discharge, because he wanted further assistance. Any mention of his wife produced a severe wave of depressive reaction, but with psychiatric assistance he gradually became willing to go through this painful process, and after three days on the psychiatric service he seemed well enough to go home.

He showed a high rate of verbal activity, was restless, needed to be occupied continually, and felt that the experience had whipped him into a state of restless overactivity.

As soon as he returned home he took an active part in his business, assuming a post in which he had a great many telephone calls. He also took over the role of amateur psychiatrist to another bereaved person, spending time with him and comforting him for his loss. In his eagerness to start anew, he developed a plan to sell all his former holdings, including his house, his furniture, and giving away anything which could remind him of his wife. Only after considerable discussion was he able to see that this would mean avoiding immediate grief at the price of an act of poor judgment. Again he had to be encouraged to deal with his grief reactions in a more direct manner. He has made a good adjustment.

With eight to ten interviews in which the psychiatrist shares the grief work, and with a period of from four to six weeks, it was ordinarily possible to settle an uncomplicated and undistorted grief reaction. This was the case in all but one of the 13 Cocoanut Grove fire victims.

MORBID GRIEF REACTIONS

Morbid grief reactions represent distortions of normal grief. The conditions mentioned here were transformed into "normal reactions" and then found their resolution.

Delay of Reaction.—The most striking and most frequent reaction of this sort is *delay* or *postponement*. If the bereavement occurs at a time when the patient is confronted with important tasks and when there is necessity for maintaining the morale of others, he may show little or no reaction for weeks or even much longer. A brief delay is described in the following example.

A girl of 17 lost both parents and her boy friend in the fire and was herself burned severely, with marked involvement of the lungs. Throughout her stay in the hospital her attitude was that of cheerful acceptance without any sign of adequate distress. When she was discharged at the end of three weeks she appeared cheerful, talked rapidly, with a considerable flow of ideas, seemed eager to return home and to assume the role of parent for her two younger siblings. Except for slight feelings of "lonesomeness" she complained of no distress.

This period of griefless acceptance continued for the next two months, even when the household was dispersed and her younger siblings were placed in other homes. Not until the end of the tenth week did she begin to show a true state of grief with marked feelings of depression, intestinal emptiness, tightness in her throat, frequent crying, and vivid preoccupation with her deceased parents.

That this delay may involve years became obvious first by the fact that patients in acute bereavement about a recent death may soon upon exploration be found preoccupied with grief about a person who died many years ago. In this manner a woman of 38, whose mother had died recently and who had responded to the mother's death with a surprisingly severe reaction, was found to be but mildly concerned with her mother's death but deeply engrossed with unhappy and perplexing fantasies concerning the death of her brother, who died twenty years ago under dramatic circumstances from metastasizing carcinoma after amputation of his arm had been postponed too long. The discovery that a former unresolved grief reaction may be precipitated in the course of the discussion of another recent event was soon demonstrated in psychiatric interviews by patients who showed all the traits of a true grief reaction when the topic of a former loss arose.

The precipitating factor for the delayed reaction may be a deliberate recall of circumstances surrounding the death or may be a spontaneous occurrence in the patient's life. A peculiar form of this is the circumstance that a patient develops the grief reaction at the time when he himself is as old as the person who died. For instance, a railroad worker, aged 42, appeared in the psychiatric clinic with a picture which was undoubtedly a grief reaction for which he had no explanation. It turned out that when he was 22, his mother, then 42, had committed suicide.

173

Distorted Reactions. The delayed reactions may occur after an interval which was not marked, by any abnormal behavior or distress, but in which there developed an *alteration* in the patient's *conduct* perhaps not conspicuous or serious enough to lead him to a psychiatrist. These alterations may be considered as the surface manifestations of an unresolved grief reaction, which may respond to fairly simple and quick psychiatric management if recognized. They may be classified as follows: (1) *overactivity without a sense of loss*, rather with a sense of wellbeing and zest, the activities being of an expansive and adventurous nature and bearing semblance to the activities formerly carried out by the deceased, as described above; (2) *the acquisition of symptoms belonging to the last illness of the deceased*. This type of patient appears in medical clinics and is often labelled hypochondriasis or hysteria. To what extent actual alterations of physiological functions occur under these circumstances will have to be a field of further careful inquiry. I owe to Dr. Chester Jones a report about a patient whose electrocardiogram showed a definite change during a period of three weeks, which started two weeks after the time her father died of heart disease.

While this sort of symptom formation "by identification" may still be considered as conversion symptoms such as we know from hysteria, there is another type of disorder doubtlessly presenting (3) a recognized *medical disease*, namely, a group of psychosomatic conditions, predominantly ulcerative colitis, rheumatoid arthritis, and asthma. Extensive studies in ulcerative colitis have produced evidence that 33 out of 41 patients with ulcerative colitis developed their disease in close time relationship to the loss of an important person. Indeed, it was this observation which first gave the impetus for the present detailed study of grief. Two of the patients developed bloody diarrhea at funerals. In the others it developed within a few weeks after the loss. The course of the ulcerative colitis was strikingly benefited when this grief reaction was resolved by psychiatric technique.

At the level of social adjustment there often occurs a conspicuous (4) *alteration in relationship to friends and relatives*. The patient feels irritable, does not want to be bothered, avoids former social activities, and is afraid he might antagonize his friends by his lack of interest and his critical attitudes. Progressive social isolation follows, and the patient needs considerable encouragement in re-establishing his social relationships.

While overflowing hostility appears to be spread out over all relationships, it may also occur as (5) *furious hostility against specific persons;* the doctor or the surgeon is accused bitterly for neglect of duty and the patient may assume that foul play has led to the death. It is characteristic that while patients talk a good deal about their suspicions and their bitter feelings, they are not likely to take any action against the accused, as a truly paranoid person might do.

(6) Many bereaved persons struggled with much effort against these feelings of hostility, which to them seem absurd, representing a vicious change in their characters and to be hidden as much as possible. Some patients succeed in hiding their hostility but become wooden and formal, with affectivity and conduct *resembling schizophrenic pictures.* A typical report is this, "I go through all the motions of living. I look after my children. I do my errands. I go to social functions, but it is like being in a play; it doesn't really concern me. I can't have any warm feelings. If I were to have any feelings at all I would be angry with everybody." This patient's reaction to therapy was characterized by growing hostility against the therapist, and it required considerable skill to make her continue interviews in spite of the disconcerting hostility which she had been fighting so much. The absence of emotional display in this patient's face and actions was quite striking. Her face had a mask-like appearance, her movements were formal, stilted, robot-like, without the fine play of emotional expression.

(7) Closely related to this picture is a *lasting loss of patterns of social interaction.* The patient cannot initiate any activity, is full of eagerness to be active—restless, can't sleep—but throughout the day he will not start any activity unless "primed" by somebody else. He will be grateful at sharing activities with others but will not be able to make up his mind to do anything alone. The picture is one of lack of decision and

initiative. Organized activities along social lines occur only if a friend takes the patient along and shares the activity with him. Nothing seems to promise reward; only the ordinary activities of the day are carried on, and these in a routine manner, falling apart into small steps, each of which has to be carried out with much effort and without zest.

(8) There is, in addition, a picture in which a patient is active but in which most of his activities attain a coloring which is *detrimental to his own social and economic existence*. Such patients with uncalled for generosity, give away their belongings, are easily lured into foolish economic dealings, lose their friends and professional standing by a series of "stupid acts," and find themselves finally without family, friends, social status or money. This protracted self-punitive behavior seems to take place without any awareness of excessive feelings of guilt. It is a particularly distressing grief picture because it is likely to hurt other members of the family and drag down friends and business associates.

(9) This leads finally to the picture in which the grief reaction takes the form of a straight *agitated depression* with tension, agitation, insomnia, feelings of worthlessness, bitter self-accusation, and obvious need for punishment. Such patients may be dangerously suicidal.

A young man aged 32 had received only minor burns and left the hospital apparently well on the road to recovery just before the psychiatric survey of the disaster victims took place. On the fifth day he had learned that his wife had died. He seemed somewhat relieved of his worry about her fate; impressed the surgeon as being unusually well-controlled during the following short period of his stay in the hospital.

On January 1st he was returned to the hospital by his family. Shortly after his return home he had become restless, did not want to stay at home, had taken a trip to relatives trying to find rest, had not succeeded, and had returned home in a state of marked agitation, appearing preoccupied, frightened, and unable to concentrate on any organized activity. The mental status presented a somewhat unusual picture. He was restless, could not sit still or participate in any activity in the ward. He would try to read, drop it after a few minutes, or try to play pingpong, give it up after a short time. He would try to start conversations, break them off abruptly, and then fall into repeated murmured utterances: "Nobody can help me. When is it going to happen? I am doomed, am I not?"

176

With great effort it was possible to establish enough rapport to carry on interviews. He complained about his feeling of extreme tension, inability to breathe, generalized weakness and exhaustion, and his frantic fear that something terrible was going to happen. "I'm destined to live in insanity or I must die. I know that it is God's will. I have this awful feeling of guilt." With intense morbid guilt feelings, he reviewed incessantly the events of the fire. His wife had stayed behind. When he tried to pull her out, she had fainted and was shoved out by the crowd. She was burned while he was saved. "I should have saved her or I should have died too." He complained about being filled with an incredible violence and did not know what to do about it. The rapport established with him lasted for only brief periods of time. He then would fall back into his state of intense agitation and muttering. He slept poorly even with large sedation. In the course of four days he became somewhat more composed, had longer periods of contact with the psychiatrist, and seemed to feel that he was being understood and might be able to cope with his morbid feelings of guiilt and violent impulses. On the sixth day of his hospital stay, however, after skillfully distracting the attention of his special nurse he jumped through a closed window to a violent death.

If the patient is not conspicuously suicidal, it may nevertheless be true that he has a strong desire for painful experiences, and such patients are likely to desire shock treatment of some sort, which they picture as a cruel experience, such as electrocution might be.

A 21-year-old woman, whose 20-month-old son was accidentally smothered developed a state of severe agitated depression with self-accusation, inability to enjoy anything, hopelessness about the future, overflow of hostility against the husband and his parents, also with excessive hostility against the psychiatrist. She insisted upon electric-shock treatment and was finally referred to another physician who treated her. She responded to the shock treatments very well and felt relieved of her sense of guilt.

It is remarkable that agitated depressions of this sort represent only a small fraction of the pictures of grief in our series.

PROGNOSTIC EVALUATION

Our observations indicate that to a certain extent the type

177

and severity of the grief reaction can be predicted. Patients with obsessive personality make-up and with a history of former depressions are likely to develop an agitated depression. Severe reactions seem to occur in mothers who have lost young children. The intensity of interaction with the deceased before his death seems to be significant. It is important to realize that such interaction does not have to be of the affectionate type; on the contrary, the death of a person who invited much hostility, especially hostility which could not well be expressed because of his status and claim to loyalty, may be followed by a severe grief reaction in which hostile impulses are the most conspicuous feature. Not infrequently the person who passed away represented a key person in a social system, his death being followed by disintegration of this social system and by a profound alteration of the living and social conditions for the bereaved. In such cases readjustment presents a severe task quite apart from the reaction to the loss incurred. All these factors seem to be more important than a tendency to react with neurotic symptoms in previous life. In this way the most conspicuous forms of morbid identification were found in persons who had no former history of a tendency to psychoneurotic reactions.

MANAGEMENT

Proper psychiatric management of grief reactions may prevent prolonged and serious alterations in the patient's social adjustment, as well as potential medical disease. The essential task facing the psychiatrist is that of sharing the patient's grief work, namely, his efforts at extricating himself from the bondage to the deceased and at finding new patterns of rewarding interaction. It is of the greatest importance to notice that not only over-reaction but under-reaction of the bereaved must be given attention because delayed responses may occur at unpredictable moments and the dangerous distortions of the grief reaction, not conspicuous at first, be quite destructive later and these may be prevented.

Religious agencies have led in dealing with the bereaved.

They have provided comfort by giving the backing of dogma to the patient's wish for continued interaction with the deceased, have developed rituals which maintain the patient's interaction with others, and have counteracted the morbid guilt feelings of the patient by Divine Grace and by promising an opportunity for "making up" to the deceased at the time of a later reunion. While these measures have helped countless mourners, comfort alone does not provide adequate assistance in the patient's grief work. He has to accept the pain of the bereavement. He has to review his relationships with the deceased, and has to become acquainted with the alterations in his own modes of emotional reaction. His fear of insanity, his fear of accepting the surprising changes in his feelings, especially the overflow of hostility, have to be worked through. He will have to express his sorrow and sense of loss. He will have to find an acceptable formulation of his future relationship to the deceased. He will have to verbalize his feelings of guilt, and he will have to find persons around him whom he can use as "primers" for the acquisition of new patterns of conduct. All this can be done in eight to ten interviews.

Special techniques are needed if hostility is the most marked feature of the grief reaction. The hostility may be directed against the psychiatrist, and the patient will have such guilt over his hostility that he will avoid further interviews. The help of a social worker or a minister, or if these are not available, a member of the family, to urge the patient to continue coming to see the psychiatrist may be indispensable. If the tension and the depressive features are too great, a combination of benzedrine sulphate, 5-10 mgm. b.i.d., and sodium amytal, 3 gr. before retiring, may be useful in first reducing emotional distress to a tolerable degree. Severe agitated depressive reactions may defy all efforts of psychotherapy and may respond well to shock treatment.

Since it is obvious that not all bereaved persons, especially those suffering because of war casualties, can have the benefit of expert psychiatric help, much of this knowledge will have to be passed on to auxiliary workers. Social workers and ministers will have to be on the look-out for the more ominous pictures, referring these to the psychiatrist while assisting the more normal reactions themselves.

ANTICIPATORY GRIEF REACTIONS

While our studies were at first limited to reactions to actual death, it must be understood that grief reactions are just one form of separation reactions. Separation by death is characterized by its irreversibility and finality. Separation may, of course, occur for other reasons. We were at first surprised to find genuine grief reactions in patients who had not experienced a bereavement but who had experienced separation, for instance with the departure of a member of the family into the armed forces. Separation in this case is not due to death but is under the threat of death. A common picture hitherto not appreciated is a syndrome which we have designated *anticipatory grief*. The patient is so concerned with her adjustment after the potential death of father or son that she goes through all the phases of grief-depression, heightened preoccupation with the departed, a review of all the forms of death which might befall him, and anticipation of the modes of readjustment which might be necessitated by it. While this reaction may well form a safeguard against the impact of a sudden death notice, it can turn out to be of a disadvantage at the occasion of reunion. Several instances of this sort came to our attention when a soldier just returned from the battlefront complained that his wife did not love him anymore and demanded immediate divorce. In such situations apparently the grief work had been done so effectively that the patient has emancipated herself and the readjustment must now be directed towards new interaction. It is important to know this because many family disasters of this sort may be avoided through prophylactic measures.

BIBLIOGRAPHY

Many of the observations are, of course, not entirely new. Delayed reactions were described by Helene Deutsch (1). Shock treatment in agitated depressions due to bereavement has recently been advocated by Myerson (2). Morbid identification has been stressed at many points in the psychoanalytic literature and recently by H. A. Murray (3). The relation of mourning and depressive psychoses has been discussed by Freud (4), Melanie Klein (5), and Abraham (6). Bereavement reactions in wartime were discussed by Wilson (7). The reactions after the Cocoanut Grove fire were described in some detail in a chapter of the monograph on this civilian disaster (8). The effect of wartime separations was reported by Rosenbaum (9). The incidence of grief reactions among the psychogenic factors in asthma and rheumatoid arthritis has been mentioned by Cobb, *et al*, (10, 11).

1. Deutsch, Helene, "Absence of Grief," *Psychoanalyt. Quart.,* 6:12, 1937.
2. Myerson, Abraham, "The use of shock therapy in prolonged grief reactions." *New England J. Med.,* 230:9, Mar. 2, 1944.
3. Murray, H. A., "Visual manifestations of personality," *Jr. Abn. & Social Psychol.,* 32:161-184, 1937.
4. Freud, Sigmund, "Mourning and melancholia." *Collected Papers,* IV, 288-317; 152-170.
5. Klein, Melanie, "Mourning and its relation to manic-depressive states." *Internat. J. Psychoan.,* 21:125-153, 1940.
6. Abraham, C., "Notes on the psycho-analytical investigation and treatment of the libido, viewed in the light of mental disorder." Selected Papers.
7. Wilson, A. T. M., "Reactive emotional disorders." *Practitioner,* 146:254-258.
8. Cobb, S., & Lindemann, E., "Neuropsychiatric observations after the Cocoanut Grove fire." *Ann. Surg.,* June 1943.
9. Rosenbaum, Milton., "Emotional aspects of wartime separations." *Family,* 24:337-341, 1944.
10. Cobb, S., Bauer, W., and Whitney, I., "Environmental factors in rheumatoid arthritis." *J. A. M. A.,* 113:668-670, 1939.
11. McDermott, N., and Cobb, S., "Psychogenic factors in asthma." *Psychosom. Med.,* 1:204-341, 1939.
12. Lindemann, Erich, "Psychiatric factors in the treatment of ulcerative colitis." *Archives of Neurology and Psychiatry,* 49:323-324, 1943.

In the last fifteen years the funeral industry has been widely criticized for encouraging financial display, causing emotional strain, and supporting apparently meaningless ritual requirements. However, most people have little first-hand knowledge about the practical or ritual activities which occur during the brief period between the time of death and the final disposition of the remains. A concise treatment of those activities is provided by sociologist Leroy Bowman, who gives a dispassionate account of the American wake, funeral service and committal service in "Group Behavior at Funeral Gatherings." It is a mistake to think that grief and mourning cease at the conclusion of the funeral; this misunderstanding may account for much of the anger that has been directed at the American funeral as an institution. Bowman's objective analysis of the social structure of formal and informal practices as well as the social variables that have led to changes in those practices provides a balanced perspective of an emotionally charged topic.

GROUP BEHAVIOR AT FUNERAL GATHERINGS

Leroy Bowman

That short, potential stir
That each can make but once,
That bustle so illustrious
'Tis almost consequence,
Is the *éclat* of death.

Emily Dickinson

The arrangements the family makes for a funeral provide typically for three, sometimes four, types of gatherings. At all of them, except the fourth, the casket containing the remains is observed by all in attendance. These are: (1) the wake, (2) the religious ceremony, (3) the committal service at which the casket is lowered into the grave, and (4) possibly the gathering at the home after the more formal and public sessions are over.

Leroy Bowman. "Group Behavior at Funeral Gatherings." *The American Funeral: A Study in Guilt, Extravagance, and Sublimity*. Washington, D.C.: Public Affairs Press, 1959.

The reasons for holding several instead of one long observance are the necessity of holding the differing stages of the funeral in rooms of suitable size, style, and equipment; the prohibitive length of time that would be required if one only meeting was held; the need to offer alternative days or hours to accommodate persons with crowded calendars; the desirability of providing separate occasions in order that groups of differing composition may attend differing types of assemblages; and lastly, the danger of blurring the impression made at any one of the occasions if it was associated too closely with the others. The gatherings vary greatly,not only in composition and affective tone, but in type of activity indulged in, the solidarity of the groups, and in leadership.

THE SOCIABLE WAKE

The wake is a period during which the embalmed body lies in the casket to be looked at by visitors. It is also designated as "lying in state." The first term originated in a custom, rarely still practiced, of relatives sitting up all night with the body. The second term, "lying in state," applied originally to the bodies of notables, as they lay on exhibition for the benefit of followers. Neither term is descriptive as applied generally today. The expressed reason for attending is to pay respects to the dead, or to offer sympathy to the close relatives who are always present. However, the "viewing of the body" and the expressions of sympathy are only the traditional and the proper performances expected of visitors. In the majority of cases they are briefly and sometimes perfunctorily accomplished. Attention then reverts, if the visitors remain for any length of time, to friendly and casual conversation with the others present. It takes up the greater part of the time usually spent at the wake.

In approximately six out of ten cases the visiting is done at the funeral parlor, in practically all other cases at the home. Visiting usually takes place in the afternoon or evening from one to four days preceding the day of the funeral service. For most groups in the east, middle west, and south, attendance during this period is large. In the region west of the Rocky Mountains bodies lie in state for but one evening before the service. Almost universally the place in which the wake is held is made as homelike and as cheerful as possible. A few touches in the décor, especially in the vicinity of the casket, indicate the presence of death, such as two pillar-like lamps and two candles encased in colored glass. In the funeral homes pictures of a religious import, such as *The Last Supper*, are often displayed.

The most striking note in the surroundings of the casket is the large number of flowers arranged in bunches or woven into floral designs. Often they are so numerous that little or no aesthetic effect is produced. The tone of funeral parlors varies from the dreary, through the garish to the elegant. Frequently the parlors are over-elaborate. The chapels in a large establishment may each be done in a period style, or according to a dominant pattern and called "The Blue Room," "The Victorian Room," etc.

The casket containing the body is sometimes placed in the dominant spot in the room or suite of rooms. Or it may be in a niche or in a room adjoining that in which the visitors congregate. Sometimes the casket cannot easily be seen from the seats or standing places of the majority of persons in the group. Clergymen or representatives of groups who come to say prayers only, or to hold a service, may stand near the casket. Sermons or talks, however, will be delivered often from a speaker's vantage point without reference to the situation of the body. The visitors who do more than make an appearance, look at the deceased and speak to a member of the family, distribute themselves in the most available spots and in formations which are most favorable for group conversation and discussion.

Typically the wake is held for the whole world of acquaintances and connections of the person who has died. It is the occasion, while he lies in state, for each individual who knew him to see him for the last time, personally to offer condolences to widow, mother or son, to tell of his connections with the one who is being honored, and to praise him. It is the opportunity also for representatives of the organizations to which he has belonged to bring word to his relatives and friends of the place he took in their work and companionship. That this occasion should be regarded in certain sectors of society, especially in certain cultural groups, as the biggest bid for recognition of a lifetime is not difficult to understand. Recognition comes seldom in these groups. The desire for it on the part of the members of the bereaved family is projected on to the dead person. That the thrill of the hour in the limelight fails to stir the deceased is obvious, but it is not altogether true that anticipation of it has no effect on him. The fact can be seen in the many references in story, drama and everyday life to a desire for a brilliant funeral.

The periods in which the body lies in state, especially those in the evening, provide opportunity for delegations of varying sizes to pay their respects. From the work shop, store, society or church come associates, or a group officially representing the job, section, committee or project. Status is one determining factor in the selection of the personnel of delegations. Frequently the job boss, or any other immediate superior comes and gives a tone of added importance to the occasion. In small communities those in attendance represent all walks of life. The strongest selective factor is church affiliation. In large communities economic status is the greatest determining factor in the composition of the attendance at the wake. Ethnic origin plays a powerful part, especially as it is associated with religious differences. This holds for national origin among minority groups, especially in the first and second generations. The ownership of the funeral parlor selected by the family corresponds usually to the race, creed and national origin of the family of the deceased, in response to common loyalties and because of greater understanding of group habits in the social activities of the wake.

In the gatherings of the wake the influence of the church is exercised in varying degrees, but, with the exception of Pentecostal groups, less than at the ceremony and the committal service. However, church groups in any denomination may appear at the wake in numbers or by representative delegations. Often in evangelical circles the minister, his assistant, or lay leaders of the church conduct short religious sessions such as prayers, Scripture readings, or songs. In groups of greatest church solidarity a sermon may be given on one of the evenings.

At wakes in Catholic groups a priest often appears to say a prayer. Some Protestant ministers refrain from attendance, feeling that the wake is purely social, and that it is best for them to wait for the serious note that will be sounded at the church service. The most formal incidents at some wakes are the services conducted by certain of the fraternal orders. Veterans groups offer formal services to be held at the wake, or military honors to be performed at the grave. There are wakes at which as many as five fraternal services have been given, although some of the larger orders provide their ceremony on condition it is the only one to be held.

Activity at the wake is predominantly social intercourse. When a large number of persons is present, as is often true in the evening, the occasion becomes a party. Some groups are more reverential or subdued than others. Some wear ordinary clothing; some "dress up." They talk about their usual interests, as well as those of the deceased. Most of them speak about the likeness to life of the face of the dead acquaintance. Some of them seem consciously to avoid mention of the body.

As in all social matters there are examples of extremes of behavior: In the Pentecostal groups revelrous lamentation is prolonged. There are degrees of conviviality to be found in different groups. Joking at the wake is practiced in more than one cultural group. The assertion that joking is more cruel than sober expression of sympathy to members of the family is not borne out by inquiry. In fact many persons defend joking as less cruel. They say they make an effort "to say silly things about ourselves and the deceased" and thus to take the minds of the bereaved family off the grievous aspects of their loss, to "tide them over the worst period." I have been unable, through many queries, to find anyone accustomed to the practice who has felt hurt by it.

Ribaldry at wakes is also a matter of degree, governed by the prevailing convivial habits of the group in question. Funeral directors report that men, especially those of certain cultural groups want to bring in food and drinks. Few establishments allow either. However one funeral home known to the author has a cafeteria on the premises. Members of the lower income groups sometimes bring soft drinks into the funeral chapels.

There are two main factors in the reduction of the hilarious aspects of the wake: (1) the more public atmosphere of the funeral parlor as compared to the home, and (2) the rules laid down by funeral directors, setting a closing hour at 9, 10, or 11 o'clock, or discouraging visiting hours after a given time. The elegance of many funeral establishments has added to the suppression of hilarity on the part of many groups.

One striking characteristic of wakes is the comparative lack of leadership in most of them. No one "starts anything" beyond the possible ushering into the proper room by an attendant at the funeral parlor, and beyond the first formality of looking at the face of the deceased and speaking to the chief mourners. The words of a visiting delegation, the prayer of a clergyman, or the service of a fraternal organization may constitute a formal ritual. On the whole, however, the discussion is informal, carried on in small casual groups.

Though emotions experienced at the wake are many and varied, it is the least emotional meeting of the series of funeral assemblages. The chief mourners usually express their gratitude for the many statements of sympathy. A large attendance swells their pride. For some families, the numerous floral pieces, the glamor of the casket, or even the mere knowledge of the costliness of the arrangements, creates a sense of prestige. The most universal wish is "to do the right thing" for the dead one. The right thing is to accord him recognition by providing for the occasion an aura of splendor. The number and importance of those in attendance magnify the sense of prestige.

For the members of the family the wake may be fatiguing, lasting, as it often does, for many hours. Often the prolonged experience is an ordeal. Little time is left the family for the routine tasks, and the consequent pressure creates tension that mounts until the day of the funeral. The funeral parlor provides for some of the satisfaction of entertaining in a spacious room, for others, however, the strangeness of its surroundings is depressing. For a very considerable number the place and the proceedings seem pretentious, out of keeping with their feelings about the mystery of life and death. The terms they use to describe the sessions of the wake include "superficial," "barbarous," "pagan." For them the lavish display is wasteful in the highest degree. Many feel revulsion at the public aspect of the wake, especially the submission of the "restored" face of the dead to the curious or morbid gaze of all who come. Some complain that the atmosphere is not that of home or church, but is charged with commercialism, at a time when commercialism should have no place.

In small towns and in isolated groups the wake is often a moving experience. In larger towns, especially when a group of theater size gathers, it is likely to become a casual matter. For the prominent citizen it becomes a public affair, devoted largely to viewing the body; for the unknown pauper it is dispensed with.

THE RITUAL SERVICE

The funeral service is the third stage of the funeral proceedings, following the preparations in the home, and the wake. It is different from the wake in almost all particulars. For one thing it is a brief ceremony as compared with the sessions of the preceding stage. It is formal in content and procedure, in the church setting in which it is held, and even in the attire of those attending. At the wake, friends and relatives are inclined to lighten the spirit of the occasion and often to avoid the mournful aspects of the death; at the funeral service the most serious of death's meanings are confronted. Except in very rare instances the service is intended to be a serious and sobering experience.

The funeral service is a ritual lying traditionally in the province of the church. Even among non-church members, the majority of persons look upon the church as the place for the holding of the service, or on a clergyman, bringing the message of the church to the funeral parlor, as the appropriate individual to officiate. There are exceptions, as in the case of brief ceremonies of the family and friends at home or in funeral parlors, in which there is no clerical leadership but rather that of the elder member, friend, or organization official. The relation of the funeral to the essential activities of the church varies among denominations and among churches within one denomination.

In some instances it is strictly a church affair and the members are all expected to put in an appearance. In others, it may be peripheral in its relation to the congregational aspect of the church, or regarded as a matter of chief concern only to the clergyman and the bereaved family.

On the whole, fewer persons attend the church service than come at one time or another to the wake. In metropolitan areas the funeral service of a prominent leader in a minority group is often the occasion for a mass demonstration of solidarity that fills the largest church and throngs the street on which it stands.

At the service emphasis is put on the seating arrangements for the participants and on the sequence of events. The casket is placed in front of the group, with the closest relatives nearest to it, and those of less connection with the deceased further back. In the church the clergyman is in the most prominent position at the altar or in the pulpit; the pall bearers and any other dignitaries of the occasion are also near the front. When the service is over the same relative status of positions is maintained in the procession to the cemetery. Events in the ritual take place in automatic sequence rather than by verbal direction of a leader. At services in mortuary homes the sequence is less fixed and the undertaker, who assumes very little prominence at a church, directs affairs more actively in his own premises.

At the wake much verbal interaction takes place. At the service practically none occurs; the audience is silent except as it may take part in responses led by the clergyman. In fact the clergyman initiates all action, except that directed by the funeral director. Activity on the part of the auditors is of an unexpressed emotional or intellectual kind.

When a eulogy is given, the keenest attention of the members of the audience is devoted to identification of each with the dead person. After the funeral, they tell of listening for items in the narration of the life or in the characterization of the eulogy with which they were familiar, or events or loyalties which they shared with the deceased. The desire to listen to a eulogy rather than to an analysis and critical evaluation of the life that is ended, comes in part from this identification, and the consequent egoistic satisfaction in praise and commendation that directly or remotely reflects on them.

However, a much stronger emotion creates or strengthens the wish to hear well of the dead. It is the wish to be well spoken at one's own funeral. Under the weight of the apprehension, whether clearly or vaguely realized as such, the individual gains some assurance through hearing words of approbation. In this connection one emotional experience at the funeral service needs to be mentioned here. This experience is the concern that is usually aroused over the mystery of life and death and the often painful reappraisal of the ideals held by the individual and the degree to which they are implemented in the routine of daily affairs. Clergymen occasionally find persons ready to affiliate or renew affiliation with the church when death has occurred in the family.

Due to the depth of feeling aroused by death in the minds of some of those in attendance, and due also to the grief of the close friends and relatives, there is always the possibility of an outburst of emotional expression, especially in the case of a few minority groups. The clergy, for the most part, take precautions to prevent the occurrence, some meet with the members of the family before the ceremony to fortify them against the emotional ordeal. Tensions of other kinds are experienced during the ceremony by some of the members of the congregation; sympathy with the bereaved, remembrance of similar losses in the past, fear or expectation of an emotional outburst, or, among those present who are not adherents of the faith expressed in the ritual, an uneasiness at participation in it.

In a gathering of any considerable size, there are also persons who are emotionally affected very little. Many persons who are deeply affected are fatigued by the contemplation of death. To meet these tensions and this fatigue clergymen reduce the service to thirty minutes or less in length. Clergymen called to officiate at a service in a funeral home, may speak voluntarily or by request for only ten minutes.

One other almost universal characteristic of funerals is the lavish display of expenditures noticeable in the costly casket. This is particularly striking at the obsequies held for the dead of low or middle income families. At services held in the chapels of undertaking establishments, the impression of conspicuous display is augmented by the mass of costly floral pieces. A real or imagined need may be served by the seemingly extravagant exhibit. Nevertheless the uninitiated observer cannot but be struck by the contrast of the social and spiritual emotions aroused by the death and emotions characterized by the superficial desire to live up to the Joneses.

A lasting impression of differences between funeral services is left by the contrasting atmosphere in which they may be held. In the home of the deceased a tone of familiarity with him and his "folks" prevails. Sympathy for the family is felt more intensely than in either of the other two settings, and simplicity of casket and procedure seems eminently appropriate. The participant's mind is apt to dwell on the family life of the deceased, its beginning and its now partial dissolution, as well as on the generation immediately preceding and the one following his. At the church the symbols of faith make their imprint, and solemnity as well as architectural grandeur seem fitting. Here not only the deceased and his family, but the gathering itself becomes merely a part of the expression of ultimate human longings. The mind of the participant in this context dwells less on the period of a lifetime and more on vast stretches of time and on the meaning of eternity. In a sense the funeral parlor is more informal than either the home or church. It symbolizes death to the participant more than they, and in greater measure holds the attention to this one unusual happening. It magnifies the present anguish and guilt and glosses over the permanence of affection and sorrow, and the continuing processes of daily living. It emphasizes, not so much the span of life nor the long stretch of time, but the short period of the funeral activities.

FINALITY OF THE COMMITTAL SERVICE

Committing the remains to the earth is a continuation of the funeral service. It is dramatic beyond any incident in the funeral period except the moment of death itself. It is packed

191

with acts and symbols of finality, and if ritual could blot out any lingering fantasy that the dead one might be seen or heard again, the committal would do so.

Fewer persons attend the committal service, partly because to do so is time consuming. This is particularly true in urban centers where the cemetery lies at a considerable distance from residential areas. In addition, many acquaintances entertain the opinion that the final act affects specifically only the closest relations and friends. On occasion, when the clergyman has been brought in to officiate at the service of a stranger, or when the journey to the grave is long, the committal service is said incongruously in the funeral parlor before the procession starts. Thereafter few but the immediate family accompany the casket. If the deceased has been prominent, or a member of a cohesive group, larger numbers of persons make the trip. It is still quite a common thing for the surviving members of the family to take pride in the number of cars in the procession.

During the last and climactic episode of the funeral series the casket is the center of attention. Lines of status are drawn as at the preceding service. The hearse leads the procession, followed by the immediate family, other relatives, near friends and others in order. The clergyman and pall bearers ride in cars near the head of the cortege. At the end of the journey the clergyman and the immediate relatives stand closest to the grave. The undertaker becomes much more prominent in the direction of the proceedings as he and his assistant instruct the pall bearers in placing the casket on the tapes and later lowering it into the grave.

The rite is brief; the trend is to make it less harrowing for those who have lived with the one who now is dead. But feelings run deep and strong and are more likely to burst out here than at any other time. Often the clergyman bolsters the closest relatives before the committal begins. As the casket is lowered and the symbolic flowers or handful of earth is thrown on the casket and particularly when the phrase "dust to dust" is heard, the tension is almost unbearable for any one who has known the deceased at all well, but especially for the family. At this moment, in certain cultural groups, a widow may attempt to throw herself on the casket and plead to go with her husband. The observer may recognize it as a role she is expected to play, and may be prepared to discount the sincerity of the act. Witnessing the enactment of just such a scene, however, leads to the firm conviction that under the cruel circumstances, the role the widow plays must be easy to assume with a maximum of tense emotion and a minimum of pretense.

The committal service might be characterized as a rite to confirm to the participants the end of their relationship to the dead, and as such it is an essential part of the celebration of death in certain religious groups. For some persons, however, it is a harrowing anticlimax to the calm sublimity of the funeral service.

THE RETURN HOME

From the moment of death, and in case of critical illness preceding it for a period before death, through the afternoons and evenings of the wake, through the tense emotional experience of the funeral service and the tragic moments of the committal service, the family has spent its physical and mental strength. The stimulus of responsibility in prominent roles has enabled the members to hold out to the end. When the cultural requirements have been met and the spotlight removed, the return to the home may signalize a let-down into more heart rending sorrow than any happening up to that time. The old relationships have been disrupted, and the new not yet entered upon. It is then that some of the neighbors or the relatives not included in the immediate family often try to make the homecoming seem less lonesome and desolate. They prepare food, either in the home of the family or in their own homes, and bring it in for the tired and hungry group. Such assistance has become a custom that is to be found in many parts of the country.

Usually few persons are present, unless many relatives have come from outside the city to remain for a gathering of the extended family. Action originates with the neighbors, relatives and close friends; and ordinarily, as in any housekeeping matter, the women take over the planning and serving of food. There is little or no formality, and a warm, intimate feeling pervades the group.

The impulse of the close associates to lessen the work and brighten the spirit of the return home does not arise solely from a rational consideration of the need of the family. It springs from a desire of practically every one who has known the family in a friendly fashion. From the hour when death is expected or has come many offer help, and many more would do so if they could think of some service that is needed.

It would appear first that some glimmering of the pressure of formal requirements of the funeral on the family is felt. Second, the sympathy that is felt finds verbal expression difficult for many persons and inadequate for many more. Occasionally the observer detects something of the feeling of guilt that the chief mourners experience also gripping in smaller measure the less intimate friends and neighbors. The wish "to do something" is its manifestation.

Societies vary in their patterns for dealing with the crisis caused by death's losses. In a cross-cultural study entitled "Bereavement and Mental Health," psychiatrist Edmund Volkhart in conjunction with Stanley Michael explores individual vulnerability to pathological grief reactions as a function of the specific cultural assumptions about death.

They conclude that the more significance the family structure places on a few individuals in a person's life, the more impact the loss of one of those persons will have. In addition, they point out that conflict arises when personal reactions are at variance with social role expectations; the rituals connected with the role may fail to provide for expression of some important needs.

BEREAVEMENT AND MENTAL HEALTH

Edmund H. Volkhart
(with the collaboration of
Stanley T. Michael)

CULTURAL PERSPECTIVES

A convenient place to begin is with the concept of culture, which is often regarded as the most important single concept in the social sciences. Although it may be defined technically in different words and used in slightly different ways, culture refers basically to the ideas, norms, values, practices, and beliefs which are historically shared by the members of an organized group or society. Each society has its own distinctive culture; and whereas at one level of abstraction there are certain universals common to all cultures, the specific contents of various cultures are amazingly diverse.[1-2]

Edmund H. Volkhart and Stanley T. Michael. "Bereavement and Mental Health." *Explorations in Social Psychiatry.* Edited by A. H. Leighton, J. A. Clausen, and R. N. Wilson. New York: Basic Books, 1957.

The concept of culture is significant in the present connection in that each individual is born into and develops within specific cultural context. By example, precept, reward, and punishment he learns most of the culture to which he is exposed.[3]

Any sociocultural system may be envisaged as being composed of a series of organized groups, of what are sometimes termed "social institutions."[4] At one level of analysis these are specific and local—i.e., *a* family, *a* school, *a* church, and so on; at another level of analysis the specific units are combined into "type" institutions—i.e., *the* family, *the* school, *the* church, and so on, indicating a particular emphasis on the typical features of each.

Each such group, or institutional unit, in turn may be regarded as an organization of "positions" or "statuses." A family, for example, is composed of husband, wife, parents, children, brothers and sisters; each status being identified by its relation to another (i.e., husband-wife, parent-child, brother-sister, etc.). These positions are, of course, occupied by particular persons, but the behavior of the persons in their relation to each other is channeled by the structure of the relationship itself. Mutual expectations arise, and the statuses of the relationships come to involve certain "roles" or role behaviors vis-à-vis each other. All of the principal social relationships, in any culture, may be regarded as interlocking roles.[5-7]

As soon as an individual is born, he begins to be a part of a social relationship (parent-child), in the setting of a particular institution (the family), which is composed, at least in part, of persons who have already been culturally trained. In their behavior toward the newcomer, much of their cultural learning will be manifest; and this is important because the individual *self* will develop primarily in interaction with family members.[8,9] The individual self, in brief, is a social self, including the "reflected appraisals of others," such roles as have been internalized, and "the residue" of an individual's experiences within his institutional and cultural framework.[10,11]

From the standpoint of a given individual, his culture is experienced by the way in which his interactions are channeled in social relationships, within institutional settings, and by the various pressures, demands, responses, and expectations of others which make themselves felt in countless life situations. Thus each individual, consciously or unconsciously, comes to adopt most of the prevailing ideas, practices, norms, values and beliefs which parents, peers, and nonfamilial adults introduce to him. In this way he has available, for practically every life-situation, a culturally determined solution.

Thus far, then, culture has been shown to be linked to individual behavior [12] by means of a series of intervening concepts: social institutions, positions and statuses, roles, and the self. At this point some general implications of the concept of culture may be suggested.

In the first place, human death is a universal and recurring event. Every culture has its own values, ideas, beliefs, and practices concerning it. An individual learns the orientations of his culture toward death; and thus when he is faced with bereavement, one factor involved is his conception of the meaning of death. In this connection many, if not most, societies throughout the world do not regard the event of death as being an inevitable fact of life; rather, it is often construed as being the result of an accident, of negligence, or of malice on the part of magicians or sorcerers.[13] Similarly, the cultural orientation of many peoples toward death is that it represents a gain for the deceased, an improvement in his prospects and status, and that mourning for his loss of life is inappropriate.[14,15] These are in marked contrast to our own prevailing beliefs, for with us death is inevitable, and the fate of the deceased is by no means as clear and as certain as it may once have been in the Christian tradition.

If, then, we assume that beliefs can influence self-perceptions and self-reactions, the kinds of beliefs that are accepted and internalized will condition bereavement reactions. By the same token, the emotional displays of bereaved persons may also be learned responses and may have nothing to do with necessary and inherent feelings of grief. Conventional bereavement behavior varies widely from culture to culture, and whether it is genuine, "natural" emotional expression or mere ritual performance is in given cases often open to question.[16-18] In some cultures, for example, our conventional sign of grief—

weeping—either is not manifest by the bereaved or is manifest in circumstances that we should regard as strange or is mingled with laughter as we understand it.

All of this raises the question, of course, as to whether the self is entirely social or whether it shares some deep-seated, indestructible fragments of humanity in general. Social scientists tend to hold the former view, whereas some branches of psychiatry tend to hold the latter. The issue cannot now be resolved, but it should be apparent that cross-cultural data can at least provide fresh perspectives on bereavement reactions and present viewpoints concerning them.

Moreover, it may not be amiss to note that cultural considerations may influence any attempt scientifically to analyze bereavement problems. Those who are familiar with, and sensitive to, cultural influences on behavior should first be wary of themselves and their work—i.e., the way in which they perceive, categorize, and explain behavioral events. For various implicit and explicit assumptions, biases, terminology and evaluations, all derived from the culture, can easily intrude upon the task at hand; they cannot all be erased, but they should at least be recognized for what they are: a curious blend of folk knowledge, rationalizations, beliefs, and ignorance. It may even be that some mental health problems we attribute to bereavement, by reason of proximity in time, have other and quite different sources.

The phenomena which we label "bereavement" and "grief" are embedded in a cultural frame of reference. Just as other peoples have their interpretaton of death, and appropriate reactions to it, so, too, do we in Western civilizations; but our own implicit interpretation is not easy for us to recognize and make explicit as a cultural rather than scientific orientation simply because we have absorbed that orientation and perceive events accordingly.

Thus, as a cultural norm and idea we tend to define a given death as a "loss" to someone, especially to close members of the family of the deceased. Almost any behavior that they then manifest is regarded as "grief"; thus the term "grief" functions, culturally, both as a descriptive label and as a satisfying interpretation based on a presumably known "cause." Moreover, we tend to regard such "grief" not only as natural but also as desirable. A bereaved person *ought* to show grief, both as a token of respect to the dead and for the sake of his own mental health—expression of grief gets it "out of the system."

It is simply generally assumed that a bereaved person[19] will be grief-stricken; but whether these displays of grief stem from internal compulsions or external demands is not usually a matter of concern. Indeed, the very source of the behavior and the imputed feelings is assumed to lie in what were satisfactory relationships with the deceased other, even though it is often well known that a given relationship, husband-wife or parent-child, fell far short of being satisfactory to one or both of the partners. At least in our culture there is a tendency to idealize the relationship which has been severed by death— and this, too, is culturally encouraged. "Don't speak ill of the dead."

In short, the behavioral phenomena characterized by the words "bereavement" and "grief" are heavily saturated with cultural assumptions. Moreover, any analyst, be he psychiatrist or social scientist, has absorbed many of these premises long before he has professed to be a scientist; to the extent that he has accepted and internalized them, his perceptions of events have therefore been previously structured, thus preconditioning the analysis through the uncritical use of conventional categories.

The point here, of course, is not the validity of the prevailing cultural interpretation of bereavement and grief, which may be correct in part or in whole, as other folk interpretations of events have been correct in the past. The point is that the cultural orientation is a matter for inquiry and verification rather than a priori, and often unwitting, acceptance.

Caution is therefore indicated. At best, words are slippery instruments of thought and expression, and this is especially true when familiar, and perhaps value-laden, terms are used.

Bereavement can be defined with sufficient precision to be useful. "Grief" on the other hand presents difficulties: the total reaction pattern of a bereaved person may be only partially an expression of grief (in the sense of felt loss), and

199

the amount of grief anyone possesses is always inferential anyway. For these reasons, the phenomena that we usually label as "grief," "sorrow," and "mourning" will here be designated by the more colorless phrases "bereavement behavior" or "bereavement reactions." Such usage will not alter any of the distress of the experience or its poignancy, but it will remind us, perhaps, that more elements than sorrow or grief are involved, and it will also facilitate cross-cultural comparisons. "Behavior" can be observed and recorded, "grief" cannot. And it is essential that as much cross-cultural perspective as possible be gained, else the purported analysis may prove to be nothing more than a technical restatement of prevailing cultural premises.[20,21]

BEREAVEMENT, FAMILY STRUCTURE, AND THE SELF

Of all the social institutions, the family and kinship systems are of the greatest importance insofar as the study of bereavement is concerned. Indeed, their structure and the manner in which they emphasize some relationships rather than others supply initial reference points for the concept of bereavement itself. Always and everywhere some persons rather than others are considered to have a special interest in a given death; but who they are, and in what relationship they stand to the deceased, are matters of cultural variability.

In our society, for example, when a married adult dies, the prevailing definition of bereaved persons includes his parents and siblings, (i.e., members of his family of orientation) and his spouse and their children (i.e., members of his family of procreation). The emphasis is placed on members of the immediate nuclear families as having suffered the main loss;[22-24] and if collateral relatives, such as cousins or aunts or uncles or "in-laws" are included, it is by special relationship rather than as part of the system. They are family members nominally, not functionally.[25]

By way of contrast, the Trobriand Islanders have a quite different scheme of family relationships and a correspondingly different concept of who constitute the bereaved.[26] Their emphasis is placed on persons related to the deceased through his mother—that is, his maternal kin of all kinds are considered to have been "closest" to the deceased and to have more of an interest in the event than any of the paternal relatives or even the spouse. A wife, for example, may "grieve" at the death of her husband, but this is usually ceremonial and obligatory rather than spontaneous, and she is not considered by others to be bereaved in the same sense as are the maternal kin.

These brief, contrasting examples of family systems indicate that, regardless of cultural variability, bereavement is an observable condition; it is not inferential; its definition, in cultural terms, can be determined. Further, bereavement is a formal status in which individuals either have or have not legitimate occupancy. It derives from family and kinship structures which place persons in necessary or preferred positions vis-à-vis each other. Thus, in some places a maternal aunt or a paternal uncle may be more important to the individual, socially and psychologically, than are his own biological or sociological parents. When they die bereavement is thrust upon him by the system.

Such considerations are important not only for purposes of initial orientation toward phenomena but also because they bear upon the development of the self in terms of whom the individual will attach himself and in what manner. That is, although different family systems may have the same positions or statuses in the abstract (i.e., mothers, fathers, aunts, siblings, etc.), the psychological value of such positions in interpersonal relations is by no means always equivalent. Some positions may be singled out according to cultural principles of descent as more important than others; and their interpersonal value will also be influenced by the size of the family unit, together with the degree to which intrafamily relations are based on different ideas of authority, punishment, need-satisfaction, and so on.

Thus, since the development of the self takes place primarily within the family context, that process will be influenced by the range, frequency, intimacy, and quality of the interactions provided by the family system. The number of "targets" for emotional attachment will vary accordingly, as will the particular statuses that will become targets. Such factors, in turn, will affect the number and kinds of identifications the self will make, the degree of dependency on others, and the general mode and strength of affective ties.[27]

If, then, the amount of self-involvement with another is a major variable in bereavement behavior, its sources must lie at least in part in the familial conditions of self-development. And if this is true, we should expect typically different bereavement behaviors in societies with different systems. There is some evidence for this interpretation, as the following examples will illustrate.

In his study of the Ifaluk people, Spiro[28] was puzzled by some features of bereavement there. When a family died, the immediate survivors displayed considerable pain and distress, which behavior was in accordance with local custom. However, as soon as the funeral was over, the bereaved were able to laugh, smile, and behave in general as if they had suffered no loss or injury at all. Their "grief" seemed to disappear as if by magic, and this too was approved by custom.

Several hypotheses might be offered to account for these events which contrast sharply with those we would expect. At one extreme, it might plausibly be argued that the brief, but intense, mourning period was sufficient to discharge all the implicated emotions (such as hostility, loss, guilt, etc.) and thus provided rapid reintegration of the self. This would assume object-relationships of a kind familiar to us but would not particularly account for the efficiency and timing of the observed behavior. At the other extreme,[29] it might be said that the displays were mere conventions, rituals, and, having little to do with emotional experience, could be turned off and on as learned. Or it might be suggested that the grief actually represented intense subjective feelings and that these persisted privately after the funeral but in a manner not easily detected by an observer.

Spiro's analysis, based on his knowledge of the total culture, is along the following lines, which involve the family system and socialization practices that prevail among the Ifaluk. There the developing child forms no exclusive emotional attachments to other family members. Child-rearing is not conducted solely in the home by parents and siblings but involves many other persons who are as important in an individual's life as are family members. The growing child and the mature adult have, therefore, diffused and dispersed their emotional ties among many persons rather than focused them on a few. Accordingly, the psychological significance of any single family member to any other family member is muted rather than intensified.

In terms of the thesis being developed here, the bereavement behavior of the Ifaluk suggests that their family system is such as to develop selves which are initially less vulnerable in bereavement than are the selves we are accustomed to. This can be explained by a consideration of how both social and psychological forces interact.

If we assume that any social relationship, mediated by physical and symbolic interaction, inevitably produces in the partners the feelings and conditions of love, ambivalence, hostility, identification, and dependence, then the Ifaluk develop selves in which these are relatively weak insofar as any given other person is concerned. The family relationships which impinged on self-development are such as to minimize personal dependence on any one person, to make a person's identifications multiple rather than exclusive, and to enable him to distribute his feelings of love and hostility more widely.

Another way of stating this is that in self-other relations among the Ifaluk, the other is not valued by the self as a unique and necessary personality. Functionally speaking, not only are the roles of others dispersed, but the roles themselves are more important psychologically than are the particular persons who play the roles vis-à-vis the self. Multiple and interchangeable personnel performing the same functions for the individual provide the individual with many psychological anchors in his social environment; the death of any one person leaves the others and thus diminishes loss.

In American society, of course, it is not so easy to describe *the* family system, for there are many sub-group variations. Nevertheless, some sociologists have discerned a trend toward the "small family system," particularly among middle-class urban populations.[30-33] To relate this system to the present problem involves considerable overgeneralization, yet for heuristic purposes it may be contrasted with the Ifaluk system.

The American small family system has several dimensions. In contrast to the extended family, it is one in which there are relatively few members and these few live together under one roof and somewhat apart from relatives and neighbors.

In terms of self-development, the small family system means a number of things. During a person's early years the range of his interactions is largely confined to his mother, father, and siblings, if any, and especially to his mother. Frequency and intimacy of contact are thereby channeled among the same few persons who become the only (and repetitive) targets for identification and dependency. Moreover, these same few sources provide the person with his most intense gratifications and frustrations, a condition that tends to maximize ambivalence as well as repressed hostility.[34] Guilt-feelings are easily aroused in connection with authority figures—especially since the person knows that he is supposed to love them, yet cannot do so all the time because they punish and frustrate him.

In these circumstances, it is likely that the self develops strong emotional attachments to the family figures and has considerable affective investment in them. These self-feelings are, however, quite complicated. To the extent that one loves his family members (and this is inculcated as a cultural value), he may feel a corresponding loss when they die—a sentiment which is reinforced by the fact that, as a cultural norm, the death of a family member is socially defined as a loss. But, in addition to the love elements and those of dependency and identification, there are intertwined with them the self-feelings of ambivalence and hostility. In bereavement the self, therefore, faces not only the problem of replacing the loss but also the one of managing these feelings of guilt and hostility.

Moreover, the small family system tends to breed over-identification and overdependence. That is to say, intrafamily experiences are such as to make it difficult for the person to separate the parental activities toward him from the particular individuals who engage in those activities. The maternal role, for example, which aunts, older sisters, or other female adults could occupy and enact, is occupied continuously by the same woman, for in the small family system there are no other persons to act as substitutes and thus disperse the emotional investment. Emotional attachments to particular persons are thereby fostered, and the person becomes dependent on their unique personalities in addition to their roles.

Furthermore, other cultural values operate in the development of the self to influence the process similarly. Not only does the child experience the same persons in the roles of father and mother, but he is taught that he can have only one father and mother—that is, the particular persons who are thus labeled. Cultural training and actual experience thus reinforce each other in such a way that specific persons continually appear to be irreplaceable, and no one is psychologically prepared to accept substitutes.

By way of contrast, it is reported of the Murngin[35] that the death of a father creates few psychological problems for his children. All their lives they have called their paternal uncles "father," and their relationships with these uncles have not differed very much from their relationships with their father. When the self develops in such a system, there is less likelihood that it will become closely attached to a particular figure; thus the sense of loss is lessened and the relationship with that figure can be more readily transferred to substitute figures.

The inference to be drawn from all this is that familial systems, by their influence on the development of the self, can enhance or reduce the initial vulnerability of persons in bereavement. This vulnerability is increased to the extent that self-involvements with others are diffuse, thus minimizing the psychological significance of any one other.

In this connection, one further feature of the small family system should be noted. Typically, a married adult belongs to two families, the one of orientation and the one of procreation. In a sense this dual membership involves a dispersion of affect and self-involvement, for the person simply has more relationships: in addition to being son or daughter, brother or sister, he is now also husband and parent. His roles have multiplied.

But, although membership in the family of orientation is officially retained, residence in a separate household usually diminishes his opportunities for interaction and continued emotional investment in parents and siblings. There simply is not so much intimate association with them as there was when he lived under the same roof. He tends, therefore, to gain some release from whatever self-feelings he had toward them by increasing his physical, social, and psychological distance from them. Thus his vulnerability vis-à-vis these family members tends to be reduced.

At the same time, through marriage, children, and a separate residence, he is again enmeshed in a small family system, but with new personnel. Now his self-involvements tend to be directed toward spouse and children, and, because of the way his self developed in the small family of orientation, his relationships with these "new" persons tend to be of the same order as were the old—i.e., exclusive attachments.

In brief, membership in the two small families does not necessarily have the same psychological effect as continued residence in an extended family may have. Dispersion of affect need not occur. Rather, it is much more likely that one's emotional investments are merely redirected from one set of figures to another; and as vulnerability to bereavement in the family of orientation diminishes, vulnerability to deaths in the family of procreation may increase.

The preceding pages have attempted to sketch some of the ideal-typical relationships between family structure, self-development, and vulnerability in bereavement. From the two polar-type family systems that were used for illustrative purposes it is suggested that the meaning of bereavement to the persons involved can be modified. In one case the degree of self-involvement with others, and therefore vulnerability in bereavement, was minimal; in the other the degree of self-involvement with others, and therefore vulnerability in bereavement, was maximal.

High vulnerability in interpersonal relationships does not, however, mean the inevitable presence of mental health problems in bereavement. Psychic stresses and strains may be multiplied, to be sure, but if these have been fostered by some social and cultural conditions, there may be other social and cultural conditions which can help to ease them.[36,37] In brief, the course and outcome of high vulnerability in bereavement may be a function not only of itself but also of the requirements and taboos that exist within the bereavement situation. This can best be indicated by considering the importance and utility of the concept of "social role" as this is applicable to bereavement reactions.

BEREAVEMENT AND SOCIAL ROLES

It has previously been indicated that the category of bereaved persons, at a given death, is culturally defined. Some relationships in the family and kinship system are included and some are not, and the inclusions and exclusions vary from culture to culture; but whenever a death evokes that category, the persons in it come to occupy a formal, legitimate status in the eyes of others as well as in their own eyes. And as is the case with other statuses, the persons in it have a new social role to play—the social role of the bereaved person.

In cross-cultural terms, the specific content of the role varies widely: weeping; personal preparation of the corpse for burial, gashing one's own body with knives or sharp sticks, protracted seclusion; fasting, wreaking vengeance on those responsible for the death, special religious obligations of prayer or sacrifice, sharp and humiliating alterations in dress and appearance, and so on.

In a given culture, some of these role behaviors may apply to all persons in the bereavement status, whereas others apply only to persons in specified relation to the deceased. For example, the widow may have some obligations which apply only to her, such as not to remarry or not to remarry within certain periods of time; or it may be that she is obliged to remarry with her next partner being culturally prescribed— e.g., a brother or cousin of the deceased husband.

Although there are great variations in the specific content of the social role of the bereaved person, one point is clear: whatever the obligations, proscriptions, or injunctions may be, they exist from his standpoint in the form of expectations, demands, and pressures from others. They are *social* obligations, immediate and potent, yet to fulfill them in a way that is both psychologically and socially satisfactory is by no means as obvious or as easy as is frequently assumed. Often the role requirements are painful in themselves, and it is also a difficult role to learn because it is not encountered frequently in the course of life and opportunities for rehearsal are scarce.

The import of this is to suggest that the conception of the bereaved person as having a social role to perform provides another perspective from which to examine mental health problems in bereavement. Such problems may be socially induced as well as psychologically induced—i.e., they may have their source in role deficiencies and difficulties as well as in the self-other relationship itself. Such a formulation suggests a number of possibilities that psychiatrists and social scientists might further explore.

The formulation, for example, opens up the possibility that some bereavement problems may be occasioned not by severe loss but by an awareness of one's inability to play the bereaved role properly[38]. If we assume that one of the role obligations is to express grief and loss and that these sentiments are imputed to the bereaved by others, the bereaved person who lacks these sentiments may be in a painfully dangerous situation as the result of guilty fear.

A hypothetical reconstruction, in terms of the present analysis, may illustrate the problem. A given role (husband, wife, mother, etc.) is culturally defined as involving considerable emotional investment in the partner who occupies the complementary role in the relationship. The role, in its ideal sense, is internalized by an individual, but his experience in the relationship contradicts the role. Inappropriate sentiments are developed—e.g., more hostility than love. Fearing the reactions of others, he remains in the relationship which, on the surface, does not deviate too far from the typical; but the hostility must be repressed and guilt over failure to meet the ideal is increased. Then, in bereavement, this individual is supposed to feel loss, and the social role he is expected to enact deals almost entirely with this imputed sentiment. He is expected to express grief. Such expectations and imputations are not congruent with his own-self-feelings, and awareness of the discrepancy between self and role[39] increases guilt. There are also no socially sanctioned avenues for the release or displacement of the hostility. There is, in short, an accumulation of pressures which come to a climax in bereavement. In such a case, which is probably quite atypical, the bereavement experience, including the incompatible role that is imposed, precipitates and crystallizes mental health problems that were already incipient. Such a case can indicate the significance of situational pressures to adopt the proper role.

In American culture, it is difficult to consider the social role of the bereaved person in other than very general terms, but it appears to center around ideas of loss and the desirability of expressing that loss and grief. The language makes "bereavement" and "loss" interchangeable terms. Individuals learn to regard bereavement as meaning loss, and this sentiment is attributed to them by others when the bereavement situation actually occurs. Thus, to the extent that this evaluation of the event has been internalized, and to the extent that the self-other relationship as personally experienced makes it possible, the psychological sense of loss will be enhanced. When this happens, the bereaved person can more or less adequately play his required role—i.e., to have some sort of episodic breakdown, express his grief conventionally, and thus behave "normally."

However, this type of role, with its emphasis on loss, grief, and expression of them, may not always be psychologically functional. And here several possibilities appear.

For example, this particular type of role of the bereaved person may conflict with other roles he has—e.g., sex roles. In our society, females are generally permitted and encouraged to be more "emotional" than males in various life situations. To the extent that women internalize this segment of their sex role, it should be easier for them to meet the requirements of "expressing grief" in their social role of the bereaved person; it simply requires a reapplication of a lifelong pattern.

Men, on the other hand, are expected and encouraged to be more stoical and restrained than women in any life emergency.[40] The role of male in our culture does not encourage emotional displays. Thus, in bereavement males may experience a conflict between their life-long training in their sex role and the immediate situational demand for emotional expression as a bereaved person.[41] It may be, therefore, that when bereaved males exhibit signs of psychic stress, in the form of intensities and distortions beyond expected levels, they are reflecting this conflict in addition to, or even instead of, the sense of loss and grief.

Our cultural emphasis on loss in bereavement, with its social role preoccupied with grief expression, provides still other problems. The social role, by concentrating on the feeling and expression of loss, thereby neglects to provide for other emotions and the needs they create. This can be formulated as follows: The emotions of a bereaved person, vis-à-vis the deceased other, consist of various degrees and intensities of the sense of loss, hostility, guilt, and the like. When these are minimal in strength, the bereaved person has a very low initial vulnerability to any mental health problems. When these are maximal and complicated, the person (unless he has a correspondingly high ego strength) has a high initial vulnerability to mental health problems in bereavement, for the stronger and more complex these self-feelings are, the greater is their tendency to create new personality needs. If a strong sense of loss is involved, there is a need for replacement; if there is much latent hostility, there is need for discharge; if guilt is strong, there is need for release or displacement. If all are present, as our family and cultural system tends to make probable, then the bereaved person is vulnerable unless his social role as a bereaved person adequately meets these needs.

In other words, the character of the self-other relationship conditions the level of initial vulnerability in bereavement. When this level is high, and new personality needs are therewith generated, the social role of the bereaved person may either lessen that vulnerability by meeting the needs or exacerbate it by failing to meet them.

From this standpoint, our preoccupation with loss and grief in bereavement may create special kinds of mental health problems of which we are only dimly aware. For example, as has been previously suggested, the significant other in our culture is significant in terms of his unique personality in addition to, or instead of, the functions he performs vis-à-vis the self. Thus, in bereavement, one loses not merely a role in his whole system of interaction but a particular person in the role. Thus, whereas we stress the sense of loss and recognize the need for replacement,[42] basically the culture creates conditions in which the deceased is irreplaceable because he cannot ever really be duplicated. The social role cannot contain a provision for "automatic replacement" because all our patterns of inter-personal relationships militate against such replacement.

In order for replacements to be accepted and acceptable, the role of the deceased must be regarded, culturally and per-sonally, as at least equal in importance to the person who plays it. Other societies have handled this problem of replacement by the devices of obligatory remarriage[43,44] or adoption. Such arrangements, though, are not merely *ad hoc*, set up to take care of bereavement problems alone. Rather, they are basic ingredients of the way in which the sociocultural system oper-ates, of the way in which interpersonal relations are perceived, valued, and practiced. Since the expectations of the partners in the social relationship do not come to include the absorption of the self in the other, it is possible for the social role of the bereaved person (i.e., as widow, widower, orphan, etc.) to include replacement of the other without particular psychic stress.

The fact that the social role of the bereaved person in our culture may not easily cope with the problem of replacement is, therefore, a local one. It is bound up in our system of inter-personal relations, the kind of selves we tend to develop, and is exaggerated by our cultural emphasis on loss. In this way the bereaved person has no automatic cultural solution to the problem of replacement.

In the same manner, the social role of the bereaved person in our culture makes no real provision for the other emotions and the personality needs they create—i.e., hostility and guilt and their release, discharge, or displacement. At least, there are no obvious segments of the role which include socially approved devices for handling those residues of guilt, hostility, and ambiv-alence. With the person left on his own, so to speak, to handle them as best he can, it is not surprising that these feelings and the unmet needs they create appear in cases of "acute" or "distorted" grief in our society.

In many cultures prevailing mourning customs may be interpreted as providing role requirements which do meet some of these emotional needs. Opler,[45] for example, has shown how the ambivalence toward relatives, which is induced by the social structure of the Apache, finds socially sanctioned displacement in mourning rites and customs. Warner[46] indicates how the obligation of the bereaved to avenge the death of the deceased provides sanctioned means of ridding guilt-feelings and hostility among the Murngin. And in anthropological literature there are many examples of the bereaved being required to inflict pain and disfigurement on their bodies—obligations which may be regarded as attempts to fasten the attention of the bereaved upon himself and therefore to hasten his emancipation from the deceased.

Such considerations lend some weight to the hypothesis that different cultures will select, from among all the possible involvements the self may have with the other, one or a few which will be dealt with in the social role of the bereaved person. Thus, if the bereavement problems of a given culture are adequately perceived, functionally adequate social roles for the bereaved may be devised which can blunt such vulnerability to breakdown as may appear. But to the extent that social and cultural conditions encourage interpersonal relationships in which overidentification, overdependence, sense of loss, hostility, guilt, and ambivalence are bred in profusion, and to the extent that the social role of the bereaved person does not take account of these feelings and the needs they inspire—to that extent bereaved persons may often be unintended victims of their sociocultural system. In our case, the sense of loss may be handled satisfactorily by the role which encourages expression of loss and grief; but the role does not, and cannot, adequately provide for replacement when this need is strong, and the added burdens of accumulated and unrelieved guilt, hostility, and ambivalence, when they are strong, can only increase vulnerability to psychic breakdown.

NOTES

1. Kluckhohn, C.: "Culture and Behavior," in G. Lindsey, ed., *Handbook of Social Psychology*. Addison-Wesley, 1954, p. 922.
2. ————————: "Universal Categories of Culture," in A. L. Kroeber, ed., *Anthropology Today*. Univ. of Chicago Press, 1953.
3. Strictly speaking, "learning" and "internalizing" should not be used as equivalents. One may "learn" a given idea or act, or how to act, without being impelled to so behave; he may simply learn that such is proper under certain circumstances. When something is "internalized," on the other hand, the implication is that the range of alternatives has been at least drastically restricted, if not eliminated. In other words, learning can be more superficial than internalization.
4. Mitra, D. N.: "Mourning customs and modern life in Bengal." *Am. J. Sociol.*, 52: 309-311, 1947.
5. Cottrell, L. S., Jr.: "The adjustment of the individual to his age and sex roles." *Am Sociol. Rev.*, 7: 618-625, 1942.
6. Parsons, T.: *The Social System*. Free Press, 1951.
7. Sarbin, T. R.: "Role Theory," in G. Lindzey, ed., *Handbook of Social Psychology*. Addison-Wesley, 1952, Chap. 6.
8. Mead, G. H.: *Mind, Self and Society*. C. W. Morris, ed. Univ. of Chicago Press, 1934.
9. Sullivan, H. S.: *The Interpersonal Theory of Psychiatry*. Norton, 1953.
10. Kluckhohn, C.: "Culture and Behavior," in G. Lindsey, ed., *Handbook of Social Psychology*. Addison-Wesley, 1954, p. 922.
11. Sarbin, T. R.: "Role Theory," in *Handbook of Social Psychology*, p. 224.
12. In a sense this can never be completely achieved to the satisfaction of psychology or psychiatry. Sapir's observations on this point are relevant: "problems of social science differ from problems of individual behavior in degree of specificity, not in kind. Every statement about behavior which throws the emphasis . . . on the actual integral experiences of defined personalities or types of personalities is a datum of psychology or psychiatry rather than of social science. Every statement about behavior which aims, not to be accurate about the behavior of an actual individual or individuals or about the expected behavior of a physically and psychologically defined type of individual, but which abstracts from such behavior in order to bring out in clear relief certain expectancies with regard to those aspects of individual behavior which various people share, as an interpersonal or 'social' pattern, is a datum . . . of social science." E. Sapir, "Why Cultural Anthropology Needs the Psychiatrist," *Psychiatry*, 1: 12, 1938.

13. Simmons, L. W.: *The Role of the Aged in Primitive Society*. Yale Univ. Press, 1945. pp. 217-220.

14. *Ibid*. pp. 223-224.

15. Sumner, W. G., and Keller, A. C.: *The Science of Society*. 3 Vols. Yale Univ. Press, 1927. Vol. 2, pg. 943 ff.

16. Durkheim went so far as to write: "Mourning is not a natural movement of private feelings wounded by cruel loss; it is a duty imposed by the group. One weeps, not simply because he is sad, but because he is forced to weep. It is a ritual attitude which he is forced to adopt . . . but which is, in a large measure, independent of his affective state."

17. Gerth, H., and Mills, C. W.: *Character and Social Structure*. Harcourt Brace, 1953. p. 20 and p. 48 ff.

18. Hartley, E. L., and Hartley, R. E.: *Fundamentals of Social Psychology*. Knopf, 1952, p. 210.

19. In one sense "bereavement" and "grief" can be defined in terms of each other, i.e., not one without the other. As will be indicated, however, clarity is gained if they are viewed independently.

20. Kluckhohn, C.: "Culture and Behavior," in G. Lindsey, ed., *Handbook of Social Psychology*. Addison-Wesley, 1954. p. 922.

21. Stainbrook, E.: "A Cross-cultural Evaluation of Depressive Reactions," in Hoch and Zubin, eds., *Depression*. Grune & Stratton, 1954.

22. Eliot, T. D.: "The adjustive behavior of bereaved families: a new field for research." *Social Forces,* 8: 543-549, 1930.

23. ————: "The bereaved family." *Ann. Am. Acad. Pol. and Soc. Sci.,* March 1932, 1-7.

24. Waller, W., and Hill, R.: *The Family*. Dryden, 1951, Chap. 22.

25. Parsons, T.: "The kinship system of the contemporary United States." *Am. Anthropologist.*

26. Malinowski, B.: *Crime and Custom in Savage Society*. Humanities Press, 1926. p. 26.

27. In a similar vein, Sarbin writes that "we would expect different kinds of self-concepts in persons whose early socializing interactions were limited to one or two parent figures from those whose early socializing interactions were more extensive."

28. Spiro, M. E.: Ifaluk: a South Sea Culture. Unpublished Ms., submitted as a final report, Coordinated Investigation of Micronesian Anthropology, Pacific Science Board, National Research Council. Human Relations Area Files, Yale University, 1949.

29. Durkheim, E.: *The Elementary Forms of Religious Life*. Free Press, 1947. p. 397.

30. Bossard, J. H. S.: *Parent and Child*. Univ. of Penn. Press, 1953.

31. Green, A. W.: "The middle class male child and neurosis." *Am. Sociol. Rev.,* 11: 31-41, 1946.

32. Parsons, T.: "Certain Primary Sources and Patterns of Aggression in the Social Structure of the Western World," in P. Mullahy, ed., *A Study of Interpersonal Relations.* Nelson, 1949, pp. 269-296.

33. ————————: "The kinship system of the contemporary United States." *Am. Anthropologist.*

34. ————————: "Certain Primary Sources and Patterns of Aggression in the Social Structure of the Western World,"in P. Mullahy, ed., *A Study of Interpersonal Relations.* Nelson, 1949, pp. 269-296.

35. Warner, W. L.: *A Black Civilization.* Harper, 1937.

36. Simmons, L. W.: *The Role of the Aged in Primitive Society.* Yale Univ. Press, 1945. pp. 217-220.

37. Spiro, M. E.: "A psychotic personality in the South Seas." *Psychiat.,* 13: 189-204, 1950. pp. 202-203.

38. This touches upon a problem raised by Rado.

39. This is in line with Sarbin's comment that "the self is what the person 'is,' the role is what the person 'does.'"

40. Anderson, J. E.: "Changes in Emotional Responses with Age," in Martin L. Reymert, ed., *Feelings and Emotions.* McGraw-Hill, 1952. pp. 424-425.

41. Thus Lindemann observed men patients who, in bereavement, appeared unable to express their grief for fear they might "break down."

42. Lindemann, E.: "Modifications in the course of ulcerative colitis in relationship to changes in life situations and reaction patterns." In *Life Stress and Bodily Disease.* Williams and Wilkins. pp. 708-710.

43. As an illustration: "The heartbroken widow would be an object of curiosity; the widow mourns her husband in the prescribed manner with, it may be, genuine but very transient grief, and takes up life against just where she left it, but in the home of her next husband." A. T. and G. M. Culwick, *Ubena of the Rivers* (London: Allen & Unwin, 1936), p. 366.

    Also: "In three deaths which I observed, the widows were married by levirate husbands on the third day after mortuary rites. In two of these the widows passed to the deceased's oldest brother; in the third, to his parallel cousin." A. R. Holmberg, *Nomads of the Long Bow.* Publications of the Institute of Social Anthropology, No. 10, Smithsonian Institute (Washington: Government Printing Office, 1950), p. 88.

44. Sumner, W. G. and Keller, A. C.: *The Science of Society.* 3 Vols. Yale Univ. Press, 1927. Vol. 3, pp. 1841-1884.

45. Opler, M. E.: "An interpretation of ambivalence in two American Indian tribes." *J. Soc. Psychol.,* 7: 82-116, 1936.

46. Warner, W. L.: *A Black Civilization.* Harper, 1937. pp. 414-415.

Extraordinary death by war, suicide, or holocaust defies reason and challenges feelings of personal immortality. Writing shortly after the destruction of World War I, in "Thoughts for the Times on War and Death," Sigmund Freud explores two factors responsible for mental distress among non-combatants during World War I. The first part of his discussion centers on the disillusionment of the war: the following selection on the altered attitude towards death. Freud likens the unconscious mind of modern man to primeval man who does not believe in his own death. While both primeval and modern man might desire the death of enemies, it is the dilemma of man that he experiences ambivalent feelings when contemplating the death of another person, especially a "loved" one.

In time of war, when the sanctions ("Thou shalt not kill") against killing are removed, the balance among unconscious tensions is upset. With the absence of war an impossibility, Freud argues for an acknowledgment of unsanctioned instincts.

THOUGHTS FOR THE TIMES ON WAR AND DEATH: OUR ATTITUDE TOWARD DEATH

Sigmund Freud

A factor to which I attribute our present sense of estrangement in this once lovely and congenial world is the disturbance that has taken place in the attitude which we have hitherto adopted toward death.

That attitude was far from straightforward. To anyone who listened to us we were of course prepared to maintain that death was the necessary outcome of life, that everyone owes nature a death [1] and must expect to pay the debt—in short, that death was natural, undeniable and unavoidable. In reality, however, we were accustomed to behave as if it were

---

Chapter II, "Our Attitudes Towards Death," from Paper XVII, "Thoughts for the Times On War And Death," in Volume 4, COLLECTED PAPERS, by Sigmund Freud, edited by Ernest Jones, M.D., authorized translation under the supervision of Joan Riviere, published by Basic Books, Inc. by arrangement with The Hogarth Press Ltd. and the Institute of Psycho-Analysis, London. For permission to reprint for the United States. For Great Britain and Canada, permission to reprint from "Thoughts for the Times on War and Death" in Volume XIV of *The Standard Edition of the Complete Psychological Works of Sigmund Freud*, revised and edited by James Strachey, with permission from Sigmund Freud Copyrights Ltd., The Institute of Psychoanalysis and The Hogarth Press Ltd.

otherwise. We showed an unmistakable tendency to put death on one side, to eliminate it from life. We tried to hush it up; indeed we even have a saying (in German): to think of something as though it were death.[2] That is, as though it were our own death, of course. It is indeed impossible to imagine our own death; and whenever we attempt to do so we can perceive that we are in fact still present as spectators. Hence the psychoanalytic school could venture on the assertion that at bottom no one believes in his own death, or, to put the same thing in another way, that in the unconscious every one of us is convinced of his own immortality.

When it comes to someone else's death, the civilized man will carefully avoid speaking of such a possibility in the hearing of the person under sentence. Children alone disregard this restriction; they unashamedly threaten one another with the possibility of dying, and even go so far as to do the same thing to someone whom they love, as, for instance: "Dear Mummy, when you're dead I'll do this or that." The civilized adult can hardly even entertain the thought of another person's death without seeming to himself hard-hearted or wicked; unless, of course, as a doctor or lawyer or something of the kind, he has to deal with death professionally. Least of all will he allow himself to think of the other person's death if some gain to himself in freedom, property or position is bound up with it. This sensitiveness of ours does not, of course, prevent the occurrence of deaths; when one does happen, we are always deeply affected, and it is as though we were badly shaken in our expectations. Our habit is to lay stress on the fortuitous causation of the death—accident, disease, infection, advanced age; in this way we betray an effort to reduce death from a necessity to a chance event. A number of simultaneous deaths strikes us as something extremely terrible. Toward the actual person who has died we adopt a special attitude—something almost like admiration for someone who has accomplished a very difficult task. We suspend criticism of him, overlook his possible misdeeds, declare that *de mortuis nil nisi bonum*, and think it justifiable to set out all that is most favorable to his memory in the funeral oration and upon the tombstone. Consideration for the dead, who, after all, no longer need it, is more important to us than the truth, and certainly, for most of us, than consideration for the living.

The complement to this cultural and conventional attitude toward death is provided by our complete collapse when death has struck down someone whom we love—a parent or a partner in marriage, a brother or sister, a child or a close friend. Our hopes, our desires and our pleasures lie in the grave with him, we will not be consoled, we will not fill the lost one's place. We behave as if we were a kind of Asra, who die when those they love die.[3]

But this attitude of ours toward death has a powerful effect on our lives. Life is impoverished, it loses in interest, when the highest stake in the game of living, life itself, may not be risked. It becomes as shallow and empty as, let us say, an American flirtation, in which it is understood from the first that nothing is to happen, as contrasted with a Continental love-affair in which both partners must constantly bear its serious consequences in mind. Our emotional ties, the unbearable intensity of our grief, make us disinclined to court danger for ourselves and for those who belong to us. We dare not contemplate a great many undertakings which are dangerous but in fact indispensable, such as attempts at artificial flight, expeditions to distant countries or experiments with explosive substances. We are paralysed by the thought of who is to take the son's place with his mother, the husband's with his wife, the father's with his children, if a disaster should occur. Thus the tendency to exclude death from our calculations in life brings in its train many other renunciations and exclusions. Yet the motto of the Hanseatic League ran: *Navigare necesse est, vivere non necesse* (It is necessary to sail the seas, it is not necessary to live.)

It is an inevitable result of all this that we should seek in the world of fiction, in literature and in the theatre compensation for what has been lost in life. There we still find people who know how to die—who, indeed, even manage to kill someone else. There alone too the condition can be fulfilled which makes it possible for us to reconcile ourselves with death: namely, that behind all the vicissitudes of life we should still be able to preserve a life intact. For it is really too sad that in life it should be as it is in chess, where one false move may force us to resign the game, but with the difference that we can start no second game, no return-match. In the realm of fiction we find the plurality of lives which we need. We die with the hero with whom we have identified ourselves; yet we survive him, and are ready to die again just as safely with another hero.

It is evident that war is bound to sweep away this conventional treatment of death. Death will no longer be denied; we are forced to believe in it. People really die; and no longer one by one, but many, often tens of thousands, in a single day. And death is no longer a chance event. To be sure, it still seems a matter of chance whether a bullet hits this man or that; but a second bullet may well hit the survivor; and the accumulation of deaths puts an end to the impression of chance. Life has, indeed, become interesting again; it has recovered its full content.

Here a distinction should be made between two groups—those who themselves risk their lives in battle, and those who have stayed at home and have only to wait for the loss of one of their dear ones by wounds, disease or infection. It would be most interesting, no doubt, to study the changes in the psychology of the combatants, but I know too little about it. We must restrict ourselves to the second group, to which we ourselves belong. I have said already that in my opinion the bewilderment and the paralysis of capacity, from which we suffer, are essentially determined among other things by the circumstance that we are unable to maintain our former attitude toward death, and have not yet found a new one. It may assist us to do this if we direct our psychological enquiry toward two other relations to death—the one which we may ascribe to primeval, prehistoric men, and the one which still exists in every one of us, but which conceals itself, invisible to consciousness, in the deeper strata of our mental life.

What the attitude of prehistoric man was toward death is, of course, only known to us by inferences and constructions, but I believe that these methods have furnished us with fairly trustworthy conclusions.

Primeval man took up a very remarkable attitude toward death. It was far from consistent; it was indeed most contradictory. On the one hand, he took death seriously, recognized it as the termination of life and made use of it in that sense; on the other hand, he also denied death and reduced it to nothing. This contradiction arose from the fact that he took up radically different attitudes toward the death of other people, of strangers, of enemies, and towards his own. He had no objection to someone else's death; it meant the annihilation of someone he hated, and primitive man had no scruples against bringing it about. He was no doubt a very passionate creature and more cruel and more malignant than other animals. He liked to kill, and killed as a matter of course. The instinct which is said to restrain other animals from killing and devouring their own species need not be attributed to him.

Hence the primeval history of mankind is filled with murder. Even today, the history of the world which our children learn at school is essentially a series of murders of peoples. The obscure sense of guilt to which mankind has been subject since prehistoric times, and which in some religions has been condensed into the doctrine of primal guilt, of original sin, is probably the outcome of a blood-guilt incurred by prehistoric man. In my book *Totem and Taboo* (1912-13) I have, following clues given by Robertson Smith, Atkinson and Charles Darwin, tried to guess the nature of this primal guilt, and I believe, too, that the Christian doctrine of today enables us to deduce it. If the Son of God was obliged to sacrifice his life to redeem mankind from original sin, then by the law of talion, the requital of like by like, that sin must have been a killing, a murder. Nothing else could call for the sacrifice of a life for its expiation. And the original sin was an offence against God the Father, the primal crime of mankind must have been a parricide, the killing of the primal father of the primitive human horde, whose mnemic image was later transfigured into a deity. [4]

His own death was certainly just as unimaginable and unreal for primeval man as it is for any one of us today. But there was for him one case in which the two opposite attitudes toward death collided and came into conflict with each other; and this case became highly important and productive of far-reaching consequences. It occurred when primeval man saw someone who belonged to him die—his wife, his child, his friend—whom he undoubtedly loved as we love ours, for love cannot be much younger than the lust to kill. Then, in his pain, he was forced to learn that one can die, too, oneself, and his whole being revolted against the admission; for each of these loved ones was, after all, a part of his own beloved self. But, on the other hand, deaths such as these pleased him as well, since in each of the loved persons there was also something of the stranger. The law of ambivalence of feeling, which to this day governs our emotional relations with those whom we love most, certainly had a very much wider validity in primaeval times. Thus these beloved dead had also been enemies and strangers who had aroused in him some degree of hostile feeling. [5]

Philosophers have declared that the intellectual enigma presented to primeval man by the picture of death forced him to reflection, and thus became the starting-point of all speculation. I believe that here the philosophers are thinking too philosophically, and giving too little consideration to the motives that were primarily operative. I should like therefore to limit and correct their assertion. In my view, primeval man must have triumphed beside the body of his slain enemy, without being led to rack his brains about the enigma of life and death. What released the spirit of enquiry in man was not the intellectual enigma, and not every death, but the conflict of feeling at the death of loved yet alien and hated persons. Of this conflict of feeling psychology was the first offspring. Man could no longer keep death at a distance, for he had tasted it in his pain about the dead; but he was nevertheless unwilling to acknowledge it, for he could not conceive of himself as dead. So he devised a compromise: he conceded the fact of his own death as well, but denied it the significance of annihilation—a significance which he had had no motive for denying where the death of his enemy was concerned. It was beside the dead body of someone he loved that he invented spirits, and his sense of guilt at the satisfaction mingled with his sorrow turned these new-born spirits into evil demons that had to be dreaded. The (physical) changes brought about by death suggested to him the division of the individual into a body and a soul—originally several souls. In this way his train of thought ran parallel with

the process of disintegration which sets in with death. His persisting memory of the dead became the basis for assuming other
forms of existence and gave him the conception of a life continuing after apparent death.

These subsequent existences were at first no more than
appendages to the existence which death had brought to a close
—shadowy, empty of content, and valued at little until later
times; they still bore the character of wretched makeshifts.
We may recall the answer made to Odysseus by the soul of
Achilles:

> For of old, when thou wast alive, we Argives honoured thee even as
> the gods, and now that thou art here, thou rulest mightily over the dead.
> Wherefore grieve not at all that thou art dead, Achilles.
> So I spoke, and he straightway made answer and said: 'Nay, seek
> not to speak soothingly to me of death, glorious Odysseus. I should choose,
> so I might live on earth, to serve as the hireling of another, of some por-
> tionless man whose livelihood was but small, rather than to be lord over
> all the dead that have perished. [6]

Or in Heine's powerful and bitter parody:

> Der kleinste lebendige Philister
> Zu Stuckert am Neckar
> Viel glucklicher ist er
> Als ich, der Pelide, der tote Held,
> Der Schattenfurst in der Unterwelt.[7]

It was only later that religions succeeded in representing
this after-life as the more desirable, the truly valid one, and in
reducing the life which is ended by death to a mere preparation.
After this, it was no more than consistent to extend life back-
wards into the past, to form the notion of earlier existences,
of the transmigration of souls and of reincarnation, all with the
purpose of depriving death of its meaning as the termination of
life. So early did the denial of death, which we have described
as a "conventional and cultural attitude," have its origin.

What came into existence beside the dead body of the
loved one was not only the doctrine of the soul, the belief in
immortality and a powerful source of man's sense of guilt, but
also the earliest ethical commandments. The first and most
important prohibition made by the awakening conscience was

"Thou shalt not kill." It was acquired in relation to dead people who were loved, as a reaction against the satisfaction of the hatred hidden behind the grief for them; and it was gradually extended to strangers who were not loved, and finally even to enemies.

This final extension of the commandment is no longer experienced by civilized man. When the furious struggle of the present war has been decided, each one of the victorious fighters will return home joyfully to his wife and children, unchecked and undisturbed by thoughts of the enemies he has killed whether at close quarters or at long range. It is worthy of note that the primitive races which still survive in the world, and are undoubtedly closer than we are to primeval man, act differently in this respect, or did until they came under the influence of our civilization. Savages—Australians, Bushmen, Tierra del Fuegans—are far from being remorseless murderers; when they return victorious from the war-path they may not set foot in their villages or touch their wives till they have atoned for the murders they committed in war by penances which are often long and tedious. It is easy, of course, to attribute this to their superstition: the savage still goes in fear of the avenging spirits of the slain. But the spirits of his slain enemy are nothing but the expression of his bad conscience about his blood-guilt; behind this superstition there lies concealed a vein of ethical sensitiveness which has been lost by us civilized men.[8]

Pious souls, no doubt, who would like to believe that our nature is remote from any contact with what is evil and base, will not fail to use the early appearance and the urgency of the prohibition against murder as the basis for gratifying conclusions as to the strength of the ethical impulses which must have been implanted in us. Unfortunately this argument proves even more for the opposite view. So powerful a prohibition can only be directed against an equally powerful impulse. What no human soul desires stands in no need of prohibition;[9] it is excluded automatically. The very emphasis laid on the commandment "Thou shalt not kill" makes it certain that we spring from an endless series of generations of murderers, who had the lust for killing in their blood, as, perhaps, we ourselves have today.

Mankind's ethical strivings, whose strength and significance we need not in the least depreciate, were acquired in the course of man's history; since then they have become, though unfortunately only in a very variable amount, the inherited property of contemporary men.

Let us now leave primeval man, and turn to the uncon-scious in our own mental life. Here we depend entirely upon the psychoanalytic method of investigation, the only one which reaches to such depths. What, we ask, is the attitude of our unconscious toward the problem of death; The answer must be: almost exactly the same as that of primeval man. In this respect, as in many others, the man of prehistoric times survives unchanged in our unconscious. Our unconscious, then, does not believe in its own death; it behaves as if it were immortal. What we call our "unconscious"—the deepest strata of our minds, made up of instinctual impulses—knows nothing that is negative, and no negation; in it contradictories coincide. For that reason it does not know its own death, for to that we can give only a negative content. Thus there is nothing instinctual in us which responds to a belief in death. This may even be the secret of heroism. The rational grounds for heroism rest on a judgment that the subject's own life cannot be so precious as certain abstract and general goods. But more frequent, in my view, is the instinctive and impulsive heroism which knows no such reasons, and flouts danger in the spirit of Anzengruber's *Steinklopferhans:* "Nothing can happen to *me!*"[10] Or else those reasons only serve to clear away the hesitations which might hold back the heroic reaction that corresponds to the unconscious. The fear of death, which dominates us oftener than we know, is on the other hand something secondary, and is usually the outcome of a sense of guilt.[11]

On the other hand, for strangers and for enemies we do acknowledge death, and consign them to it quite as readily and unhesitatingly as did primeval man. There is, it is true, a distinction here which will be pronounced decisive so far as real life is concerned. Our unconscious does not carry out the killing; it merely thinks it and wishes it. But it would be wrong so completely to undervalue this psychical reality as compared with factual reality. It is significant and momentous enough. In our unconscious impulses we daily and hourly get rid of anyone who stands in our way, of anyone who has offended or injured us. The expression "Devil take him!," which so often comes to people's lips in joking anger and which really means "Death take him!," is in our unconscious a serious and powerful death-wish. Indeed, our unconscious will murder even for trifles; like the ancient Athenian code of Draco, it knows no other punishment for crime than death. And this has a certain consistency, for every injury to our almighty and autocratic ego is at bottom a crime of *lèse-majesté*.

And so, if we are to be judged by our unconscious wishful impulses, we ourselves are, like primeval man, a gang of murderers. It is fortunate that all these wishes do not possess the potency that was attributed to them in primeval times;[1][2] in the cross-fire of mutual curses mankind would long since have perished, the best and wisest of men and the loveliest and fairest of women with the rest.

Psychoanalysis finds as a rule no credence among laymen for assertions such as these. They reject them as calumnies which are confuted by conscious experience, and they adroitly overlook the faint indications by which even the unconscious is apt to betray itself to consciousness. It is therefore relevant to point out that many thinkers who could not have been influenced by psychoanalysis have quite definitely accused our unspoken thoughts of being ready, heedless of the prohibition against murder, to get rid of anything which stands in our way. From many examples of this I will choose one that has become famous:

In *Le Père Goriot*, Balzac alludes to a passage in the works of J. J. Rousseau where that author asks the reader what he would do if—without leaving Paris and of course without being discovered—he could kill, with great profit to himself, an old mandarin in Peking by a mere act of will. Rousseau implies that he would not give much for the life of that dignitary. *"Tuer son mandarin"* has become a proverbial phrase for this secret readiness, present even in modern man.

There are also a whole number of cynical jokes and anecdotes which reveal the same tendency—such, for instance, as the words attributed to a husband: "If one of us two dies, I shall move to Paris.[13] Such cynical jokes would not be possible unless they contained an unacknowledged truth which could not be admitted if it were expressed seriously and without disguise. In jest—it is well known—one may even tell the truth.

Just as for primeval man, so also for our unconscious, there is one case in which the two opposing attitudes towards death, the one which acknowledges it as the annihilation of life and the other which denies it as unreal, collide and come into conflict. This case is the same as in primal ages: the death, or the risk of death, of someone we love, a parent or a partner in marriage, a brother or sister, a child or a dear friend. These loved ones are on the one hand an inner possession, components of our own ego, but on the other hand they are partly strangers, even enemies. With the exception of only a very few situations, there adheres to the tenderest and most intimate of our love-relations a small portion of hostility which can excite an unconscious death-wish. But this conflict due to ambivalence does not now, as it did then, lead to the doctrine of the soul and to ethics, but to neurosis, which affords us deep insight into normal mental life as well. How often have physicians who practise psychoanalysis had to deal with the symptom of an exaggerated worry over the well-being of relatives, or with entirely unfounded self-reproaches after the death of a loved person. The study of such phenomena has left them in no doubt about the extent and importance of unconscious death-wishes.

The layman feels an extraordinary horror at the possibility of such feelings, and takes this aversion as a legitimate ground for disbelief in the assertions of psychoanalysis. Mistakenly, I think. No depreciation of feelings of love is intended, and there is in fact none. It is indeed foreign to our intelligence as well as to our feelings thus to couple love and hate; but Nature, by making use of this pair of opposites, contrives to keep love ever vigilant and fresh, so as to guard it against the hate which lurks behind it. It might be said that we owe the fairest flowerings of our love to the reaction against the hostile impulse which we sense within us.

To sum up: our unconscious is just as inaccessible to the idea of our own death, just as murderously inclined toward strangers, just as divided (that is, ambivalent) towards those we love, as was primeval man. But how far we have moved from this primal state in our conventional and cultural attitude toward death!

It is easy to see how war impinges on this dichotomy. It strips us of the later accretions of civilization, and lays bare the primal man in each of us. It compels us once more to be heroes who cannot believe in their own death; it stamps strangers as enemies, whose death is to be brought about or desired; it tells us to disregard the death of those we love. But war cannot be abolished; so long as the conditions of existence among nations are so different and their mutual repulsion so violent, there are bound to be wars. The question then arises: Is it not we who should give in, who should adapt ourselves to war? Should we not confess that in our civilized attitude toward death we are once again living psychologically beyond our means, and should we not rather turn back and recognize the truth? Would it not be better to give death the place in reality and in our thoughts which is its due, and to give a little more prominence to the unconscious attitude toward death which we have hitherto so carefully suppressed? This hardly seems an advance to higher achievement, but rather in some respects a backward step—a regression; but it has the advantage of taking the truth more into account, and of making life more tolerable for us once again. To tolerate life remains, after all, the first duty of all living beings. Illusion becomes valueless if it makes this harder for us.

We recall the old saying: *Si vis pacem, para bellum*. If you want to preserve peace, arm for war.

It would be in keeping with the times to alter it: *Si vis vitam, para mortem*. If you want to endure life, prepare yourself for death.

NOTES

1. A reminiscence of Prince Hal's remark to Falstaff in *I, Henry IV*, v. 1: "Thou owest God a death." This was a favorite misquotation of Freud's. See, for instance, *The Interpretation of Dreams*, Standard Ed., 4, 205, and a letter to Fliess of February 6, 1899 (Freud, 1950a, Letter 104), in which he explicitly attributes it to Shakespeare.

2. To think something unlikely or incredible.

3. The Asra in Heine's poem ("Der Asra," in *Romanzero*, based on a passage in Stendhal's *De l'amour*) were a tribe of Arabs who "die when they love."

4. Freud, *Totem and Taboo*, Essay IV, Standard Ed., *13*, 146 ff.

5. *Ibid.*, Essay II, Standard Ed., *13*, 60 ff.

6. *Odyssey* XI, 484-91, Trans., A. T. Murray.

7. Literally: "The smallest living Philistine at Stuckert-am-Neckar is far happier than I, the son of Peleus, the dead hero, the shadow-prince in the underworld." The closing lines of "Der Scheidende," one of the very last of Heine's poems.

8. Freud, *op. cit.*, Standard Ed., *13*, 66 ff.

9. Cf. Frazer's brilliant argument quoted in *Totem and Taboo*, Standard Ed., *13*, 123.

10. "Hans the Stone-Breaker"—a character in a comedy by the Viennese dramatist Ludwig Anzengruber (1839-89).

11. Fuller discussions of the fear of death will be found in the closing paragraphs of *The Ego and the Id* (1923*b*) and at the end of Chapter VII of *Inhibitions, Symptoms and Anxieties* (1926*d*).

12. Freud, *op. cit.*, Essay IV, Standard Ed., *13*, 85 f, S.F. XIV—U.

13. This is also quoted in Freud's *The Interpretation of Dreams* (1900*a*), Standard Ed., *5*, 485.

Suicide, like war, distorts the mourning process by emphasizing the ambivalence marked by Freud in the previous paper. Psychiatrist Albert Cain summarizes the legacy of suicide, emphasizing the psychological vulnerability of the survivor as he is tormented by feelings of personal responsibility in addition to the normal reactions of pain, anger and guilt. Society offers no explanation or absolution for the death; rather, it stigmatizes the mourner, depriving him of support.

SURVIVORS OF SUICIDE

Albert C. Cain

The papers included in this book speak of and for the survivors of suicide, of their torment and their desperate need for psychological assistance. Seen at varying ages, individually or as a family, in different settings, at widely varying intervals following the suicide, in highly divergent forms of study or intervention, the survivors of suicides nevertheless spoke a story with many major convergences: The authors of these papers underline that there are qualitative and quantitative features in the stresses impinging upon the family survivors of suicide that range significantly beyond those typical of bereavement per se. They are struck by the severity of psychopathology found in the survivors, and by the intrinsic vulnerability of suicide survivors. They are not only aware of, but quick to insist upon the *multiplicity* of *pre-suicide* and *post-suicide* determinants of the survivor's personality and psychopathology. They are emphatic in balancing discussions of the obvious direct pathogenic impact of suicide itself with references to *preexisting* profoundly pathogenic influences (grossly evidenced, for instance, in the effects upon the family members of an eventual suicide's prior alcoholism, repeated desertions, acting out, borderline psychosis, depression, raw marital strife, and such—

conditions often reported in the pre-suicide behavior of those who eventually commit suicide). So too do they spell out many powerful *post-suicide* secondary and tertiary pathogenic forces.[1] From these reports there evolves, frame by frame, a picture of the legacy of suicide that is simultaneously cognitive and affective, that captures the complex individual intrapsychic sequelae, placing these in turn within a powerful interpersonal and familial field of forces, and using a wide angle lens, within the larger social milieu of clan, neighbors and society.

The reactions portrayed, complex and individual as they are, can perhaps be clustered and capsuled as follows:

1. *Reality distortion*—massive, insistent use of denial and repression; tangled webs of evasions, contradictory beliefs, deliberate lies; concealment and anxiety-clouded confusion of memory, fantasy, and "imposed" redefinitions of reality . . . often elaborated into family myths , misconceptions, and varying disorders of reality linkage (feelings of unreality, derealization, weakened capacity for or commitment to reality testing, marked ego-splitting).

2. *Tortured object-relations*—desperate lonely neediness; disillusioned and doubt-filled distrust of human relationships; a hunger for, yet fear of closeness; a repetitive need to reenact separations, drive loved objects away, replay experiences of estrangement and reunion (or conversely, within the same dynamic configuration, ferocious determination to maintain crucial object-relations at any and all costs).

3. *Guilt*—visible quite directly, or in blaming and accusations, or in more symptomatic form; utterly irrational or painfully appropriate; focused variously on general anger and death wishes, specific acts, feelings that one could or should have prevented the suicide, a pervasive sense of complicity, or a sense of having been blamed by the suicidal individual for his despair; guilt variously fused with, displaced to or serving as screen guilt for other earlier guilts from myriad developmental sources.

4. *Disturbed self-concept*—compounded of a sense of shame, dishonor, and stigma; of having been cast away, abandoned, unwanted; of being worthless, unlovable if not bad or rotten; of being helpless, vulnerable; of being eternally unsure of self or others.

5. *Impotent rage*—intense yet admitting of little socially acceptable discharge; multiplied by the frequent sense of rejection

and deliberate desertion, with its core narcissistic insult; fed by the social "branding" and at times ostracism, the intense frustration of ongoing needs, and the enforced facing of old and huge new burdens alone.

6. *Identification with the suicide*—often the result of a commingling of archaic introjective mechanisms and interpersonal tugs and pulls toward redefinition of self and family role;[2] masked or overt, accepted or fiercely defended against; the identification variously focusing upon personality features of the suicide, the threatening of suicide, the bodily sensations of the suicidal act, the committing of suicide—even the specific act of suicide itself in like manner, setting, or anniversary date.

7. *Depression and self-destructiveness*—bred of the guilt, shame, rage, unmet yearning and unresolved grief delineated above, depression in its many faces is paramount: in active self-hatred, in states of hollow emptiness and deadness; in apathy, withdrawal, and immobilization; in sadness and despair; these depressive processes, exacerbated by the identification processes noted, are visible in implacably self-destructive ways of life and a remarkable incidence of direct suicidal behavior—suicidal impulses, fantasies, threats, preoccupation,[3] repeated suicidal attempts and completed suicides.

8. *Search for meaning*—driven, endless repetitions and reconstructions of different versions of the events preceding the suicide, and a groping quest for the "meaning" of the suicide. Spared temporarily for some by avoidance, suppression, flights into activity, spared for others by rigid, abrupt foreclosure of all but one unthreatening interpretation or construction; for many a struggle, too often alone, for a fixed sense of the specific suicidal events, the why of it, and the fit of the experience itself with the larger order of life. For too many this floundering search to construct a meaning, an interpretation of suicide, of *the* suicide, provides too few answers not colored with guilt, with perceived responsibility, with despair beyond redefinition or reparation.

9. *Incomplete mourning*—given the potent factors of denial, concealment, and evasion in the face of suicide, the shame and guilt-engendered avoidance of communication, and the mutual withdrawal of and from friends, neighbors and relatives (with consequent lack of opportunity for reassurance, reality testing, catharsis, shared grieving, and social support), the gradual working through of mourning is severerely hampered if not made impossible; thus the survivor of suicide is peculiarly vulnerable to the crippling effects of unresolved

mourning so richly described initially outside the realm of suicide (Bowlby, 1961, 1963; Lindemann, 1944).

It is also apparent from the studies presented here that these psychological processes neither originate nor evolve in an interpersonal vacuum.[4] Quite the contrary. They are often shaped by and amidst family interactions contorted by individuals too deeply preoccupied with their own grief to be helpful to each other, brimming with needs to blame and externalize, contending with newly erupted affects and problem behavior in themselves and each other, abruptly forced into significantly restructuring delicately intertwined family roles and sometimes required to learn utterly new roles and skills, caught between divergent if not conflicting patterns or pace of grief reactions among family members, urgently pressed to replace previous highly cathected modes of interpersonal relationship and sources of need-gratifications, buffeted as well by major practical problems which weigh toward further dissolution of the already harshly rent family structure.

These family processes are seen as still further contextually influenced by and infused with the prevalent values, constructions, taboos, and orientations toward suicide of a society whose proffered meanings of suicide tend to be at best ambiguous and fertile with the seeds of blame; a society whose attitudes toward suicide are basically punitive; a society which affords virtually no institutions or mechanisms for relieving the unique burdens bequeathed the suicide's bereaved. And ultimately a social milieu is portrayed which surrounds suicide and its survivors with the mark of *stigma*; stigma whose familiar accompaniments of shame, disgrace, social avoidance, and cloaked communication (if not forthright malignant blaming and ostracism) multiply the intrinsically formidable tasks of mourning and coping with the suicide death of a family member.

NOTES

1.   One can no more suggest that the substantial psychopathology seen is *purely* the product of, for example, parent suicide than one could claim that Oedipus' fall, torment, and commitment

to self-destruction was purely or primarily the product of Jocasta's self-hanging!

2. Most vividly seen with the young children of suicides, whose surviving parent suddenly imposes identification—"mis-identification" in John Benjamin's fortunate term—with the dead parent upon them.

3. Reference here to suicidal preoccupation is not only to preoccupation with one's own suicide, but a pervasive interest in and often effort to involve oneself with suicidal individuals (evident in the number of survivors of suicide—family suicides or those of other intimates—who volunteer and often helpfully serve as lay staff in suicide prevention agencies).

4. It has been suggested that accumulating evidence of psychopathology in survivors of suicide attests to the validity of the concept that a primary motive of suicide is to damage others— blame them, accuse them, cause sorrow, regret and trouble. This concept is, of course, key to Adlerian approaches to suicidal behavior (Ansbacher, 1970). "Revenge suicides" are well known and have been a normal social mechanism in a number of societies (Westermarck, 1906; Jeffreys, 1952; Murphy, 1954; Noyes, 1968). There are dramatic clinical cases of openly hostile, vengeful suicides on record, and many instances in which such motives and fantasies are not difficult to discern. In many others, however, no such motivation is apparent. But more to the point, it must be emphasized here that the "survivor" materials presented in this volume provide *no direct evidence* whatsoever as to the nature and meaning of the prior suicides per se. To infer from the effects on survivors simply and linearly to the suicides' *intention* is *a distortion of clinical inference and a misuse of survivor data.*

Personal responses to an individual's death are as complex as the relationship with him in life. Anger and guilt as well as sorrow must find a place in any mourning process. But the mourner's expression of anger and guilt is often difficult for others to accept. On occasion the mourner may find a vehicle for the expression of his feelings, whether socially acceptable or not, and a means to resolve the irrational contradictions of his emotions through writing. Sylvia Plath, a master poet of the twentieth century, has often explored the chaotic emotions surrounding death, her own and that of others. In "Daddy," a mourning poem of a sort, the speaker gives vent to strong feelings of anger and merges the response to an individual death symbolically to the holocaust experience of the Jews in World War II.

DADDY

Sylvia Plath

You do not do, you do not do
Any more, black shoe
In which I have lived like a foot
For thirty years, poor and white,
Scarcely daring to breathe or Achoo.

Daddy, I have had to kill you.
You died before I had time—
Marble-heavy, a bag full of God,
Ghastly statue with one grey toe
Big as a Frisco seal

And a head in the freakish Atlantic
Where it pours bean green over blue
In the waters off beautiful Nauset.
I used to pray to recover you.
Ach, du.

In the German tongue, in the Polish
    town
Scraped flat by the roller
Of wars, wars, wars.
But the name of the town is common.
My Polack friend.

Says there are a dozen or two.
So I could never tell where you
Put your foot, your root,
I never could talk to you.
The tongue stuck in my jaw.

It stuck in a barb wire snare.
Ich, ich, ich, ich.

I could hardly speak.
I thought every German was you.
And the language obscene

An engine, an engine
Chuffing me off like a Jew.
A Jew to Dachau, Auschwitz, Belsen
I began to talk like a Jew.
I think I may well be a Jew.

The snows of the Tyrol, the
    clear beer of Vienna
Are not very pure or true.
With my gypsy ancestress and
    my weird luck

And my Taroc pack and my Taroc
  pack
I may be a bit of a Jew.

I have always been scared of *you*,
With your Luftwaffe, your gobbledygoo.
And your neat moustache
And your Aryan eye, bright blue.
Panzer-man, panzer-man, O You—

Not God but a swastika
So black no sky could squeak through.
Every woman adores a Fascist,
The boot in the face, the brute
Brute heart of a brute like you.

You stand at the blackboard, daddy,
In the picture I have of you,
A cleft in your chin instead of your
  foot
But no less a devil for that, no not
Any less the black man who

Bit my pretty red heart in two.
I was ten when they buried you.
At twenty I tried to die
And get back, back, back to you.
I thought even the bones would do.

But they pulled me out of the sack,
And they stuck me together with glue.
And then I knew what to do.
I made a model of you,
A man in black with a Meinkampf
  look

And a love of the rack and the screw.
And I said I do, I do.
So daddy, I'm finally through.
The black telephone's off at the root,
The voices just can't worm through.

If I've killed one man, I've killed
  two—
The vampire who said he was you
And drank my blood for a year,
Seven years, if you want to know.
Daddy, you can lie back now.

There's a stake in your fat black heart
And the villagers never liked you.
They are dancing and stamping on
  you.
They always *knew* it was you.
Daddy, daddy, you bastard, I'm
  through.

Violent and untimely death create special problems for both survivors and the larger society. A culture's death rituals should be flexible to provide for a wide range of those needs. In "Religious Symbolism in Limbu Death-by-Violence," anthropologist Rex L. Jones describes a special death ritual that the Limbu of Nepal perform after a violent or accidental death. Summarizing the funeral as a "symbolic battle with death," Jones shows how the Limbu ritual brings the chaos of unexpected death under control and interprets the otherwise senseless occurrence of death.

RELIGIOUS SYMBOLISM IN LIMBU DEATH-BY-VIOLENCE

Rex L. Jones

INTRODUCTION

Religions display a tremendous variety of rituals and myths that deal with the destiny of the human soul, with the diagnosis of disease, and with curing and healing, all of which indicates a preoccupation with the dying and decaying human body. The rites of passage at birth, puberty, and death, which are almost universal in human society, may be viewed as attempts to symbolically order the natural process of a decaying universe embodied in the life cycle of a human being. Fertility cults, agricultural rituals, and hunting magic further display an attempt on the part of man to control the life and death process itself through a symbolic control of nature and a creation of order and purpose to existence. Even national and tribal rituals, or rituals of state, designed on the surface to further the political process such as coronations of royalty, independence day celebrations, world renewal ceremonies, or honorific rituals for important political figures and heroes are filled with

"Religious Symbolism in Limbu Death-by-Violence," R. L. Jones, *Omega - Journal of Death and Dying,* Volume 5, Number 3, Fall, 1974. Copyright © Baywood Publishing Company, Inc.

the intent to symbolically create political and societal order. A survey of salvation movements, millenarian cults, or messianic dreams reveals an obsession on the part of men to bring order out of chaos and create a world free of disease, poverty, suffering, and death. Finally, religious ecstasy and mysticism, regardless of the sociological functions, display an attempt on the part of man to gain eternal life, free from death and the endless cycle of suffering and decay.

In the forefront of this obsession with order and decay stands the religious leader—the prophet, the shaman, the medicine man, and priest. The prophet through visions, dreams, and revelations encapsulizes and transmits to his followers a world of perfection, free from disease, poverty, suffering, and death. Through his charisma, this perfected universe becomes a living reality, attainable for the faithful and the true believer. The shaman and medicine man symbolize the same principle. In their initial illness through possession and the trance they encounter illness, death, and destruction. Eventually, generally through an apprenticeship, they learn to control this chaotic state of the universe which is embodied in their own life. They soon learn to summon the spirit world at will and transform its supernatural power into a controlled secular power with which they manipulate the potentially destructive forces of the secular world. By controlled ecstasy they bring order to the lives of men. The priest, in a less dramatic fashion, accomplishes the same thing. Through ritual, prayer, and petition he summons divine order to a troubled world. The prophet, shaman, and priest merely represent "stages" of the religious process, ecologically adapted to the needs of men. In their role as religious leaders, they symbolize the longing for order and perfection in a disordered and imperfect world.

As an illustration of this principle, I propose to briefly examine concepts of death as expressed in a death ritual which I observed while doing fieldwork among a Tibeto-Burman speaking people of eastern Nepal, the Limbu. The ritual is not a normal death ritual, even by Limbu definitions, since it concerns an accidental, violent death, but it nevertheless makes clear much of the esoteric symbolism in normal Limbu funeral practices and reveals more clearly the uncertainty and hopelessness that death brings, and the Limbu's attempts to abolish it.

The Limbu of eastern Nepal number approximately 150,000 people. Today, they live in a multi-ethnic mountain community dominated politically and economically by caste Hindus, especially Brahmans and Chetris. This domination is relatively recent, having occurred in the last two centuries as a result of conquests by the Hindu monarchy of central Nepal. Large scale immigrations of caste Hindus and other ethnic groups followed the conquest, and today it is estimated that Limbus number less than twenty-five per cent of the population of their indigenous homeland, frequently referred to as Limbuan. Because of complex land tenure rights and relative political autonomy enjoyed in the nineteenth and twentieth century, Limbus have maintained a cultural and ethnic identity that differs considerably from their Hindu neighbors and conquerors. Although they have adopted a subsistence pattern based on wet rice agriculture that is almost indistinguishable from that of the Hindus in the area, they retain many features of the southeast Asian culture complex. This is especially evident in the distinctions made between normal deaths of old age and disease and abnormal deaths by accident or in childbirth.

Origins of Life and Death in Limbu Mythology

In Limbu mythology, God, *Porokmi Yambami* (Brahmā) created the first man (*Tāpunāmā Wāhināmā*) by mixing ashes and the droppings of chickens. He then breathed life into his creation and the man moved, but he could not talk. God took the tongue of a fish and made man's tongue so that he could speak. Thus, man is composed of the four basic elements of fire, earth, air, and water symbolized by ashes, dung, the breath of God, and the fish that live in water. The life principle identified with the breath of God is indestructible, but one's corporeal existence is perishable and returns eventually to the basic elements. Originally, say the Limbu, God made a man of gold and silver, but he could not make him speak. Had God accomplished his task with the first creation, man would have eternal life, but for the price of speech, he pays with death. Death is, therefore, inevitable, but there are many ways of dying.

Thus, normal deaths of old age or disease are accepted as inevitable, as the work of God, or rather as a result of his failure to create a perfect man. Abnormal deaths by violence, accident, or in childbirth are caused by the failures of men who are tempted by evil spirits. Out of envy and jealousy of the living, these spirits cause men to die prematurely. The spirits of men who die normally go to a land of the dead, after their bodies have been given a proper burial and they have been pacified with a period of mourning and a feast. The souls of men who die abnormally remain on earth, near their homes or places of death, to harass and plague the living, and out of jealousy and envy, they cause others to die in the same fashion.

The spirits of those who die by violence or accident (soghā), women who die in childbirth (*sugut*), and stillbirths (*susik*), originated in mythological times as a result of the desires and failures of men. One version of a myth tells how the first woman, *Tāpunāmā-Wāhināmā*, out of loneliness sought a child. She was impregnated by a storm and gave birth to a male child. On reaching weaning age, the boy was required to fend for himself and set out with a dog on a hunting expedition. After hunting all day without success, he decided to return home. On his return he came to a ridge where there were eight paths. Before he could decide which path to take, night fell and the boy died of hunger. He was, henceforth, known as *Susik Yongdong* and his spirit remained on earth to plague the human fetus, presumably causing it to die of hunger in the womb. The myth goes on to describe how the dog that accompanied the boy returned to *Tāpunāmā-Wāhināmā* with the news of her child's death. She began to cry and in her agony she went to look for her son. On discovering him, only his bones were left. She buried the bones and returned home. On her way she passed a large lake where she sat to rest. While resting, night came on and she fell asleep. In her dream her dead child's soul came and had intercourse with her. She was blinded by this act and soon died. Her spirit became the *Sugut* and remained on earth to cause women to die in childbirth.

Another myth is given to account for the origins of the *soghā* spirit. After the creation of the world, a boy and his sister decided to build a house. The boy went into the woods to cut a tree for the wood they needed. After repeated failures to cut the tree, his sister came to help him. She made offerings of food, liquor, and beer at the base of the tree and only then was the boy able to fell the tree. With the help of friends he brought it back to the village, and by accident it fell and killed his sister. For several nights the sister's spirit came to haunt her brother because he failed to give her a mourning feast. Finally, he called in a shaman who, with the help of his tutelary spirit, was able to trap the angry spirit. The spirit spoke to him and told him that she could only be held for three years at which point she would assume a number of forms that would be dangerous for the living. She would appear in the form of a bull's horns and kill unsuspecting men; she would enter trees and fall on people; she would sit in the mouth of a dog and bite people; or she would cause travelers to fall off trails and die. From that time forward, men have been plagued with accidental and violent deaths caused by *soghā* spirits. Only a shaman who knows the proper ritual is able to capture and control these spirits.

In the above mythological accounts unexpected and violent deaths are explained symbolically through the *failures of men*. Generally, such deaths originate with incestuous desire, greed, envy, or other asocial acts. These same qualities are attributed to the spirit forms—*soghā, sugut,* or *susik.* The Limbu identify evil in other contexts with similar asocial qualities of envy and jealousy. Suicide is thought to be the most extreme manifestation of these qualities. Indeed, death by "accident" or violence is equated with death by suicide; both result from the failures of men.

DEATH RITUALS

The death rituals for those who die by suicide, violence or childbirth parallel the mythological accounts. Such deaths are treated differently from normal deaths of old age or disease.

In a normal death the deceased is washed, clothed, and laid out on a bamboo stretcher. An all-night vigil takes place over the body. On the following day, the body is carried to a cemetery. A grave is dug, and a coffin of rocks constructed in the base of the grave. The body is lowered into the grave, the coffin sealed, and the deceased's possessions are tossed on top of the coffin. The grave is filled and a marker placed on top. Following the funeral close relatives enter a period of mourning—four days for a male and three days for a female. During this period the immediate male relatives of the deceased, the sons, brothers, fathers, or husbands are isolated inside the deceased's home clothed only in a white cotton garment. They are not allowed to speak to non-patrilinear relatives or to eat foods coated in salt or oil. At the end of the mourning cycle a feast for the dead is prepared and attended by relatives, neighbors, and friends of the family. The principal mourners shave the hair from their bodies and sit in front of the feast while one or more shamans give a funeral oration to the guests. After the offerings have been made to the deceased's spirit, the guests are fed and the period of pollution is ended.

Without analyzing the details of this ritualized period of mourning, certain points emerge. All death is dangerous to the living, especially to close kinsmen. This danger is averted through prescribed ritual. Close relatives undergo a social death through isolation and are reborn at the mourning feast, where their connections to the deceased are severed. Death itself, though God-given and therefore unpredictable and inevitable, is made meaningful. Through ritual symbolism the living have exerted a control over death and reordered the universe by reaffirming social relations.

In abnormal deaths, the dangers are multiplied. Such deaths are brought about by human failure symbolized by the *soghā, sugut,* and *susik* spirits. In such situations, the entire world of man is threatened by disorder and inexplicable chaos. Society itself seems doomed by the forces of greed, envy, and jealousy. Because of these perceived dangers such deaths are given a different ritual treatment. I witnessed the procedures of such a death ritual only once while in the field. The following summarized account is presented as an illustration.

Death by Violence

After an extremely severe monsoon storm in the beginning of October, 1968, that lasted for three days and nights,
my wife Shirley and I woke to learn that about midnight a
landslide had crushed a house just below ours, killing two
people, an old woman and a young girl of about three or four
years. Three others in the house at the time had somehow
escaped. When we arrived the bodies of the woman and young
girl were laid out on bamboo stretchers on the front porch of
the deceased woman's son's house, which was about 100 feet
adjacent to the one that had been destroyed. A specialized
shaman called a *mangba* had been called to the house along
with his apprentice helper. The two were squatting under a
tree facing the bodies. A number of onlookers (about 80 to
100 in all) had gathered at the scene. Unlike a normal Limbu
funeral where those in attendance are almost invariably Limbus,
most of whom are related by patrilinear descent or marriage,
this crowd was *multi-ethnic* in composition. I noted several
Brahmans and Chetris and a few Newar from the nearby Ba-
zaar as well as representatives of the menial castes of leather-
workers, tailors and blacksmiths. The Limbus themselves were
represented by many who were unrelated to the deceased either
by marriage or descent. The crowd was a hodge-podge of curious people who happened to live close enough to witness the
event. It was much like a crowd one would expect to find at a
particularly disastrous car accident in Times Square, Manhattan
—a congregation of the curious from all walks of life having
little more in common than insatiable curiosity with death and
a nearness to the disaster. I think this is worth mentioning
because it demonstrates an important contrast between the two
types of Limbu death rituals. At a normal funeral the attendance mirrors Limbu social structure in that the majority show
a kinship relationship to the deceased. In an abnormal funeral
the attendance reflects the unpredictable situation of chaos
in the random and unordered composition of the crowd.
Shortly after we arrived, the shaman and his apprentice
took charge of the proceedings. They began to chant and beat

their percussion instruments, a drum and brass plate. Almost as a signal the bodies were lifted and carried along a path toward the ridge above, followed by the crowd. The shamans danced on the spot where the bodies had lain and followed the funeral procession, beating their instruments constantly. At the top of the ridge near a Limbu cemetery, the procession stopped. The *mangba* ran to several of the graves, danced around them, and returned to the crowd. The procession then continued past the cemetery along a path leading into a forested area. The shaman and his apprentice followed, repetitiously chanting and drumming. In a clearing in the forested area the entire procession stopped and several men began immediately, without ceremony, to dig the graves. While the digging was in process, the crowd sat near the bodies talking and chatting amidst the wailing of close relatives. On completion of the work, the bodies were rapidly lowered into the grave. Their eyes, ears, and noses were covered. I was told later that they were buried face down.

Again the contrasts to a normal funeral should be noted. In a normal funeral the bodies are laid near the grave while it is being dug and their faces shaded by a white cloth; in the abnormal funeral, the bodies are unshaded. In a normal funeral, a coffin of stones is constructed in the grave; in the one witnessed above, no coffin was constructed. In a normal burial, the bodies are buried face up in an extended position; in the one under description, they are buried face down. In a normal burial the orifices of the body are uncovered; in an abnormal funeral, the eyes, ears, and nose are covered. Finally, in a normal funeral, the deceased is buried in a cemetery in a plot "purchased" and consecrated by a shaman; in an abnormal funeral, the deceased is buried in a grave dug in the forest and the plot is neither "purchased" nor consecrated by the shaman. In a normal funeral the grave is marked; in the one being described, the grave is left unmarked.

After the burial, the procession broke into confusion. The participants engaged in a mock battle with sticks on the path leading back toward the ridge past the cemetery. This particular mock battle threatened to lead to a real fight when two of the participants began to hit each other in earnest, each claiming that the other had hit him in anger rather than in jest. They were controlled by the crowd, which had by this time reached a crossroads leading back to the scene of the accident. The shaman and his apprentice again took control of the procession. The *mangba* sacrificed a chicken and placed it next to a bottle of liquor in the middle of the road, as an offering to the spirits of the dead woman and child.

The *mangba* and his apprentice began to dance around the offering, simulating a trance, with the stated purpose of sealing off the road to prevent the *soghā* spirits from escaping. No one was allowed to stand between the offering and the burial ground, for fear the spirits, who were not yet fully under the control of the *mangba*, might attach themselves to the unfortunate participant. On completion of this rite, the *mangba* then marked each participant on the forehead with a piece of charcoal as a protection against the powers of the *soghā* spirit. Many who had accompanied the procession returned to their homes. The remainder followed the *mangba* in procession back to the house of the deceased woman's son.

On arrival at the house, the shaman and his apprentice danced around the house. Again chaos broke out. Many of the onlookers standing in a terraced field just above the courtyard of the house began throwing pumpkins, squashes, and other garden produce on those unfortunate enough to be standing in the courtyard. The deceased woman's son tossed many of the dead woman's possessions into the pile of debris. In the middle of this confusion two men dragged a squealing pig that belonged to the deceased into the courtyard and decapitated it with a Nepali bushknife, basking many of the onlookers with the blood of the animal. The *mangba* and his apprentice continued their dance on the front porch of the house. A number of women strained beer for those in the procession as is customary after a normal burial. Many drank their beer and went home. A few stayed to assist in the preparations for the ritual to capture and "kill" the *soghā* spirits, which was to take place during the night. Gradually, the crowd diminished and the few that remained sat around discussing the events that had taken place. The lull continued until nightfall. After a short spell, I went to my house and ate.

244

When I returned shortly after dark, the meat from the slaughtered pig was being prepared for the fifteen or twenty people who remained. All were Limbus, but only about half were related to the deceased. The *mangba* and his apprentice sat on the porch of the house, smoking and drinking beer, waiting for the meal to be prepared. Others were cutting and stripping bamboo to be used in the construction of a special altar in the courtyard of the deceased's woman's son's house.

A bonfire was lit, and a few feet from it, a small mound about four to six feet in diameter and about three or four inches in height was erected. On this mound two large bamboo branches about twelve feet high were crossed and tied together. From the ground to the point where the branches crossed a three-step ladder was built. Circling the edge of the mound a small "x"-shaped fence was constructed and left open at one end. A cloth banner and sword were stuck into the mound near the base of the branches, and oil flames, a leaf-plate of rice, and a vase of flowers completed the altar. A small hole about six inches in depth was scooped out next to the altar. The *soghā* spirits were to be lured into this hole and "killed" by fire.

After the *mangba* had eaten he entered the house and began chanting. While he chanted the sons of the deceased woman strung two small necklaces (*mālā*) of seed pods and placed them on the altar as symbols of those who had just been killed. The *mangba* then approached the altar in the courtyard and seated himself in front of the opening. The apprentice sat next to him and began drumming. Gradually, the drumming and chanting increased until both men arose and began a dance around the altar. At the climax of the dance, the *mangba* blew a bone whistle intended to summon the *soghā* spirits. The dance continued for fifteen or twenty minutes until the two shamans sat down to rest in front of the altar. They repeated this procedure on occasion until long past midnight, with the stated purpose of gradually gaining control over the *soghā* spirits.

Finally, at about three a.m., one of the women brought a dish of corn flour that was heated over the fire, while another participant lit three bamboo torches. The *mangba* and his helper arose and began to beat the brass plate. An onlooker grabbed the banner and sword from the altar and flailed them wildly about. Another grabbed a long stick and beat it randomly in the air. Suddenly, the shaman and helper ran around the house followed by the holders of the torches, the corn flour, and the weapons. The procession continued past the house that had been destroyed and up the trail towards the top of the ridge, flinging the corn flour at the torches and beating at the *soghā* spirits. A fence of fire was erected at the crossroads, and the *soghā* spirits were chased by the group toward the altar. When the group, led by the shamans, returned to the altar, coals from the fire were casually tossed into the hole where the *soghā* spirits were thought to have hidden, and the performance ended. The participants drank beer and went home.

The funeral for those killed by the landslide ended with the above events. No period of mourning was observed, nor did the surviving relatives observe a period of fasting or the customary pollution rites. A mourning feast for the dead was ignored.

The expressed purpose of the entire ritual described above was to "kill" the *soghā* spirits. During my questioning of the events, I learned that the phrase, "to kill the spirits," was only a metaphor for "capturing" them, since a spirit cannot be killed in a literal sense. Depending upon the powers of the *mangba* and upon his having performed the ritual properly, the spirits remain harmless for three years. At the end of each three-year period the ritual must be repeated to insure the safety of those living in the vicinity of the accident. If the *mangba* fails in his performance, the spirits remain loose and harass the living, possibly causing further deaths by violence.

CONCLUSIONS

The death ritual just described emphasizes in dramatic fashion the chaos unleased by unexpected death in Limbu society. This chaos is symbolized again and again in events that lead up to the "killing" of the *soghā* spirits. The entire ritual oscillates between periods of social and psychological chaos and systematic exertion of control over the participant's behavior by the shaman and his apprentice. The ritual is punctuated and held together by the shaman's chanting, drumming, and dancing. The role of the shaman is to bring order to a society threatened by unexpected and unpredictable death. In this capacity he functions as both political and religious leader. He controls the participants by leading them from one stage of the ritual to the next, and in his final act of "killing" the *soghā* spirits, he exerts control over the supernatural realm.

The ritual itself, from beginning to end, may be likened to a dramatic performance designed to stamp out death or, at the very least, to make death intelligible, meaningful, and predictable. It might be described quite simply as a symbolic battle with death. Death, especially death by accident or violence, is the mark of a chaotic universe, a "universe in ruins." The death ritual is the Limbu's attempt to capture and order this chaos in his own terms.

In the death ritual "chaos vs. order" is symbolized in a number of instances. The bodies are buried in the forest rather than a cemetery, showing the contrast between unordered and ordered space. The funeral occurs immediately without delay and without a period of mourning or pollution, thereby contrasting time in terms of the unexpected and the expected. A mock battle ensues, emphasizing anarchy as opposed to an ordered society.

Underneath the symbolism of this death ritual is a reality that cannot be tolerated for any length of time by the human mind—the reality that life has no other purpose than "being." The symbolism does not express this reality; it denies it. By contrasting chaos and order the ritual offers a dialectical synthesis of the two and tells us finally that the situation of death itself is now under control. God and man are once again in charge. An imperfect world of chaos, inexplicable events, and anarchy are replaced by order, explanations, and social control.

QUESTIONS

1. Define each of the following terms used in this chapter. The starred words are concepts the writers expect the reader to know already. If you are not familiar with them, consult a dictionary.

*traumatic experience
*syndrome
normal grief reaction
  (grief syndrome)
*psychoneurotic
  grief work
*identification
*conversion symptom
  anticipatory grief
*culture
*norm
*value
*status position
*social role
*kinship system
*socialization

*ambivalence
*family of orientation, of
  procreation
*taboo
*role requirement
*shaman
*patrilineal, matrilineal
  descent
  wake
  committal service
  eulogy
  embalming
*Psychoanalytic School
*the unconscious
*object-relations
  incomplete mourning

2. a. As Lynn Caine found herself a new widow, she quickly became aware of a new role expectation. She was determined to be the "ideal American widow," full of courage and restraint. Outline the characteristics of the admired American widow.

b. Volkart and Michael describe how the cultural role expectation can be at odds with the experience of the mourner and result in pathology. In what ways does the American stereotype provide support for the widow? In what ways does it block expression of her needs?

3. In his noted paper, "Mourning and Melancholia," Freud considered identification with the deceased to be a necessary temporary component of the grief work, a factor that could become distorted under certain circumstances. Lindemann lists identification as a part of normal grief that in its extreme forms may indicate pathology. Compile a list of different kinds of behavior that might be considered identification, beginning with the examples given by Lindemann and Albert Cain.

4. Lindemann and Cain describe in detail how the mourning process can fail to resolve loss. What different forms can "pathological grief" take? What kinds of behavior might indicate to you that a bereaved person was reacting in a psychologically unhealthy manner? What factors would you need to take into account in making your determination?

5. a. As expected death after a long illness becomes more frequent in our country, family and friends are more likely to begin an anticipatory grief reaction before death occurs. Recalling the discussions of Kubler-Ross and Lindemann, outline the benefits and the dangers involved in beginning to mourn while the terminally ill patient is still alive.

b. Under these circumstances, the needs of the mourner would no longer be met by the social role demands of the bereaved as we know it. Contrast the kinds of role behavior that would be appropriate following sudden unexpected death with those following a long terminal illness. How might the funeral rites be changed to reflect these differences in needs?

6. In providing his overview of funeral customs Bowman makes several generalizations. Examine "Group Behavior at Funeral Gatherings" closely to identify some of those generalizations and in each case suggest a procedure by which you could test their validity.

7. Jones describes the Limbu shaman as an intermediary who restores order in a world distorted by death. Grief reflects this disruption in the social order. As the role of religion has declined for many in America, who is most often looked to for support? Compare and contrast the functions of modern day helpers to those of the shaman.

8. Outline the relationship between the special Limbu funeral Jones describes and Limbu creation myths.

9. It has become a cliché to criticize American funeral practices for denying death. More importantly, they have been criticized for depriving the mourner of his grief. Consider the variety of responses described by Bowman. In what ways do they represent denial of grief? Does the funeral, as you know it, promote healthy grieving? Suggest three specific changes that could be made in the funeral to better meet the psychological needs of mourners.

10. Many critics of the modern funeral advocate replacing the traditional service with the body present with a memorial service at which the body is not present. What psychological advantages and disadvantages do you see to having the body of the deceased as the focal point of the funeral service?

11. Sigmund Freud has written, ". . . at bottom no one believes in his own death, or, to put the same thing in another way, that in the unconscious every one of us is convinced of his own immortality." How does Freud reach this conclusion? Do you agree? What evidence would you offer for your view?

12. Freud discusses the role of drama and literature in man's attempt to reconcile himself with death. What is this role? Do you agree with Freud's interpretation? Why or why not?

13. Consider the war novel as a literary genre. Using war novels you know, what attitudes toward death can you find expressed, both directly and indirectly? What examples of guilt do you find when characters encounter the death of another?

14. Bereavement after suicide is considered an especially high risk grief period. What special supports do the survivors of suicide need? How could you provide for their particular reactions?

15. a. "Daddy is a mourning poem. Cite lines in the poem that exemplify anger and guilt.

    b. "Holocaust" is a term now used to refer to the Jewish experience of persecution and execution in the concentration camps of Germany in World War II. Consider the use of holocaust imagery in "Daddy." What is its effect in setting the tone of the poem? What analogy is suggested between the holocaust and bereavement?

PROJECTS FOR FURTHER STUDY

1. Lynn Caine poignantly portrays the feelings of helplessness of the widowed, whose needs are too often overlooked. Using recent journal articles, investigate the "Widow to Widow" program described by Phyllis Silverman, in *Helping Each Other in Widowhood*. Information on a similar program, "Journey's End," is available from the Ethel Percey Andrus Gerontology Center, University of Southern California. What supports are offered in your community? What specific services would be helpful to the widowed? Try to interview three widows (perhaps through a church group) on their experience of bereavement in order to generate a specific list of problems and needs.

2. a. Although the funeral is one of our most conservative rituals, it is subject to change, as is any social institution. Interview some older relatives on funeral customs they recall from their youth. How have funeral customs changed over the last fifty years? Have attitudes towards funeral customs also changed? Why?

   b. Not only the social customs but the ritual itself also change. Study the new funeral liturgies both in the church and in the secular funeral. For example, the funeral industry is developing the "Life Centered" funeral; ideas for personalized services are suggested in Ernest Morgan's *A Manual of Death Education and*

252

Simple Burial. Compare and contrast the orientation, the symbols, and the styles of the newer liturgies with the more traditional.

3. Writers such as Jessica Mitford, in *The American Way of Death*, and Ruth Mulvey Harmer, in *The High Cost of Dying*, cite examples of financial abuses in the funeral industry. To protect the "consumer" from unnecessary expenses, they advocate the development of non-profit memorial societies. Visit a funeral home to investigate the typical funeral costs in your area. If there is also a memorial society in the area, compare the services offered by each and their costs. The following resources may be useful in gathering information.

"The Price of Death: A Survey Method and Consumer Guide for Funerals, Cemeteries and Grave Makers" contains a suggested procedure for conducting a survey of prices and services, including questionnaire forms with instructions for their use. This consumer handbook is available from the U. S. Government Consumer Information Center, Pueblo, Colorado, 81009.

Information in various forms about traditional funerals is available from the National Funeral Director's Association, 135 W. Wells Street, N.W., Washington, D.C., 20036.

Information about memorial societies is available from the Continental Association of Funeral and Memorial Societies, Inc., 1828 L Street, N.W., Washington, D.C., 20036.

4. In the nineteenth century the word "cemetery" began to replace the traditional generic terms, "graveyard," or "burial ground"; a shift which reflected the fact that the cemetery had become a cultural institution. Visit a local cemetery to see how death is presented: identify as many different representations of death as you can, both individual symbols (e.g., ornaments and headstones) and the

253

symbolism of the place itself (e.g., the setting and architectural styles). Where you find inscriptions on the headstones, collect representative examples of different styles of epitaphs. What different themes do you find? What information is typically given about the deceased? Besides serving as a disposition site for bodies, what other social, religious or personal functions does a cemetery serve? serve?

Before beginning these exercises please read "Note to Instructor" on page xiii

STRUCTURED EXERCISES

1. This exercise is designed to synthesize the information about funeral customs provided by the papers in Chapter Three. The exercise can be modified either to allow further investigation of the function of funerals or to put the student in a position to experience his own feelings about funerals.

    a. Imagine that you have died with everything in your life as it is right now. Design a personalized funeral or memorial service for yourself. Describe in detail the arrangements you would like: the time the service would be held; the kind of gathering it would be; the setting where it would be held; who would be there; what would occur during different parts of the gathering; whether there would be music and flowers, and if so, what kind; and so on. Even if you want a traditional religious funeral, describe the details; there are still many options such as choice of hymns or prayers which personalize such a service.

        This exercise could be written up before class discussion, or it could be done in class as a visualization exercise once the class is familiar with what goes on at a funeral. In class discussion, try to compare and contrast the themes that emerge from the different descriptions as well as focusing on the personal feelings of loss.

b. The eulogy is the traditional funeral oration which reviews the life of the deceased and represents a formal farewell from the community. Assume that everything in your life is as it is right now and write your own eulogy. How would you sum up your life at this point?

In order to share the experience with the class, you could form small groups to read the completed eulogies, either by passing them around to be read silently, or by reading them aloud to the group. A second alternative for sharing the eulogies would be to have each person take turns at lying on a table, eyes closed, imagining a funeral setting in as much detail he wishes appropriate, while his eulogy is read aloud. After all the eulogies have been read, discuss your reactions both to composing the eulogy and then to hearing it read. What has the process told you about yourself and your goals?

c. The epitaph is the brief statement placed on a memorial marker. What would yours be? Explain your choice to the class. Do they agree with its appropriateness for you?

2. To explore your personal reactions to loss, picture the most important person in your life. Suppose he or she were to die tomorrow. Take ten minutes to decide on responses to the following questions. Use a worksheet to make notes if you wish.

a. What would you miss most about that person?

b. What one thing do you wish you had had a chance to tell that person?

c.   What one thing do you wish you could have heard from that person?

d.   What one thing would you have wanted to change in the relationship?

e.   What was the happiest moment you recall sharing with that person?

f.   What was the most painful moment, before now, the two of you shared?

g.   What circumstances (time, place, event) do you expect to bring the most painful memories?

When everyone has completed the questions, you may share the responses either as a class or in smaller groups. During this part of the exercise, you may discuss your reactions to actually doing the exercise, how you selected the person you chose, and what you learned from the experience.

FOR FURTHER READING

The following books and papers provide in-depth coverage of the topics introduced in this chapter.

Freud, S. Mourning and Melancholia. In J. Strachey (ed.) *The Complete Psychological Works,* Vol. 14. London: Hogarth, 1966.

Goody, J. *Death, Property and the Ancestors.* Stanford, California: Stanford University Press, 1962.

Gorer, G. *Death, Grief, and Mourning.* Garden City, N.Y.: Doubleday, 1965.

Grollman, E. A. (ed.) *Concerning Death: A Practical Guide for the Living.* Boston: Beacon Press, 1974.

Habenstein, R. W. and Lamers, W. M. *Funeral Customs the World Over,* Milwaukee: National Funeral Directors Association, 1960.

Krystal, H. (ed.) *Massive Psychic Trauma.* New York: International Universities.

Lamm, M. *The Jewish Way of Death and Mourning.* New York: Jonathan-David, 1972.

Lifton, R. J. *History and Human Survival.* New York: Random House, 1970.

Mitford, J. *The American Way of Death.* New York: Simon & Schuster, 1963.

Morgan, E. *A Manual of Death Education and Simple Burial*, rev. 7th edition. Burnsville, N. C.: The Celo Press, 1976.

Parkes, C. M. *Bereavement: Studies of Grief in Adult Life*. New York: International Universities Press, 1972.

Pincus, L. *Death and the Family*. New York: Pantheon, 1975.

Schoenberg, B., Carr, A., Peretz, D. and Kutscher, A. (eds.) *Loss and Grief: Psychological Management in Medical Practice*. New York: Columbia University Press, 1970.

Silverman, P., Mackenzie, D., Pettipas, M. and Wilson, E. *Helping Each Other in Widowhood*. New York: Health Sciences Publishing, 1975.

Stannard, D. E. (ed.) *Death in America*. Philadelphia: University of Pennsylvania Press, 1975.

4
Death
and the Child

INTRODUCTION

As recently as the sixteenth century, Montaigne could write to a friend in terms that surprise the modern reader, "I have lost two or three children in infancy," he explained, "not without regret, but without great sorrow." Yet with the probability that several children born to any one family would die before reaching the age of majority, families could not allow themselves to become too attached to children whose hold on life was still fragile.

In twentieth-century America, decreased infant mortality, control of childhood diseases and vastly improved health conditions have rendered the death of a child a rare tragedy: at once a senseless waste, an affront to pride in medical progress and a haunting intimation of mortality. The child is not only regarded as a person from the moment of birth (or conception as is often evidenced in arguments against abortion), he is often seen as the center of the family unit, the natural recipient of extensive care and the tangible representation of the hopes of those around him. There is considerable variety in contemporary styles of child-rearing, but, common to most, is the dedication of adults to protect their children from all that is harmful. And, as one might have predicted from studies of adult attitudes, the discussion of death has most often been considered as something harmful, thereby requiring protection for children. Indeed the taboo against the discussion of death with children has been so effective that as Simon Yudkin notes in his paper, "Children and Death," children today know more about their origin than their end.

There is more than parental tenderness, however, that restrains the discussion of death with children, and makes even less likely the discussion of the child's own death. Such a discussion poses a threat to one's own hold on life. Faced with the death of a parent, or a friend, a person recognizes the possibility of his own death, but when confronted with the death of a child (someone who has shared fewer years), the arbitrary power of death becomes unavoidable. The person is forced to concede not only that he *will* die at some time, but that he *might die at any time.*

Current Research

Thus, it comes as no surprise that widespread study of children and death followed well after studies of the dying adult were conducted. Recent work on the subject of children and death has taken three forms: research in the social sciences directed to an understanding of children's conceptions of death and their mourning reactions, medical studies oriented to improved reflections in treatment for terminally ill children and popular children's literature and films which have been designed to bring their presentations of death to children into line with the best available research.

Research in the Social Sciences

As developmental psychology has moved from a normative to a structural approach, beginning with renewed interest in the studies of Jean Piaget, considerable research into the child's formation of the concepts of *life* and *death* has followed. Sylvia Anthony (1940, 1972), observing school-age children's play and fantasy found death a common theme, and the child's discovery of death to be simply an incident in the normal day-to-day process by which a child explores his environment. Maria Nagy, working in Hungary, traced a developmental sequence in children's theories concerning the nature of death. Nagy found that the child who, at the age of four, might pour water on a dead animal to "make it alive," grows into the six-year-old, telling tales of the boogeyman, and then becomes the nine-year-old, at once forced to accept the inevitability of death and ready to mock it with jokes and gestures.

But to say that the child's discovery of death in the abstract is more exploratory than emotional is not to suggest that children feel little emotional response to particular deaths. On the contrary, when a child loses a significant person in his life, Shambaugh (1961) warns that "every defense will be mobilized to ward off the impact and that every new object relationship as it develops will be influenced by the fact that an earlier one was lost." Agreement on the child's capacity to mourn, however, is not unanimous. According to Martha Wolfenstein, the young child, though he may be aware of death, is not developmentally ready to begin the work of mourning. She suggests that adolescence, a period when the individual comes to see time as irreversible, and when he gives up a major love object, his parents, is a trial mourning period and a necessary pre-condition to actual mourning. John Bowlby, however, suggests that mourning can be divided into three phases — protest, despair, and detachment — and that it may occur at least in its first phase, as early as six months of age. The research into the child's understanding of death and capacity to mourn has been joined recently by a growing number of observations of the dying child and his family in the hospital environment.

The Dying Child

The care of the dying child, or adolescent, presents a doctor with one of his most difficult tasks, yet as recently as 1968 William Easson, a child psychiatrist, noted that in most cases "the physician or physician-to-be was given little understanding of the management of the dying child." Though new research on the dying child is still scant, beginning in 1960, a small number of psychiatrists and pediatricians began documenting the dying child's awareness of impending death. In addition, they recognized that the child's awareness of his death was often

265

accompanied by withdrawal and denial of the diagnosis on the part of both parents and hospital staff. Currently, research into the support systems needed by the dying child and his family has burgeoned, resulting in a text on the subject and a hefty, internationally edited volume in child psychiatry.

Literature and Film

The past quarter century, which has been so productive in studies of child development, has been equally abundant in children's literature. At one time the subject of death was presented primarily to motivate children through fear to good behavior. Later it was avoided altogether.

> A little child
> That lightly draws its breath
> And feels its life in every limb
> What should it know of death?
> *Wordsworth*

It has more recently been presented in a realistic manner which acknowledges the child's understanding of death and often reflects the complexities of his reactions toward it.

Some works such as *Charlotte's Web* portray death as a necessary part of the cycle of nature; others like *Anna and the Old One* or *My Grandpa Died Today* present death within the family unit. A smaller portion are those books that represent the death of a child, for example, *A Taste of Blackberries* and *The Brothers Lionheart*. The interest in the presentation of death to children has not been confined to books, for both film and television portrayals have appeared in the past few years. So great has been the activity in this field, in fact, that the danger of exploitation of emotion, always present in marketing for children and equally likely in presentations of death for any audience, lurks dangerously close. To identify these works that will be most conducive to understanding, we must seek enduring simplicity, those books which Paul Hazards notes will "distill from all kinds of knowledge, the most difficult and the most necessary — that of the human heart."

ENCOUNTER

THE FIRST TIME SOMEBODY YOU KNEW DIED

The statements below are the recollections of elementary school children. Thinking back on your own childhood, when was the first time you encountered the death of somebody close to you? Picture the time, recalling who died. Was it a person or a pet? How old were you at the time? What did you think was the cause of death? Did that death make you worry about your own health or safety?

"I remember when I was five years old my uncle died. Then a lot of people came to the funeral and there was many flowers inside the box and outsi too. I got to tuch him and he was very cold then my mother told me why he was that cold. He was cold because some people take out al there things from inside. I went to tell someone els and he told me the same thing. And know I had believed her. Everybody was cring that my tears came out. Sins that time I did not want to go to a funeral ever again."

"When my granmather died I died too."

"My father went to Vietnam and he was Berly to go in the jungle and he step om pungy stikes and I was very sad sow they gave me all of his guns begde boots and his very owm money everybody loved him in the force so my mother crying and she told me that I was the man for the house."

"My Great grand father died when he was having a heart attack. My Great Grand mother was very sad and had to marry again."

"After a person is buride He will always be with you. And if you will not belief me ask your parents."

The selections on the preceding page were written by children between the ages of nine and twelve, the time when children begin to understand death as an irreversible and inevitable occurrence. The children's responses are typical in their simple realism, their puzzled efforts to understand what death means and their ultimate reliance on parental authority.

In 1948, Maria Nagy investigated the theories of death that children construct by conducting a field study of 378 children in Budapest. Nagy, a structuralist in the tradition of Piaget, hypothesized that children's theories about the nature of death would reflect changing states of development as the children matured. In her study she found that very young children do understand death though they understand it to mean something very different from the concepts of the older child or adult. The following paper outlines developmental stages in the child's evolving conception of death. Though Nagy herself refers to categories within her study as "stages," the categories are not mutually exclusive.

THE CHILD'S THEORIES
CONCERNING DEATH

Maria Nagy

INTRODUCTION

The Problem and Its History

Death is immemorial man's eternal problem. Life, the other great problem, gains its significance and its value only through death. Life and death are not two extremes, irreconcilable opposites which the human mind joins artificially into one formula. The relation between life and death is organic, for man as individual behaves in a quite identical way, that is, according to his nature, toward these two apparently contradictory facts.

Maria Nagy. "The Child's Theories Concerning Death." *Journal of Genetic Psychology*, LXXIII (1948), 3-27. (Vol. 73).

He who does not know how to live is also not capable of dying. And he who fears death is really terrified of life.

Every work on folk psychology which aims at being complete deals with not only the people's attitude toward life, but also its conception of death, as one is not to be understood without the other. Psychopathology is therefore concerned with the abnormal preoccupations with death, for only by abolishing these can a healthy behavior in life be attained. Psychologists, working with the age of adolescence, fundamentally examine everything which turns the adolescent attention toward death, for just those apparently inhibiting factors indicate the resolution of new life vigors.

Child psychology in the last half century has carried out research in every phase of the child's life, but cognizance of the child's conception of death is still isolated. Yet it is quite certain that the child connects life and death, indeed it is just in childhood that the individual develops his behavior in respect to death.

If we wish to investigate experimentally the child's attitude toward death, the theme must necessarily be divided into detailed questions. Among the questions connected with death, in the present study I wish to deal with only one. *What does the child think death to be, what theory does he construct of the nature of death?*

According to Reik's observations, the child thinks of death as temporary and gradual. Chadwick analyzes more the child's feelings in relation to death, not the understanding rendered by a definition of death. Graber found that to the child death and sleep were the same, so death is not known for what it is. Gerard carried out observations on three children. He also stated that death's finality was unknown to them. According to Stern, at the age of 10 death is not understood realistically; either they believe in physical survival, or in the Great Reaper. Wechsler and Schilder's experiments show that death is considered as a violent phenomenon. Cousinet investigates the idea of death genetically and distinguishes three stages. In the first stage the child denies death; in the second the truth is taken into account, he considers the process as similar to illness. Finally, in the third stage, it becomes quite concrete, the child considers it a peculiar process taking place in the living. It is unfortunate that these three stages were not indicated according to age and that he does not show their frequency. Finally, Weber deals with the recognition of the signs of death and finds that the child considers death a destroying-force which cuts him off from life and his family. In the literature of psychoanalysis there are many references to the child's attitude toward death, as it seeks the origin of all forms of behavior in childhood, hence the attitude toward death also. According to one of Freud's instinct-groupings which distinguishes the instinct of life and that of death, they are disposed to explain every manifestation of a person's life through its fundamental relationship to life and death. But his hypotheses tend rather toward the instinctive factors, they do not investigate the theories concerning the nature of death.

From the above it appears that further examination of the child's attitude toward death is necessary, as previous authors, with the exception of Cousinet, do not give the course of development and deal principally with feelings in connection with death. I, however, *wish to investigate, from the genetic standpoint, the theories concerning the nature of death of children from three to ten years of age.*

Method and Material

The material was assembled in three ways: (1) written compositions, (2) drawings, (3) discussions.

1. *Compositions* were written by children from seven to ten. I go into the class with the teacher. "Do you know why I have come, children? I know that you can write very nice compositions. I am curious about them. It will be a little strange, but certainly you will do it very cleverly. *Write down everything that comes into your minds about death.*" (I repeat slowly, twice.) It is not allowed to ask questions. Work time, one hour. The eventual questions and general attitudes are noted.

2. In one of the schools, after the compositions were finished, the children began of their own accord to make drawings

about death. This gave the idea of having separate drawings. The six to ten year olds did this in the same school. I announce that there will be secret drawing. "Who can cleverly separate himself from the others, so that no one can see what he is doing?" In an instant they surround themselves with their satchels, with their blocks. It is not necessary to give special instructions, they themselves discover how to sketch death. The bigger ones wrote an explanation of the text (see drawing that follows).

THE FIRST DEATH

1. *The death-man.* "Smokes a pipe in his joy. He is happy if he has work, work received from the good God."

2. *The sun.* It is so black because "the sun is also in great mourning. In nice weather it looks on the world and sees what happens. In bad weather the good God tells him." The child also personifies the sun. The world is for people. The duty of the sun is to follow people with its attention. Cosmic factors also take part in human suffering.

3. *Weeping willow.* "It is sad because it is beside a grave, that is why it keeps its branches lowered. Since the first man died it has always been sad." The ideas are explained by the same factors as in the case of the sun.

4. *Eva.* Weeps for the dead. In her handkerchief is the little girl's monogram.

5. *Guardian-angel.* 6. *Mourning angel.* Not only man and nature but also supernatural beings take part in the mourning.

3. The discussions were made with two somewhat varying methods with three to six and seven to ten year olds. I began with the ten year olds and descended gradually, in order to accustom myself to their way of speaking, among the smaller ones. With the seven to ten year olds I talked separately, one by one, in a quiet place. I hide my writing behind some object so

that they do not see that I take notes of what they say. As introduction I merely say, "You wrote a very clever composition, that is why I called you here. It will be easier now than last time, because you needn't write, only talk. *Tell me all you can think of about death.*" If they were perplexed I encouraged them: "Just think, surely lots of interesting things will come to mind." I let them speak freely. If they said anything I had them explain it. With that I always take care that my questions are indefinite, that is to say, suggest nothing. I emphasize, it was not an interrogation, but the child's spontaneous expression artificially brought out. The aim of the questions posed was just, in fact, that I should know the exact meaning of the child's expressions and not give them an arbitrary interpretation.

When the child runs out of something to say I ask questions. The questions were assembled and composed on the basis of the compositions. The range of questions was as follows: (a) What is death? (b) Why do people die? (c) How can one recognize death? (d) Do you usually dream? Tell me about a dream about death! Naturally only those of the questions were put concerning which free discussion had not dealt.

Then I discuss with them the doubtful points in the composition and drawings if I have so far not got an answer about them. Finally I ask them, if any thing more has come to mind, to tell it.

With the three to six year olds the situation was more difficult as I had no composition on which to base the discussion. As at that age there is still no concentrated thinking, instead of direct announcement of the object I was obliged to choose an indirect route. And first of all I try to create some contact with the child. I ask him to tell me something, and perhaps I will tell him a story.

Then when I see the moment has arrived, I ask him to tell me about the *table.* If he understood the instructions he must then tell about the following words: *death, life, birth, brother.* Naturally I linger longest on the word death and try to get it discussed the most. When necessary I ask questions. My questions are the same as for the bigger children, only differently drawn up.[1]

The distribution of the experimental material is shown in Table 1.

TABLE 1

| Age | Distribution of material according to age | | | | | | | | |
	3	4	5	6	7	8	9	10	Total
Composition	–	–	–	–	63	81	93	57	294
Drawing	–	–	–	8	9	9	12	2	40
Discussion	7	13	16	26	32	23	29	5	151
Total	7	13	16	34	104	113	134	64	484

Thus we have a total of 484 protocols from 378 children, 51 per cent of the children were boys, 49 per cent girls. They are selected from different religions, different schools and social levels. The material was collected in Budapest and its environs.

RESULTS[2]

What is death? Among the children from three to ten the replies given to this question can be ranged in three groups. As the different sorts of answers can be found only at certain ages, one can speak of stages of development. The child of less than five years does not recognize death as an irreversible fact. In death it sees life. Between the ages of five and nine death is most often personified and thought of as a contingency. And in general only after the age of nine is it recognized that death is a process happening in us according to certain laws. The frequency of the three degrees in the different age limits is illustrated in Table 2 and Table 3.

TABLE 2 (N gives the frequency in absolute values)

| Age | What is death? (Composition) | | | | | | | | | |
| | 7 | | 8 | | 9 | | 10 | | Total | |
	N	%	N	%	N	%	N	%	N	%
2nd stage	12	92.3	21	91.3	27	71	4	16.7	65	65.3
3rd stage	1	7.7	2	8.7	11	29	20	83.3	34	34.7
Total	13	100	23	100	38	100	24	100	98	100

273

First Stage: There Is No Definitive Death

In the first stage the child does not know death as such. He attributes life and consciousness to the dead. There are two variations of this affirmation, which I discuss the one after the other. According to one group, death is a departure, a sleep. This entirely denies death. The other group already recognizes the fact of death but cannot separate it from life. For that reason it considers death either gradual or temporary.

TABLE 3

	What is death? (Discussion)									
Age	3		4		5		6		7	
	N	%	N	%	N	%	N	%	N	%
1st stage	6	85.7	7	50	6	33.3	2	7.8	–	–
2nd stage	1	14.3	7	50	12	66.7	21	80.7	19	57.6
3rd stage	–	–	–	–	–	–	3	11.5	14	42.4
Total	7	100	14	100	18	100	26	100	33	100

Age	8		9		10		Total	
	N	%	N	%	N	%	N	%
1st stage	–	–	–	–	–	–	21	12.9
2nd stage	14	53.8	16	53.3	2	22.8	92	56.4
3rd stage	12	46.2	14	46.7	7	77.8	50	30.7
Total	26	100	30	100	9	100	163	100

A. Death a departure, a sleep. B. Jolan (3, 11):[3] "The dead close their eyes because the sand gets into them."

The child had heard something about the eyes of the dead being closed. It explained this by an exterior cause. The dead person voluntarily, defensively, closes its eyes.

Sch. Tomy (4, 8): "It can't move because it's in the coffin."

"If it weren't in the coffin, could it?"

"It can eat and drink."

Like the first with the closing of the eyes, here too the immobility is the consequence of exterior compulsive circumstances. It doesn't move because the coffin does not permit it.

He considers the dead as still capable of taking nourishment.

Sch. Juliska (5, 10) had already seen a dead person. "Its eyes were closed, it lay there, so dead. No matter what one does to it, it doesn't say a word."

"After ten years will it be the same as when it was buried?"

"It will be older then, it will always be older and older. When it is 100 years old it will be exactly like a piece of wood."

"How will it be like a piece of wood?"

"That I couldn't say. My little sister will be five years old now. I wasn't alive yet when she died. She will be so big by this time. She has a small coffin, but she fits in the small coffin."

"What is she doing now, do you think?"

"Lying down, always just lies there. She's still so small, she can't be like a piece of wood. Only very old people."

In the beginning she sees the matter realistically. The dead person cannot speak. The closed eyes do not necessarily mean the cessation of sight. The dead person is compared to a piece of wood. In all probability she wanted thus to express immobility. Later it comes out that young people grow in the grave. The growth is not great. She says her sister is five years old because she herself is five.

B. Irèn (4, 11): "What happens there under the earth?"

"He cries because he is dead."

"But why should he cry?"

" Because he is afraid for himself."

She feels that death is bad. Perhaps she has had the experience of seeing the dead mourned. She transfers this sentiment to the dead themselves. They also mourn for themselves.

V. Juliska (5, 3): "What is your father doing now under the earth?"

"He lies there. Scratches the earth, to come up. To get a little air."

She knows of the reclining state of the dead. She imagines that in the earth it must be difficult to breathe. The dead person scratches the earth away, to get air.

T. Pintvöke (4, 10): "A dead person is just as if he were asleep. Sleeps in the ground, too."

"Sleeps the same as you do at night, or otherwise?"

"Well — closes his eyes. Sleeps like people at night. Sleeps like that, just like that."

"How do you know whether someone is asleep or is dead?"

"I know if they go to bed at night and don't open their eyes. If somebody goes to bed and doesn't get up, he's dead or ill."

"Will he ever wake up?"

"Never. A dead person only knows if somebody goes out to the grave or something. He feels that somebody is there, or is talking."

"Are you certain? You're not mistaken?"

"I don't think so. At funerals you're not allowed to sing, just talk, because otherwise the dead person couldn't sleep peacefully. A dead person feels it if you put something on his grave."

"What is it he feels then?"

"He feels that flowers are put on his grave. The water touches the sand. Slowly, slowly, he hears everything. Auntie, does the dead person feel it if it goes deep into the ground?" (i.e. the water).

"What do you think, wouldn't he like to come away from there?"

"He would like to come out, but the coffin is nailed down."

"If he weren't in the coffin, could he come back?"

"He couldn't root up all that sand."

Death is on the one hand identified with sleep, on the other hand is supposed to be in connection with the outside world. The dead person has knowledge of what goes on in the world. It does not merely think, but also feels.

B. Evi (6,5): "Between sleeping and death there isn't any difference."

She identifies sleep and death.

J. Mancika (3, 11): "What does he do, since he is in the coffin?"

"Sleeps. Covered with sand. It's dark there."

"Does he sleep as we do at night, or differently?"

"He puts sand there, lies on it. If you die the bed will be sandy, then the sheet will be black."

The dead person lives, as he himself prepares the sleeping place. The grave is a bed, the dead person also has sheets. Death is sleep.

H. Gàspàr (8, 5):[4] "People think dead persons can feel."

"And can't they?"

"No, they can't feel, like sleep. Now, I sleep, I don't feel it, except when I dream."

"Do we dream when we're dead?"

"I think we don't. We never dream when we're dead. Sometimes something flashes out, but not half as long as a dream."

"What flashes out?"

"Some little kind of thought, some little kind of dream. Pictures disappear in front of him. But they're so short, much less than when we're asleep."

This child has at times a quite realistic conception of death. He states definitely that the dead do not feel nor think. Later, however, he thinks that thoughts and pictures flash out before the dead person.

F. Robi (9, 11): "I was six years old. A friend of my father's died. They didn't tell me, but I heard. Then I didn't understand. I felt as when Mother goes traveling somewhere — I don't see her any more."

He feels the same about news of death as about traveling. The dead person resembles the absent, in that he sees neither of them.

Summary. As we see, in general these children do not accept death. To die means the same as living on, under changed circumstances.

Death is thus a departure. If someone dies no change takes place in him. Our lives change, inasmuch as we see him no longer, he lives with us no longer.

This, however, does not mean that the children have no disagreeable sentiments in relation to death, because for them the most painful thing about death is just the separation itself.[5]

To the child the association Death-Departure exists also in the inverse sense. If anyone goes away it thinks him dead. Jaehner states that his children thought that whenever their father went away they were going to bury him, as they already knew the connection between death and burial.

Most children, however, are not satisfied, when someone dies, that he should merely disappear, but want to know where and how he continues to live. As all the children questioned knew of funerals, they connected the facts of absence and funerals. In the cemetery one lives on. Movement is to a certain degree limited by the coffin, but for all that the dead are still capable of growth. They take nourishment, they breathe. They know what is happening on earth. They feel it, if someone thinks of them, and they even feel sorry for themselves. Thus the dead live in the grave. Most children, however, feel too — and have therefore an aversion for death — that life is limited, not so complete as our life. Some of them consider this diminished life exclusively restricted to sleep. While here they identify death with dreams, from seven years on they liken it to sleep. But as the child's sense of reality increases, the more it feels and knows the difference between the two.

According to psychoanalysis, to the unconscious sleep and death are the same. Both satisfy the desire to return into the mother's womb. In death and in sleep the separation stops and the unity with the mother, which was complete in the intra-uterine life, is restored. In the child both are the same, because in him the desire is more openly shown than in adults and the so-called "birth trauma" is still fresh.

In primitive peoples too we find widespread examples of the identification of death and sleep. The natives of West Africa, for example, have no special word for sleep. The verb for sleep is written "to be half dead." If the dead live they think it principally in that in dreams they can return and visit us. And the extent to which death to them is merely a removal is also shown by the fact that in very many places food and drink are put beside the deceased, and even clothing and arms. Servants and wives are buried with them, that there should be someone to look aften them in the after-life.

But even within our cultural regions these primitive forms are often found, if not otherwise than in our expressions. If someone dies we say he has "passed on." The deceased returns to his dear "mother-earth." We "take our leave" of the dead, wish him "peaceful repose." And if our feelings were consistent, that there was only a dead body in the grave, our funeral rites would lose much of their meaning.

Finally I must answer the question, what impels the children to the denial of death? What endeavour brings about the identification of death with departure, or with sleep? In early infancy, that is, under five, its desires guide the child even at the price of modifying the reality. Opposition to death is so strong that the child denies death, as emotionally it cannot accept it.

B. Death is gradual, temporary. There are among children of five and six those who no longer deny death, but who are still unable to accept it as a definitive fact. They acknowledge that death exists but think of it as a gradual or temporary thing.

L. Bandika (5, 6): "His eyes were closed."

"Why?"

"Because he was dead."

"What is the difference between sleeping and dying?"

"Then they bring the coffin and put him in it. They put the hands like this when a person is dead."

"What happens to him in the coffin?"

"The worms eat him. They bore into the coffin."

"Why does he let them eat him?"

"He can't get up any longer, because there is sand on him. He can't get out of the coffin."

"If there weren't sand on him, could he get out?"

"Certainly, if he wasn't very badly stabbed. He would get his hand out of the sand and dig. That shows that he still wants to live."

In the beginning the child sees realistically. He does not say, like the previous children, that "he closes his eyes," but that the eyes were closed. He sees only exterior differences between sleep and death. This would again be evidence of a denial of death, if immediately afterwards he had not begun to speak of worms. He does not state that the dead cannot move, merely that the sand hinders them in moving. On the other hand, he attributes a desire for life to the dead person — though only when he is not "very badly killed." Thus there are degrees of death.

T. Dezsö (6, 9): "My sister's godfather died and I took hold of his hand. His hand was so cold. It was green and blue. His face was all wrinkled together. He can't move. He can't clench his hands, because he is dead. And he can't breathe."

"His face?"

"It has goose-flesh, because he is cold. He is cold because he is dead and cold everywhere."

"Does he feel the cold or was it just that his skin was like that?"

"If he is dead he feels too. If he is dead he feels a tiny little bit. When he is quite dead he no longer feels anything."

Again the explanation begins realistically. The dead person cannot move or breathe. Quite cold. He explains the cause of the cold childishly. He is cold because it is chilly. He feels the cold, however, only when not entirely dead. This has no relation to the process of the death agony, as he saw his sister's godfather only at the funeral.

That gradualness in death is not merely a matter of insufficiency of expression and is not related to the processes of death can be seen from the case of a ten year old, to whom this early childish impression remained as an incoherent element in what otherwise was an entirely realistic conception:

"Until he disappears from the earth he knows everything. Until they have thrown three shovels-ful, three handsful of earth on him, he knows if they say anything about him."

In the beginning he describes realistically the physical changes which take place in death and then, after all, states that until he is put into the earth the dead person knows everything. Thus the time between dying and being buried is a transitory state between life and death.

Pr. Ibolya (5): "His eyes were shut."

"Why?"

"Because he couldn't open them. Because he is in the coffin. Then, when he wakes up, then they take him out of the coffin. They put somebody else in."

"When they take him out of the coffin what happens to him?"

"If I die my heart doesn't beat."

In death the action of the heart stops. On the other hand, she states too that death is sleep. But not eternal sleep, because the dead person awakens.

280

Gr. Pityu (6): "He stretched out his arms and lay down. You couldn't push down his arms. He can't speak. He can't move. Can't see. Can't open his eyes. He lies for four days."

"Why for four days?"

"Because the angels don't know yet where he is. The angels dig him out, take him with them. They give him wings and fly away."

"What stays in the cemetery?"

"Only the coffin stays down there. Then people go there and dig it up. They take out the coffin for it to be there if somebody dies. If they couldn't make one quickly it would be there. They clear it up, good and bright."

"What happens to him in Heaven?"

"If it's a woman, she does the cleaning. If it's a man, then he'll be an angel. He brings Xmas trees . . . bakes cakes in the sky and brings toys. It's bad to go to Heaven, because you have to fly. It's a good thing to be in Heaven. You can't get wet, don't get soaked if it rains. It only rains on the earth."

"Well, what are you going to do if you ever get there?"

"I'm going to bake cakes, the whole year. Each angel has got his own stove."

"Won't there be an awful lot of cakes, if you bake the whole year round?"

"Lots of houses. Lots of children. If the cakes are done we can play hide-and-seek. Then the children hide in the clouds. You can hide very well up there. One flies up, the other flies down."

He describes death realistically. The activities of life are missing. He says that one remains only four days in the tomb, then goes to heaven.[6] Thus death lasts four days. He imagines heavenly life in a quite childish way. They play and eat cakes. The question of rain came up because there was a great rainfall at the time of the questioning, he got wet and went home from the kindergarten.

Summary. As we see, the children of the second group already accept death to a certain extent. The distinction between life and death is, however, not complete. If they think of death as gradual, life and death are in simultaneous relation; if it is temporary, life and death can change with one another repeatedly.

These conceptions are of a higher order than that which entirely denies death. Here, namely, the distinction between the two processes has already begun. Furthermore, beside their desires the feeling for reality also plays a role. Thus occurs the compromise solution, that while death exists it is not definitive.

Rivers tells of similar experiences in the Solomon Islands. There is a word — the "mate" — which they translate as death, though it cannot be used as the contrary of "toa," which is the expression for life. "Mate" is not only the dead person but the dying, even the old and the sick, those who, in the opinion of the natives, should already have died. "Mate"-ness is a state which can last for years. It is not the period before death, because for them there is no death but a transition between the two modes of existence. The person designated as in a state of "mate" is accorded funeral rites. Thus with them the burial is not the burial of the dead body but a festive transposition from the "toa" state into the "mate" state. It is a great turning point in life, one of several, such as for instance pubescence, the founding of a family. As we see, in this conception life and death are confused just as in the children's ideas.

Second Stage: Death—a Man

In the second stage the child personifies death. This conception is to be found in the whole of childhood, but seems characteristic between the ages of five and nine. The personification of death takes place in two ways. Death is imagined as a separate person, or else death is identified with the dead. When death is imagined as a separate person we again find two conceptions. Either "the reaper" idea is accepted, or a quite individual picture is formed of the death—man. The ways of personifying death are shown, in respect to their frequency, in Table 4.

TABLE 4

Personification of death		
	Discussion	Composition
Distinct person: the reaper	31 } 67	27 } 49
original	36	22
The dead	31	16
Total	98	65

Br. Marta (6,7): "Carries off bad children. Catches them and takes them away."

"What is he like?"

"White as snow. Death is white everywhere. It's wicked. It doesn't like children."

"Why?"

"Because it's bad-hearted. Death even takes away men and women too."

"Why?"

"Because it doesn't like to see them."

"What is white about it?"

"The skeleton. The bone-skeleton."

"But in reality is it like that, or do they only say so."

"It really is, too. Once I talked about it and at night the real death came. It has a key to everywhere, so it can open the doors. It came in, messed about everywhere. It came over to the bed and began to pull away the covers. I covered myself up well. It couldn't take them off. Afterwards it went away."

"You only pretend it was there. It wasn't really there."

"I was ill then. I didn't go to the kindergarten. A little girl always came up. I always quarreled with her. One night it came. I always took raisins, though it was forbidden."

"Did you tell your mother?"

"I didn't dare to tell my mother, because she is anyhow afraid of everything."

"And your father?"

"Papa said it was a tale from the benzine tank. I told him it wasn't any fairy-tale."

In the description of the skeleton-man his color is important. He carries people off because he is bad-hearted. So dying is considered a bad thing. Death was seen in feverish dreams. Since then she is convinced that it exists. Talk of death causes its magical advent. Death came too because she had done wrong. So there is a relationship between sin and death.

K. Karoly (7, 8): "Death is a living being and takes people's souls away. Gives them over to God. Death is the king of the dead. Death lives in the cemetery and can be seen only when he carries off some persons's soul. There is a soul in death."

"How do you mean that?"

"He can go where he likes."

"What is death like?"

"White. Made of a skeleton. It's covered with a white sheet."

"How do you know it's like that?"

"Because once I saw a play and I saw it there."

"And in reality death is like that?"

"Alive he couldn't be drawn, because there isn't any such man who is made only of a skeleton. Who wants to can't see him and who doesn't want to sees him."

"How do you know it's like that?"

"It has already been experienced."

"People didn't just make it up? It's truly so?"

"It's really like that."

Death is king and in the service of God. Only the dying can see him. The ability to move about derives from the soul. He considers death impossible to draw.

P. Géza (8, 6): "Death comes when somebody dies, and comes with a scythe, cuts him down and takes him away. When death goes away it leaves footprints behind. When the footprints disappeared it came back and cut down more people. And then they wanted to catch it, and it disappeared."

Death is so much a person that it even leaves footprints. Like a child, it teases people. He wants to exterminate death.

B. Tibor (9,11): "Death is a skeleton. It is so strong it could overturn a ship. Death can't be seen. Death is in a hidden place. It hides in an island."

He thinks of death in fairy-tale style. It hides on an island. Its strength is tremendous. Death is invisible. He doesn't say whether it is invisible of itself or whether it is only that people don't see it.

V. Peter (9, 11): "Death is very dangerous. You never know what minute he is going to carry you off with him. Death is invisible, something nobody has ever seen in all the world. But at night he comes to everybody and carries them off with him. Death is like a skeleton. All the parts are made of bone. But then when it begins to be light, when it's morning, there's not a trace of him. It's that dangerous, death."

"Why does it go about at night?"

"Because then nobody is up and it can come undisturbed."

"Is it afraid of people?"

"No. It doesn't want people to see it."

"Why?"

"Because they would be frightened of it."

Death is invisible because it goes about at night. Others imagine death as ill-intentioned; this child supposes it to have good intentions. It goes about secretly because it does not want to frighten people.

V. Imre (7, 7): "What is death? A ghost. Invisibility. Ugly. Full of skeletons."

"Is the skeleton invisible?"

"The skeleton doesn't show because it is invisible too. When one draws the skeleton then it can be seen."

Death is a person. Why the skeleton is invisible and how the invisibility can be drawn, he doesn't say.

B. Gyuszika (4,9): "Death does wrong."

"How does it do wrong?"

"Stabs you to death with a knife."

"What is death?"

"A man."

"What sort of a man?"

"Death-man."

"How do you know?"

"I saw him."

"Where?"

"In the grass. I was gathering flowers."

"How did you recognize him?"

"I knew him."

"But how?"

"I was afraid of him."

"What did your mother say?"

"Let us go away from here. Death is here."

He imagines death as a man whom he saw when gathering flowers. He could be recognized by his fearfulness. Afterwards he says he would like to know death's address; he would go and shoot him. Kill the death-man, that we should not die is the children's reiterated desire.

K. Pityu (6, 1): "Puts on a white coat, and a death-face."

"Who?"

"Death. Frightens children."

"Has he frightened you already?"

"I'm not afraid. I know it's just a man who has put on a death-face. He was in the circus once."

"Now don't tell me about that man, but about real death. What is death, really?"

"Real death? I don't know. It has big eyes and white clothes. It has long legs, long arms."

"But that's not really death. That is an 'uncle' dressed up like death."

"No. I went to church. I saw the real death. He went toward the Nepliget (a park)."

"You are mistaken. That was a man dressed up like death."

"But death has eyes as big as the squares on this table. Death is also only a man, only it has bigger eyes."

Death is the same as an actual, existing person. He can be recognized by his big eyes.[7] At one time he can distinguish death from that which he sketches, at other times he cannot. The circus plays a large role in the formation of ideas of death of children in the suburbs.

Sz. Daisy (8, 3): "It's like a man."

"How?"

"Well, when its time comes it dies. Then it comes down from Heaven and takes him away."

"Who?"

"Death?"

"It's like a man?"

"Sort of like a man. Lives up in Heaven."

"Is death good?"

"I think it's bad, because it stops people from living."

"In what is it like a man?"

"It's like a man in its body. In its way of thinking it's different. People think that death is bad. Then death thinks now it is going to do good if it takes people up to Heaven."

"Then does it think too that it is doing good when it takes people to Hell?"

"No. People are afraid of death, but death isn't afraid of

itself. It certainly takes them up in some kind of carriage. It surely takes a lot of people at a time. So it couldn't take them otherwise than in a carriage."

Death is a man, living in Heaven. In body he resembles mankind, in thought he is different.

B. Ildiko (7, 11): "Death can't be seen, like the angels can't be seen, because they are spirits. I imagine death is a bad man's skeleton brought to life."

"How do you mean?"

"A spirit like that. If you catch him it's like air."

"Is it different somehow from our souls?"

"Once death died. And then it was a bad man's soul. It kills people once they are very old."

"Only old people?"

"If they are ill. Death gives illness, and bacilli, too."

"Why did that man become death?"

"Because he was a specially, terribly bad man. He did every sort of wickedness. He stole, and everything all his life. God wanted that he should be death."

"Why is death a spirit?"

"Death has to have a soul too, so he can move, because if people hadn't souls they couldn't move."

"How is it different from our souls?"

"I don't know. Somehow I can't express it. Death is a skeleton and a soul. A person is skeleton, soul and skin. There's flesh on him."

Death is temporary, otherwise a dead person could not be brought to life. Death became death as a punishment. The death-man spreads illness. The soul is the principle of motion. Quite an individual idea. A tendency to fabulizing is apparent, but belief in the personal nature of death is a serious conviction.

H. Gabriella (7, 9): "Whoever dies the death angels carry away. The death angels are great enemies of people. Death is the king of the angels. Death commands the angels. The angels work for death."

Death is the angels' king.

T. Stefi (7, 6): "What is death? A ghost. You can't see him, he just comes, like that. Like something that flies in the air."

"What is a ghost?"

"Somebody invisible. An invisible man. In the form of a ghost. Comes in the air."

Death is an invisible man, that is, a ghost.

Szm. Gyula (8, 3): "Death is not a living person, it takes away the souls of the dead. It keeps watch over the dead. Death is like a spirit. Death doesn't go about by day, but by night."

"What is that, a spirit?"

"An invisible person."

"Why invisible?"

"Because he isn't dressed and doesn't go among people."

"Why does he go about only at night?"

"Because by day he can't go among people."

"Why?"

"Because they would be frightened of him."

"Aren't they frightened of him at night?"

"They aren't afraid of him at night because at night people sleep. Death isn't a living person."

"What is it then?"

"Death is alive, too."

Death being a person not living means that it is invisible, as it goes about at night.

M. Imre (9, 9): "They always draw death with a skeleton and a black cloak. In reality you can't see him. In reality he's only a sort of spirit. Comes and takes people away, he doesn't care whether it's a beggar or a king. If he wants to, he makes them die."

"What is that, a sort of spirit?"

"You can't see him."

He makes a distinction between drawing and the reality, but still personifies death. Death is a spirit. In this he understands the same as the others in spirit, or ghost, that is, invisible.

Sz. Marianne (9, 7): "He takes people's lives."

"How?"

"Not the way they always draw it. He comes there."

"What is death?"

"It is a spirit that doesn't exist. It isn't on earth either, it's in the sky. People don't see it. It is an invisible spirit."

"Spirit?"

"You can't see it. It's air."

She does not accept the usual drawings of death. Death is a spirit and invisible. In the sky. She says it is non-existing because it has no body.

H. Gàspàr (8, 5): "I don't think it's the same as in the picture. The reality is different from the picture. Only people die, there isn't any death itself. I don't know if it's alive, if it is a person. If it is a man it is like the woodcutter. It has a white cloak on, a scythe in its hand, as one imagines it in a picture. It's not something you can see."

"In reality what is it like?"

"I think it is only a picture. But perhaps in reality too it is a sort of invisible person. I'm not sure if there is really any such thing."

"If there is, where is it?"

"Spirit forms haven't any country."

"Haven't angels either?"

"Yes, but they are good spirits. I only mean the bad ones. Bad men haven't any home. They come and go, wander about, loiter around, doing damage."

"Is death a bad spirit?"

"Yes."

"Why?"

"Because somehow it's cold. I imagine it would be terrible if you saw it. You would kneel down, implore it, pray to it, and still death would make you die. I've often imagined I ran away from death."

"How, ran away?"

"In my room, by myself, I imagine it. I don't dare to go out. I shut the door after myself, so he can't catch me. It's as if he were there. I play like that, often."

"Is it a game?"

"I don't know. I often pretend about him."

"Are you afraid, when you are alone?"

"No, I just pretend to myself."

"The whole thing isn't true?"

"No."

"Why are you afraid, if it isn't true?"

"Somehow I'm afraid. Death is the most powerful lord in

the world, except the good God. Death is a companion of the devil. Death is like a ghost. If death has servants then the ghosts are its servants. If death dances, then a lot of ghosts come in white cloaks and dance the ghost-dance. It could be so beautiful."

"What would be beautiful about it?"

"I don't know, but there's something so beautiful about it. Something so suitable. Death and ghosts go together, like fairies and angels. Spirits and the devil go together with death. But the most terrible of all is death."

"Do you often think of death?"

"I often do. But such things as when I fight with death and hit him on the head, and death doesn't die. Death hasn't got wings."

"Why?"

"I imagine somehow that he hasn't. The angels have, and the fairies in the stories, but death hasn't. But he can fly, for all that. He can fly without wings, too. Death has got some kind of invisible wings. In reality they can't be seen."

In the beginning he denies that death is a personal reality, then after all imagines it. These are characteristic day-fantasies. He runs away from death, hits it on the head, but it doesn't die.

Sz. Jozsef (9, 10): Already accepts death quite realistically. He tells how at home he always plays ghosts with the smaller children. He shakes the bushes and says that death is going about there. On that the small children run away, while he gathers up their toys and the whole playground is his. He stretches cords so the little ones cannot come back. After, all, what happened to him once?

"I stayed there, lying on the ground. I fell into the cord myself. I stayed for a quarter of an hour lying on the ground. Only later I dared to get up. I was afraid that death was really there and perhaps I would die too."

He doesn't believe in the death-man, and yet he began to be afraid of him in an evening's play. Fifteen per cent of the children questioned stated that they were accustomed to think about death at evening. They supposed, therefore, a relationship between death and darkness. This connects with the examples already mentioned, where the children often imagine that it is "usual" to die at night. The deathman also principally goes about at night.

The third form of personification of death is when death is identified with the dead. This group consequently uses the word for death in place of the word for the dead person. This is the more extraordinary, as in Hungarian the two words are essentially different and even in sound could never be confounded as in other languages (Der Tot — tot; la mort — mort; death — the dead). The word for dead person instead of the word for death occurs in every discussion, every writing.

W. Làszlo (6, 8): "It is a superstition about death, because it doesn't go about at night, anywhere. It's in its coffin. Death isn't true. It isn't true that it goes about on earth and cuts people down."

"Then where is it?"

"It's in the coffin, always. Death lies in the coffin."

He doesn't believe in death as a distinct personality. He identifies death and dead people.

A. Carla (7, 11): "Death can't speak, nor move. I was often at the cemetery. It's very sad."

"What is sad?"

"When I see a grave there's a death in it. That's sad."

"Is death in the grave, or a dead person?"

"A dead person. . .I never saw death, only heads and bones."

"What is death?"

"A dead person, who hasn't any flesh any more, only bones."

According to her twin brother, Béla: "Death is a skeleton."

"Is it real, or is it only that one makes an image like that of it?"

"It exists, too. If a person dies, that will be death."

Death as identified with the dead exists for both twins.

B. Miklos (8, 2): "Death can't talk. Death can't talk, because it isn't alive. Death has no mind. Death can't think because there isn't any mind in him. Death can't write because there isn't any soul in him. Death can't read because there is no living soul in him."

"What is the difference between death and the dead?"

No answer.

"What are the dead?"

"The person who dies."

"What is death?"

No reply.

In a childish way he describes in detail all the things the dead cannot do. His ideas of life and soul are confused. He cannot express the difference between death and the dead, nor define death.

E. Laci (8, 8): "What is death? A being, dead of old age or illness."

Complete identification.

M. Mària (9, 6): "What is death? Soul. I, if I die too, I am soul, not a body."

Death is again identified with the dead person. Diverging from the usual, she considers characteristic not the destruction of the body but the endurance of the soul.

Summary. In the second stage of development, in general between five and nine, the children personify death in some form. Two-thirds of the children belonging to this group imagine death as a distinct personality. Either they believe in the reality of the skeleton-man, or individually create quite their own idea of the death-man. They say the death-man is invisible. This means two things. Either it is invisible in itself, as it is a being without a body or it is only that we do not see him because he goes about in secret, mostly at night. They also state that death can be seen for a moment before, by the person he carries off.

Compared with the first stage, where death is denied, here we find an increase in the sense of reality as contrary to their desires. The child already accepts the existence of death, that is its definitiveness. On the other hand, he has such an aversion to the thought of death that he casts it away. From a process which takes place in us death grows to a reality outside us. It exists but is remote from us. As it is remote our death is not inevitable. Only those die whom the death-man catches and carries off. Whoever can get away does not die.

Of the children in the second stage of development again one-third thought of death as a person and identified it with the dead. These children use the word death for the dead. In this conception, too, is evident a desire to keep death at a distance. Death is still outside us and is also not general.

It is surprising how little the literature on this subject deals with the personification of death, though the tendency to personify is in general well known at certain stages of a child's development. Only E. Stern mentions it concerning ten year olds but does not see its universal significance nor deal with its motives.

Third Stage: Death the Cessation of Corporal Activities

In general it is only after the age of nine that the child reaches the point of recognizing that in death is the cessation of corporal life. When he reaches the point where death is a process operating within us he recognizes its universal nature.

F. Eszter (10): "It means the passing of the body. Death is a great squaring of accounts in our lives. It is a thing from which our bodies cannot be resurrected. It is like the withering of flowers."

Death is the destruction of the body. She mixes the natural explanation with the moral, also considers death a reckoning.

Cz. Gyula (9, 4): "Death is the termination of life. Death is destiny. Then we finish our earthly life. Death is the end of life on earth."

He expresses its regularity by the word destiny.

F. Gàbor (9, 11): "A skull portrays death. If somebody dies they bury him and he crumbles to dust in the earth. The bones crumble later, and so the skeleton remains altogether, the way it was. That is why death is portrayed by a skeleton. Death is something that no one can escape. The body dies, the soul lives on."

He knows that the portrayal of death is not death itself. Indeed, he also explains why the skeleton became the symbol of death. Death is universal.

Sz. Tamàs (9, 4): "What is death? Well, I think it is a part of a person's life. Like school. Life has many parts. Only one part of it is earthly. As in school we go on to a different class. To die means to begin a new life. Everyone has to die once, but the soul lives on."

It is comprehensible; he sees eternal mystery beyond the physical changes.

SUMMARY

I investigated how children from three to ten think of death. I employed written compositions, drawings, and discussion alike in collecting the data, and 484 protocols from 378 children were at my disposition. In the present study the material has not been fully worked up; I only desired to answer the question of what death is to the child, what theories he constructs as to the nature of death. I found three stages of development. The first is characteristic of children between three and five. They deny death as a regular and final process. Death is a departure, a further existence in changed circumstances. There are ideas too that death is temporary. Indeed distinction is made of degrees of death.

The child knows itself as a living being. In his egocentric way he imagines the outside world after his own fashion, so in the outside world he also imagines everything, lifeless things and dead people alike, as living. Living and lifeless are not yet distinguished. He extends this animism to death too.

In the second stage, in general between the ages of five and nine, death is personified, considered a person. Death exists but the children still try to keep it distant from themselves. Only those die whom the death-man carries off. Death is an eventuality. There also occur fantasies, though less frequently, where death and the dead are considered the same. In these cases they consistently employ the word death for the dead. Here death is still outside us and not universal. The egocentric, otherwise called anthropocentric, view, therefore, plays a role not only in the birth of animism, but in the formation of artificialism too. Every event and change in the world derives from man. If in general death exists, it is a person, the death-man, who "does" it. We get no answer, naturally, as to why, if death is bad for people, he does it.

Finally, in the third stage, in general around nine years, it is recognized that death is a process which takes place in us, the perceptible result of which is the dissolution of bodily life. By then they know that death is inevitable. At this age not only the conception as to death is realistic, but also their general view of the world. Negatively this means that animistic and artificialistic tendencies are not characteristic and egocentrism is also much less.

As we see, the theory the child makes of death faithfully reflects at each stage a general picture of its world. To conceal death from the child is not possible and is also not permissible. Natural behavior in the child's surroundings can greatly diminish the shock of its acquaintance with death.

NOTES

1. In the schools I frequented the most I everywhere got the name "Auntie Death," though the schools had no connection with one another.

2. In the present study I do not give the complete results of the material collected, only that dealing with the nature of death.

3. The age is significant. The child was past 3 years and 11 months old.

4. The age of the children who took part equally in written composition and discussion was reckoned from the time of writing the composition. The discussions took place three months later than the compositions.

5. As control I asked 30 older children what was the most terrible thing about death, and they all answered that it was the separation.

6. This is not belief in a life in the world beyond, but simply living on, because while the former know about the body's dissolution, the latter fantasy does not know it.

7. This child also has remarkably large eyes. Many of them drew the death-person as themselves.

In the selection from James Agee's Pulitzer Prize-winning novel, A Death in the Family, *two children work to understand the sudden death of their father, a tragedy that has effectively disordered their universe. The children mull over the explanations given them by adults and pool their own reflections to conclude that God, the death-man, has carried their father off. In the following discussion between the children and their Aunt Hannah, Catherine typifies the response of a young child as she listens to all the explanations yet denies the finality of death with her question, "When is Daddy coming home?" Rufus, for his part, moves toward a more mature understanding of death as physical cessation when he realizes that it was not God, but a concussion that killed his father.*

selection from
A DEATH IN THE FAMILY

James Agee

Catherine did not like being buttoned up by Rufus or bossed a-round by him, and breakfast wasn't like breakfast either. Aunt Hannah didn't say anything and neither did Rufus and neither did she, and she felt that even if she wanted to say anything she oughtn't. Everything was queer, it was so still and it seemed dark. Aunt Hannah sliced the banana so thin on the Post Toasties it looked cold and wet and slimy. She gave each of them a little bit of coffee in their milk and she made Rufus' a little bit darker than hers. She didn't say, "Eat"; "Eat your breakfast, Catherine"; "Don't dawdle," like Catherine's mother; she didn't say anything. Catherine did not feel hungry, but she felt mildly curious because things tasted so different, and she ate slowly ahead, tasting each mouthful. Everything was so still that it made Catherine feel uneasy and sad. There were little noises when a fork or spoon touched a dish; the only other noise was the very thin dry toast Aunt Hannah kept slowly crunching and the fluttering sipping of the steamy coffee with which she wet each mouthful of dry crumbs enough to swallow it. When Catherine tried to make a similar noise sipping her milk, her Aunt

Hannah glanced at her sharply as if she wondered if Catherine was trying to be a smart aleck but she did not say anything. Catherine was not trying to be a smart aleck but she felt she had better not make that noise again. The fried eggs had hardly any pepper and they were so soft the yellow ran out over the white and the white plate and looked so nasty she didn't want to eat it but she ate it because she didn't want to be told to and because she felt there was some special reason, still, why she ought to be a good girl. She felt very uneasy, but there was nothing to do but eat, so she always took care to get a good hold on her tumbler and did not take too much on her spoon, and hardly spilled at all, and when she became aware of how little she was spilling it made her feel like a big girl and yet she did not feel any less uneasy, because she knew there was something wrong. She was not as much interested in eating as she was in the way things were, and listening carefully, looking mostly at her plate, every sound she heard and the whole quietness which was so much stronger than the sounds, meant that things were not good. What it was was that he wasn't here. Her mother wasn't either, but she was upstairs. He wasn't even upstairs. He was coming home last night but he didn't come home and he wasn't coming home now either, and her mother felt so awful she cried, and Aunt Hannah wasn't saying anything, just making all that noise with the toast and big loud sips with the coffee and swallowing, *grrmmp,* and then the same thing over again and over again, and every time she made the noise with the toast it was almost scary, as if she was talking about some awful thing, and every time she sipped it was like crying or like when Granma sucked in air between her teeth when she hurt herself, and every time she swallowed, *crmmp,* it meant it was all over and there was nothing to do about it or say or even ask, and then she would take another bite of toast as hard and shivery as gritting your teeth, and start the whole thing all over again. Her mother said he wasn't coming home ever any more. That was what she said, but why wasn't he home eating breakfast right this minute? Because he was not with them eating breakfast it wasn't fun and everything was so queer. Now maybe in just a minute he would walk right in and grin at her and say, "Good morning, merry sunshine," because her lip was sticking out, and even bend down and rub her cheek with his whiskers and then sit down and eat a big breakfast and then it would be all fun again and she would watch from the window when he went to work and just before he went out of sight he would turn around and she would wave but why wasn't he right here now where she wanted him to be and why didn't he come home? Ever any more. He won't come home again ever any more. Won't come home again ever. But he will, though, because it's home: But why's he not here? He's up seeing Grampa Follet. Grampa Follet is very, very sick. But Mama didn't feel awful then, she feels awful now. But why didn't he come back when she said he would? He went to heaven and now Catherine could remember about heaven, that's where God lives, way up in the sky. Why'd he do that? God took him there. But why'd he go there and not come home like Mama said? Last night Mama said he was coming home last night. We could even wait up a while and when he didn't and we had to go to bed she *promised* he would come if we went to sleep and she promised he'd be here at breakfast time and now it's breakfast time and she says he won't come home ever any more. Now her Aunt Hannah folded her napkin, and folded it again more narrowly, and again still more narrowly, and pressed the butt end of it against her mouth, and laid it beside her plate, where it slowly and slightly unfolded, and, looking first at Rufus and then at Catherine and then back at Rufus, said quietly, "I think you ought to know about your father. Whatever I can tell you. Because your mother's not feeling well."

Now I'll know when he *is* coming home, Catherine thought.

All through breakfast, Rufus had wanted to ask questions, but now he felt so shy and uneasy that he could hardly speak. "Who hurt him?" he finally asked.

"Why nobody hurt him, Rufus," she said, and she looked shocked. "What on earth made you think so?"

Mama said so, Catherine thought.

"Mama said he got hurt so bad God put him to sleep," Rufus said.

Like the kitties, Catherine thought: she saw a dim, gigantic old man in white take her tiny father by the skin of the neck and put him in a huge slop jar full of water and sit on the lid, and she heard the tiny scratching and the stifled mewing.

"That's true he was hurt, but nobody hurt him," her Aunt Hannah was saying. How could that be, Catherine wondered. "He was driving home by himself. That's all, all by himself, in the auto last night, and he had an accident."

Rufus felt his face get warm and he looked warningly at his sister. He knew it could not be that, not with his father, a grown man, besides, God wouldn't put you to sleep for *that,* and it didn't hurt, anyhow. But Catherine might think so. Sure enough, she was looking at her aunt with astonishment and disbelief that she could say such a thing about her father. Not in his *pants,* you dern fool, Rufus wanted to tell her, but his Aunt Hannah continued: "A *fatal* accident"; and by her voice, as she spoke the strange word, "fatal," they knew she meant something very bad. "That means that, just as your mother told you, that he was hurt so badly that God put him to sleep right a-way."

Like the rabbits, Rufus remembered, all torn white bloody fur and red insides. He could not imagine his father like that. Poor little things, he remembered his mother's voice comforting his crying, hurt so terribly that God just let them go to sleep.

If it was in the auto, Catherine thought, then he wouldn't be in the slop jar.

They couldn't be happy any more if He hadn't, his mother had said. They could never get well.

Hannah wondered whether they could comprehend it at all and whether she should try to tell them. She doubted it. Deeply uncertain, she tried again.

"He was driving home last night," she said, "about nine, and apparently something was already wrong with the steering mech—with the wheel you guide the machine with. But your father didn't know it. Because there wasn't any way he could know until something went wrong and then it was too late. But one of the wheels struck a loose stone in the road and the wheel turned aside very suddenly, and when . . . " She paused and went on more quietly and slowly: "You see, when your father tried to make the auto go where it should, stay on the road, he found he couldn't, he didn't have any control. Because something was wrong with the steering gear. So, instead of doing as he tried to make it, the auto twisted aside because of the loose stone and ran off the road into a deep ditch." She paused again. "Do you understand?"

They kept looking at her.

"Your father was thrown from the auto," she said. Then the auto went on without him up the other side of the ditch. It went up an eight-foot embankment and then it fell down backward, turned over and landed just beside him.

"They're pretty sure he was dead even before he was thrown out. Because the only mark on his whole body," and now they began to hear in her voice a troubling intensity and resentment, "was right — here!" She pressed the front of her forefinger to the point of her chin, and looked at them almost as if she were accusing them.

They said nothing.

I suppose I've got to finish, Hannah thought; I've gone this far.

"They're pretty sure how it happened," she said. "The auto gave such a sudden terrible jerk" — she jerked so violently that both children jumped, and startled her; she demonstrated what she saw next more gently: "that your father was thrown forward and struck his chin, very hard, against the wheel, the steering wheel, and from that instant he never knew anything more."

She looked at Rufus, at Catherine, and again at Rufus. "Do you understand?" They looked at her.

After a while Catherine said, "He hurt his chin."

"Yes, Catherine. He did," she replied. "They believe he was *instantly* killed, with that one single blow, because it happened to strike just exactly where it did. Because if you're struck very hard in just that place, it jars your whole head, your brain so hard that — sometimes people die in that very instant." She drew a deep breath and let it out long and shaky. "Concussion of the brain, that is called," she said with most careful distinctness, and bowed her head for a moment; they saw her thumb make a small cross on her chest.

She looked up. "Now do you understand, children?" she

asked earnestly. "I know it's very hard to understand. You please tell me if there's anything you want to know and I'll do my best to expl—tell you better."

Rufus and Catherine looked at each other and looked a-way. After a while Rufus said, "Did it hurt him bad?"

"He could never have felt it. That's the one great mercy" (or is it, she wondered); "the doctor is sure of that."

Catherine wondered whether she could ask one question. She thought she'd better not.

"What's an eight-foot embackmut?" asked Rufus.

"Em-bank-ment," she replied. "Just a bank. A steep little hill, eight feet high. Bout's high's the ceiling."

He and Catherine saw the auto climb it and fall backward rolling and come to rest beside their father. Umbackmut, Catherine thought; em-*bank*-ment, Rufus said to himself.

"What's instintly?"

"Instantly is — quick's that"; she snapped her fingers, more loudly than she had expected to; Catherine flinched and kept her eyes on the fingers. "Like snapping off an electric light." Rufus nodded. "So you can be very sure, both of you, he never felt a moment's pain. Not one moment."

"When's. . . " Catherine began.

"What's. . . " Rufus began at the same moment; they glared at each other.

"What is it, Catherine?"

"When's Daddy coming home?"

"Why good *golly*, Catherine," Rufus began; "Hold your tongue!" his Aunt Hannah said fiercely, and he listened, scared, and ashamed of himself.

"Catherine, he *can't* come home," she said very kindly. "That's just what all this means, child." She put her hand over Catherine's hand and Rufus could see that her chin was trembling. "He died, Catherine," she said. "That's what your mother means. God put him to sleep and took him, took his soul away with Him. So he can't come home . . . " She stopped, and began again. "We'll see him once more," she said, "tomorrow or day after; that I promise you," she said, wishing she was sure of Mary's views about this. "But he'll be asleep then. And after that we won't see him any more in this world. Not until God takes us away too.

"Do you see, child?" Catherine was looking at her very seriously. "Of course you don't, God bless you"; she squeezed her hand. "Don't ever try too hard to understand, child. Just try to understand it's so. He'd come if he could but he simply can't because God wants him with Him. That's all." She kept her hand over Catherine's a little while more, while Rufus realized much more clearly than before that he really could not and would not come home again: because of God.

"He would if he could but he can't," Catherine finally said, remembering a joking phrase of her mother's.

Hannah, who knew the joking phrase too, was startled, but quickly realized that the child meant it in earnest. "That's it," she said gratefully.

But he'll come once more, anyway, Rufus realized, looking forward to it. Even if he *is* asleep.

"What was it you wanted to ask, Rufus?" he heard his aunt say.

He tried to remember and remembered. "What's kuh, kuh-kush, kuh. . . ?"

"Con-cus-sion, Rufus. Concus-sion of the brain. That's the doctor's name for what happened. It means, it's as if the brain were hit very hard and suddenly, and joggled loose. The instant that happens, your father was — he. . ."

"Instantly killed."

She nodded.

"Then it was that, that put him to sleep."

"Hyess."

"*Not* God."

Catherine looked at him, bewildered.

Working from a developmental understanding of death much like that of Maria Nagy, Simon Yudkin, a British pediatrician, notes that in Western culture death has gradually been banished as a subject for discussion with children and at the same time medical advances have resulted in greatly increased control of childhood disease. Consequently, now more than ever, children are shielded from information about death and dying and in the absence of information they are likely to fill in with fantasy. Here, Yudkin urges that children be given a chance to talk about their fears of death so that the origins of those fears can be recognized and the children reassured.

selection from
CHILDREN AND DEATH
Simon Yudkin

SUMMARY

Some children who are ill are afraid of dying. They should be given an opportunity to show their fears and to talk about what death means to them so that the origin of their worries can be made clear and so that they can be reassured. The child with a fatal illness may not know that he is dying and may respond predictably to unusual behavior by his parents, who do know that he is dying. But dying children may also fear death and must be given an opportunity to talk about it. Often the fear is about some fantasy that concerns death and about which reassurance can be given. Whether older children should be told that they are in fact going to die is a question for which I have no answer.

The death of a child in a ward should be treated with dignity and solemnity, not furtively or with secrecy. The parents

Simon Yudkin, "Children and Death." *The Lancet.* 1967, i, 37.

of a dying child need sympathy and understanding and confidence in their doctor. This is not increased by a willingness to subject the child to useless therapy. More research is needed about children's attitude to death and of sick children's fear of death. Cross-cultural studies would be valuable in helping to decide how much the fear of death is determined by the real facts of the children's lives and deaths and how much by pure and universal fantasy.

INTRODUCTION

How is it that we have come to regard death as a forbidden word? It was not always so. In the Middle Ages, fathers took little notice of their children until their survival seemed assured. Even mothers did not always regard the death of their babies as an unmitigated tragedy. Aries (1962)[1] quotes the comforting (*sic*) words of a neighbor to a woman who had given birth to her sixth "brat": "before they are old enough to bother you, you will have lost half of them or perhaps all of them." Montaigne wrote: "I have lost two or three children in their infancy, not without regret, but without great sorrow" (Aries 1962). Two or three! As recently as the 1930s I remember that mothers of large families talked with some equanimity of having "buried two or three children." The bereaved parent is rare in Britain nowadays and does not seem to talk in the same way. Does familiarity breed contempt, or at least acquiesence? What is the attitude to death amongst children and adults in countries where most people die before the age of thirty? Is it different for the children, for example in many parts of Africa and Asia, who must see death around them much oftener than children in this country? Does the attitude change as death gets further and further away? Does the emphasis of our own culture on the individual and on close relationships make for deeper or greater grief? In *The Meaning of Death* Mandelbaum (1959)[2] writes that in some cultures, where group behavior and group loyalty loom larger than individual interpersonal relationships, individual grief seems to be almost lost in elaborate ritual: other cultures, on the other hand, still allow, or even encourage, expressions of individual grief.

The attitude of the person who is himself dying must presumably be affected by the prevailing beliefs about death and a possible after-life, but are not touched on in this book; references to this aspect of the problem are scanty and mostly literary rather than scientific.

In the eighteenth and nineteenth centuries, children in this country were not excluded from problems of life and death. They knew about the death of brothers and sisters as as of parents, and apparently accepted these as part of the natural order of things. The death of children or adults from disease or violence appeared in many stories, not only in those written for adults but also in those written especially for children. It is true that the tendency was to use death as a warning against wrongdoing or as a religious admonition, but the ease with which children were disposed of in stories for the young is remarkable. In *Dangerous Sports, A Tale Addressed to Children Warning Them Against Wanton, Careless, Or Mischevious Exposure To Situations From Which Alarming Injuries So Often Proceed* published in 1808 (Avery 1965),[3] almost every activity of daily life seems likely to end in death or severe injury (the two were used almost interchangeably). The religious attitude consisted often of awful warnings of the horrors of hell. Dr. Isaac Watt's *Divine and Moral Songs for Children* (1715)[4] promised this future for a disobedient child:

"The ravens shall pick out his eyes
And eagles eat the same."

And the Rev. Cares Wilson, publisher in the 1830s of a regular juvenile magazine *The Children's Friend,* warned his readers to prepare themselves for death during an epidemic of "hooping cough" by saying to themselves:

"Perhaps I may soon die, and then where will my soul go? Will it go to heaven, or will it be cast down into hell, where there will be weeping, and wailing, and gnashing of teeth?" (Avery 1965).

When not used as warnings of brimstone and hell, children's deaths were used as exemplary records of piety. *Examples For Youth, In Remarkable Instances Of Early Piety In Children And Young Persons, Members Of The Society Of*

Friends, published in 1892, described the last illness and dying moments of pious children of various ages.

CONTEMPORARY ATTITUDES

In our own culture and in this generation, death seems to have been banished and has replaced sex as our most prohibited biological subject. The Victorian child had death in his prayers and his precepts; modern children are more likely to be taught about their origin than about their departure from this world. Doctors are as bad as other groups in prohibiting talk of death. Throughout most of my medical career I never heard the subject discussed at all, and articles about death, especially death in childhood, have appeared in medical journals only during the past few years. Each general practitioner, house physician and house surgeon, each registrar and consultant has to deal with dying patients and with their relatives, but has to act without the benefit of advice or of previous discussion. So far as hospitals are concerned, many of the doctors simply avoid the issue, leaving the job to the equally untrained nursing staff.

Our gradual banishment of death as a respectable subject has coincided with and may indeed be related to the very success of medicine itself. We have, after all, been able to prevent or cure many diseases which killed people in their early and middle lives: we have been especially successful with the diseases of childhood. A child born now in one of the favored countries of the world is expected to survive to the age of 65 or 70 years with nothing more than a series of relatively minor illnesses. Not surprisingly, most medical writing about death come from geriatricians, and the few that deal with death in childhood come from clinics for children with malignant disease (Davis 1964).[5] The death of a child from an illness in Britain nowadays is an affront to our pride. Our job is to prevent or cure disease, not accommodate with death; the more successful we are the more our comparatively few failures produce in us a deep emotional reaction. Perhaps we are more able to help the parents of a child who has been killed in an accident than those of a child dying of an illness: the first is someone else's responsibility; death from disease we think of as ours. Yet sometimes we are helpless and some children will die despite all we can do, and we know they will die.

THE ATTITUDE OF CHILDREN TO DEATH

There is some understanding about the attitude of adults to the realization that they are dying (Hinton 1963),[6] but practically nothing is known about the attitude of children. We know very little about how the child thinks of death, even if it does not apply to himself. My views, which are similar to those of Nagy (1948),[7] are little more than tentative.

The very young child has no concept of death and does not appear to distinguish between short-term separation and death: when a person a small child knows and loves goes away, the difference between a permanent and a short disappearance is not understood. Infants who are cared for by a number of different people are likely to take some time to learn the difference between them and to be really upset about the absence of one of them, but it is obvious that a child learns very quickly to distinguish between lasting and brief absences. In other words, he learns both from his own quite real experience and from his gradual appreciation of time.

As he grows beyond the age of two or three, he will soon learn that some things "die" or are "dead." In this country these are usually his pets, and he learns that "dead" things have characteristics which are different from things which are alive. His own reaction is very often one of curiosity rather than concern, and his parents may respond to his questions by being either shocked or matter-of-fact according to their own feelings and understanding. A child is very unlikely to see a dead person; the chances are, if a near relative or friend does die, that he will be told that the person has "gone away," "gone on a long journey," or "gone up to heaven." Even if the word "death" is mentioned, our embarrassment and annoyance if the child talks of death of people that he knows in the same way that he talks of the death of his pets must be both confusing and disturbing. It also shows how this is our modern veneer of pretending to answer all children's questions in a matter-of-fact way and how inconsistent is our relatively straightforward response to a child's talk of sex with our reaction to his talking about death.

The child of, say, three to seven years has therefore begun to appreciate some of the facts about death, such as not breathing, being buried, and not returning. They also have fantasies about death, and fact and fantasy mingle, with the facts adding terror to fantasy. The child knows what it is like to hold his breath and can picture what it might be like to be put in a box and covered with earth. Death may be thought of as being just like this, only worse. A dead person might, when he opens his eyes again and wakes up, find that he is in a box and buried or that he will never be able to breathe again even if he wants to.

Death is also often personified, as something done to a person by another or by God and may be thought of as the arch punishment for himself or for others. Children of this age often play with death ("bang, bang, you're dead) in an attempt to come to terms with their fear. At this age particularly, children's fantasies make their use of words vastly different from ours and we must tread delicately if we are to step into the world of their fears and try to help them. Nevertheless, the fear of death is usually remote in an acutely ill child. At this age he is usually more afraid of discomfort and pain than of the idea that he might die.

The older child gradually develops a more realisitic appreciation of death and dying. Grief and mourning about the death of loved ones takes on a more adult aspect. Yet, on the whole, fear of death for himself is relatively remote. Even the most desperately ill children often seem unable to conceive that they will not recover. Of course, almost all acutely ill children in such a country as Britain do recover, and what I have said may very well not be true of children in Africa or Asia. In Britain also, in earlier times, children apparently often expected to die and some evidently prepared themselves for death.

"How can we tell that we shall ever live to grow up? Many children die much younger than us; and if we do not think of preparing for death, what will become of of us?" says a child in Mrs. Cameron's *History of Margaret Whyte, or The Life and Death of a Good Child* (Avery 1965). But even in Britain now there are exceptions. A few children do suffer terribly from a fear of dying, often without good physical cause, and we must always be aware of this possibility. On the whole, however, the school child takes his illnesses calmly and often almost impersonally.

Both reality and anxiety are more strikingly developed about the time of puberty and after, and from about the age of twelve on one sometimes finds children who are intensely anxious about quite trivial conditions and who, with sensitive understanding, will often reveal a fear of some serious or fatal illness. At the same time, children at puberty and later are more able to adjust to an illness affecting them which is, in fact, fatal and do so with the same mechanisms of defence, denial, anger, sadness, and so on that adults do.

REFERENCES

1. Aries, P. (1962) *Centuries of Childhood;* p. 38. London.
2. Mandelbaum, D. G. (1959) in *The Meaning of Death.* London.
3. Avery, G. (1965) *Nineteenth Century Children;* chap. 13. London.
4. Watts, I. (1715) *Divine and Moral Songs for Children,* cited by M. King Hall. *The Story of the Nursery;* p. 157. London, 1955.
5. Davis, J. (1964) *Devl. Med. Child Neurol.* ,Vol. 6, 286.
6. Hinton, J. M. (1963) *Q. Jl. Med.*, Vol. 32, 1.
7. Nagy, M. (1948) *J. Genet. Psychol.*, Vol. 73, 3.

Though the subject of death had appeared in children's literature of the eighteenth and nineteenth centuries, it was usually presented as a prod to moral behavior. Frequently, children were urged to behave well in life in order to avoid eternal punishment thereafter. In recent years, however, death has returned to children's literature as a subject for realistic presentation and open consideration. Often in works such as Charlotte's Web, *it is an animal that dies, but the following piece by Joan Fassler demonstrates that even the death of a family member can be presented to children so as to allay rather than arouse fears. In* My Grandpa Died Today, *the child who serves as the narrator, describes his feelings of loss and grief as well as his personal means of honoring his grandfather's memory.*

MY GRANDPA DIED TODAY

Joan Fassler

My grandpa was very, very old. He was much, much older than me. He was much older than my mother and father. He was much older than all my aunts and uncles. He was even a little bit older than the white haired bakery-man down the block.

My grandpa taught me how to play checkers. And he read stories to me. And he helped me build my first model. And he showed me how to reach out with my bat and hit a curve ball. And he always rooted for my team.

One day, grandpa and I took a long slow walk

Joan Fassler. *My Grandpa Died Today.* New York: Human Sciences Press, 1971.

together. Grandpa stopped to rest awhile. "David," he said, "I am getting very old now. And surely I cannot live forever." Then grandpa put his arm around my shoulders and went on talking in a soft voice. "But I am not afraid to die," he said, "because I know that you are not afraid to live." And I nodded my head in a thoughtful way, even though I did not understand what grandpa meant.

Just two days later grandpa sat down in our big white rocking chair. And he rocked himself for a little while. Then, very softly, very quietly, grandpa closed his eyes.

And he stopped rocking.
And he didn't move any more.
And he didn't talk any more.
And he didn't breathe any more.
And the grownups said that grandpa died.

My mother cried and cried. And my father cried and cried. And many people came to our house. And they cried, too. And they took grandpa away and buried him.

More people kept coming to our house. And they pulled down all the window shades. And they covered all the mirrors. And our whole house looked as if it was going to cry. Even the red shingles on the roof. Even the white shutters at the windows. Even the flagstone steps going up to the door. And everyone was very sad.

I was sad, too. I thought about my grandpa and about all the things we used to do together. And, in a little while, I discovered a funny, empty, scary, rumbly kind of feeling at the bottom of my stomach. And some tears streaming down my cheeks.

Somehow, I didn't feel like sitting in the living room with all the gloomy grown-ups. So I walked quietly into my own room, and I took out some of my favorite toys. Then I did two jig-saw puzzles and colored three pictures. And I rolled a few marbles very slowly across the floor.

The grownups didn't mind at all. They came in and smiled at me. And someone patted me gently on my head. It was almost as if they all knew that grandpa and I must have had some very special talks together.

The next day was still a very sad day at our house. Late in the afternoon, I heard a soft knock at the door. My best friend, Bobby, wanted to know if I could play ball. And again the grownups didn't seem to mind. So I left our sad, sorry house. And Bobby and I walked slowly down to the park.

Almost too soon, it was my turn at bat. I looked around and saw that the bases were loaded. Then I took a deep breath, and tried to forget about the rumbly feeling at the bottom of my stomach. I planted my feet firmly on the ground. I grasped the bat with two steady hands. I watched the ball whizz towards me. And, SMACK, I hit it high and far.

And then I ran. I ran with every bit of strength and power and speed inside my whole body.

And it was a grand slam home run!

And somehow, right there on the field, in the middle of all the cheers and shouts of joy, I could *almost* see my grandpa's face breaking into a happy smile. And that made me feel so good inside that the rumbles in my stomach disappeared.

And the solid hardness of the ground under my feet made me feel good inside, too. And the warm touch of the sun on my cheeks made me feel good inside, too.

And, it was at that very moment, that I first began to understand why my grandpa was not afraid to die. It was because he knew that there would be many more hits and many more home runs for me. It was because he knew that I would go right on playing, and reading, and running, and laughing, and growing up.

Without really knowing why, I took off my cap. I stood very still. I looked far, far away into the clear blue sky. And I thought to myself, "Grandpa must feel good inside, too."

Then I heard the umpire calling, "Batter-up!" And we went on with the game.

In "Children and Death," Simon Yudkin noted that while there is some research on the attitudes of adults to the realization that they are dying, very little is known about the attitudes of children in the same circumstances. Yet without an understanding of the child's awareness of his illness and his responses to his condition, both family and medical personnel are to provide support for the child. To investigate ways of assisting the families of terminal children, a research team composed of four pediatric hematologists, a child psychiatrist, and a social worker conducted a retrospective study of twenty families in whch a child had died of leukemia. The following paper reports the attitudes of the families towards the medical staff and the impact of the illness and death of the child on his parents, siblings and grandparents.

CHILDHOOD LEUKEMIA: EMOTIONAL IMPACT ON PATIENT AND FAMILY

C.M. Binger, A.R. Ablin, R.C. Feuerstein, J.H. Kushner, S. Zoger, and C. Mikkelsen

Terminal illness makes a heavy impact upon all concerned, family and professionals. Particular effects of terminal illness and loss have been the subject of numerous studies.[1-4]

Lindemann points out that among adults the grief reaction is a syndrome with psychologic and somatic symptomatology, including somatic distress, a preoccupation with the image of the deceased, feelings of guilt, hostile reactions and the loss of previous patterns of conduct. How long the acute symptoms last seems to depend upon how quickly a person breaks his bonds with the one who has died, returns himself to his diminished human environment and forms new relationships. Lindemann also described the "anticipatory grief reaction" that occurs upon the initial diagnosis of a fatal disease.

A child's concept of death varies with his age; so, too, does

Reprinted with permission from *The New England Journal of Medicine*, Vol. 280, pages 414-418, Feb. 20, 1969.

his anxiety about his illness. Whether he grieves and how he grieves is also related to his maturation and point of development. Whatever the age of a patient whose illness is terminal, honesty and truthfulness are important from those who work with him. The workers, too, must maintain the patient in hope and reassure him that there will be relief from pain. The patient must be assured that he will not be isolated and that those upon whom he depends will not desert him.

To prepare themselves more fully to support families who face the crisis of a child's death, four pediatric hematologists, a child psychiatrist and a social worker undertook a retrospective study of families who had lost a child from acute leukemia. This paper summarizes the findings of the group, indicates how these findings have been used in their ongoing work with such families and describes their application by other professionals who face this problem.

THE STUDY

The pediatric hematology records revealed that 23 children had died of leukemia between January, 1964 and December, 1966. The parents of these children were asked to come to be interviewed by the child psychiatrist regarding the impact of the crisis and its after-effects upon their lives. Twenty families agreed to come. The interview, which lasted for two to three hours, elicited information including the following: limited family data; details surrounding the diagnosis; short-term and long-term effects upon patient, parents, siblings and family constellation; relation with doctors and other professional personnel; sources of support during stress; terminal phase and death; the funeral; and after-effects. The structure and the content of the interviews were managed with considerable freedom in an effort to make this interview a helpful or even therapeutic experience for these families. The interviews were transcribed and analyzed, and the results compiled.

THE CLINIC

Inpatient and outpatient care was carried out through the De-

315

partment of Pediatrics house staff at the medical center with supervision by us. History, physical findings and laboratory data were included in the discussion of the findings and recommendations at the end of each visit.

In the past two years, supportive efforts have been enriched by the regular presence of a child psychiatrist and a psychiatric social worker at the initial conference and in the hematology clinic. Families are also invited to return two or three months after the child's death to discuss their reactions to the crisis, the autopsy report and current stresses.

FINDINGS

Learning the Diagnosis

In the 16 cases the diagnosis of leukemia had already been revealed to the parents or was strongly suspected by them at the time they were referred. In eight families, one or both parents thought their child might have had leukemia before any mention of it by a physician. Most of the parents had sensed something seriously wrong with the child before the diagnosis was discussed or confirmed.

Reactions immediately upon diagnosis ranged from loss of control to outward calm and resignation. Many parents described this as the hardest blow they had to bear throughout the course of illness. During the first days or weeks after hearing the diagnosis, most parents experienced symptoms and feelings of physical distress, depression, inability to function, anger, hostility and self-blame (the "anticipatory grief reaction"). These gradually subsided and were followed by acceptance and resolution to meet all the special needs of the child. Persistent overt denial of the diagnosis or "shopping around" was not encountered. There was denial of the diagnosis by relatives (especially grandparents) and friends rather than among the parents themselves.

The Initial Conference

Whether or not the diagnosis had been known before referral, members of the team discussed many aspects of both

316

diagnosis and disease with the parents. Specific topics included what was known about etiology, heredity, therapy, ultimate prognosis, problems to be anticipated, possible sources of help, means to support the affected child and his siblings, the function of the clinic, current research and reasons for hope. All families expressed appreciation for the frankness and honesty of this initial discussion, and eight specifically singled it out as one of the major sources of help. Several parents who had received their information piecemeal elsewhere made reference to the anxieties specifically provoked by unanswered questions.

Attitudes Toward Professional Personnel

In general, most parents were well satisfied with the clinic and the professional team: nine families specifically mentioned the "panel" of specialists as a source of reassurance.

When parents complained, the discontent was far more frequent with inpatient than with outpatient care. Usually, this was not for any recurrent or basic shortcoming in care but upon a specific situation, whether real or imagined: a doctor's "choking" a child while trying to stop a nosebleed: a nurse's slowness in lending a mother a dime to call her husband for what she considered to be an emergency: a doctor who was "too busy" caring for another child to answer a question: and the premature discharge of a child who had to be rehospitalized on the following day.

Even good intentions and scrupulous care cannot wholly eliminate such situations. When the child is in relapse and ill enough to require hospitalization, parents and physicians experience a significant increase in strain and tension, and the grief reaction becomes more manifest. Professional personnel, when they understand the attitudes of parents and are prepared to respond to their needs, become a valuable source of help instead of becoming enmeshed in a pattern of mutual hostility and recrimination.

Six of the 20 families believed that, as death approached, the professional staff became more remote. The child seemed to become progressively isolated both in a physical sense (because of leukopenia and infections, most of the children were on isolation precautions terminally) and in the sense that he was "avoided" (a word used by several parents) by the staff.

The professional has his own problems in coping with the imminent death of a child. He is distressed and often feels guilty about the failure of therapy. Simultaneously, he is troubled by his own fears and anxieties about death and feels inadequate to support the dying child and his parents. Faced with these conflicts, he often avoids the patient or family or makes himself unapproachable by presenting a facade of busyness, impatience or formality. Thus, at a time when most needed, the professional often assumes a neutral or even negative role in contacts with the family of the dying child.

The parents with the most negative attitudes toward the professional staff were those whose children had had the shortest course of illness. These children were usually the sickest, did not have remissions and were contantly a source of distress to parents and staff.

In contrast with negative attitudes toward inpatient care were the many positive remarks on the support received from the professional staff. In particular, parents appreciated being allowed to participate in the care of the child and being granted complete freedom of visiting privileges.

Impact on Patients

Most children above four years of age, although not told directly of the diagnosis, presented evidence to their parents that they were aware of the seriousness of their disease and even anticipated their premature death. The parents of 14 children tried to shield them from the diagnosis; during the course of the illness 11 of these children indicated their sense of impending death. Younger children, though not expressing fear of death per se, manifested concern about separation, disfigurement or hurt.

Only two of the teenagers were told that they had leukemia for which there was currently no known cure. There was no evidence during the course of the illness or in the interview with the family after death that they had greater difficulty coping than their counterparts to whom nothing had been said directly. Both these families reported a more meaningful relation with their child than they had ever experienced before. They thought this change was due largely to their frank discussion of the diagnosis and the open communication within their families.

As parents attempted to protect their children from the concerns of the illness, older leukemic children attempted similarily to protect their parents; the children who were perhaps the loneliest of all were those who were aware of their diagnosis but at the same time recognized that their parents did not wish them to know. As a result, there was little or no meaningful communication. No one was left to whom the child could openly express his feelings of sadness, fear or anxiety.

Impact on Parents

From the initial diagnosis through the illness of a child and his subsequent death, parents manifested all aspects of "anticipatory" as well as subsequent grief reactions, such as intellectualization, irritability, depression, somatization, denial and frenzied activity.We had not previously been aware of the silent, intense worry of some parents about the circumstances under which their child might die.

The circumstances surrounding a child's terminal illness should be discussed with parents early in the course of the treatment, for parental fantasies are often much worse than actual fact. At first thought, to discuss death might seem needlessly cruel, but parents are troubled by the specific circumstances of this eventuality. A frank discussion does much to relieve months of anxiety. It becomes obvious to all when the child is in a preterminal or, finally, a terminal state, so that the family and professionals will not be left unprepared.

The fathers found many ways to absent themselves from painful involvement with their troubled families. This type of behavior is a coping mechanism, and often indicates the father's need for additional support. Although others may look upon such behavior as expressing a lack of interest or concern, it is a way of avoiding the pain of an ongoing involvement with the dying child. Such avoidance, however, often leaves the mother bereft of much needed support. Fathers who manifest this

319

type of behavior should be helped to express their painful feelings and to look at the effect on their families of this method of coping.

Impact on Siblings

In approximately half the families one or more previously well siblings showed significant behavioral patterns that indicated difficulty in coping. Problems described by parents included an onset of severe enuresis, headaches, poor school performance, school phobia, depression, severe separation anxieties and persistent abdominal pains. Several siblings complained of the preoccupation of parents and friends with the ill child. Often, siblings had feelings of guilt and fear that they too might suffer a fatal illness; they misinterpreted their parents' preoccupation with the sick child as rejection of themselves. In their own way, they had "anticipatory grief reactions." Supportive therapy and counseling for parents and siblings should be considered an essential aspect of total care.

Impact on Grandparents

Ten families stated that one or both sets of grandparents were a burden or hindrance during the course of the child's fatal illness. In many other families the grandparents offered considerable support. Negative interactions reflected to a considerable extent past relations between parents and grandparents. Grief reactions or the grandparents' lack of knowledge also contributed to the ineffectiveness in helping the parents of the child. Grandparents are welcomed to the clinic to discuss concerns with us; like parents, they grieve and need help in coping with their feelings.

Sources of Support to Parents

The physician was only one of a number of sources for simultaneous support.

In 15 families, *parents* turned to each other. The quality of this support seemed to be related to the previous state of the marriage. In others, each parent in handling his own grief was unable to be helpful to the spouse.

If there was a meaningful relation with the *clergy* before the illness, it seemed to continue throughout; de novo introduction of clergy at this time seemed to be of little help. Although only a small number of families received help from clergy, personal religion and religious concepts seemed to be of considerable help. Three families made no comment about the role of religion; 10 expressed negative feelings and disappointment in religion as a source of support during this time.

The *referring physician* was a source of help in nine families and in six of minimal or no help; in one the parents were openly antagonistic. Sometimes, the referring physician seemed to lose contact with the parents and left patient management to the hospital specialists, or in other ways provided only minimal support to the family. Often, the parents of a leukemic child resented the person who first made the diagnosis.

This feeling may be a factor in the parents' resentment toward the referring physician; another may be that the parents of a child with a serious or terminal illness leave the referring physician to seek the "best" or "most specialized" medical service, and since criticism of their choice is a criticism of their own judgment, it is easier to criticize the referring physician than the "superspecialist." Sometimes, a close relation between the referring physician and parents can be inadvertently impaired by the university physician, who takes over the entire management.

The *social worker* was of considerable help to many parents by offering practical assistance in solving financial, housing and transportation problems and as someone who was always available to listen to parental worries, anxieties and other painful feelings. She was introduced at the initial interview as a member of the "leukemia team" and helped greatly in subsequent contacts with the parents and family of the leukemic child.

Parents of other leukemic children, as they waited in the clinic, often discussed common problems and gave significant support to one another. They often formed strong bonds, which continued long after their children expired — despite extreme differences in background, residence, race or economic status. Of 15 families who mentioned the possible role of parents of other leukemic children, 11 expressed positive feelings toward these relations. Although the Oncology-Hematology Clinic makes communication possible among people with similar problems, burdens are sometimes increased by inappropriate sharing of sorrows. Efforts are now made to introduce families to each other if a need seems to be present.

The hospital physician, house officer and nursing staff were a major source of support to most families. Often, the parents became dependent upon a senior physician or house staff member and called on him during times of need. The private telephone number of one of the staff hematologists is now given so that someone whom the family members know will always be available to them.

Fifteen families expressed positive feelings toward the *mortician or funeral director.* Their experience with grief reactions makes them skilled in offering solace to grieving families.

The Child's Death

The actual death was not always the most important event in the *parents'* recollection of the child's illness. Often, the time of the initial diagnosis was equated with death, and it was then that grieving began. The parents of 10 children expressed a sense of relief as well as grief at the time of the child's death. Some were relieved that the child's suffering was at an end; others felt released from long standing worry over when and how the child would die. Four couples recalled intense anger concerning circumstances surrounding their child's death, which was directed against medical personnel, house staff, nurses, physicians or religious personnel. Such reactions should be taken as expressions of grief, not as personal insults.

Siblings' reactions to the death were manifested in varying ways. Some of the children cried and verbalized their grief directly. Others seemed to work out their grief through play activities. Another group of children seemed on the surface to be unconcerned at the time of death only to over-react to a subsequent loss (delayed grief reaction) some months later. Still another group tended to contain their grief only to show marked behavioral changes subsequently. Siblings often felt responsible in some way for the death, or thought they would also die of leukemia. During this period of general confusion and turmoil, the parents may not be able to deal effectively with these feelings, but professionals should be sensitive to them and offer assistance.

Aftereffects

In 11 families, one or more members had emotional disturbances that were severe enough to interfere with adequate functioning and required psychiatric help. None had required such help before. These emotional disturbances included several cases of severe depression requiring admission to a psychiatric hospital, a conversion reaction wherein a man was temporarily unable to talk, divorce, severe psychosomatic symptoms and the behavioral changes in siblings mentioned above. In other families, milder disturbances occurred in both the adults and the children.

Physicians should be alert to the families that might be particularly vulnerable so as to help them through this period.

Suggestions by Parents

All parents considered it important to treat the child "normally" during the illness. They advised that the family "live day to day," "enjoy the child," "not give special privileges" and "not be overprotective." They also expressed a need for more time to talk to doctors about matters other than medical management of the disease. Nineteen families thought that more specific information about the terminal events should have been given to them.

Parents made no clear-cut recommendations about whether a child under nine years of age should be told the diagnosis. In retrospect, all three families with an affected child over this age would have told the child the diagnosis early in the course of the illness. Most families would have told the older siblings of the diagnosis and prognosis.

DISCUSSION

A crisis of this kind is admittedly a major challenge for any family. Still, the fact that in 50 per cent of the families at least one member reacted so strongly to the crisis as to need psychiatric help was somewhat startling. From the point of view of preventive mental health the question remains how these untoward reactions could have been anticipated and prevented.

It is a grave error to think that a child over four or five years of age who is dying of a terminal illness does not realize its seriousness and probable fatality. Repeatedly, experience has shown us otherwise. We have seen the pathetic consequence of the loneliness of a fatally ill child who has no one with whom he may talk over his serious concerns because his parents are frequently trying to shield him from the diagnosis. His siblings or contemporaries also almost never act as a sounding board for release of his tensions. Whereas dying adults can express some of their feelings to their spouses, to mature and respected friends, to the clergy or to doctors, the dying child may have to deal alone with his fears, concerns and apprehensions and also cope with his own inner scheme of fantasies and "white lies" developed by his parents so that meaningful communication between the child and adults is prevented. The question is not whether to talk about the diagnosis and prognosis (the child usually senses it), but rather how to let the child know that his concerns are shared and understood and that there is willingness to talk about them with him. Reassuring him that everything possible will be done, that each discomfort that can be alleviated will be, and that all are ready to help in every possible way will allay many apprehensions.

Hope rests not only on life or death. Recognizing with the child what he already knows (that he has a fatal illness) opens up communication without which hope cannot be conveyed. Though he knows the worst that can happen, hope can yet be imparted. He knows that lies will not be told to him, that he will not be deserted physically or emotionally, and that he can voice aloud his feelings of sadness, fear, helplessness, loss and anxiety. Older ill children can be told about current research and prognosis, and their co-operation can be enlisted in medical efforts to help them. Adults can give them the support they so clearly need.

Each parent and sibling reacts to a fatal illness individually, in a manner consistent with his own personality structure, past experience, current crises, and the particular meaning or special circumstances associated with the loss threatening him. To help them, one must know each one and his relation to his or her family, how they react to the initial diagnosis, how their grief process begins and how they cope. One should know, too, something of their beliefs about life, death and religion, their response to previous crises, and their current burdens and sources of support.

Our own efforts to help parents and siblings begin with a team approach at the initial conference conducted by one of the pediatric hematologists and with the house officer, child psychiatrist and social worker participating. Most often the diagnosis has already been shared with the family by the house officer directly responsible for care of the child. The conference occurs in the hospital when the family has had the opportunity to adjust to this initial impact. This meeting is open-ended and sets the stage for help to the family throughout the course of the child's illness. During it we attempt to anticipate questions and to elucidate diagnoses, prognoses and methods of treatment. The conference also provides an opportunity for us to know the family and for them to know us. They are not told how to manage their lives but are helped to arrive at the solution most adequate for them and encouraged to express feelings. We expect to leave the conference with greater sensitivity toward the family. They, in turn, learn that we are not only concerned about the medical aspects of the illness, but are engaged with them as human beings who are facing a crisis, and that our efforts to help will be steady and continuous.

As a result of our study, we have become aware of the importance of inviting families to return to the clinic after the child's death. At this follow-up interview, a summary of the autopsy report is given to them, their reactions to the child's death are reviewed, current stresses are discussed, and all the family members are encouraged to express their thoughts and feelings. Such interviews seem to lead to healthful resolutions of

325

grief.

Who, however, provides help for the professional personnel? They are dedicated and accustomed to making young patients well. When they cannot do so, they feel intense frustration, and their own anxieties concerning death and dying are exacerbated. Anxiety, depression and irritability sometimes ensue. As a child nears death, many professional personnel tend to cope with their own anxieties by avoiding the patient and family when both need support most. For the professional staff to talk with one another periodically about their own emotions and reactions to the work is necessary and useful. They should examine and discuss their own emotional reactions continually, as they affect their interaction with the child and his family. Thus, the professional enables himself to undertake the comprehensive approach to the dying child.

NOTES

1. Bergman, A. G., and Schulte, C. J. A. "Care of child with cancer." *Pediatrics* Vol. 40 (3):492-546, Part 2, 1967.
2. Cain, A. C., Fast, I., and Erickson, M. E. "Children's disturbed reactions to death of sibling." *Am. J. Orthopsychiat.* Vol. 34:741-752, 1964.
3. Friedman, S. B., Chodoff, P., Mason, J. W., and Hamburg, D. A. "Behavioral observations on parents anticipating death of child." *Pediatrics* Vol. 32:610-625, 1963.
4. Furman, R. "Death and the young child: some preliminary considerations." *Psychoanalyt. Stud. Child.* Vol. 19:321-333, 1964.
5. Hamovitch, M. B. *The Parent and the Fatally Ill Child.* (Los Angeles: Delmar Pub. Co., 1964).
6. Harrison, S. I., Davenport, C. W., and McDermott, J. F. "Children's reactions to bereavement: adult confusions and misperceptions." *Arch. Gen. Psychiat.* Vol. 17:593-597, 1967.
7. Karon, M., and Vernick, J. "Approach to emotional support of fatally ill children." *Clin. Pediat.* Vol. 7:274-280, 1968.
8. Lindemann, E. "Symptomatology and management of acute grief." *Am. J. Psychiat.* Vol. 101:141-148, 1944.
9. Morissey, J. R. "Death anxiety in children with fatal illness." In *Crisis Intervention.* Edited by E. Parod. (New York: Family Service Association of America, 1965), p. 324-338.
10. *Idem.* Note on interview with children facing imminent death. *Social Case Work.* Vol. 44:208, 1963.

11. Siggins, L. D. "Mourning: critical survey of literature." *Internat. J. Psycho-Analysis* Vol. 47:14-25, 1966.
12. Somit, A. J. and Green, M. "Psychologic considerations in management of deaths on pediatric hospital services. I." Doctor and child's family. *Pediatrics* Vol. 24:106-112, 1959.
13. *Idem.* "Pediatric management of dying child. II. Child's reaction to fear of dying." In *Modern Perspectives in Child Development.* Edited by A. J. Solnit and S. A. Provence (New York: International Univ. Press, 1963). p. 217-228.
14. Vernick, J. and Karon, M. "Who's afraid of death on leukemia ward?" *Am. J. Dis. Child.* Vol. 109:393-397, 1965.

Since little is known about the age at which fatally ill children are aware of their condition, Eugenia Waechter administered a standardized anxiety scale to sixty-four hospitalized children between the ages of six and ten. Her findings indicate that despite efforts to shield a child from a knowledge of the seriousness of his illness, the anxiety of those close to him is likely to alter the emotional climate in the family to such a degree that the child will develop suspicions and fears about his condition. Often the child will feel that his awareness of his condition is knowledge that he is not supposed to have, so the silence of those around him isolates him from needed support. Waechter dismisses the much-debated question of whether or not a child should be told if his condition is terminal, as she argues that the seriously ill child should be able to discuss any concerns or questions that he does have.

CHILDREN'S AWARENESS OF FATAL ILLNESS

Eugenia H. Waechter

No one's emotions are left untouched by the death of a patient, but the death of the very young is particularly poignant because it speaks silently of unfulfilled promise and destroyed hopes. To defend ourselves, we may unconsciously avoid children with fatal illness and leave them largely alone to deal with their fears and anxieties at a time when comfort, nearness, and sympathetic understanding are most important to them.

Researchers have been reporting that fatally ill children do not, as a rule, experience or express anxiety about death until after the age of ten. And they infer that until then, children are not aware of what is happening to them.[1-4]

I didn't believe them.

To test my own hypothesis I set up a study based on the assumption that, despite widespread efforts in our society to shield children with fatal illness from awareness of their diagnoses or prognoses, the anxiety of meaningful adults is conveyed to them through the false cheerfulness or evasiveness of those around them. The child might believe that if he expresses fear of death openly, he may risk loss of human contact. Therefore, research that relies on a child's overt expression of anxiety or fears about death, mutilation, or separation might get an incomplete or distorted picture of the actual concerns of the seriously ill child.

The subjects for my study were 64 children between the ages of six and ten, divided into four groups matched for age, race, social class and family background. In one group were three children with leukemia, six with neoplastic diseases, six with cystic fibrosis, and one with progressive septic granulomatosis. In the second group were children with a chronic disease, but good prognosis; in the third, children with a brief illness. These groups were tested in the hospital. Testing of the fourth group, non-hospitalized children, was carried out at an elementary school selected after the data had been completed for the three groups of hospitalized children.

A General Anxiety Scale for Children that measured concerns in many areas of living was administered to each hospitalized child.[5] Each child was also shown a set of eight pictures and asked for stories about the pictures to elicit indirect and fantasy expression of the child's concerns related to present and future body integrity. Four of the pictures were selected from the Thematic Apperception Test and four were specifically designed for the study.[6]

Interviews with the parents of each hospitalized child were tape recorded to gather data on the variables that I believed would influence the quality and quantity of fatally ill children's concerns related to death. These were the child's previous experience with death, the religious devoutness within the family, the quality of maternal warmth toward the child and the opportunities the child had had to discuss his concerns or the nature of his illness with his parents, professional personnel, or other

In one of the projective tests to elicit the fantasies of dying children ages six to ten the author asked them to tell stories about these pictures. They often gave the characters their own diagnosis and symptoms, and 63 percent related their stories to death.

meaningful adults.

Analysis of the results of the General Anxiety Scale showed that the total scores of the children with fatal illness were twice as high as the scores of the other hospitalized children, supporting the prediction that although only two of the 16 children had been told their prognoses, the generalized anxiety was extremely high in all cases.

Children with poor prognoses told substantially more stories relating to threat to body integrity than did the comparison groups, indicating that they were more preoccupied with death, and suggesting that the denial may not be an effective or complete defense in blocking awareness and in minimizing fear and anxiety in such an extreme situation.

Those children who were threatened with death discussed loneliness, separation, and death much more frequently in their fantasy stories, although none of them did so directly either to me or to other hospital personnel.

A most striking finding was the dichotomy between the child's degree of awareness of his prognosis, as inferred from his imaginative stories, and the parent's belief about the child's awareness. As mentioned previously, only two of the 16 subjects in the fatally ill group had discussed their concerns about death with their parents, yet the proportion of stories related to death told by these children was 63 percent. The children often gave the characters in the stories their own diagnoses and symptoms; they frequently depicted death in their drawings; and occasionally they would express awareness of their prognoses to persons outside their immediate family. This dichotomy suggests that knowledge is communicated to the child by the change in affect which he encounters in his total environment after the diagnosis is made and by his perceptiveness of other nonverbal clues. It also implies a deepening of isolation when the child becomes aware of the evasiveness which meets expression of his concern.

I found a highly significant correlation between the total score on the projective test and the degree to which the child had been given an opportunity to discuss his fears and prognosis. This supports the prediction that giving the child such opportunity does not heighten death anxiety; on the contrary, understanding acceptance and conveyance of permission to discuss any aspect of his illness may decrease feelings of isolation, alienation, and the sense that his illness is too terrible to discuss completely.

The degree of awareness, as influenced by the opportunities the child has had to discuss his illness with his parents, is influenced by the immediacy of the threat of death, or the chronicity of the disease, and by the extent to which the cooperation of the child is necessary in the treatment regimen. The immediacy to parents of the threat of the child's death affects both the intensity of anxiety communicated to the child and the quality of his particular concerns. Children with illnesses which run a fairly rapid course are not often allowed to learn of their diagnoses (adults consider this a protective measure), whereas children with cystic fibrosis or other chronic handicapping conditions may become more aware of and knowledgeable about both their medical regimens and their ultimate prognoses.

Many parents are deeply troubled about the best procedure to follow with their child. Frank discussion with their child about the possibility of imminent death would arouse, they believe, feelings they couldn't cope with. Although my purpose in the interview with the parents was to elicit specific information, it also gave parents an opening to discuss their feelings and concerns about their child's prognosis. Many parents asked for further interviews. They needed to discuss these questions with an empathetic counselor.

The data about religious instruction and previous experience with death lacked a variability suitable for drawing conclusions about specific effects of either. Trends, however, indicated that both influences do affect the response of children with fatal illness. The religious devoutness of parents does not seem to affect the quantity of anxiety as expressed by children, but does influence the quality of their concerns and the manner in which they cope with their fears. Previous experience with death may also influence children's fantasy about their own future, depending on the manner in which they were supported during the former incidents.

Some illustrations from the data may highlight these children's awareness of their diagnoses and prognoses and their fears of the future.

One six-year-old boy in the terminal stages of leukemia had discussed his illness with his parents in terms of "tired blood." He told me the following story after looking at a picture of a woman entering a room with her face in her hands:

This is about a woman. She's somebody's mother. She's crying because her son was in the hospital, and he died. He had leukemia. He finally had a heart attack. It just happened. . . he died. Then they took him away to a cemetery to bury him, and his soul went up to heaven.
This woman is crying. But she forgets about it when she goes to bed. Because she relaxes and her brain relaxes. She's very sad. But she sees her little boy again when she goes up to heaven. She's looking forward to that. She won't find anybody else in heaven—just her little boy that she knows..

This story illustrates this boy's awareness of the present

and probable future, the influence of religious instruction on his fantasy and ways of dealing with his concerns, and the quality of loneliness and separation he is experiencing. His sense of helplessness to alter events and certainty about an inevitable future are apparent.

One eight-year-old girl with cystic fibrosis told the following story after examining a picture of a small child in bed with a nurse standing nearby:

> One girl was reading a book in the hospital. The nurse was over by the bed. The girl's name was Becky. She had the bad coughing. She had trouble with her lungs. She had lung congestion. The nurse is looking at her chart. Becky is thinking they're going to do an operation. Becky is only eight years old. She thinks they're going to hurt her and she doesn't want it. And they did give the operation. They gave her a sleeping shot. She didn't like shots. The same nurse always came in, because she knew what to do. Becky died. Then her mother came to see her and they told her she died. But the mother didn't like to hear that.

This story illustrates further the identification which was apparent as the children viewed the pictures, and in this case, the child's projection of her feelings onto the mother. In many instances, though the clues were purposely vague, the children attributed their own diagnoses and symptoms to the characters in their story and thus communicated their concerns and fears. Again, a sense of helplessness is apparent in this story — of inability to alter events, fear of mutilation and pain, certainty about an inevitable future, sadness and separation, yet reliance on those in her environment as giving the only assistance available to her.

Some comments in the stories not only indicated the helplessness a child may feel, but also reflected the view of an environment which is nonsupportive and in some occasions actively hostile, punishing, and impeding anxiety reduction and recovery of a sense of body integrity. A seven-year-old boy with cystic fibrosis commented in a story:

> The little boy had to stay in the hospital because the doctor wanted it. He got a shot in the back; a big needle. He was scared of shots, and didn't want it. And the doctor did it hard. His lungs are gone — he can't

breathe. His lungs got worse and he didn't get well. He died and he was buried with a big shovel.

These statements also communicate the child's fear, his perspective regarding treatment procedures, his sensing that body integrity and intactness cannot be regained, and his feeling of incompleteness in body image. Despondency regarding the future is poignant and loneliness is apparent in the concluding sentence.

In other stories, this boy made statements such as "They [hospital personnel] put a tent on him and freeze him, too," "The nurse turned off the lights and the door was closed, and he was lonesome and scared," "The little boy's very sick – he's mad too, because he wanted to go home." Statements like these illustrate some children's real concern about what they see as unsupportiveness in an environment they are incapable of escaping. They may not appreciate the therapeutic intent of hospital personnel and are preoccupied with fear, loneliness, and anger. Other statements this boy made, such as, "The boy is thinking he hopes he gets well – he's thinking he might not get well and die," highlight very real anxiety about nonbeing, though he had never discussed this overtly with anyone. When coupled with the loneliness he also expressed, it is possible to imagine his fear that he might die in an alien and hostile environment, separated from all those who care about him.

The sense of loneliness is accentuated because of the young child's sense of time as stretching interminably between parental visits. One six-year-old girl commented. "She has to be in the hospital for long days and never gets to see her Mommy and Daddy. She's very lonesome." She also said in one of her stories that the child character "got sick by not coughing up the mucus,"which tells us not only that she has received instruction about her condition (cystic fibrosis), but also that young children often assume responsibility for the causality of their illness whether warranted or unwarranted and may feel guilt in addition to their fears.

Strong feelings of anger and hostility may also accompany the loneliness associated with the question, "Why did this have to happen?" And these feelings may be accentuated by sensed prohibitions against revealing suspicion or knowledge of the diagnosis. An eight-year-old girl who had very recently been diagnosed as having a malignant tumor of the femur and whose mother was determined that she should never be told the diagnosis, nevertheless indicated preoccupation with death in all eight of her stories, angrily concluding almost every story with the death of the main character and remarking, "And nobody cared — not even her mother!" Another story ended with the statement, "She was very lonesome before she died because nobody cared." Such statements give us insight into the manner in which evasiveness or uneasy cheerfulness may be interpreted by children. That this girl was aware of the meaning of the alterations in the emotional climate surrounding her can be seen in this story:

> She's in the hospital, and the doctor is talking to her mother and father. She's sick — she's got cancer. She's very, very sick. She's thinking she wishes she could go home. She had an operation at the hospital, but she didn't want it because she wanted to get out of the hospital. This little girl dies — she doesn't get better. Poor little girl. This girl at the hospital — she has cancer. Her hip is swollen and her bone's broken. This little girl in the picture died, and then they buried her. And then she went up to heaven. She didn't like it there — because God wasn't there.

Conclusion

It seems clear that frequently denial or the protectiveness of adults may not be entirely effective in preventing children with fatal illness from experiencing anxiety or in keeping awareness of their diagnoses and probable prognoses from them. The question of whether a child should be told that his illness is fatal is meaningless; rather questions and concerns which are conscious to the child threatened with death should be dealt with in such a way that the child does not feel further isolated and alienated from his parents and other meaningful adults. There should be no curtain of silence around his most intense fears. These feelings of isolation may also be relieved by efforts designed to keep the child closer, both spatially and emotionally, to others on pediatric wards.

Support must also be made available for them during and

following actual encounters with death on pediatric wards. They need support that allows introspective examination of attitudes and fears related to death in general and to the death of children in particular.

THE GENERAL ANXIETY SCALE FOR CHILDREN

1. When you are away from home, do you worry about what might be happening at home?
2. Do you sometimes worry about whether your body is growing the way it should?
3. Are you afraid of mice or rats?
4. Do you ever worry about knowing your lessons?
5. If you were to climb a ladder, would you worry about falling off it?
6. Do you worry about whether your mother is going to get sick?
7. Do you get scared when you have to walk home alone at night?
8. Do you ever worry about what other people think of you?
9. Do you get a funny feeling when you see blood?
10. When your father is away from home, do you worry about whether he is going to come back?
11. Are you frightened by lightning and thunderstorms?
12. Do you ever worry that you won't be able to do something you want to do?
13. When you go to the dentist, do you worry that he may hurt you?
14. Are you afraid of things like snakes?
15. When you are in bed at night trying to go to sleep, do you often find that you are worrying about something?
16. When you were younger, were you ever scared of anything?
17. Are you sometimes frightened when looking down from a high place?
18. Do you ever worry when you have to go to the doctor's office?
19. Do some of the stories on radio or television scare you?
20. Have you ever been afraid of getting hurt?
21. When you are home alone and someone knocks on the door, do you get a worried feeling?
22. Do you get a scary feeling when you see a dead animal?
23. Do you think you worry more than older boys and girls?
24. Do you worry that you might get hurt in some accident?
25. Has anyone ever been able to scare you?
26. Are you afraid of things like guns?
27. Without knowing why, do you sometimes get a funny feeling in your stomach?
28. Are you afraid of being bitten or hurt by a dog?
29. Do you ever worry about something bad happening to someone you know?

30. Do you worry when you are home alone at night?
31. Are you afraid of being too near fireworks because of their exploding?
32. Do you worry that you are going to get sick?
33. Are you ever unhappy?
34. When your mother is away from home, do you worry about whether she is going to come back?
35. Are you afraid to dive into the water because you might get hurt?
36. Do you get a funny feeling when you touch something that has a real sharp edge?
37. Do you ever worry about what is going to happen?
38. Do you get scared when you have to go into a dark room?
39. Do you dislike getting in fights because you worry about getting hurt in them?
40. Do you worry about whether your father is going to get sick?
41. Have you ever had a scary dream?
42. Are you afraid of spiders?
43. Do you sometimes get the feeling that something bad is going to happen to you?
44. When you are alone in a room and you hear a strange noise, do you get a frightened feeling?
45. Do you ever worry?

Adapted from Sarason, S. B., and Others. *Anxiety in Elementary School Children.* New York, John Wiley and Sons, 1960.

The author marked the "yes's," counted them, and compared the scores of dying children with two control groups of hospitalized children. Dying children showed twice as much anxiety.

NOTES

1. Knudson, A.G., and Natterson, J.M. Participation of parents in the hospital care of their fatally ill children. *Pediatrics* 26:482-490. Sept. 1960.
2. Morrissey, J.R. Death anxiety in children with a fatal illness. In *Crisis Intervention.* ed. by H.J. Parad. (New York. Family Service Association of America, 1965), pp. 324-338.
3. Natterson, J.M., and Knudson, A.G. Observations concerning fear of death in fatally ill children and their mothers. *Psychosom. Med.* 22: 456-465, Nov.-Dec. 1960.
4. Richmond, J.B. and Waisman, H.A. Psychologic aspects of management of children with malignant diseases. *Am. J. Dis. Child.* 89:42-47, Jan. 1955.
5. Sarason, S.B. and others. *Anxiety in Elementary School Children.* (New York. John Wiley and Sons, 1960).
6. Murray, H.A. *Thematic Apperception Test.* (Cambridge, Mass., Harvard University Press, 1943).

QUESTIONS

1. Define:

   statistical distribution   hematology
   death-man   anxiety scale
   concussion   thematic apperception test
   egocentric   projective test
   fantasy

2. The children's statements, "The First Time Somebody I Knew Died," which appear at the beginning of this chapter, represent individual attempts to make sense of death. Examine each selection, separating accurate from inaccurate information and hypothesize how the ideas were formed.

3. In each of the three developmental stages that Maria Nagy outlines, the child is likely to hold some beliefs that will be carried into adult life either as factual errors or more subtly, in attitudes. List euphemisms that parallel the child's notion of death as 1) nonexistent, as 2) sleep and as 3) a person.

4. *A Death in the Family* and *My Grandpa Died Today* both present a young boy faced with the death of a close family member, a father in the former and a grandfather in the latter. Though this chapter presents only a small section of

A Death in the Family much of the mourning process is depicted. Compare and contrast the grief reactions of the boys in the two works. Consider the degree of loss, the practical implications of the loss, the "appropriateness" of the death, the information the boy has been given about the death, as well as each boy's efforts to cope with his loss.

5.   Many of the professionals represented in this chapter (Yudkin, Binger, *et al.,* Waechter) advocate honesty in communications with children who are fatally ill. Yet they do not necessarily equate that honesty with a decision to inform a terminal child of his diagnosis. Outline the factors to be considered and the kind of information to be given if a child is to be informed of a terminal diagnosis.

6.   In the retrospective study conducted by the Binger research team, most families indicated that they had accepted the terminal diagnosis for their child as his "death." But with continued medical advances in the treatment of leukemia, extended remission is a more likely possibility. And the impact of this "Lazarus syndrome" is often difficult for families. Outline the possible difficulties for the family when a child who had been diagnosed as terminal continues in an unexpected and extended remission. In your outline, consider the impact on the patient (his social development, peer relationships, academic pursuits), his siblings, and his parents.

7.   Recalling the discussion of appropriate death in Chapter One, review the reactions of the parents studied by Binger, *et. al.,* and list the factors that could make death of a child appropriate.

8.   The papers by Yudkin, Binger, *et. al.,* and Waechter suggest a need for increased communication with children who are seriously or fatally ill. Outline five changes in hospital care as you know it that might foster increased communication.

9. Eugenia Waechter discusses a number of reactions that terminally ill children express either verbally or non-verbally. List these reactions and compare them to the reactions of a dying adult as outlined by Kubler-Ross in Chapter Two.

PROJECTS FOR FURTHER STUDY

1. Interview three children on the subject of the death of a favorite pet. Allow their discussion to range freely, asking questions only when necessary to continue the discussion. Analyze each set of interview responses in terms of the developmental stages outlined by Maria Nagy.

2. Using the card catalog of your local children's library, compile a bibliography of children's literature where the primary subject is death. Expand the bibliography through annotation: include such details as date of publication, developmental level of audience, point of view from which the story is told, conceptualization of death, religious or cultural setting, object of death, portrayal of the mourning reaction.

3. Much as attitudes about death and dying are rooted in childhood, so are attitudes towards the aging process and the aged shaped at an early age. To explore children's attitudes towards aging, ask five or six children, "Who is the oldest person you know?" and "What do they most like to do?" Then have each child draw a picture of that person involved in his or her favorite activity. Ask each child to tell you about the picture. Compare the pictures and the oral reports that you gather from the children. Note both the similarities and the differences in their accounts and suggest possible reasons for each.

Before beginning these exercises please read "Note to Instructor" on page xiii

STRUCTURED EXERCISES

1. Select five members of the class to role-play the following situation before the rest of the class:

    The parents of a seven year-old leukemic boy are meeting with a health care team consisting of the child's physician, nurse and social worker. The child has reentered the hospital in the terminal phase of his painful illness; he has previously experienced three spontaneous remissions and returned home, only to fall dangerously ill and return to the hospital each time. A fourth remission is not expected. The group must decide whether to begin the child on an expensive new experimental treatment. Although the treatment is not expected to be able to control the disease for the child, it might keep him alive for up to six months longer, and its use in this case would add to medical knowledge and possibly improve the survival rate of other sick children. However, the parents and the two younger brothers of the child have prepared themselves for his death at each return to the hospital. The emotional strain of the dramatic recoveries is reflected in the worsening relationship between the parents and in behavior problems in the children. The father is working a second job to help pay the medical bills. The mother alternates between wanting to keep her child alive at all costs and wanting to release him from pain. The doctor is committed to saving and prolonging life if at all possible, especially in the case of a child. The nurse has cared for the child during each hospitalization and considers herself to have the primary responsibility for caring for the child. The social worker has given the parents financial counseling and has tried to give them psychological support during the long illness.

The five students are to reach a group decision whether to prolong the child's life. After the decision has been made, each should describe to the class how he felt about his role as the discussion progressed. Then the class as a whole should discuss their reactions, answering the following questions:

a. What criteria did the group use to reach the final decision?

b. What additional information would you have liked to have had?

c. Should anyone else have been included in the decision-making?

d. What factors contributed most to the difficulties in making the decision?

2. Set aside a class session for a study group on children's literature. Bring a large selection of children's books which deal with death or have students each bring two books they have read. Divide the class into groups of five. Circulate the books within each group so each person can read all the books in the group. Allow twenty minutes for reading them, and have the groups discuss their reactions to the books. Did they find them enjoyable? realistic? Was the dialogue realistic? Were the characters credible? How threatening was the death? Was there any resolution for the grief? Would the student read the book to a child? Why? or Why not? Did they agree with the conception of death?

FOR FURTHER READING

The following books and papers provide in-depth coverage of the topics introduced in this chapter.

Anthony, E.J. and Koupernik, C. (eds.) *The Child in His Family, Vol. II: The Impact of Disease and Death.* New York: Wiley, 1973.

Anthony, Sylvia. *The Discovery of Death in Childhood and After,* New York: Basic Books, 1972.

Furman, E. A. *Child's Parent Dies: Studies in Childhood Bereavement.* Princeton, N.J.: Yale University Press, 1974.

Grollman, E.A. (ed.) *Explaining Death to Children.* Boston: Beacon Press, 1967.

Lindgren, Astrid. *The Brothers Lionheart,* Leicester: Brockhampton, 1975.

Mills, G.C., Reisler, R., Jr., Robinson, A.E., and Vermilye, G. *Discussing Death: A Guide to Death Education.* Homewood, Ill.: ETC Publications, 1976.

Smith, Doris Buchanan. *A Taste of Blackberries,* New York: Thomas Y. Crowell, 1973.

Stein, Sarah B. *About Dying.* New York: Walker and Company, 1974.

White, E.B. *Charlotte's Web.* New York: Harper and Row, 1952.

Wolf, Anna. *Helping Your Child To Understand Death,* New York: Child Study Press, 1973.

Wolfenstein, M. and Kliman, G. (eds.) *Children and the Death of a President.* New York: Doubleday, 1965.

5

Choices and Decision in Death

INTRODUCTION

Given an extended period of dying, would you prefer to be at home, or in the hospital? Would you want to be maintained on life-extending machinery? To what extent? What do you want to happen to your body after death? Can you imagine any cause that might motivate you to sacrifice your life in martyrdom or that would motivate you to sacrifice your life in an altruistic act? Are there any conditions under which you might choose to end your own life?

The discovery of the role of decision in death is not recent, but the range of possible choices is continually expanding. Treatments of the element of personal decision in death in earlier centuries occasionally included references to martyrdom, but more often were limited to a discussion of suicide, an option that was rarely considered responsible.

Suicide

Apart from isolated accounts of honorable death, as in battle, both Greek and Roman culture generally opposed suicide on ethical grounds. In Athens, for instance, those who attempted suicide were punished with removal of one hand, generally the hand that had been instrumental in the attempt. The milder Roman censure of suicide was strengthened with the influx of the Christian tradition which judged suicide an offense against the cmmandment, "Thou shalt not kill."

From the Middle Ages through to the eighteenth century, penalties against suicide continued in the form of confiscation of property, degradation of the corpse and prohibition against burial in consecrated ground. Though the legal sanctions against suicide have fallen into disuse, the social censure against a suicide attempter or the bereaved "survivor" of a suicide continues.

It was not until the nineteenth century that suicide was studied as a medical problem, often as a form of insanity. In 1897, Emile Durkheim began to study suicide within the context of societal disorganization and alienation. More recently, psychology has taken the study of suicide into an investigation of the nature of personal motivation and levels of intention, thereby expanding the study of self-murder into one of self-destructive behaviors.

Elective Death

The debate over the role of decision in death extends far beyond the issue and frequently centers on the right of the dying patient to determine the manner of his own death. Euthanasia, which once meant simply "the good death" is now associated with elective death, in the face of imminent natural death. In this context, the ethical dilemmas that were posed with the issue of suicide are multiplied; for, with euthanasia, in the sense of voluntary death, the responsibility for decision usually extends beyond the dying person to those around him.

Implicit Choice

Choices related to death are made regularly both in the social context and in a personal realm. In the larger framework of society, the decision to enter a war, no matter how just the cause, to impose the death penalty on a convicted criminal or even to accelerate the progress of environmental pollution is an exercise of choice. Likewise, the personal decision to undertake a rescue operation in spite of personal hazard, or even to persist in a life-endangering behavior challenges mortality.

Reverence for Life

Decisions in death, and their counterpart, reverence for life, forces a reexamination of ethical principles. The abilities to create living organisms under laboratory conditions, on the one hand, and to terminate prenatal life through abortion on the other, call for an evaluation of responsibility in the generation and termination of life. Ethical issues which once may have been reserved for the philosopher have entered the domain of the scientist and press with an immediacy on the common man. Confronted with the intubation of the helpless who, if conscious at all, seem aware only of pain and hopelessness, how is one to weigh the relative merits of the quality of life against its quantity, or, as some have suggested, against its costs—both psychological and financial. Any study of elective death must draw freely on the best available information in all disciplines. In the future, the number of choices associated with death is destined to increase, and a continued study of death and dying can make implicit choices *explicit.* Continued examination is not without its hazards, however. As Bob Patrick wonders, in the final selection of this chapter, about the effects of continued proximity to physical death, we might ask what the effects of intellectual familiarity with death will be. Will the study of death and dying be popularized to the point of defeating its purpose by exploiting innate fears? Or, in taming death will we regularize decisions with mundane practicality, and rob death of its mystery?

ENCOUNTER

SUICIDE PACT

Dr. and Mrs. Henry P. Van Dusen, leaders in American theological life, swallowed overdoses of sleeping pills last month in the bedroom of their Princeton, N.J., home in an effort to carry out a suicide pact.

Mrs. Van Dusen died. Dr. Van Dusen vomited up the pills and died 15 days later on Feb. 13, apparently of a heart ailment, in the Carrier Clinic in Belle Meade, N.J.

Dr. Van Dusen, the former president of Union Theological Seminary, and his wife—both members of the Euthanasia Society and advocates of an individual's right to terminate his or her own life—had entered into the pact rather than face the prospect of debilitating old age.

Mrs. Van Dusen was 80 years old when she died on Jan. 28. Her husband was 77. Although reportedly depressed, the Van Dusens were convinced that their suicide attempt carried no burden of sin but rather the promise of after-life.

Friends and associates had known of the couple's suicide effort, but details about the incident did not become widely known until yesterday.

Kenneth A. Briggs. "Suicide Pact Preceded. Deaths of Dr. Van Dusen and His Wife." *New York Times,* February 25, 1975. © 1975 by the New York Times Company. Reprinted by permission.

In a letter they left behind, the Van Dusens said there were many old people who would die of natural causes if not kept alive medically and expressed the resolve not to "die in a nursing home."

The Van Dusens, whose prominence peaked while Dr. Van Dusen served as president of the seminary from 1945 until his retirement in 1963, said that they had led "happy lives" but that poor health no longer permitted them to "do what we want to do."

A worsening arthritic condition had made Mrs. Van Dusen lame. Five years ago, Dr. Van Dusen suffered a severe stroke which limited his physical activity and prevented him from speaking normally. For the vigorous, articulate Presbyterian scholar and his active wife, the setbacks were serious impediments to living the kind of useful, productive lives to which they had become accustomed.

1. The Van Dusens' act highlights the issue of the individual's right to choose death. Do you believe that this right exists? Under what circumstances?

2. Had you been in circumstances similar to the Van Dusens' would you have made the same choice?

3. Consider the person discovering the Van Dusens within a reasonable period after they had taken the sleeping pills. Would that person have a moral obligation to revive them? Would the obligation be any different for a friend, relative or family doctor?

In choosing their time of death, the Van Dusens took a stand on a long-debated issue: the issue of whether or not an individual has the right to terminate his life. Though some major writers (Epicurus, Thomas More, John Donne and Montaigne among them) have presented the arguments in favor of the individual's right to choose his dying, the main current of Western thought has held that the proprietary right over human life rests with divine authority, or the state (often seen as the earthly representative of the divine order) rather than with the individual.

In the following paper, Joseph Fletcher, a medical ethicist, argues that human needs validate human rights so that, in certain situations, a man has the right to end his own life. Fletcher bases his views on what he terms a 'pragmatic situation ethic' and urges that the issue of when to terminate life be examined in the context of changing conditions.

ELECTIVE DEATH

Joseph Fletcher

> Vex not his ghost: O, let him pass! He
>   hates him
> That would upon the wrack of this
>   tough world
> Stretch him out longer.

Shakespeare

Since we shoulder our responsibility for birth control, a feature of every civilized culture, can death control be far behind? If we have a right to initiate a life deliberately, may we not terminate one? Depending, of course, upon the circumstances?

There are really two questions here, one factual and one moral. In what follows, the thrust is toward answering both of them in the affirmative. To a certain extent these questions are

---

Joseph Fletcher. "Elective Death." *Ethical Issues in Medicine*. Edited by E. Fuller Torey. Boston: Little, Brown and Company, 1968.

mutually penetrating. In actual fact the practice of death control is increasing, due to medical pressures and human needs so great that they provide their own moral justification. And as the practice is further justified by the situation, it is more easily and sensibly encouraged and disinhibited. It is exactly in this sense that I use the term *right*—as something justified pragmatically by the situation. Those who entertain any notion that there are some rights which are simply given in the very nature of things, above and beyond circumstances or human needs, will not be happy about everything I am about to say, and they ought to be alerted.

What is to be said to a nurse who is upset and suffers an acute anxiety reaction, unable to carry out her duty, because an intern, on instructions from a staff surgeon and a resident, has told her that a patient in the recovery room is to be "let go," and that she is to turn off the intravenous fluids and the oxygen? (Often only the slower strategy of starvation is used, without suffocation.) What is a man to do whose father has been lying virtually unconscious for four years in a hospital bed, following a massive cerebral hemorrhage? The patient cannot eat or speak; is incontinent, shows no neurological evidence of interpersonal communication and is kept going with tube feeding by around-the-clock private nurses. The patient's son would feel guilt about suggesting that the doctors bring it to a close, yet he also feels guilty about the expense ($40,000 a year), the wasted resources that other things and people need, and his father's distressingly subhuman status. After all, is the patient anymore his father?

Years ago, in 1954, I wrote that there is a logical contradiction in the Hippocratic Oath, subscribed to by the medical profession. As I saw it then, the Oath illogically promises two incompatible things, both to relieve suffering and, as I put it, to "Prolong and protect life." [1] But I was mistaken. Actually, there is not a word in that pious old apprenticeship agreement about either relieving suffering or prolonging life. Instead, the promise is to seek the "benefit of the sick," leaving the meaning of "benefit" unstipulated. The vitalistic idea that preserving life is the *summum bonum* of medicine appears nowhere in the Oath, except eisegetically (i.e., when read into it). On the contrary, making life sacrosanct was more likely a Pythagorean taboo, different from the empirical temper of Hippocrates and his case-minded approach. In place of such moral metaphysics, he said, in a famous maxim, "Life is short and art is long, the occasion fleeting, experience fallacious and judgment difficult." He knew the relativity of ethical decision. In fact, some of his disciples engaged in direct euthanasia on the same grounds that Plato, Socrates, Epicurus, and the Stoics approved it.[2]

In any case, what appeared to be ethical to whomever it was who wrote the Oath is not an eternal verity. Almost certainly it was not Hippocrates, as Edelstein has now made abundantly clear.[3] There is no reason to take that unknown moralist's understanding of right and wrong or good and evil as a permanent model of conscience for all times and all conditions. What is right or good does not transcend changing circumstances; it arises out of them.

When biologists predict that by, let us say the year 2100, men will be free of hunger and infectious diseases, able to enjoy physical and mental life to the age of 90 or 100, replacing defective parts of the body as need develops, cyborg fashion, we can hope that the frequency of treatment situations posing the question of elective death will be cut down. But sooner or later it will arise for many patients, no matter what the longevity norm may become. Paradoxically, modern medicine's success in prolonging life has itself directly increased the incidence of death control decisions in the chronic and terminal ills of the American people. Those over 65 are expected to increase from 18.5 million in 1966 to 24.5 million in 1980—something in the order of one out of every eight persons.

Novels in the classic tradition have drawn a picture of the deathbed scene where the elderly "pass on," surrounded by their families and friends, making their farewell speeches and *meeting* death instead of being overtaken or snatched by it. This model of death has become almost archaic. Nowadays, most of the time, death comes to people (even the young and middle aged) in a sedated and comatose state; betubed nasally, abdominally, and intravenously; and far more like manipulated objects than like moral subjects. A whole fascinating array of devices—surgical, pharmacological, and mechanical—is brought into play to stave death off clinically and biologically. Yet ironically, by their dehumanizing effects these things actually hasten personal death, i.e., loss of self-possession and conscious integrity. They raise in a new form the whole question of "life" itself, of how we are to understand it and whether the mere minimum presence of vital functions is what we mean by it.

For many people contemplating modern medicine's ability to prolong life (or, perhaps, to prolong death), death itself is welcome compared to the terrors of senility and protracted terminal treatment. Patients actually look for doctors who will promise not to allow them to "go through what mother did" or "lie there as Uncle John was made to." They are beginning to ponder ways of *escaping* medical ministrations; the white coats of our doctors and their paramedical attendants are taking on a grimmer hue, a new and less benign image. This is bound to increase as medicine's victories continue. It is a success problem, not a failure problem! The predominant illnesses become degenerative and chronic, not acute or infectious. Disorders in the metabolic group, cardiovascular ills, renal problems, and malignancies—these fill our hospital beds.

DEATH: ENEMY AND FRIEND

In all talk of elective death—that is, chosen or moral dying rather than fatal or amoral dying (*moral* always means the voluntary as against the involuntary or helpless)—the basic issue is whether human beings are always to regard death as an enemy, never as a friend. Is death never to be welcomed? May we never choose to go out and meet it? Dr. Logan Clendenning years ago, in his popularizing effort to make knowledge a part of the public's weaponry against illness, thought of it as being sometimes a friend. He wrote, "As I think it over, death seems to me one of the few evidences in nature of the operation of a creative intelligence exhibiting qualities which I recognize as mind stuff. To have blundered onto the form of energy called life showed a sort of malignant power. After having blundered on life to have conceived of death was a real stroke of genius." [4]

The logic of this is to either fight off or make an ally of *mortis*, as it happens to suit human needs. This is exactly what all medicine does; it either uses or outwits all biological forces for the sake of humanly chosen ends. Medicine is, at bottom, an interference with blind, brute nature. Three hundred years ago Thomas Sydenham called it "the support of enfeebled and the coercion of outrageous nature." Medicine refuses to "leave in God's (nature's) hands what must be" in everything else but death. Why should it stop there? Maurice Maeterlinck was sure that "there will come a day when science will protest its errors and will shorten our sufferings."[5] And that day is at hand, precisely because of the achievements of medical science and the pressures such achievements create to rethink our values and our view of man.

Medicine's primary *raison d'etre* is, in Albert Schweitzer's phrase, "reverence for life." Life is its business. This, however, is very far from absolutizing the vital spark regardless of human personality and its claims. To subordinate every other consideration to bare sentience is to make biological life, as such, an idol. It is the vitalistic error. Respiration, circulation, reflexes, and the like, are not ends in themselves. Can it not be that life in its fullest meaning includes death, and that, since death is certain to come whether it does so constructively or willy-nilly, the only real question open to us is how it comes, as a good death ("euthanasia") or a bad death ("dysthanasia")?

Dr. David Karnofsky, who did so much for the Sloan-Kettering Institute, put the point of view of radical vitalism very clearly, at a meeting of the American Cancer Society in 1961. He opposed letting the patient go under any circumstances, arguing that the practice of keeping the patient alive is endorsed by "state planners, efficiency experts, social workers, philosophers, theologians, economists and humanitarians." Apart from this being a pretty wild *omnium gatherum* (practically everybody in the helping professions), the accusation is symptomatic of the embattled, almost paranoid mentality of many physicians. Karnofsky's main professed reason for preserving life by any and all means as long as possible was the old statistical absurdity about "something might turn up at the last minute, some new discovery or an inexplicable remission." But what is more irresponsible than to hide from decision-making behind a logical possibility that is without antecedent probability?

As an example of "ethical" medicine, Dr. Karnofsky cited a patient with cancer of the large bowel. After a colostomy followed by recurrence, x-ray treatment was used; radioactive phosphorus checked abdominal fluids, and an antibiotic stopped broncho-pneumonia. Metastases ended liver function in spite of innumerable delaying actions, stupifying or traumatic, until the end "came." The patient was kept alive for ten months, but might otherwise have died in a matter of days or weeks. Was it right or wrong to add ten months? Was it more life or more death that was added? Who was benefited? What were the benefits? For Dr. Karnofsky, the obligation to maintain biological function or "life" was not a question of weighing benefits and forfeits. For him what is right or good was intrinsic; and life as such, per se, was precious—of greater value than anything else. This is the fundamental question in all cases of ethical concern, not only in life and death. Is the worth or desirability of thing or action inherent and intrinsic, regardless of the situation; or do right and good depend contingently and extrinsically upon the situation? If you take the intrinsic position, then some if not all obligations are absolute and universal; if you take the extrinsic view, all are relative. Karnofsky, like many others, was an absolutist. I am not. On the absolutist view some things are never open to responsible decision and choice; in "situation ethics" everything is.

IMPORTANT DISTINCTIONS

It is at this point that we need to pause to make distinctions of some practical importance. In the management of terminal illness there are two distinct moral problems, closely related but by no means the same. One is the classic issue over *euthanasia*; the other, and by far the more pressing in its frequency, is "letting the patient go" or, as I have called it, *anti-dysthanasia.* [6] The classic debate was about "mercy killing," i.e., doing something directly to end a life graciously when it would otherwise go on (active euthanasia, it is sometimes called). The more pressing and more common issue is whether one may graciously refrain from procedures, not *doing* something but *omitting* to do something, so that death will come (in some circles this is called *passive euthanasia*). This second problem is the one that our success with prolongation and resuscitation forces upon us daily in hospitals all around the world. Possibly the best way to put the distinction with its various sides is to speak of euthanasia in four terms:

1. *Direct voluntary*, as when a patient consciously chooses to end it all, with or without medical intervention. Such is the case of the patient who sneaks an overdose or is left one within reach, or who swallows a Kleenex or pulls out a tube. It is deliberately done and consciously willed by the patient.

2. *Indirect voluntary*, as when a patient before reaching an unconscious or comatose state (while still competent and with a *mens sana* even if not *in corpore sano*) gives leave to his medical servants to use discretion about letting death come. This, too, the patient has willed, yet his death is not directly done but indirectly by ceasing opposition to it. Such is the case of those who, after consultation, "pull the plug" at some point of diminishing returns.

3. *Indirect involuntary*, as when a patient's wishes are not known and yet doctors and/or family and friends *choose for him* to stop fighting off death. Such is the case when the pain, subhuman condition, irreversibility, cost, injustice to others, and the like, combine to outweigh the benefits of keeping him alive. This third form is far and away the most typical and frequent situation—indirect euthanasia, without the patient's past or present opinion in the account, except as it might be presumed.

4. *Direct involuntary*, as when a patient's wishes are not known, yet in the judgment of physicians, family, or friends it seems better to them to end his life by a "mercy killing" than to let it go on, as it will. Such a case would be a decerebrated person, perhaps one whose cerebral cortex has been shattered in an auto accident, in "excellent health" biophysically, fed by indwelling nasal tubes, unable to move a muscle, suffers no pain but only reacts by reflex to a needle prick. I know one such, a young man

358

(who now looks like a little child), and his mother says, "My son is dead." Another case would be an obstetrician's decision not to respirate a monster at birth, or a "blue baby" deoxygenated beyond tolerable limits of cyanosis or brain suffocation.

Some moralists have tended to put great store by the distinction between "direct" and "indirect" actions, Roman Catholics, for example. They argue that it is one thing morally to *do* an act such as ending a life by "bare bodkin" (as Shakespeare put it), and another thing altogether to *permit* a life to end by starvation, as when an intravenous therapy is discontinued. To others this seems a cloudy and tenuous distinction. Either way the intention is the same, the same end is willed and sought. And the means used do not justify the end in one case if not the other, nor are the means used anything that *can* be justified or "made sense of" except in relation to the gracious purpose in view. Kant said, as part of his practical reason, that if we will the end, we will the means. Whether euthanasia is direct or indirect, voluntary or involuntary, is ethically something that *depends upon the facts in the situation,* not upon some intrinsic principle regardless of the realities. This is the shape of the tension between empirical and metaphysical moralities.

Curiously enough, in view of the religious and philosophical differences which divide moralists and ethicists, this matter of an alleged obligation to make the maintenance of a patient's life the supreme obligation is one around which moralists are pretty well united against the publicly professed opinion of the medical profession. (Note, I say "publicly.") That is, we find that Catholic, Protestant, Jewish, and humanist teachings all have a place for euthanasia in one form or another. Archbishop Temple,[7] the Anglican theologian, once said of pacifism what can be said of Karnofsky's radical vitalism, that it "can only rest upon a belief that life, physiological life, is sacrosanct. That is not a Christian idea at all; for, if it were, the martyrs would be wrong. If the sanctity is *in* life, it must be wrong to give your life in a noble cause as well as to take another's . . . Of course, this implies that, *as compared to some things,* the loss of life is a small evil; and, if so, then, *as compared to some other things,* the taking of life is a small injury."

Catholic moralists, and most orthodox Jews and most orthodox Protestants, are opposed to euthanasia in forms # 1 and # 4 (see previous list); i.e., they rule out as immoral any direct methods of ending a life in order to end suffering and waste. But they allow forms # 2 and # 3, the indirect strategies. Catholic theologians refuse to call the indirect forms "euthanasia," and they add a further *caveat* or limitation. Pius XII[8] and his interpreters have restricted even the indirect forms (both of which they justify) to permission to cease and desist from the use of "extraordinary" treatments only, where there is no reasonable hope of benefit. All ordinary treatments must continue without letup. Usually, *extraordinary* procedures are taken to be those that are expensive, painful, or inconvenient.[9]

The difficulty with this is, like so much else, due to the rapid advance of medical science and of the medical arts. Ordinary and extraordinary are very relative terms as the weaponry of health and control of nature's pathologies sweeps on. Look at how quickly penicillin ceased to be extraordinary, and also sulpha drugs and electronic cardiac devices such as the pacemakers. In no time prosthetic implants will be old hat. There is no way to establish a consensus (even if desirable) as to the defining features of an extraordinary treatment. Is it mortality rate, pain, inconvenience, expense, effectiveness, competence, subject's life expectancy (a lung removed in a child is not the same as in an old person), frequency, or what? And so it goes.

Those who live by situation ethics, and this includes many liberal Jews and Protestants and humanists (this writer being one), are ethically prepared to employ euthanasia in all four forms, depending in every actual case upon the circumstances. Nevertheless, no matter what rhetoric and doctrine are used at the theoretical level, there can be no doubt that in practice there is an increase of responsible situational decision making in proportion to the increase of the problem's occurrence in our hospitals. By now, due to greater longeviy and medical know-how, it is an everyday, almost routine thing. Considerations of income and experience, especially in teaching hospitals, may tend to soft-pedal the issue and discourage it, but profit, training, and research are only brakes; they do not stop the trend to elective death. The frightening pressures of population only add to it. Sooner or later we shall be forced back on "statistical" morality. Speaking of a situation not unlike ours in America, the British medical journal *Lancet*[10] says: "If the average length of a patient's stay in a hospital is two weeks, a bed in that hospital occupied for a year could have been used by 26 other patients . . . In a country without a surplus of hospital beds, an irrevocably unconscious patient may sometimes be kept alive at the cost of other people's lives."

OBJECTIONS

In *Morals and Medicine* I have identified and thoroughly discussed ten different objections to euthanasia. I will not attempt to retrace all of that ground but there are some elements in the traditional opposition to euthanasia (we can call it *elective death*, if we prefer) that keep cropping up. The objection that it is suicide is only an epithet which is not really in question. The objection that it is murder only begs the question, since the problem is precisely whether a *felo de se* for medical cause is to be held an unlawful killing or not. When people cite the Ten Commandments they often fail to note that the decalogue prohibits murder, not killing as such, and this too ties in with the whole question of licit and illicit dying and killing. Obviously the Jews, as well as their Christian cousins, have not been in any significant numbers vegetarians or pacifists or opposed to capital punishment.

Once a bishop castigated me for saying that by wanting to release those caught in a painful and incurable condition I was ignoring the theologically alleged benefit spiritually ("the redemptive effect") of suffering, as in Jesus' crucifixion. The bishop himself ignored the fact that sacrificial suffering is voluntary and chosen and conscious. There is nothing redemptive going on *in most instances* of terminal misery and loss of human functions. And when it is said that given the right to choose death too many would do it impulsively or connive and encourage it in others for selfish reasons (e.g., "to get the deed to the old home place"), what reply is needed other than *abusus non tollit usum*, the abuse of a thing does not rule out its use? Otherwise we should always have to repress any research, innovation, and development which enlarges our human control over the conditions of life, since all such power can be used for ill as for good.

Some say that if our society and culture tolerated suicide in such cases as we have mentioned the result would be a cheapening of life and weakening of our moral fiber.[11] They seem to think that all interest would be lost, for example, in intensive care units, and nobody would respond to emergency Code 90 calls! If there is danger of becoming hardened by the practice of death control, by the same token there is danger of becoming hardened by the constant practice of prolonging life beyond any personal or human state. Pope's lines on vice cut two ways: "Yet seen too oft, familiar with her face, We first endure, then pity, then embrace." It is at least possible that euthanasia could not have half the demoralizing influence of stockpiling and planning to use weapons of mass extermination, even "tactical" bombs, and the total war of modern military technology. Besides, not every human being cries, *Timor Mortis conturbat me* (the fear of death confounds me); there are the pure in heart who fear not. "It is safe," said C. S. Lewis, "to tell the pure in heart that they shall see God, for only the pure in heart want to."[12] The fear of the hereafter, among religious believers and skeptics alike, is nearly gone except for primitives and a few doctrinaire incorrigibles.

Perhaps the most anomalous stance in the whole developing discussion is the official or formal position of the medical fraternity, as taken in the American Medical Association and similar groups, that what they are opposed to only is making euthanasia *legal*. That is, they want to use their own discretion, as they are already doing, but they do not want any public acknowledgment that they have any such discretion or ever use it. The fact is, of course, that even in the case of euthanasia in form #3, doctors are vulnerable to malpractice suits ("failure to do what is of average competence and practice"). Hence the essentially scared and "phony"discussion in medical circles, and a tightly bound fraternal refusal to testify in court adversely to a fellow physician no matter what the charge or the facts. In this matter as in so many others, the law, and the conventional wisdom, are hopelessly antediluvian when see in the light of medicine's progress. But the day is coming when doctors will recognize that just as they are slowly accepting the morality of terminating some lives at the beginning (abortion) for therapeutic reasons of mental, emotional, and social well-being, so they should be terminating for these reasons some lives at the ending, i.e., therapeutic euthanasia.

It would be unfair to the morally muscle-bound and false to the facts to urge the case for euthanasia in any of its forms as if there were no difficulties. The finest diagnosticians and prognosticians are sometimes baffled. At best the safest way to describe a professional person, whatever his field, is as an educated guesser. We cannot be "sure" that the "hopeless" case is really hopeless. Resuscitation procedures now have greatly increased our chances of reviving drowned people or frozen people who not long ago were beyond help. So also with cardiac arrests, anoxia, some cerebral vascular lesions, spontaneous hypoglycemia, and the like. The exciting thing about medicine is that even though it magnifies the problem of medical initiative in death for the aged and the chronic, it reduces it for the young and the acute. Yet there is no escape from the necessity of decision, case by case. This is as true for "ending it all" or "letting him go" as for whether to operate or not. Nothing is certain but death itself, on its own terms or ours. But if in the face of man's finite knowledge and understanding of health, life, and death, even our physicians cannot make good *"guess-timates,"* then we are indeed trapped in a merely fatalistic web. But if they have a truly creative competence, as I believe they have, then why refuse them the initiative late and not early? What does it mean to "have" a doctor?

WHAT IS DEATH AND WHEN?

Back and behind this very human and crucial question of when death is to be accepted lies the question, "When *is* death?" And, in a way, *what* is death? Even the most pragmatic value problems presuppose profound philosophical or theological commitments. The outmoded legal definition of death nearly completely misses the mark in these days of biochemistry and death control, and of genetic control. Almost certainly the heart-and-lungs definition, by which life is supposed to be present if there is clinically detectable breathing or heartbeat, will have to go. We cannot use mad Lear's test of Cordelia's corpse: "Lend me a looking glass; If that her breath will mist or stain the stone, Why then, she lives."

The philosophy of elective death turns its advocates in the direction of determining death as present, or life gone, when a patient's EEG (electroencephalographic tracing) has remained flat for say 24 hours, regardless of other criteria such as respiration or heartbeat.[13] This is certainly a long enough anoxia or cessation of the bioelectric activity of the brain to establish cerebral death, *and cerebral death is death*. This is reported to have been adopted by the French Academy of Medicine, and neurologists everywhere (e.g., Clarence Carfoord of Sweden) advocate it.

The point to note is that modern medical thinking, using a conceptual apparatus drawn from scientific method, no longer regards life and death as *events*. They are seen and understood now as points along a biological continuum. This makes nonsense of much of the old-fashioned abortion debate about when conception occurs, at insemination or fertilization or development of the embryo to certain stages, and so on along the pregnancy line. In the same way it undercuts the argument about when death "occurs," because death is a *process,* not an event. And the core of it is not sentience of the body or some arbitrary minimum of vital functions; *it is the person, and mental function.* When mind is gone, in the degenerative process, and with it the homeostasis of the organism, then life is gone: death has come. Then, at least, if not before, let the battle stop.

It is this problematic character of both life and death, medically regarded, that lends so much interest to a suggestion from Dr. Charles K. Holling[14] of the College of Medicine in the University of Cincinnati: "Hospitals of the future may well have 'death boards.' Applications for permission to discontinue the artificial measures by which life is being maintained might be made to such boards either by the patient who is in possession of his mental faculties or by his next-of-kin." Such review boards could well have an ombudsman, an intelligent lay participant. Dr. Holling is using a model from the "TA" boards of hospitals, those that make decisions in cases of therapeutic abortion.

Bernard Shaw has Sir Patrick say, in *The Doctor's Dilemma*, "All professions are conspiracies against the laity." The old gambit of writing prescriptions in Latin to keep patients from knowing what they say will not work any longer. Medicine is not a "mystery" any more, and its practitioners no longer have a craft of which everybody else is totally ignorant. This is the age of science, and that means a unity of knowledge and freedom of exchange. Repressed knowledge does not stay repressed, as the growing membership of the Nuclear Nations Club attests. Among other things this means that the doctors are no longer alone or isolated in their decision making. In situation problems about terminal cases the physician does not have to cast his own vote alone and uncounted with others. Nor, given medicine's great gains, is the range of decisions as narrow as it once was. When we have to reckon with death, we need not always only glimpse it over our shoulder as we run. Indeed, if we run we are lost.

FATALITY OR INTEGRITY

There are deep-rooted psychic inhibitions which prevent us from seeing our problem in a rational and responsible perspective. There is, or has been, too much *mystique* and superstitious metaphysics about it. But now it presents itself as a challenge to human control, as distinguished from supernatural or natural and fatalistic control. It is a question of responsible control of life, not merely of health and well-being but of being itself. It is time we confronted theology's blanket denunciation of suicide and medicine's uncritical opposition to death.[15]

In the final analysis there are three postures we can assume. The one with the most tradition is absolutist. In its theological form it has been expressed in terms of a divine monopoly theory of life and death. It says that God is the creator of each person ("soul") and reserves to himself the right to decide when life shall come (as against birth control) and when death shall come (as against euthanasia). A much studied treatise in this old tradition says death control is "a violation of the property rights of Jesus Christ."[16] If the absolutist posture takes a nontheological shape it becomes radical vitalism or a sort of naturalistic mystique about life as the highest good and death the worst evil, regardless of the situation. It is the first posture, the absolutist one, which lends itself to accusations of "playing God" when elective death is discussed.

The second posture is the one of stoic indifference or anomie. Because it finds no meaning in existence, it assigns no real value to it and can as easily embrace endurance of life at its worst as repudiation of life at its best.

In between these two extremes of absolutism and adiaphorism lies the pragmatic situation ethic. It finds life good sometimes, and death good sometimes, depending upon the case, the circumstances, the total context. In this view life, no more than any other good thing or value, is good in itself but only by reason of the situation; and death, no more than any other evil, is evil in itself but only by reason of the situation. This is the method by which medicine makes decisions, and there is every reason why it should do so from first to last.

NOTES

1. Fletcher, J., *Morals and Medicine* (Princeton: Princeton University Press, 1954).
2. Williams, G., *The Sanctity of Life and the Criminal Law* (New York: Alfred A. Knopf, 1957).
3. Edelstein, L., *The Hippocratic Oath* (Baltimore: Johns Hopkins University Press, 1943).
4. Clendenning, L., *The Human Body* (3rd ed.) (New York: Alfred A. Knopf, 1941).
5. Jacoby, G. W., *Physician, Pastor and Patient* (New York: Paul B. Hoeber, 1936).
6. Fletcher, J., Death and medical initiative. *Folia Medica* (Tufts University) 7:30, 1962.
7. Temple, W., *Thoughts in War Time* (London: Macmillan & Co., 1940).

8. Pope Pius XII, *Acta Apostolicae Sedis* 49:1027, 1957.
9. Kelly, G., *Medico-Moral Problems* (St. Louis: Catholic Hospital Association, 1958).
10. The prolongation of dying. Editorial. *Lancet* 2:1205, December 8, 1962.
11. Shils, E., The sanctity of life. *Encounter* 28:39, 1967.
12. Rhoads, P. S., Management of the patient with terminal illness. *J.A.M.A.* 192:661, 1965.
13. Hamlin, H., Life or death by EEG. *J.A.M.A.* 190:112, 1964.
14. Hofling, C. K., Terminal decisions. *Mediczl Opinion and Review* 2:1, 1966.
15. Hillman, J., *Suicide of the Soul* (New York: Harper & Row, 1964).
16. Koch, A., and Preuss, A., *Handbook of Moral Theology* (St. Louis: Herder, 1924).

The research of Michael L. Peck and Carl I. Wold of the Los Angeles Suicide Prevention Center leads the discussion of elective death into a general study of self-destructive behavior. Peck and Wold believe that suicidal behavior patterns vary directly with an individual's age and life experience; consequently, a variety of methods for both evaluating and managing suicidal crises is needed.

In the full paper, "The Suicidal Patient," Peck and Wold present case examples of suicidal threats arising from various life crises. The following excerpt illustrates an instance where a typical need of adolescence to resolve the conflict of dependence versus independence is aggravated by the impending death of a parent and the family's refusal to discuss the death openly.

THE SUICIDAL PATIENT: ADOLESCENT SUICIDE

Michael L. Peck and Carl I. Wold

The authors' clinical and research experience have suggested that suicidal behaviors are not part of the unitary psychodynamic and symptom picture, but rather can be seen as dealing with conflicts and life-style issues that may be peculiar to an individual's age or experiences. Out of this assumption grows the conviction that somewhat different treatment approaches are necessary for more favorable outcomes within the various syndromes.

The first suicide syndrome to be discussed is that of the adolescent depression. The major conflict area involved here is that of dependence versus independence. It frequently occurs out of the adolescent feeling his dependency needs have not been

From *Problems in Psychotherapy: An Eclectic Approach.* Edited by W. Klopfer and M. Reed. Washington, D.C.: Hemisphere Publishing Corporation, 1974.

gratified on the one hand, and pushing himself or being pushed to move toward greater independence before he is ready. The context of the onset of this suicidal crisis or episode is generally within the family constellation, and frequently suicidal behavior occurs primarily as a need to communicate the strong feelings of frustration, hopelessness, and the blocked channels of expression.

ADOLESCENT SUICIDE SUBGROUP

Evaluation Phase

Laurie is a 15-year-old girl who was first seen at the Suicide Prevention Center following a telephone call by her stepmother. Laurie was described as miserable to live with, manipulative and unhappy, and she was now threatening to injure herself. At the outset of the office interview, it was apparent that many conflicts existed between the girl and her stepmother, Mrs. Z. Mrs. Z stated that she had married Laurie's father two years ago when the girl was 13. Although Laurie still had strong love for her mother, who had died three years earlier, she seemed to welcome and accept Mrs. Z. into the family. Their relations were reported to be quite positive for six or eight months. The usual family problems began to develop at this point and conflicts and disputes over discipline and gaining father's attention became more frequent and aggravated. Mr. Z. was described by his wife as trying to settle these conflicts fairly and objectively, but she said that Laurie grew more and more demanding.

Things became worse, according to Mrs. Z., about six months earlier when Laurie began behaving most erratically, manifesting severe mood swings and appetite and sleep irregularities, and began talking about how unhappy she was. This culminated, two days prior to the call to the Suicide Prevention Center, in Laurie ingesting a handful of aspirin in front of her father and stepmother. The reason given by Laurie for this action, both to her parents and to the therapist, was that she was miserable and wanted to die.

Laurie's version of the past two years was not dissimilar from her stepmother's. From her point of view, however, she described her unhappiness beginning about a year ago when she became aware that her stepmother was taking more and more of her father's time away from Laurie. The final event that contributed to her increasing unhappiness and apparent depression occurred about five months ago when she learned that most of her friends were going to attend a different high school several miles away, while she found out that she would have to attend the high school nearest her home and would know relatively few people. Laurie stated that this was really the core of her unhappiness and if somehow she could attend high school with her close friends, the other issues in the home would be less unpleasant.

Physically, Laurie was a rather pleasant looking, somewhat plump adolescent girl, who had not yet completed her development of breasts and hips, and so had a slight trace of a preadolescent appearance. She rarely smiled, did not speak in an animated manner, and appeared somewhat clinically depressed to the therapist. She emphasized that she, in fact, did not want to die at the present time, but was very unhappy and wished things could change.

The therapist inquired as to where the father was at this time, and why he could not come to the session. Mrs. Z. replied that Mr. Z. was not well and hopefully he would come to the next session. At this point, the therapist offered some encouragement that things could be worked out, that both Laurie and her family might need to be somewhat more flexible in trying new things in order to deal with Laurie's unhappiness and the repercussions that it had had in the family. They both agreed and then the therapist suggested that Mr. and Mrs. Z. might discuss with Laurie the possibility of Laurie going to the high school of her choice and try to work this out with the high school administration. If Laurie could organize her own transportation, Mrs. Z. thought this plan might be implemented and would also be satisfactory to Mr. Z. They agreed to discuss it that night and an appointment was made for the entire family for the following week.

The following week Laurie and Mrs. Z. returned, again without Mr. Z. present. Mrs. Z. stated that he was still not well enough to come in. The therapist this time chose to first interview Laurie alone. She seemed as depressed as the prior week and expressed no feelings of relief for her unhappiness nor hope that there was any relief in sight. When the therapist inquired as to how their discussion about the schools had worked out, she stated that she could go to the high school of her choice and that did make her feel better that night, but she had been unhappy and depressed ever since. When the therapist asked Laurie to give her impressions as to how her father viewed all that had been going on, she burst into tears. She blurted out the fact that her father was, in fact, very ill, suffering from a terminal disease and that he was not expected to live past six or seven months. She stated that she tried so hard not to worry or upset him but she couldn't help the terrible feelings of fright and depression that overcame her and had been occurring ever since she had found out about her father's condition six months ago. She viewed herself as being abandoned and because of her rather tenuous relationship with her stepmother felt that she would have nowhere to live and no one who would accept her. It was clear to the therapist at this point that the depression in Laurie stemmed from the anticipation of loss, the feeling of insecurity and being abandoned, and the strong sense of frustration over the general *collusion* among all the family members not to discuss father's impending death with anyone or amongst themselves. The suicidal gesture, then, on Laurie's part, represented an attempt to get this particular issue out in the open.

Active Intervention Phase

The therapist called Mrs. Z. into the office and explained to her what had been discussed. Although Mrs. Z. seemed somewhat surprised and disappointed that Laurie had revealed this family secret, she quickly agreed to a family conference with the therapist, which would be held in the family's home since the father was too ill to travel.

The goals at this point changed rapidly from that of arranging short-term changes in Laurie's environment in order to relieve her symptoms, to a family discussion oriented toward the long-term future of this girl, that is, what would happen to her after her father died.

Resolving the crisis

Six family sessions were held in which the therapist learned that Laurie's feelings about her stepmother not wanting her if her father was no longer in the picture were correct. Inquiry as to whom she could live with revealed an aunt and uncle who enthusiastically and warmly stated that they would welcome Laurie into their home. Following this, several individual sessions were conducted with Laurie alone, focusing on her feelings of loss, first in regard to her mother's death three years ago and now in connection with her father's anticipated death, and her feelings of insecurity. It was clear, however, that with certain aspects of her future more secure, the knowledge that she would have a home where she would be welcome was a tremendous factor in alleviating the depressive symptoms. Laurie decided to terminate therapy about four months after she first came to the Suicide Prevention Center, feeling much stronger and more competent, and having lost the hopeless feeling of impending doom and chronic feeling of unhappiness.

Three months later her father did, in fact, die and she moved in with her aunt and uncle. She called the therapist on this occasion, and went to see him three more times. She appeared to handle the crisis quite well and although she experienced a period of several weeks of grief and mourning, did not enter a clinical depression, nor did she again express suicidal feelings.

Some comments at this point will be made in regard to some of the choice points and decision processes during the course of treatment.

Summary

The first decision that was made by the therapist was to see Mrs. Z. and Laurie together for the first interview. This probably delayed obtaining the important material about Laurie's father's impending death. On the second interview the decision was made to see Laurie alone first, which permitted her to discuss this material. It is apparent that in the presence of her stepmother, Laurie felt a need to maintain the collusion of keeping the family secret.

The next choice point and decision that accompanied it was regarding suicidal behavior and the potential danger attached to this. The therapist made the evaluation of suicide potential and decided that the immediate risk was low and correctly discerned the meaning of the suicidal gesture as a communication rather than a strong desire to end her life. Because of this, customary suicide prevention precautions such as the family watching Laurie closely and removing dangerous items from the house, antidepressant medication, hospitalization and the offering of another appointment immediately, such as the next day, were ruled out. In the case of a high suicide risk with an adolescent, when the danger is acute and there appears to be no significant relief from the initial interview, all of these alternatives must be considered as important.

The next choice point came at the end of the session when the therapist suggested a discussion that night among the family oriented toward the relief of the unhappy feelings through environmental manipulation, i.e., changing high schools. This was an important step even though it did not lead to a direct alleviation of her unhappiness. It provided Laurie with the feeling that the therapist took her seriously, had her interests at heart, and was willing to intervene actively in helping her. It is quite possible that this laid the groundwork for Laurie's feeling of sufficient trust in the therapist so that next time she could open up as to what was really troubling her and be confident that he would respond to that with as much concern and activity.

The next treatment decision of importance, as was mentioned above, was the therapist's decision to see Laurie alone. The last crucial decision to making progress toward remission of her frustrations and feelings of hopelessness was the therapist's decision to go into the home, to conduct family therapy sessions, and to initiate an open discussion of the vital issues. The therapist's active approach was maintained throughout the sessions, which were oriented toward helping the entire family find a solution to Laurie's insecurities.

Had the therapist decided on the alternative of remaining in the office situation and seeing Laurie alone, or seeing Laurie and her stepmother occasionally, it is unlikely that the situation could have been resolved as effectively. The conspiracy of silence that was present, which was so frustrating to Laurie, probably could not have been broken through without complete family participation.

Suicide notes are typically unrevealing, perhaps because the act of ending one's life requires such concentrated psychic effort. Sylvia Plath's final note, for instance, was stark in its brevity: "Please call Dr._____," with a phone number following. Yet the poetry preceding her death stands as articulate testimony to her increasing preoccupation with self-destruction. In like manner, the final poems of Anne Sexton portray her analyzing a decision to die.

Anne Sexton, who later followed Sylvia Plath in suicide, also analyzes the decision to die in her writings. In the following poem, ironically titled, "Suicide Note" Sexton reviews her life in relation to the desire to "go now/without old age or disease/wildly but accurately."

SUICIDE NOTE

Anne Sexton

You speak to me of narcissism but I reply that it is a matter of my life.

Artaud

At this time let me somehow bequeath all the leftovers to my daughters and their daughters.

Anonymous

Better,
despite the worms talking to
the mare's hoof in the field;
better,
despite the season of young girls
dropping their blood;

Anne Sexton. "Suicide Note." *Live or Die.* Boston: Houghton Mifflin Company, 1966.

better somehow
to drop myself quickly
into an old room.
Better (someone said)
not to be born
and far better
not to be born twice
at thirteen
where the boardinghouse,
each year a bedroom,
caught fire.

Dear friend,
I will have to sink with hundreds of others
on a dumbwaiter into hell.
I will be a light thing.
I will enter death
like someone's lost optical lens.
Life is half enlarged.
The fish and owls are fierce today.
Life tilts backward and forward.
Even the wasps cannot find my eyes.

Yes,
eyes that were immediate once,
Eyes that have been truly awake,
eyes that told the whole story—
poor dumb animals.
Eyes that were pierced,
little nail heads,
light blue gunshots.

And once with
a mouth like a cup,
clay colored or blood colored,
open like the breakwater
for the lost ocean
and open like the noose
for the first head.

Once upon a time
my hunger was for Jesus.
O my hunger! My hunger!
Before he grew old
he rode calmly into Jerusalem
in search of death.

This time
I certainly
do not ask for understanding
and yet I hope everyone else
will turn their heads when an unrehearsed fish
   jumps
on the surface of Echo Lake;
when moonlight,
its bass note turned up loud,
hurts some building in Boston,
when the truly beautiful lie together.
I think of this, surely,
and would think of it far longer
if I were not . . . if I were not
at that old fire.

I could admit
that I am only a coward
crying *me me me*
and not mention the little gnats, the moths,
forced by circumstance
to suck on the electric bulb.
But surely you know that everyone has a death,
his own death,
waiting for him.
So I will go now
without old age or disease,
wildly but accurately,
knowing my best route,
carried by that toy donkey I rode all these years,
never asking, "Where are we going?"

We were riding (if I'd only known)
to this.

Dear friend,
please do not think
that I visualize guitars playing
or my father arching his bone.
I do not even expect my mother's mouth.
I know that I have died before—
once in November, once in June.
How strange to choose June again,
so concrete with its green breasts and bellies.
Of course guitars will not play!
The snakes will certainly not notice.
New York City will not mind.
At night the bats will beat on the trees,
knowing it all,
seeing what they sensed all day.

June 1965

t is possible to make the choice to die in more ways than are generally realized. Edwin Shneidman, a thanatologist well-known for his work in suicide and suicide prevention, suggests that it is important to consider the degree of conscious or unconscious intention in bringing about one's own death.

In his analysis of intentionality in death-related behaviors, Shneidman counters the notion that our age is one of denial with his claim that the prospect of "megadeath in the nuclear age" has instead produced a death-oriented society. Yet, he concludes, the consequences of such an orientation are more often romanticization than acceptance of death.

THE ENEMY

Edwin S. Shneidman

This may be an age of youth but it is also an age of death. Death is in the air; none of us is more than minutes away from death by nuclear incineration. Life has become both more dear and more cheap. And if it can be taken by others it can also be thrown away by oneself. Senseless killing and the wanton destruction of one's own mind reflect the same debasement of man's basic coin: life itself. In the Western world we are probably more death-oriented today than we have been since the days of the Black Plague in the 14th Century.

The young reveal an acute sensitivity to life-and-death issues. I believe that they can best be seen as children of The Bomb. At Harvard last year my course on death was scheduled in a room with 20 chairs. Having been for over 20 years one of the few researchers who concentrated on death phenomena—my original focus was on suicide prevention—I had to come to assume that only a few would want to deal with the subject. To my surprise more than 200 undergraduates from Radcliffe and Harvard showed up for the first session. Much of my recent work grew out of the introspective reports and papers completed by the participants in that course. The students' painful awareness of death, long before the season regarded as appropriate, has helped me to grasp the difference between individual death as it has long been perceived and the prospect of megadeath in the nuclear age.

At first thought, "death" is one of those patently self-evident terms, the definition of which need not detain a thoughtful mind for even a moment. Every mature person knows instinctively what he means by it. A dictionary defines death as the act or event or occasion of dying; the end of life. As far as the person himself is concerned death is his end—the cessation of his consciousness.

In spite of death's seemingly self-evident character, reflection tells us that it might take a lifetime fully to understand the word "death." As Percy Bridgman pointed out, where either consciousness or loss of consciousness (including death) is involved, we must distinguish between *your* private experiences and *my* private experiences. You (privately) can experience my (public) death; we can both (privately) experience someone else's (public) death; but neither of us can experience his own (inexperienceable) death. You can never see yourself unconscious, hear yourself snore or experience your own being dead, for if you were in a position to have these experiences you would not, in fact, be unconscious, asleep or dead.

If you can never experience your own death, it follows logically that you can never experience your own *dying*. "Now, wait a minute," you might say. "Granted that I cannot experience my being dead but obviously I am still alive while I am dying and, unless I am unconscious, I can experience that." The fact is that you can never be *certain* that you are dying. "Dying" takes its only legitimate meaning from the fact that it immediately precedes death. You may think that you are dying—and survive, in which case you were not dying at that time. You can of course at the present moment keenly experience your *belief* that you are dying, and the experience can be deathly real. You can also in the present anticipate what will happen after you are dead. But these anticipations are at the time they occur always present-moment live experiences.

All this is not to gainsay the fact that people are often correct in thinking that they are dying because they do then die. During an extended period of dying (or supposed dying), a person, unless he is massively drugged or in a coma, is very much alive. The interval of dying is a psychologically consistent, often exaggerated extension of the individual's personality and life-style. His idiosyncratic ways of coping, defending, adjusting and interacting remain with him, coloring his inner life and characterizing his behavior. A standard textbook on clinical medicine succinctly states: "Each man dies in a notably personal way."

Termination is the universal and ubiquitous ending of all living things, but only man, because he can talk about his introspective life, can conceptualize his own cessation. Death is the absence of life—and life, *human* life, is the life of the self, the life of mind. Your life is the full accounting of your personal diary, your memory bank, including your experience of the present moment. It is the life of your mind as you look out on the world and reflect upon yourself. Of course by "the life of the mind" I do not mean to limit the notion only to those aspects of mind amenable to immediate or conscious recall.

Death is the stopping of this life. Bridgman said that ". . . my own death is such a different thing that it well might have a different word." I propose that we use the word *cessation*. Cessation ends the potentiality of any (further) conscious experience. It is essentially synonymous with the conclusion of conscious life.

In order to have a full appreciation of the role of cessation, we must understand a few additional terms:

Termination is the stopping of vital physiological functions, including such gross measures as the heartbeat or the exchanges of gases between the person and his environment and such refined measures as what we now call "brain death." Physiological termination is always followed shortly by psychological cessation. The converse however is not always true: it is possible for (private) cessation to occur hours or even days before (public) termination. For example when a person's skull is crushed in an accident, cessation occurs at the instant he loses consciousness for the last time, but he might be kept alive in a hospital as long as he breathes and brainwave patterns are traced on the EEG. But his life ended the instant his mind was destroyed. Loved ones and hospital personnel saw him "alive" in the hospital but that could be an experience only for them. Because the moment of "death" is socially defined by termination, we need that concept even in a psychological approach to death.

Interruption is the stopping of consciousness with the expectation of further conscious experience. It is, to use two contradictory terms, a kind of temporary cessation. Sleep—dreamless sleep—is perhaps the best example of an interruption. Other interruptions include unconsciousness, stupor, coma, fainting, seizures and anesthetic states, and can last from seconds to weeks. By definition the last interruption of a man's life is cessation.

Continuation is the experiencing the stream of temporally contiguous events. Our lives are thus made up of one series of alternating states of continuation and interruption.

As one would imagine, *altered continuation* implies the continuation of consciousness in a way that is different from an individual's usual or modal style of functioning. Examples would be intoxication, drugged states, hypnotic states, malingering, role-playing, spying, feigning and even "unplugging." "Unplugging"—a term suggested to me by Professor Erving Goffman—is getting out of one's ordinary track of life by drifting, seceding or uncorking, such as burying yourself in a book, going on a *Wanderjahr*, watching a Western or, more actively, going on an escapade, a binge or an orgy—in short, escaping, as opposed to sweating it out.

A neglected aspect of death is the role of the individual in his own demise. The current traditional (and in my view, erroneous) conceptualization that views death as an experience—noble, religious, frightening, beneficent, malign—makes too much of the individual's role in his own death. We have already decided that for the chief protagonist, death is not an experience at all. But there is still another traditional view of death that, curiously enough, makes too little of man's role in his own demise. That view can be seen in the way we conceptualize death in our official records.

In the Western world "death" is given its operational meaning by the death certificate. The death certificate can be divided into three parts, reflecting the three basic kinds of information that it is intended to convey: a) the top third of the certificate identifies the decedent; b) the second third of the certificate relates the cause or causes of death. The international manual lists around 140 possible causes of death, including pneumonia, meningitis, myocardial infarction; c) the last third of the certificate is perhaps the most important for our interests. It is intended to tell us *how* the person died. It normally indicates one of four conceptual crypts into which each of us is eventually placed. I call this world-wide taxonomic scheme the NASH classification of death, standing for the four *modes* of death: natural, accidental, suicidal and homicidal. The main terms can be combined or modified; e.g., "Accident-Suicide, Undetermined" or "Probable Suicide."

It is evident that the *cause* of death does not automatically tell us the *mode* of death. "Asphyxiation due to drowning" or "barbiturate overdose" does not tell us whether the death was accidental or suicidal or homicidal. This NASH scheme tends to obscure rather than to clarify the nature of human death.

Much of this anachronistic classification can be traced to the 1600s, when the English crown was interested in assigning blame. Natural and accidental deaths were by definition acts of nature or of God. The survivors could only be pitied and the legitimate heirs would come into their rightful inheritances. On the other hand, the culprit must be identified and punished in homicidal and suicidal deaths. Suicide was *felo-de-se*, a felony against the self, and the crown took the dead man's goods. The coroner's judgment thus could affect the fortunes of a family. From the beginning, certification of the mode of death served quasi-legal functions with distinct monetary overtones.

This anachronistic omission of the part that a man plays in his own death ties us to seventeenth-century Cartesian thinking and keeps us from enjoying the insights of contemporary psychology and psychiatry. In order to put man back into his own dying—a time of life when he is very much alive— we shall need to call upon social and behavioral science.

It can be argued that most deaths, especially in the younger years, are unnatural. Perhaps the termination of life might properly be called natural only in cases of death in old age. Consider the following confusions: if an individual (who wishes to live) has his chest invaded by a lethal steering wheel, his death is called accidental; if he is invaded by a lethal virus, his death is called natural; if his skull is invaded by a bullet in civilian life, his death is called homicidal. A person who torments an animal into killing him is said to have died by accident, whereas one who torments a drunken companion into killing him is called a victim of homicide. An individual whose artery bursts in his brain is said to have died with a cerebral-vascular accident, whereas it might make more sense to call it a cerebral-vascular natural.

In light of these confusing circumstances, I have proposed that we supplement the NASH classification by focusing on the *intention* of each person *vis-à-vis* his own death, that all human deaths be divided among those that are a) intentioned, b) subintentioned or c) unintentioned.

Intentioned

In an intentioned death, the individual plays a direct and conscious role in effecting his own demise. Persons who die intentioned deaths can be divided into a number of subcategories:

1. *Death-seeker.* He has consciously verbalized to himself his wish for an ending to all conscious experience and he acts to achieve this end. The criterion for

a death-seeker does not lie in his method—razor, barbiturate, carbon monoxide. It lies in the fact that *in his mind* the method will bring about cessation, and in the fact that he acts in such a manner that rescue is unlikely or impossible. An individual's orientation toward death shifts and changes. A person who was a death-seeker yesterday might take tender care of his life today. Most of the individuals who are death-seekers ("suicidal") are so for relatively brief periods; given appropriate surcease and sanctuary they will soon wish to live.

2. *Death-initiator*. He believes that he will die in the fairly near future or he believes that he is failing and--not wishing to accommodate himself to a less-effective and less-virile image of himself—does not wish to let death happen to him. Rather *he* wants to play the dominant role; he will do it for himself, at his own time and on his own terms. In investigations among persons in the terminal stages of disease, it has been found that some, with remarkable and totally unexpected energy and strength, take out their tubes and needles, climb over the bedrails, lift heavy windows and jump. When we look at the occupational history of such individuals we see that they have never been fired—they have always quit.

3. *Death-ignorer*. Some people who kill themselves believe that one can effect termination without cessation. But in our contemporary society even those who espouse a religious belief in a hereafter still put the label of "suicide" on a person who has shot himself to death. This is so probably because, whatever *really* happens after termination, the survivors are still left to mourn in the physical absence of the deceased. Thus this subcategory of death-ignorer or, perhaps better, death-transcender, contains those persons who, from their point of view, terminate themselves and continue to exist in some other manner.

The concept of death-ignoring is necessary; otherwise we put ourselves in the position of making comparable a man who shoots himself in the head in the belief that he will meet his dead wife in heaven and a man who travels to another city with the expectation of being reunited with his spouse. We must consider that cessation is final as far as the human personality that we can know is concerned.

4. *Death-darer.* He bets his continuation (i.e., his life) on a relatively low probability of survival. Regardless of the outcome a person who plays Russian roulette—in which the chances of survival are only five out of six—is a death-darer, as is the uncoordinated man who attempts to walk the ledge of a tall building. The rule of thumb is, it is not what one does that matters but the background (of skill, prowess and evaluation of his own abilities) against which he does it.

Unintentioned

At the other extreme an unintentioned death is any cessation in which the decedent plays no significant role in effecting his own demise. Here death is due entirely to trauma from without, or to simple biological failure from within. At the time of his cessation the individual is going about his own business (even though he may be hospitalized) with no conscious intention of hastening cessation and with no strong conscious drive to do so. What happens is that something occurs—a cerebral-vascular accident, a myocardial infarction, a neoplastic growth, a malfunction, an invasion—whether by bullet or by virus—that for him has lethal consequences. *It* happens to *him*.

Most traditional natural, accidental and homicidal deaths would be unintentioned, but no presently labeled suicidal deaths would be. Persons who die unintentioned deaths can be subcategorized as follows:

1. *Death-welcomer.* Although he plays no discernible (conscious or unconscious) role in hastening or facilitating his own cessation, he could honestly report an

introspective position of welcoming an end to his life. Very old persons, especially after long, painful, debilitating illness, report that they would welcome the end.

2. *Death-accepter*. He has accepted the imminence of his cessation and is resigned to his fate. He may be passive, philosophical, resigned, heroic or realistic, depending on the spirit in which this enormous acceptance is made.

3. *Death-postponer*. Most of the time most of us are death-postponers. Death-postponing is the habitual orientation of most human beings toward cessation. The death-postponer wishes that cessation would not occur in the foreseeable future; that it would not occur for as long as possible.

4. *Death-disdainer*. Some individuals, when they consciously contemplate cessation, are disdainful of death and feel that they are above involvement in this implied stopping of the vital processes. They are in a sense supercilious toward death. Most young children in our culture, aside from their fears about death, are probably death-disdainers—as well they might be.

5. *Death-fearer*. He fears death—and even topics *relating to death*—to the point of phobia. He fights the notion of cessation, seeing reified death as something to be feared and hated. His position may relate to his wishes for omnipotence and to his investment in his social and physical potency. Hypochondriacs are perhaps death-fearers. (A physically well death-fearer might, when he is physically ill, become a death-facilitator.)

Imagine five older men on the same ward of a hospital, all dying of cancer, none playing an active role in his own cessation. Yet it is possible to distinguish different orientations toward death among them: one wishes not to die and is exerting his will to live (death-postponer); another is resigned to his cessation (death-accepter); the third will not believe that death can take him (death-disdainer); still another, although he takes no steps to hasten his end, embraces it (death-welcomer); and the fifth is frightened and forbids anyone to speak of death in his presence (death-fearer).

6. *Death-feigner*. It is of course possible to shout "Fire!" where there is no conflagration. It is also possible to yell or to murmur "Suicide!" when clearly there is no lethal intention. Calls like "Fire!," "Suicide!" or "Stop thief!" mobilize others. They are grab-words; they force society to act in certain ways. An individual who uses the semantic blanket of "Suicide!" in the absence of lethal intent is a death-feigner. A death-feigner stimulates a self-directed movement toward cessation. He might ingest water from an iodine bottle or use a razor blade without lethal possibility or intent. He may seek some of the secondary gains that go with cessation-oriented behavior. These gains usually have to do with activating other persons—usually the "significant other" person in the neurotic dyadic relationship with the death-feigner.

Subintentioned

The most important death category—the one that I believe may be characteristic of a majority of deaths—is the *subintentioned* death, in which the decedent plays some covert or unconscious role in hastening his own demise. The evidence lies in a variety of behavior patterns that include poor judgment, imprudence, excessive risk-taking, neglect of self, disregard of medical regimen, abuse of alcohol, misuse of drugs—ways in which an individual can advance the date of his death by fostering the risk of his own dying.

Subintention is a somewhat mysterious concept, resting as it does on the powerful idea of unconscious motivation. It is "the subterranean miner that works in us all." The question is, as Herman Melville asked, ". . . can one tell whither leads his shaft by the ever shifting, muffled sound of his pick?"

Many deaths certified as natural have a subintentional quality about them. Many of us know of cases in which persons with diabetes, peptic ulcers, colitis, cirrhosis, Buerger's disease or pneumonia have, through psychologically laden commission, omission, disregard or neglect, hastened their own demise. In addition "voodoo deaths," inexplicable deaths in hospitals (especially in surgery), and some sudden declines in health can be considered subintentioned. There is a notion that the speed at which some malignancies grow may be related to deep inner psychological variables.

And if some natural deaths are subintentioned (and thus not entirely natural), many deaths certified as accident are even more so—and not entirely accidental. A run of inimical events in one person's life can hardly be thought to be purely accidental. Sometimes we see someone drive a car as though he were afraid that he might be late for his own accident; he may be hurling himself toward a subintentioned death. Many automobile fatalities are not quite accidents and may not comfortably be called suicides; they can be more meaningfully understood as subintentioned deaths.

Some suicides show aspects of the subintentioned death category. (This is especially true for many cases certified as probable suicides.) Indeed the entire concept of subintentioned death—which asserts the role of the unconscious in death— is similar in many ways to Karl Menninger's concepts of chronic suicide, focal suicide and organic suicide, except that Menninger's ideas have to do primarily with self-defeating ways of continuing to live, whereas the notion of subintentioned death is a way to stop the process of living. Cases of subintentioned death may in general be said to have permitted suicide.

Many fatal incidents certified as homicides might be better considered subintentioned deaths. It is obvious that in some close dyadic pairs (married couples, lovers, friends), the victim—like the chief mate of the *Town-Ho* in *Moby Dick*— "sought to run more than half way to meet his doom." To provoke another person to kill you is an indirect participation, at some level of personality functioning, in the manipulation of one's date of death.

The hypothesis that individuals may play unconscious roles in their own failures and act in ways that are inimical to their own welfare seems to be too well documented from both psychoanalytic and general clinical practice to be safely ignored. Often death is hastened by the individual's seeming carelessness, imprudence, foolhardiness, forgetfulness, amnesia, lack of judgment or another psychological mechanism. Included in the subintention category would be many patterns of mismanagement and brink-of-death living that result in death.

Subintentioned death involves the psychosomatics of death; that is, cases in which essentially psychological processes (fear, anxiety, derring-do, hate, etc.) seem to play some role in exacerbating the catabolic processes that bring on termination (and necessarily cessation). Several types make up the subintentioned death groups:

1. *Death-chancer*. If a death-darer has only five chances out of six of continuing, then a death-chancer's chances are significantly greater but still involve a realistic risk of dying. It should be pointed out that these categories are largely independent of method in that most methods (like razor blades or barbiturates) can legitimately be thought of as intentioned, subintentioned or unintentioned depending on the circumstances. Individuals who "leave it up to chance," who "gamble with death," who "half-intend to do it," are subintentioned death-chancers.

2. *Death-hastener*. He unconsciously exacerbates a physiological disequilibrium so that his cessation (which would ordinarily be called a natural death) is expedited. This can be done either in terms of his life-style (the abuse of his body, usually through alcohol, drugs, exposure or malnutrition), or through the mismanagement or disregard of prescribed reme-

dial procedures. Consider the diabetic who mismanages his diet or his insulin, the individual with
cirrhosis who mismanages his alcoholic intake, the
Buerger's-disease patient who mismanages his nico-
tine intake. Closely allied to the death-hastener
is the death-facilitator who, while he is ill and his
psychic energies are low, is somehow more than
passively unresisting to cessation, and makes it easy
for termination to occur. Some unexpected deaths
in hospitals may be of this nature.

3. *Death-capitulator.* By virtue of some strong emotion,
usually his great fear of death itself, he plays a psychological role in effecting his termination. In a sense,
he scares himself to death. This type of death
includes voodoo deaths, the deaths reported among
southwestern Indians and Mexicans in railroad-spon-
sored hospitals who thought that people went to
hospitals to die, and other cases reported in psychiatric and medical literature.

4. *Death-experimenter.* A death-experimenter often
lives on the brink of death. He consciously wishes
neither interruption nor cessation, but—usually by
excessive use of alcohol and/or drugs—he pursues a
chronically altered, often befogged continuation.
Death-experimenters seem to wish for a benumbed
or drugged consciousness. They will often experiment
with their self-prescribed dosages (always increasing
them), taking some chances of extending the benumbed conscious state into interruption (coma)
and even (usually in a lackadaisical way) running
some minimal but real risk of extending the interruption into cessation. This type of death is traditionally thought of as accidental.

It is important to distinguish between subintention and
ambivalence. Ambivalence is perhaps the single most important
psychodynamic concept for understanding death—or any of
life's major psychological issues. Ambivalence represents at least
two simultaneous movements within the mind of one person
toward divergent, even opposite, goals. Examples of such

contradictory activities would be loving and hating the same person, yearning for both autonomy and dependence, and, at rock bottom, moving toward both life and death. The concomitant movement toward each of these diverse goals is genuine in its own right. One can ingest pills, genuinely wishing to die, and at the same time entertain earnest fantasies of rescue. The paradigm of suicide is one of the deepest ambivalence; to cut one's throat and to cry for help—in the same breath.

On the other hand subintention does not emphasize the dual character of man's behavior so much as, in its own way, it emphasizes the unconscious aspects of man's being. Subintentioned acts, whether toward death or toward the expansion of life, are essentially movements toward outcomes that are not conscious goals. They are life's maneuvers that well up out of unconscious motivations and thus are more subtle in their appearance and more difficult to account. Is smoking suicidal? Drinking? Driving? Skiing? These questions cannot be answered yes or no. The answer is "It depends," and it may depend on a number of factors including the individual's orientations toward death and toward others in his life.

With some passionate emphasis Arnold Toynbee makes the point that death is essentially dyadic—a two-person event— and that as such the survivor's burden is the heavier. When he considers his own situation, he writes:

"I guess that if, one day, I am told by my doctor that I am going to die before my wife, I shall receive the news not only with equanimity but with relief. This relief, if I do feel it, will be involuntary. I shall be ashamed of myself for feeling it, and my relief will, no doubt, be tempered by concern and sorrow for my wife's future after I have been taken from her. All the same, I do guess that, if I am informed that I am going to die before her, a shameful sense of relief will be one element in my reaction. . This is, as I see it, the capital fact about the relation between living and dying. There are two parties to the suffering that death inflicts; and, in the apportionment of this suffering, the survivor takes the brunt."

In focusing on the importance of the dyadic relationship in death, Toynbee renders a great service to all who are concerned with death, particularly with suicide. The typical suicide is an intensely dyadic event. The crucial role of the "significant other" in prevention of suicide is one aspect of the new look in suicidology.

Although it is difficult to take a stance counter to Toynbee, I believe that in emphasizing the dyadic aspect of death he seems to leap from a sentimental attitude of burden-sharing in a love relationship—the noble husband's wish to save his beloved wife from the anguish of bereavement—to an unnecessarily romantic view of death itself. In cases of absolutely sudden and precipitous deaths, the total sum of dyadic pain is borne by the survivor (inasmuch as the victim cannot experience any of it). But in protracted dying the present pain and anguish involved in the frightening anticipation of being dead may very well be sharper for the dying person than the pain suffered then and afterward by the survivor. The algebra of death's suffering is complicated.

For all his wisdom I believe that Toynbee indulges in the romanticization of death. In my view the larger need is to de-romanticize death and suicide.

Certainly one of the most remarkable characteristics of man's psychological life is the undiluted and enduring love affair that each of us has with his own consciousness. Trapped as he is within his own mind, man nurtures his conscious awareness, accepts it as the criterion for mediating reality, and entertains a faithful life-long dialogue with it—even (or especially) when he takes leave of his senses. Often man communicates with his mind as though it were a separate "other," whereas he is really communicating with himself. Indeed, the other to whom he talks is in large part what he defines himself to be. Death peremptorily decrees an abrupt, unwelcome and final adjournment and dissolution of what Henry Murray has aptly called "the Congress of the mind." Death—i.e., being —is total cessation, personal nothingness, individual annihilation. Should one traffic with one's greatest mortal enemy, rationalize its supposed noble and saving qualities and then romanticize it as an indispensable part of dyadic life?

One difficulty with death is that within himself each man is noble—indestructible and all-surviving. Being conscious is all one has. That is what one's life is. Consciousness defines the duration and the scope of life, and the scope can be rich or the scope can be arid, a partial death that can come long before one's cessation.

Our current attitudes toward death are unconscionably sentimental. The several notions—of "heroic death," "generativity" and "wise death" in mature old age—are culture-laden rationalizations, as though the cerebrator could ever be truly equanimous about the threat of his own naughtment or his annihilation.

Although there are undoubtedly special circumstances in which some individuals either welcome their own cessation or are essentially indifferent to it, for almost everyone the heightened probability of his own cessation constitutes the most dire threat possible. By and large the most distressing contemplation one can have is of his own cessation. Much of religion is tied to this specter—and perhaps all of man's concern with immortality. We must face the fact that completed dying (i.e., death or cessation) is the one characteristic act in which man is forced to engage.

In this context, the word *forced* has a special meaning. It implies that a characteristic that death shares with torture, rape, capital punishment, kidnapping, lobotomy and degradation ceremonies is the quality of impressment. The threat of being reduced to nothingness can be viewed reasonably only as the strongest and the most perfidious of forced punishments.

In all this I do not believe that I am echoing Dylan Thomas' "Do not go gentle into that good night. Rage, rage against the dying of the light." Rather I am saying that one should know that cessation is the curse to end all curses, and *then* one can, as he chooses, rage, fight, temporize, bargain, compromise, comply, acquiesce, surrender, welcome or even embrace death. But one should be aware of the dictum: Know thine enemy.

Death is not a tender retirement, a bright autumnal end "as a shock of corn to his season" of man's cycle. That notion, it seems to me, is of the same order of rationalization as romanticizing kidnapping, murder, impressment or rape.

Nor does it mollify the terror of death to discuss it in the honorific and beguiling terms of maturity, postnarcissistic love, ego-integrity or generativity, even though one can only be grateful to Erik Erikson for the almost perfectly persuasive way in which he has made a generative death sound ennobling and nearly worthwhile.

I wonder if it would not be better to understand generativity as reflecting pride and gratitude in one's progenitors and perhaps even greater pride and faith in one's progeny, without the necessity of deriving any pleasure from one's own finiteness and the prospect of one's demise. There is (or ought to be) a reasonable difference between experiencing justifiable pride in what one has been and is and has created, on the one hand, and, on the other hand, feeling an unwarranted equanimity when one reflects that he will soon no longer be. Maturity and ego integrity relate to the former; the latter is supported largely by the romantic, sentimental rationalization that one's cessation is a blessing. Such a rationalization is nothing less than psychologically willing what is biologically obligatory. It may be more mature to bemoan this fact and regret it.

All this means that death is a topic for the tough and the bitter—people like Melville, in "The Lightning-Rod Man": "Think of being a heap of charred offal, like a haltered horse burned in his stall; and all in one flash!" Or Camus, especially in Meursault's burst of antitheistic and antideath rage just before the end of *The Stranger*.

A look at another culture might throw some light on this problem. When I was in Japan a few years ago, it seemed to me that one of the most pervasive religio-cultural features of the country was the romantically tinged animism that infused the religious thinking. It was not a more primitive feeling, but rather a more personal and spirited feeling, especially about nature. For example the Japanese feelings about a cherry tree in its ephemerally beautful bloom seemed totally different from the feelings that an average American would muster on looking at a blossoming apple tree. The Japanese closeness to nature, akin to deification, seems to lead to a special Japanese feeling toward death—which I would have to call romanticization.

When I addressed a group of Japanese university students,

one youth asked me if I could give him any reason why he should not kill himself if he sincerely believed that he would then become one with nature. The very quality of this question illustrates this animizing and romanticizing of death. Further I recall a young engineer who sat beside me on the new Tōkaidō train and wrote out: "Cherry blossoms is blooming quickly and scattering at once. Better to come to fruition and die like the blossom." He added: "We have had many great men among our forefathers whose deeds remind us of the noble characteristics of cherry blossoms."

In this country, the romanticization of certain types of homicides is an especially troublesome part of our national heritage. The honorifics go to the man with the gun. We have glamorized our rural bandits and our urban gangsters. The romanticized myth of the Western frontier, built around the image of the man with a gun, has set its homicidal stamp on our culture. The problem for television may not be the effects of violence but the effects of the romanticization of violence.

This romanticization of death goes to the beginnings of our national history. We depict our revolutionary heroes as Minutemen with rifles—as though it were primarily guns that had won the war. Perhaps more appropriate monuments at Lexington and Concord—we have even lost the meaning of the word "concord"—might have been statues of Paine and Jefferson seated, with pens. Unquestionably these representations would have implied quite different values and might have shaped our culture in a somewhat different direction. Our recent inability to amend our gun laws in the wake of a series of catastrophic assassinations has been a national disaster and a grisly international joke, highlighting our irrational tie to our own essentially anti-intellectual legends of romanticized homicide.

Romantic notions of death are obviously related to suicide. Individuals who are actively suicidal suffer—among their other burdens—from a temporary loss of the view of death-as-enemy. This is the paradox and the major logical fallacy of self-inflicted death. It capitulates to the decapitator.

Suicidal folk have lost sight of the foe: they sail with full lights in the hostile night. They are unvigilant and forgetful. They behave in strange, almost traitorous ways. They attempt to rationalize death's supposed lofty qualities and—what is most difficult to deal with—to romanticize death as the noblest part of dyadic love. Loyal-to-life people are inured against nefarious propaganda leading to defection. One should not traffic with the enemy. Suicidal individuals have been brainwashed—by their own thoughts.

How could the de-romanticization of death help suicidal persons? Would it be salutary or beneficial to embark on programs of deromanticizing death in our schools—with courses in "death education"—or in our public media? In the treatment of the acutely suicidal person what would be the effects of directing his mind to a view of death as an enemy? Would such a psychological regimen hasten the suicide, have no effect at all, or would it make a death-postponer of him? In my own mind, the nagging question persists: would not this type of effort, like practically every other earnest exhortation in this alienated age, itself be doomed to an untimely figurative death?

But perhaps even more important is the question: how would the de-romanticization of death reduce the number of those especially *evil* deaths of murder, violence, massacre and genocide? Here, paradoxically, I am a trifle more optimistic. If only we can recognize that our three crushing national problems—the black citizen, the war in Vietnam, and the threat of nuclear death—all contain the common element of dehumanizing others (and, concomitantly, brutalizing and dehumanizing ourselves), then acting out of the urgent need to reverse our present national death-oriented course, we might bring new dimensions to life. But in order to avert the death of our own institutions we shall, in addition to being the home of the brave and the land of the free, have to become the country of the humane.

Shneidman's categories of subintentioned death include those natural and accidental deaths where the decedent seems to catalyze a situation which results in his own death. In the news story that follows, New York Times writer Jon Nordheimer traces the path of a young Congressional Medal of Honor winner from a moment of valor in Vietnam to his perplexing death as a criminal in Detroit. The report illustrates the complex effects of the hero's wartime encounter with death, his instinctive act of altruism followed by a series of violent actions and his enduring sense of survivor guilt, which culminate in his own death.

FROM DAKTO TO DETROIT: DEATH OF A TROUBLED HERO

Jon Nordheimer
(*The New York Times*, May 26, 1971)

DETROIT, May 25—A few tenants living in the E. J. Jeffries Homes, a dreary public housing project in Corktown, an old Detroit neighborhood, can still remember Dwight Johnson as a little boy who lived in one of the rust-brown buildings with his mother and baby brother. They think it strange, after all that has happened to Dwight, to remember him as a gentle boy who hated to fight.

Dwight Johnson died one week from his 24th birthday, shot and killed as he tried to rob a grocery store a mile from his home. The store manager later told the police that a tall Negro had walked in shortly before midnight, drawn a revolver out of his topcoat and demanded money from the cash register.

The manager pulled his own pistol from under the counter and the two men struggled. Seven shots were fired.

Four and one-half hours later, on an operating table at Detroit General Hospital, Dwight (Skip) Johnson died from five gunshot wounds.

Ordinarily, the case would have been closed right there, a routine crime in a city where there were 13,583 armed robberies last year.

But when the detectives went through the dead man's wallet for identification, they found a small white card with its edges rubbed thin from wear. "Congressional Medal of Honor Society—United States of America," it said. "This certifies that Dwight H. Johnson is a member of this society."

The news of the death of Sgt. Dwight Johnson shocked the black community of Detroit. Born out of wedlock when his mother was a teenager and raised on public welfare, he had been the good boy on his block in the dreary housing project, an altar boy and Explorer Scout, one of the few among the thousands of poor black youngsters in Detroit who had struggled against the grinding life of the ghetto and broken free, coming home from Vietnam tall and strong and a hero.

The story of Dwight Johnson and his drift from hero in Dakto, Vietnam, to villain in Detroit is a difficult one to trace. The moments of revelation are rare. There were, of course, those two brief episodes that fixed public attention on him: 30 minutes of "uncommon valor" one cold morning in combat that earned him the nation's highest military decoration, and the thirty-second confrontation in the Detroit grocery that ended his life.

Oddly, they are moments of extreme violence, and everyone who knew Dwight Johnson—or thought he did—knew he was not a violent man.

Now that the funeral is over and the out-of-town relatives have gone home and the family conferences that sought clues to explain Dwight's odd behavior have ended in bitter confusion, his mother can sit back and talk wistfully about the days when Skip was a skinny kid who was chased home after school by the Corktown bullies.

"Mama," he would ask, "what do I do if they catch me?" His mother would place an arm around his thin shoulders and draw him close, "Skip," she would say, "don't you fight, honey, and don't let them catch you." The boy would look downcast and worried. "Yes, Mama," he'd say.

"Dwight was a fabulous, all-around guy, bright and with a great sense of humor," reflected Barry Davis, an auburn-haired Californian who flew with his wife to Detroit when he heard on a news report that Dwight had been killed. Three others who had served with him in Vietnam, all of them white, also came, not understanding what aberration had led to his death.

'Fighting Words'

"I can remember our first day at Fort Knox and Dwight was the only colored guy in our platoon," Barry Davis recalled. "So we're in formation and this wise guy from New Jersey says to Dwight, 'Hey, what's the initials N.A.A.C.P. stand for?'

"And Dwight says, "The National Association for the Advancement of Colored People.'

"And this wise guy from New Jersey says, 'Naw, that ain't it. It stands for Niggers Acting As Colored People.'

"And I said to myself, 'Wow, those are fighting words,' but Dwight just laughed. From then on he was just one of the guys. As it turned out, Dwight liked this wise guy from New Jersey in the end as much as he liked anybody."

Most of the men who served with Sergeant Dwight Johnson remembered him that way—easy-going, hard to rattle, impossible to anger.

Another Side

But Stan Enders remembers him another way. Stan was the gunner in Skip's tank that morning in Vietnam three years ago, during the fighting at Dakto.

"No one who was there could ever forget the sight of this guy taking on a whole battalion of North Vietnamese soldiers," Stan said as he stood in the sunshine outside Faith Memorial Church in Corktown three weeks ago, waiting for

400

Skip's funeral service to begin.

Their platoon of four M-48 tanks was racing down a road toward Dakto, in the Central Highlands near the Cambodian border and the Ho Chi Minh Trail, when it was ambushed. Communist rockets knocked out two of the tanks immediately, and waves of foot soldiers sprang out of the nearby woods to attack the two tanks still in commission.

Skip hoisted himself out of the turret hatch and manned the mounted .50-caliber machine gun. He had been assigned to this tank only the night before. His old tank, and the crew he had spent 11 months and 22 days with in Vietnam and had never seen action before, was 60 feet away, burning.

"He was really close to those guys in that tank," Stan said. "He just couldn't sit still and watch it burn with them inside."

Skip ran through heavy crossfire to the tank and opened its hatch. He pulled out the first man he came across in the turret, burned but still alive, and got him to the ground just as the tank's artillery shells exploded, killing everyone left inside.

'Sort of Cracked Up'

"When the tank blew up Dwight saw the bodies all burned and black, well, he just sort of cracked up," said Stan.

For 30 minutes, armed first with a .45-caliber pistol and then with a submachine gun, Skip hunted the Vietnamese on the ground, killing from five to 20 enemy soldiers, nobody knows for sure. When he ran out of ammunition, he killed one with the stock of the machine gun.

At one point he came face to face with a Communist soldier who squeezed the trigger on his weapon aimed point-blank at him. The gun misfired and Skip killed him. But the soldier would come back to haunt him late at night in Detroit, in those dreams in which that anonymous soldier stood in front of him, the barrel of his AK-47 as big as a railroad tunnel, his finger on the trigger, slowly pressing it.

"When it was all over," Stan said, walking up the church steps as the funeral service got under way, "it took three men and three shots of morphine to hold Dwight down. He was raving. He tried to kill the prisoners we had rounded up. They took him away to a hospital in Pleiku in a straightjacket."

Stan saw Skip the next day. He had been released from the hospital and came by to pick up his personal gear. His Vietnam tour was over and he was going home.

No one there would know anything about Dakto until 10 months later, at the White House Medal of Honor ceremony.

Sergeant Johnson returned home in early 1968, outwardly only little changed from the quiet boy named Skip who had grown up in Detroit and been drafted. Even when he and other black veterans came home and could not find a job, he seemed to take it in stride.

He had been discharged with $600 in his pocket, and it was enough to buy cigarettes and go out at night with his cousin, Tommy Tillman, and with Eddie Wright, a friend from the Jefferies Homes, and make the rounds to the Shadowbox or the Little Egypt, to drink a little beer and have a few dates.

And at home no one knew about the bad dreams he was having. They would have to learn about that later from an Army psychiatrist.

If anyone asked him about Vietnam, he would just shake his head, or laugh and say, "Aw, man, nothing happened," and he would change the subject and talk about the girls in Kuala Lumpur where he went for R & R, or the three-day pass he spent in Louisville, Ky., drinking too much whiskey for the first time in his life and ending up in jail.

Out Before Tet

He returned home just as the Communist Tet offensive erupted in Vietnam, and everyone talked about how lucky he had been to get out before things got hot. They teased him then about his lackluster military career.

"When he came home from Vietnam he was different, sure, I noticed it, all jumpy and nervous and he had to be doing something all the time, it seems," said Eddie Wright. "But mostly he was the same fun-time guy."

Carmen Berry, a close friend of Katrina May, the girl Skip started dating after his discharge, thought she detected nuances of change she attributed to the same mental letdown she had seen in other Vietnam veterans.

"They get quiet," she said. "It's like they don't have too much to say about what it was like over there. Maybe it's because they've killed people and they don't really know why they killed them."

"The only thing that bugged me about Skip then," reflected his cousin Tommy, "and the one thing I thought was kind of strange and unlike him, was the pictures he brought back. He had a stack of pictures of dead people, you know, dead Vietnamese. Color slides."

In the fall he started looking for a job, along with Tommy Tillman.

"We'd go down to the state employment agency every day and take a look at what was listed," his cousin recalled. "Skip was funny; he wouldn't try for any of the hard jobs. If we wrote down the name of a company that had a job that he didn't feel qualified for, he wouldn't even go into the place to ask about it. He'd just sit in the car while I went in.

"Or if he did go in some place, he'd just sit and mumble a few words when they'd ask him questions. It was like he felt inferior. He'd give a terrible impression. But once we got back in the car, it was the same old Skip, laughing and joking."

A Pair of M.P.s

One day in October two military policemen came to his house. His mother saw the uniforms and before opening the door whispered urgently, "What did you do?"

"I didn't do nothing, honest, Ma," he answered.

The M.P.'s asked Skip a few questions. They wanted to know what he was doing and if he had been arrested since his discharge. Fifteen minutes after they left, the telephone rang. It was a colonel, calling from the Department of Defense in Washington. Sergeant Johnson was being awarded the Medal of Honor, he said. Could he and his family be in Washington on November 19 so President Johnson could personally present the award?

One week later, on Nov. 19, 1968, they were all there in the White House, Skip tall and handsome in his dress-blue uniform, his mother, Katrina and Tommy Tillman. The President gave a little speech. The national election was over, the Democrats had lost, but there were signs of movement at the Paris peace talks.

"Our hearts and our hopes are turned to peace as we assemble here in the East Room this morning," the President said, "All our efforts are being bent in its pursuit. But in this company we hear again, in our minds, the sound of distant battles."

Five men received the Medal of Honor that morning. And when Sergeant Johnson stepped stiffly forward and the President looped the pale blue ribbon and sunburst medal around his neck, a citation was read that described his valor.

Later, in the receiving line, when his mother reached Skip, she saw tears streaming down his face.

"Honey," she whispered, "what are you crying about? You've made it back."

After he officially became a hero, it seeemed that everyone in Detroit wanted to hire Dwight Johnson, the only living Medal of Honor winner in Michigan. Companies that had not been interested in a diffident ex-G.I. named Johnson suddenly found openings for Medal of Honor Winner Johnson.

Among those who wanted him was the United States Army.

"The brass wanted him in the Detroit recruiting office because—let's face it—here was a black Medal of Honor winner, and blacks are our biggest manpower pool in Detroit," said an Army employee who had worked with Skip after he rejoined the service a month after winning the medal. "Personally, I think a lot of promises were made to the guy that couldn't be kept. You got to remember that getting this guy back into the Army was a feather in the cap of a lot of people."

Events began moving quickly then for Skip. He married Katrina in January (the Pontchartrain Hotel gave the couple its bridal suite for their wedding night), and the newlyweds went to Washington in January as guests at the Nixon inaugural. Sergeant Johnson began a long series of personal appearances across Michigan in a public relations campaign mapped by the Army.

'A Hot Property'

In February, 1,500 persons paid $10 a plate to attend a testimonial dinner for the hero in Detroit's Cobo Hall, cosponsored by the Ford Motor Company and the Chamber of Commerce. A special guest was Gen. William C. Westmoreland, Army Chief of Staff and former commander of United States forces in Vietnam.

"Dwight was a hot property back in those days," recalled Charles Bielak, a civilian information officer for the Army's recruiting operations in Detroit. "I was getting calls for him all over the state. Of course, all this clamor didn't last. It reached a saturation point somewhere along the way and tapered off."

But while it lasted, Skip's life was frenetic. Lions Clubs . . . Rotary . . . American Legion. Detroit had a new hero. Tiger Stadium and meet the players. Sit at the dais with the white politicians. Be hailed by the black businessmen who would not have bothered to shake his hand before. Learn what fork to use for the salad. Say something intelligent to the reporters. Pick up the check for dinner for friends. Live like a man who had it made.

'Like a Couple of Kids'

But Leroy May, the hero's father-in-law, could still see the child behind the man.

"Dwight and Katrina were a perfect match—they both had a lot of growing up to do," he said. "They didn't know how to handle all the attention they got in those early days. They'd go out to supper so much Katrina complained she couldn't eat any more steak. I had to take them out and buy them hot dogs and soda pop. They were just like a couple of kids."

Bills started piling up. "They were in over their heads as soon as they were married," Mr. May said.

Everyone extended credit to the Medal of Honor winner. Even when he bought the wedding ring, the jeweler would not take a down payment. Take money from a hero? Not then. Later, the Johnsons discovered credit cards.

At first they lived in an $85-a-month apartment. But Katrina wanted a house. Skip signed a mortgage on a $16,000 house on the west side of Detroit. Monthly payments were $160.

'Ghetto Mentality'

In the spring of 1970, he wrote a bad check for $41.77 at a local market. The check was made good by a black leader in Detroit who was aghast that the Medal of Honor winner had gotten himself into a financial hole.

"I went to see him and told him he couldn't go on like this," said the man, a lawyer who asked to remain anonymous. "I said he was young and black and had the Medal of Honor. He could do anything he wanted. I tried to get him to think about a college and law school. The black businessmen would pick up the tab. He wouldn't have any part of it."

Looking back on this meeting, the lawyer said he suspected Skip was burdened by a "ghetto mentality" that limited his horizons. His world had been a public housing project and schools a few blocks away. Now, suddenly, events had thrust him outside the security of his boyhood neighborhood into a world dominated by whites.

He was paralyzed, the lawyer speculated, by an inability to formulate a plan of action in this alien culture that he had been transported to by something that happened on the other side of the globe.

"What does he do when he's introduced to Bunkie Knudsen, the president of Ford?" asked the lawyer. "Does he come across strong and dynamic because he knows there is a $75,000-a-year job waiting for him if he makes a good impression? And what happens to him when he just stands there and fumbles and doesn't know if he should shake hands or just nod his head? He was forced to play a role he was never trained for and never anticipated."

Tommy Tillman remembers how Skip would take several friends downtown to the Pontchartrain Hotel for an expensive meal and sit fumbling with the silverware, watching the others to see what fork to use first. "I'd say to him, 'Shoot, man, what do you care? Go ahead and use anything you want.'

"I wondered how he must feel when he's the guest of honor at one of those fancy meetings he was all the time going to."

It was about this time the stomach pains started.

'A Nervous Stomach'

"It was all that rich food he was eating," said his father-in-law. His mother recalled that "Skip always did have a nervous stomach."

He began staying away from his job as a recruiter, missed appointments and speaking engagements. "It got so I had to pick him up myself and deliver him to a public appearance," said Mr. Bielak. "I had to handcuff myself to the guy to get him someplace. It was embarrassing. I couldn't understand his attitude."

Last summer it was decided that Sergeant Johnson should report to Selfridge Air Force Base, not far from Detroit, for diagnosis of stomach complaints.

From Selfridge he was sent in September to Valley Forge Army Hospital in Pennsylvania. An Army psychiatrist later mulled over his notes on the patient and talked about them:

Maalox and bland diet prescribed. G. I. series conducted. Results negative. Subject given 30-day convalescent leave 16 October 1970. Absent without leave until 21 January 1971 when subject returned to Army hospital on own volition. Subsequent hearing recommended dismissal of A.W.O.L. charge and back pay reinstated. Subject agreed to undergo psychiatric evaluation. In cognizance of subject's outstanding record in Vietnam, the division's chief psychiatrist placed in charge of the case. Preliminary analysis: Depression caused by post-Vietnam adjustment problem.

In February, Eddie Wright bumped into Skip on a Detroit street.

"I just got out of Valley Forge on a pass."

"How things going there?"

"They got me in the psycho ward."

"Huh, you got to be kidding."

"No, man, they think I'm crazy."

During the convalescent leave, Sergeant Johnson borrowed $4,992 from a Detroit credit union. In his wallet he had a cashier's check for $1,500, the back pay the Army had awarded him. Most of his time he spent at home on the pass but when he went out he would drive to the Jefferies Homes and play basketball with the teenagers after school.

New Friends

"He was a big man down there with the kids," recalled his cousin. "We had all lived in the project and had been on welfare, just like these kids there today, and we were like heroes because we had broken out of there. We had made it to the outside world, and to them we were big successes. We had made it.

"Skip was something special. He had that medal, and they were proud of him. He'd be down there five minutes and the kids would come around and say, 'Hey man, ain't you Dwight Johnson?'"

His old high school crowd was concerned about some of his new friends, though. "They were strung out on drugs, and they just seemed to be hanging around Skip for his money," said his mother. "I asked him one night if he was taking anything, and he rolled up his sleeves and showed me there were no tracks [needle marks]. 'Ma,' he said, 'I'm not taking a thing.'"

On his return to the hospital, he began analysis with the chief attending psychiatrist.

Subject is bright. His Army G.T. rating is equivalent of 120 I.Q. In first interviews he does not volunteer information. He related he grew up in a Detroit ghetto and never knew his natural father. He sort of laughed when he said he was a "good boy" and did what was expected of him. The only time he can remember losing his temper as a youth was when neighborhood bullies picked on his younger brother. He was so incensed grownups had to drag him off the other boys. In general, there is evidence the subject learned to live up to the expectations of others while there was a build-up of anger he continually suppressed.

The Army hospital is actually in Phoenixville, Pa., several miles from Valley Forge. It is the principal treatment center for psychiatric and orthopedic patients in the Northeast, with 1,200 beds now occupied.

Because of the large number of amputees and wheelchair patients, the hospital has only two floors and is spread over several acres. Long oak-floored corridors run in all directions, connected by covered walkways and arcades. Someone once measured the hospital and found there were seven miles of corridors in a maze-like jumble. To prevent patients from losing their way, wards are painted different colors.

Dressed in hospital blue denims, the warrior-hero walked the labyrinth late at night, wrestling with the problems that tormented his mind and drained his spirit.

"The first day Dwight arrived here, the hospital's sergeant major brought him to us," said Spec. 6 Herman Avery, a tall Negro with a flat face and close-set eyes, who was master of the ward Dwight was first assigned to at the hospital. "It was the first time the sergeant major ever did that. We got the message. This guy was something special.

"Well, practically the first night he's here they dress him up and take him over to the Freedoms Foundations in Valley Forge to shake hands. When he got back he told me that if they ever did that again he would go A.W.O.L."

Further Evaluation

There was further psychiatric evaluation.

Subject expressed doubts over his decision to re-enter the Army as a recruiter. He felt the Army didn't honor its commitment to him. The public affairs were satisfactory to him at first, but he started to feel inadequate. People he would meet would pump his hand and slap his back and say, "Johnson, if you ever think about getting out of the Army, come look me up." On several occasions he contacted these individuals and they didn't remember him. It always took several minutes to remind them who he was.

Back in Detroit on leave on one occasion, his mother asked him to drive her to a doctor's appointment. In the office, an off-duty black Detroit policeman, Ronald Turner, recognized the Medal of Honor winner. When he asked for an account of his experience in Vietnam, Skip replied: "Don't ask me anything about the medal. I don't even know how I won it."

Later, the policeman reported, Skip complained that he had been exploited by the Army. He told him that ever since he won the medal he had been set on a hero's path as an inspiration to black kids.

Others recalled how upset he had become when his recruiting talks at some black high schools in Detroit had been picketed by militants who called him an "electronic nigger," a robot the Army was using to recruit blacks for a war in Asia.

With his psychiatrist, he began to discuss his deeper anxieties.

Since coming home from Vietnam the subject has had bad dreams. . He didn't confide in his mother or wife, but entertained a lot of moral judgment as to what had happened at Dakto. Why had he been ordered to switch tanks the night before? Why was he spared and not the others? He experienced guilt about his survival. He wondered if he was sane. It made him sad and depressed.

Skip signed out of the hospital on March 28 on a three-day pass to Philadelphia. The next day the newspapers and television were filled with reports of the conviction of First Lieut. William L. Calley Jr. on charges of murdering Vietnamese civilians. Skip turned up in Detroit a few days later and never returned to the Army hospital.

He settled in at home once again and dodged the telephone calls from the Army.

"How can you take punitive action against a Medal of Honor holder?" asked a major at the hospital who tried to convince him to return.

The Army did contact the Ford Motor however, which had been letting Skip use a Thunderbird for the past two years. Ford picked up the car on the theory that without it he might be inconvenienced enough to return to the hospital. Instead, he cashed the cashier's check for $1,500, his Army back pay, and bought a 1967 Mercury for $850.

He changed his unlisted phone number to avoid the Army callers and a growing number of bill collectors.

By April, his house mortgage had not been paid for the previous nine months, and foreclosing proceedings had been started. He owed payments on his credit union loan.

The car had to go into the garage for brake repairs on Wednesday, April 28, and Skip was told it would cost $78.50 to get it out. The same day Katrina entered a hospital for removal of an infected cyst and he told the admitting office clerk he would pay the $25 deposit the next day.

Lonely and depressed at home, Skip telephoned his cousin. "Let's go out and grab some beers," he said. But his cousin was busy.

He made another phone call that night and spoke to a friend in the Army. "I have a story I'm writing and I want you to peddle it for me," he said. "It starts out like this:

"Sgt. Dwight Johnson is dead and his home has been wiped out. . . ."

On April 30, Skip visited Katrina at the hospital. She said they were asking about the hospital deposit. He left at 5:30, promising to return later that evening with her hair curlers and bathrobe.

"He was just the same old Dwight, just kidding and teasing," his wife recalled. "When he was going, he said 'Ain't you going to give me a little kiss good-by?' He said it like a little boy with his thumb in his mouth. So I kissed him and he went."

A Plea for a Ride

When Eddie Wright got home from work that night about 9 o'clock, he got a call from Skip. He said he needed a ride to pick up some money someone owed him and wanted to know if Eddie could get his stepfather to drive him. He said he would pay $15 for the ride.

Around 11 o'clock, Eddie, his mother and his stepfather picked up Skip at his home. At his direction they drove west for about a mile to the corner of Orangelawn and Prest.

411

"Stop here," Skip told him, getting out of the car. "This guy lives down the street and I don't want him to see me coming."

The family waited in the car for 30 minutes. They became nervous, parked in a white neighborhood, and as Eddie explained later to the police—it may have looked odd for a car filled with blacks to be parked on a dark street. "So we pulled the car out under a streetlight so everybody could see us," he said.

At about 11:45 a police car pulled up sharply and two officers with drawn pistols got out. "What are you doing here?" they asked.

"We're waiting for a friend."

"What's his name?"

"Dwight Johnson."

"Dwight Johnson's on the floor of a grocery store around the corner," the officers said. "He's been shot."

'I'm Going to Kill You'

"I first hit him with two bullets," the manager, Charles Landeghem, said later, "But he just stood there, with the gun in his hand, and said, 'I'm going to kill you. . . .'

"I kept pulling the trigger until my gun was empty."

Skip's psychiatrist recalled one of the interviews with him.

The subject remembered coming face to face with a Vietnamese with a gun. He can remember the soldier squeezing the trigger. The gun jammed. The subject has since engaged in some magical thinking about this episode. He also suffers guilt over surviving it, and later winning a high honor for the one time in his life when he lost complete control of himself. He asked: "What would happen if I lost control of myself in Detroit and behaved like I did in Vietnam?" The prospect of such an event apparently was deeply disturbing to him.

The burial at Arlington National Cemetery took place on a muggy and overcast day. The grave, on a grassy slope about 200 yards east of the Kennedy Memorial, overlooks the Potomac and the Pentagon, gray and silent, to the south.

The Army honor guard, in dress blues, carried out its assignment with precision, the sixth burial of the day for the eight-man unit, while tourists took photographs at a discreet distance from the grieving family.

For a few days after the burial, the family weighed the possibility that Skip had been taking narcotics in the last few months of his life and the demands of drugs had sent him into the grocery store with a gun. But the autopsy turned up no trace of narcotics.

Eddie Wright and his family were released by homicide detectives after questioning, even after Eddie could not produce any plausible reason why his best friend had carried out a bizarre crime and implicated him at the same time.

The dead man's mother was the only one who uttered the words that no one else dared to speak.

"Sometimes I wonder if Skip tired of this life and needed someone else to pull the trigger," she said late one night in the living room of her home, her eyes fixed on a large color photograph of her son, handsome in his uniform, with the pale blue ribbon of his country's highest military honor around his neck.

Many acts of altruism require considerable personal risk, yet whether they are "death risking," or perhaps even "death seeking" behaviors is difficult to determine from external circumstances. Bob Patrick, an emergency service patrolman, has chosen a profession that necessitates repeated encounters with death. Secure in his career decision, and effective in his profession, Patrick, nevertheless, ponders what effect the continued exposure to violent death will have on his sensitivity. Will his work, he wonders, harden him to the point where he can no longer feel emotion in his own life? What repercussions will there be to living so intimately with death?

selection from
WORKING
Studs Terkel

"BOB PATRICK"

Harold's son. He is thirty-three, married, and has a child. He has been a member of the city police force for six years. For the past three years he has been an emergency service patrolman.

"Emergency service is like a rescue squad. You respond to any call, any incident; a man under a train, trapped in an auto, bridge jumpers, psychos, guys that murdered people and barricaded themselves in. We go in and get these people out. It is sometimes a little too exciting. I felt like I wasn't gonna come home on two incidents."

He finished among the highest in his class at the police academy, though he was "eleven years out of high school." Most of his colleagues were twenty-one, twenty-two. "I always wanted to be with the city. I felt that was the best job in the world. If I wasn't a cop, see, I don't think I could be anything else. Oh, maybe a truckdriver."

I got assigned to foot patrolman in Bedford-Stuyvesant. I never knew where Bedford-Stuyvesant was. I heard it was a low, poverty-stricken area, and it was a name that people

---

Studs Terkel. "Bob Patrick." *Working.* New York: Pantheon Books, a division of Random House, Inc., 1972.

feared. It's black. Something like Harlem, even worse. Harlem was where colored people actually grew up. But Bedford-Stuyvesant is where colored people migrated from Harlem or from North Carolina. They were a tougher class of people.

Myself and two friends from the neighborhood went there. We packed a lunch because we never really ventured outside the neighborhood. We met that morning about six o'clock. We had to be in roll call by eight. We got there a quarter after six. We couldn't believe it was so close. We laughed like hell because this is our neighborhood, more or less. We were like on the outskirts of our precinct. It was only ten minutes from my house.

When we got our orders, everybody said, "Oh wow, forget it." One guy thought he was going there, we had to chase him up three stories to tell him we're only kidding. He was ready to turn in his badge. Great fear, that was a danger area.

I was scared. Most people at Bedford-Stuyvesant were unemployed, mostly welfare, and they more or less didn't care too much for the police. The tour I feared most was four to twelve on a Friday or Saturday night. I'm not a drinker. I never drank, but I'd stop off at a bar over here and have a few beers just to get keyed up enough to put up with the problems we knew we were gonna come up against.

I would argue face to face with these people that I knew had their problems, too. But it's hard to use selective enforcement with 'em. Then get off at midnight and still feel nervous about it. And go for another few drinks and go home and I'd fall right to sleep. Two or three beers and I would calm down and feel like a husband again with the family at home.

I rode with a colored guy quite a few times. They would put you in a radio car and you'd be working with an old-timer. One of the calls we went on was a baby in convulsions, stopped breathing. The elevator was out of order and we ran up eight flights of stairs. This was a colored baby. It was blue. I had taken the baby from the aunt and my partner and I rushed down the stairs with the mother. In the radio car I gave the baby mouth to mouth resuscitation. The baby had regurgitated and started breathing again. The doctor at the hospital said what-

415

ever it was, we had gotten it up.

The sergeant wanted to write it up because of the problem we were having in the area. For a white cop doin' what I did. But I didn't want it. I said I would do it for anybody, regardless of black or white. They wrote it up and gave me a citation. The guys from the precinct was kidding me that I was now integrated. The mother had said she was willing to even change the baby's name to Robert after what I did.

The guy I worked with had more time on the job than I did. When we went on a family dispute, he would do all the talking. I got the impression that they were more aggressive than we were, the people we were tryin' to settle the dispute with. A husband and wife fight or a boyfriend and a husband. Most of the time you have to separate 'em. "You take the wife into the room and I'll take the husband into the other room." I looked up to my partner on the way he settled disputes. It was very quick and he knew what he was doing.

I've been shot. The only thing I haven't been in Bedford-Stuyvesant is stabbed. I've been spit at. I've been hit with bottles, rocks, bricks, Molotov cocktails, cherry bombs in my eye . . . I've gotten in disputes where I've had 10-13's called on me. That would be to assist the patrolman on the corner. Called by black people to help me against other black people.

After three years at Bedford-Stuyvesant he was assigned to the emergency service patrol. "Our truck is a $55,000 truck and it's maybe $150,000 in equipment. We have shotguns, we have sniper rifles, we have tear gas, bullet-proof vests, we have nets for jumpers, we have Morrissey belts for the patrolman to hold himself in when he gets up on a bridge. we have Kelly tools to pry out trapped people, we give oxygen . . ."

Fifty to seventy-five percent of our calls are for oxygen. I had people that were pronounced DOA by a doctor—dead on arrival. We have resuscitated them. I had brought him back. The man had lived for eight hours after I had brought him back. The doctor was flabbergasted. He had written letters on it and thought we were the greatest rescue team in New York City. We give oxygen until the arrival of the ambulance. Most of the time we beat the ambulance.

We set up a net for jumpers. We caught a person jumping from twenty-three stories in Manhattan. It musta looked like a postage stamp to him. We caught a girl from a high school four stories high. If it saves one life, it's worth it, this net.

A young man was out on a ledge on a six-story building. He was a mental patient. We try to get a close friend to talk to him, a girl friend, a priest, a guy from the old baseball team . . . Then you start talkin' to him. You talk to him as long as you can. A lot of times they kid and laugh with you—until you get too close. Then they'll tell you. "Stop right where you are or I'll jump." You try to be his friend. Sometimes you take off the police shirt to make him believe you're just a citizen. A lot of people don't like the uniform.

You straddle the wall. You use a Morrissey belt, tie it around with a line your partner holds. Sometimes you jump from a ledge and come right up in front of the jumper to trap him. But a lot of times they'll jump if they spot you. You try to be as cautious as possible. It's a life. . .

Sometimes you have eleven jobs in one night. I had to shoot a vicious dog in the street. The kids would curse me for doin' it. The dog was foaming at the mouth and snapping at everybody. We come behind him and put three bullets in his head. You want to get the kids outa there. He sees the cop shooting a dog, he's not gonna like the cop.

We get some terrible collisions. The cars are absolutely like accordions. The first week we had a head-on collision on a parkway. I was just passing by when it happened and we jumped out. There were parents in there and a girl and a boy about six years old. I carried the girl out. She had no face. Then we carried out the parents. The father had lived until we jacked him out and he had collapsed. The whole family was DOA. It happens twenty-four hours a day. If emergency's gonna be like this, I'd rather go back to Bedford-Stuyvesant.

The next day I read in the papers they were both boys, but had mod haircuts. You look across the breakfast table and see your son. My wife plenty times asked me, "How can you do that? How can you go under a train with a person that's severed the legs off, come home and eat breakfast, and feel . . .?" That's what I'm waiting for: when I can go home and not feel anything for my family. See, I have to feel.

A patrolman will call you for a guy that's DOA for a month. He hanged himself. I'm cuttin' him down. You're dancing to get out of the way of the maggots. I caught myself dancing in the middle of the livingroom, trying to get a ring off a DOA for a month, while the maggots are jumping all over my pants. I just put the damn pants on, brand-new, dry cleaned. I go back to the precinct and still itch and jump in the shower.

And to go under a train and the guy sealed his body to the wheel because of the heat from the third rail. And you know you're gonna drop him into the bag. A sixteen-year-old kid gets his hand caught in a meat grinder. His hand was comin' out in front. And he asks us not to tell his mother. A surgeon pukes on the job and tells you to do it.

One time we had a guy trapped between the platform and the train. His body was below, his head was above. He was talking to the doctor. He had a couple of kids home. In order to get him out we had to use a Z-bar, to jack the train away from the platform. The doctor said, "The minute you jack this train away from the platform, he's gonna go." He was talkin' and smokin' with us for about fifteen minutes. The minute we jacked, he was gone. [Snaps fingers.] I couldn't believe I could snuff out life, just like that. We just jacked this thing away and his life. And to give him a cigarette before it happened was even worse.

While you're en route to the job, to build yourself up, you say, this is part of the job that has to be done. Somebody's gotta do it. After this, there couldn't be nothing worse. No other job's gonna be as bad as this one. And another job comes up worse. Eventually you get used to what you're doin'.

Homicides are bad. I seen the medical examiner put his finger into seventeen knife wounds. I was holding the portolight so he could see where his finger was going. Knuckle deep. And telling me, "It's hit the bone, the bullet here, the knife wound through the neck." I figure I've seen too much. Jeez, this is not for me. You wouldn't believe it. Maybe I don't believe it. Maybe it didn't hit me yet.

I'm afraid that after seein' so much of this I can come

home and hear my son in pain and not feel for him. So far it hasn't happened. I hope to God it never happens. I hope to God I always feel. When my grandmother passed away a couple of months ago, I didn't feel anything. I wonder, gee, is it happening to me?

One time a guy had shot up a cop in the hospital and threw the cop down the stairs and his wheel chair on top of him. He escaped with a bullet in him. He held up a tenement in Brownsville. They called us down at three o'clock in the morning, with bullet-proof vests and shotguns. I said to myself, this is something out of the movies. The captain had a blackboard. There's eight of us and he gave each of us a job: "Two cover the back yard, you three cover the front, you three will have to secure the roof."

This guy wasn't gonna be taken alive. Frank and me will be the assault team to secure the roof. We're loaded with shotguns and we're gonna sneak in there. We met at four o'clock in the morning. We're goin' up the back stairs. On the first stairway there was a German shepherd dog outside the doorway. The dog cowered in the corner, thank God. We went up three more stories. We secured the roof.

We could hear them assaulting in each apartment, trying to flush this guy out. He fled to the fire escape. As he was comin' up, we told him to freeze. Tony, it was all over. He started to go back down. We radioed team one in the back yard. We heard shots. The rooftops had actually lit up. The assault man had fired twenty-seven bullets into this guy and he recovered. He's still standing trial from what I heard. This was one of the jobs I felt, when I was goin' up the stairs, should I give my wife a call? I felt like I had to call her.

If a perpetrator's in a building, you either talk to him or contain him or flush him out with tear gas rather than runnin' in and shoot. They feel a life is more important than anything else. Most cops feel this, yes.

I went on the prison riots we had in the Tombs. I was the first one on the scene, where we had to burn the gates out of the prison, where the prisoners had boarded up the gates with chairs and furniture. We had to use acetylene torches.

My wife knew I was in on it. I was on the front page. They had me with a shotgun and the bullet-proof vest and all the ammunition, waiting to go into the prison.

I wonder to myself, Is death a challenge? Is it something I want to pursue or get away from? I'm there and I don't have to be. I want to be. You have chances of being killed yourself. I've come so close . . .

I went on a job two weeks ago. A nineteen-year-old, he just got back from Vietnam on a medical discharge. He had ransacked his parents' house. He broke all the windows, kicked in the color television set, and hid upstairs with a homemade spear and two butcher knives in one hand. He had cut up his father's face.

We were called down to go in and get this kid. He tore the bannister up and used every pole for a weapon. We had put gas masks on. All the cops was there, with sticks and everything. They couldn't get near him. He kept throwing down these iron ash trays. I went up two steps and he was cocking this spear. We cleared out all the policemen. They just wanted emergency, us.

If you wait long enough, he'll come out. We had everybody talk to him, his mother . . . He didn't come out. The sergeant gave orders to fire tear gas. I could hear it go in the windows. I went up a little further and I seen this nozzle come out of his face. I said, "Sarge, he's got a gas mask on." We fired something like sixteen cannisters in the apartment. When he went back to close one of the doors, I lunged upstairs. I'm very agile. I hit him in the face and his mask went flying. I grabbed his spear and gave him a bear hug. He just didn't put up any resistance. It was all over.

The patrol force rushed in. They were so anxious to get this guy, they were tearing at me. I was tellin' him, "Hey, fella, you got my leg. We got him, it's all over." They pulled my gas mask off. Now the big party starts. This was the guy who was agitating them for hours. "You bum, we got you." They dragged him down the stairs and put him in a body bag. It's like a straitjacket.

When we had him face down a patrolman grabbed him

by the hair and slammed his face into the ground. I grabbed his wrist, "Hey, that's not necessary. The guy's handcuffed. he's secure." I brushed the kid's hair out of his eyes. He had mod long hair. My kid has mod hair. The guy says, "What's the matter with you?" I said, "Knock it off, you're not gonna slam the kid."

The neighbors congratulated me because the kid didn't get a scratch on him. I read in the paper, patrolman so-and-so moved in to make the arrest after a preliminary rush by the emergency service. Patrolman so-and-so is the same one who slammed the kid's face in the ground.

I'm gonna get him tonight. I'm gonna ask if he's writing up for a commendation. I'm gonna tell him to withdraw it. Because I'm gonna be a witness against him. The lieutenant recommended giving me a day off. I told my sergeant the night before last the lieutenant can have his day off and shove it up his ass.

A lot of the barricade snipers are Vietnam veterans. Oh, the war plays a role. A lot of 'em go in the army because it's a better deal. They can eat, they can get an income, they get room and board. They take a lot of shit from the upper class and they don't have to take it in the service.

It sounds like a fairy tale to the guys at the bar, in one ear and out the other. After a rough tour, a guy's dead, shot, people stabbed, you go into a bar where the guys work on Wall Street, margin clerks. "How ya doin? What's new?" You say, "You wouldn't understand." They couldn't comprehend what I did just last night. With my wife, sometimes I come home after twelve and she knows somethin's up. She waits up. "What happened?" Sometimes I'm shaking, trembling. I tell her, "We had a guy . . ." (Sighs.) I feel better and I go to bed. I can sleep.

The one that kept me awake was three years ago. The barricaded kid. The first night I went right to sleep. The second night you start thinking, you start picturing the kid and taking him down. With the kid and the tear gas, the sergeant says, "Okay fire." And you hear the tear gas . . . Like you're playing, fooling around with death. You don't want to die, but you're comin' close to it, to really skin it. It's a joke, it's not happening.

I notice since I been in emergency she says, "Be careful." I hate that, because I feel jinxed. Every time she says be careful, a big job comes up. I feel, shit, why did she say that? I hope she doesn't say it. She'll say, "I'll see you in the morning. Be careful." Ooohhh!

Bad accidents, where I've held the guys' skulls . . . I'm getting used to it, because there are younger guys comin' into emergency and I feel I have to be the one to take charge. 'Cause I seen a retired guy come back and go on a bad job, like the kid that drowned and we pulled him out with hooks. I'm lookin' to him for help and I see him foldin'. I don't want that to happen to me. When you're workin' with a guy that has eighteen years and he gets sick, who else you gonna look up to?

Floaters, a guy that drowns and eventually comes up. Two weeks ago, we pulled this kid out. You look at him with the hook in the eye . . . You're holdin' in because your partner's holdin' in. I pulled a kid out of the pond, drowned. A woman asked me, "What color was he?" I said, "Miss, he's ten years old. What difference does it make what color he was?" "Well, you pulled him out, you should know." I just walked away from her.

Emergency got a waiting list of three thousand. I have one of the highest ratings. I do have status, especially with the young guys. When a guy says, "Bob, if they change the chart, could I ride with you?" that makes me feel great.

I feel like I'm helpin' people. When you come into a crowd, and a guy's been hit by a car, they call you. Ambulance is standing there dumbfounded, and the people are, too. When you give orders to tell this one to get a blanket, this one to get a telephone book, so I can splint a leg and wrap it with my own belt off my gun, that looks good in front of the public. They say, "Gee, who are these guys?"

Last week we responded to a baby in convulsions. We got there in two minutes. The guy barely hung up the phone. I put my finger down the baby's throat and pulled the tongue back. Put the baby upside down, held him in the radio car. I could feel the heat from the baby's mouth on my knuckles. At the hospital the father wanted to know who was the guy in the car. I gave the baby to the nurse. She said, "He's all right." I said, "Good." The father was in tears and I wanted to get the hell out of there.

This morning I read the paper about that cop that was shot up. His six-year-old son wrote a letter: "Hope you get better, Dad." My wife was fixin' breakfast. I said, "Did you read the paper, hon?" She says, "Not yet." "Did you read the letter this cop's son sent to his father when he was in the hospital?" She says, "No." "Well, he's dead now." So I read the part of it and I started to choke. I says, "What the hell . . ." I dropped the paper just to get my attention away. I divided my attention to my son that was in the swing. What the hell. All the shit I seen and did and I gotta read a letter . . . But it made me feel like I'm still maybe a while away from feeling like I have no feeling left. I knew I still had feelings left. I still have quite a few jobs to go . . .

QUESTIONS

1. Define each of the following terms used in this chapter. The starred words are concepts the writers expect the reader to know. If you are not familiar with them, consult a dictionary.

cessation
termination
interruption
continuation
altered continuation
intentioned death
unintentioned death
subintentioned death
romanticization
generativity
elective death
death control
*a right
*moral
vitalistic error
active euthanasia
passive euthanasia
direct euthanasia
indirect euthanasia
voluntary euthanasia
involuntary euthanasia

radical vitalism
dysthanasia
"mercy killing"
empirical morality
*morals
*ethics
situation ethics
*humanism
"ghetto mentality"
*G.I. series
*magical thinking
*clinical depression
body bag
to "take someone down"
*truism
probabilism
proportionality
pragmatic heresy
heroics
moral dying

2. Opponents of euthanasia often argue that an acceptance of elective death would ultimately result in a "cheapening of life." But Joseph Fletcher claims that "prolonging life beyond any personal or human state" is just as likely to end in a mockery of life. Write brief arguments for each side of the following debate resolution: That prolongation of life beyond natural limits undermines respect for life.

3. Shneidman infers conscious or unconscious motivation from the patterns of behavior that he presents as illustrations of orientations toward death. Describe five cases of death where you might infer "subintention." List the criteria you would use in determining the appropriateness of your inference. Consider how you might test the hypothesis that someone was "rushing to his own funeral"?

4. a. In "Suicide Note," Anne Sexton writes:

    But surely you know that everyone has a death,
    his own death
    waiting for him.
    So I will go now
    without old age or disease . . .

    Do you share her view? Why, or why not?

   b. To what extent do you think that the writings prior to an author's death reveal his motivation?

5. Much of the discussion of death in the poetry of Anne Sexton centers on the "tools" of death. Using the views outlined in Shneidman's paper, "The Enemy," develop an explanation for why suicides may discuss method more than decision.

6. Review the paper by Michael Peck and Carl Wold to identify the predisposing and personality factors in Laurie's self-destructive threats. In doing so, be careful to differentiate

these factors from the immediate causes. Study the description of Laurie's behavior to find examples of ambivalence, frustrated dependence and indirect communication.

7. a. Shneidman condemns the romanticization of death for blurring the realization that death is "the enemy." What does he mean by the term *romanticization?* If death is viewed as "the enemy," can acceptance be possible? Explain.

   b. To what extent do you believe that our culture romanticizes death? Choose one of the following themes and describe an example of its romanticization in the media or in literature.

8. The condition of the Medal of Honor winner, Dwight Johnson, was diagnosed by an army psychiatrist as "depression caused by a post-Vietnam adjustment problem." Re-read Freud's explanation of the distortion of psychic balance in times of war (Chapter Three) to identify elements in Johnson's Vietnam experience that might have contributed to his post-Vietnam condition.

9. a. The continuum of choices suggested by the range of papers in this chapter extends to a consideration of altruism and martyrdom. List several examples of altruistic acts involving risk (e.g. the donation of an organ to a child, fighting a forest fire). How would you explain the difference between altruism and martyrdom? Are there contemporary martyrs? If so, give examples and state what benefits their martyrdom produced.

   b. What are the possible motivations for the acts you listed in 9a? Try to apply Shneidman's descriptive categories of orientations toward death to your examples. Would you describe the individuals in your examples as death-seeking? Why, or why not?

10. The selections in Chapter Five return the reader to the central question of Chapter One, "What is an appropriate death?" Identify both the implicit and the explicit conceptions of death that are expressed by the Van Dusen's, Fletcher, Anne Sexton, Shneidman, Dwight Johnson and Bob Patrick. Compare and contrast their views. Describe the role of "choice" in each view.

11. How have your own ideas of what makes death appropriate changed since your first discussions in the context of Chapter One?

PROJECTS FOR FURTHER STUDY

1. In recent years many communities have developed "hot lines," and "suicide prevention centers," to meet the crisis of suicide or attempted suicide. The movement has greatly increased our understanding of the demographics and the dynamics of suicide, thereby improving our chances of preventing suicide.

    a. Research the dynamics of suicide, differentiating between the long term personality and adjustment of the suicide victim and the precipitating events which most commonly precede a suicide attempt. The Los Angeles Suicide Prevention Center has developed a procedure for rating the "lethality" of a suicide threat as a means of evaluating the immediate, self-destructive potential of a suicide threat. From your own research construct a description of a high lethality suicide attempter, a low lethality attempter. Include in your profile, personality factors, existing sources of psycho-social support, and the immediate motivation for the suicide attempt. Lethality scales and crisis intervention are covered extensively in the collection of papers contained in *The Cry for Help*, edited by Farberow and Shneidman.

428

b.   Community "hot lines" deal with many personal crises besides suicide and they are often staffed by student volunteers working under professional supervision. Suicide prevention centers, on the other hand, are specialized efforts to deal with self-destructive behaviors and, consequently, are staffed by a higher proportion of health care professionals to lay volunteers. Visit a suicide prevention center or "hot line" in your area to research the training that lay volunteers receive, the concrete steps they are trained to take, the point at which a referral to a professional is made, and the steps that the professional is likely to take.

2.   In *Deaths of Man*, Edwin Shneidman relates his conception of subintentioned death to that of "equivocal death," a death in which the victim's actual intention of ending his own life may not be clear. Procedures for a "psychological autopsy" have been developed from a study of suicidology, gerontology, and the psychosocial aspects of cancer. The psychological autopsy evaluates the contribution of conscious and unconscious factors in death from various causes.

a.   Investigate the procedures for a psychological autopsy. What variables are studied? What information is gathered? From whom? What significant factors enter into the final decision? What purposes can such an investigation serve? The psychological autopsy in cases of equivocal suicide is discussed in *Cry for Help* and *Deaths of Man*; a more general treatment of deaths from cancer in old age is found in *The Realization of Death*, by Avery Weisman.

b.   Jon Nordheimer's article on Dwight Johnson is, in a sense, a psychological autopsy. Review Nordheimer's report to identify the crucial elements of a psychological autopsy. What additional information would you need in order to reach a conclusion about the degree of subintention in the case of Johnson? Do you agree with the mother's final statement?

3. Death has proved a most abundant theme in literature; so much so, that one can develop categories for the study of literary presentations of death—e.g. death in the war novel, death and disease, death and self-definition and death in poetry. Decide, as a class, which categories you will use, then select one work to study individually. Read the work carefully and then develop a critique of the presentation of death in that work. Include in your report, responses to the following:

    a. Why did you select this particular work?

    b. How was death portrayed in the work? (Who died? Why? With what effect on the other characters?)

    c. To what extent was the presentation of death realistic? Clinical?

    d. What attitudes does the author convey about death?

    e. What symbols of mortality are used in the work?

    f. What are your reactions to the presentation of death in the work?

After all students have completed their individual reports, the class can divide into groups on the basis of the categories they previously decided to study. In the small groups, each student can report on the work he read, then the group members can work together to identify features in the presentation of death that are common to the specific category. The bibliographic references that follow may serve as a beginning.

Death in the War Novel

Catton, Bruce. *A Stillness at Appomatox*. New York: Doubleday & Co., Inc., 1954.

Crane, Stephen. *The Red Badge of Courage*. New York: Grosset & Dunlap 1952.

Deighton, Len. *Bomber*. New York: Signet, 1971.

Remarque, E. *All Quiet on the Western Front*. Boston: Little Brown & Co., 1958.

Death and Disease

Alsop, S. *Stay of Execution*. New York: Lippincott, J. B. & Co., 1973.

Craven, Margaret. *I Heard The Owl Call My Name*. New York: Doubleday Books, 1973.

Lund, D. *Eric*. New York: Lippincott, J. B. and Co., 1974.

Solzhenitsyn, A. *Cancer Ward*. New York: Farrar, Straus & Giroux Inc., 1969.

Death and Self-definition

de Beauvoir, Simone. *A Very Easy Death*. New York: Warner Books Inc., 1973.

Fuentes, Carlos. *The Death of Artemio Cruz*. New York: Farrar, Straus & Giroux Inc., 1964.

Plath, S. *The Bell Jar*. New York: Harper & Row Inc., 1971.

Shaw, Bernard. *Saint Joan*. New York: Penguin, 1951.

Death in Poetry

Plath, Sylvia. *Ariel*. New York: Harper & Row, 1966.

Sexton, Anne. *The Death Notebooks*. Boston: Houghton and Mifflin, 1974.

Tennyson, A. *In Memoriam*. Norton, W. W. & Co., Inc., 1974.

STRUCTURED EXERCISES

1. The bureaucracy of death throws a harsh light on death's aftermath. The objective details of death that are required for the official forms which accompany the disposition of the body offer a sharp contrast to what Shneidman has described as the "romanticization of death." In order to focus on the *facts* of death, assume that you have died in some chosen manner at some future time. Now, take fifteen minutes to visualize the circumstances of "your death" and complete the Certificate of Death found in the Appendix at the end of this book.

   After each member of the class has finished, break up into groups of four to discuss the results of the exercise. Answer the following questions.

   a. How did you die? When? Where?

   b. What was the mode of death? The cause of death?

   c. Was there an autopsy? Why, or why not?

   d. How might others assess the "intentionality" of your death? On what would they base their assessment?

   e. What effect has this exercise had on you? How has it affected your attitude toward the physical facts of death?

432

2. As the medical choices in extending life have increased the general public has become more aware of the choices that must be made. The last several years have seen the growing interest in documents such as the "Living Will," although at the present time they have no legal status. Some states (Kansas and Florida, among them) are debating legislation which is often referred to as "Dignity in Death" or "Right to Die" legislation. One such bill provides for a legally binding "Directive to Physicians" (See Appendix C). Such proposals respond to the individual's fear of being forced to endure unnecessary prolongation of life, and his desire for a voice in medical decision-making, but the full implications of a particular proposal may go unnoticed until it is applied to specific situations.

Three illustrative cases are given below. Working as a class, discuss each case. Refer to the directive given in Appendix C and answer the questions following each example. Compare and contrast the three cases, considering the relative suitability of the directive to each.

At the end of your discussion list any changes you would propose to the directive or the safeguards you would write into a "Right to Die" law.

Case 1

As a result of a drug overdose, a 16 year old boy has remained in a deep coma for six months. His physician judges the coma to be irreversible but cannot state that recovery at a distant time in the future is impossible. In the meanwhile, the boy is unable to breathe without mechanical aid from a respirator, although there is evidence of residual sub-cortical functioning (i.e., he does not meet the criteria for brain death). The boy's parents are reluctant to let their son go, but continued financial burdens threaten the stability of the home.

　　　　1. Does continued maintenance on a respirator meet the criterion for a "life-sustaining procedure" as given in the proposal (see Appendix A)?

433

2.   If you were the parents, would you want the boy to be maintained on the respirator? For how long?

3.   A teenager is unlikely to consider signing a document like a living will and is legally too young to sign a directive such as the one given in Appendix A. If the boy had indicated in previous discussions with his parents that he would not have wanted to be maintained indefinitely on a respirator, what action would you recommend?

Case 2

Mr. V., age 48, is suffering from a malignant brain tumor and is in a semi-comatose state. He has been referred by the family physician to the tumor ward of a Veteran's Administration hospital for terminal care. The VA oncologist suggests to Mrs. V. that a new drug might have some positive effects: an "extraordinary" treatment but one without painful side effects. Mrs. V. gives permission for treatment and subsequently Mr. V. recovers sufficiently to live comfortably for another twelve months.

1.   From the description, do you consider that the drug represented a "life-sustaining procedure" as defined in the proposal?

2.   If you were Mrs. V., what would you have decided, regardless of whether Mr. V. had signed such a directive?

3.   If Mr. V. had signed the directive six months earlier, in his current semi-comatose condition would there be a way to allow his receiving the treatment?

Case 3

A 68 year old grandmother with terminal bone cancer is being maintained on heavy doses of pain-relieving drugs. Since the cancer has not spread to vital organs, she faces an indeterminate period of intense pain before death occurs, most likely from a complication of the cancer such as pneumonia. In the course of her long illness she has reached the limit of her physiological tolerance to narcotics; increasing the dosage to alleviate her pain is likely to result in a fatal overdose. She has indicated unwillingness to sign the directive. Her husband is urging the physician to act to prevent further suffering, yet the doctor realizes the serious risk to the patient in administering higher doses of drugs.

1.   As an observer what do you feel the doctor should do? Would your response differ if you were the husband? The patient?

434

2. How do you believe the final decision should be made?

3. Had the woman signed the directive, what options, if any, would the doctor have?

FOR FURTHER READING

The following books and papers provide in-depth coverage of topics introduced in this chapter.

Alvarez, A. *The Savage God: A Study of Suicide.* New York: Random House, 1972.

Cutler, D. R. (ed.) *Updating Life and Death.* Boston: Beacon Press, 1969.

Farberow, N. L. and Shneidman, E. S. (eds.) *The Cry for Help.* New York: McGraw-Hill, 1961.

Gorovitz, S., Jameton, A. L., Macklin, R., O'Connor, J. M., Perrin, E. V., St. Clair, B. P., and Sherwin, S. (eds.) *Moral Problems in Medicine.* Englewood Cliffs, N.J.: Prentice-Hall, 1976.

Lifton, R. J. *Home from the War: Vietnam Veterans: Neither Victims nor Executioners.* New York: Simon and Schuster, 1973.

Maguire, D. C. *Death by Choice.* New York: Doubleday and Company, 1974.

Menninger, K. *Man Against Himself.* New York: Harcourt Brace and World, 1966.

Perlin, S. (ed.) *A Handbook for The Study of Suicide.* New York: Oxford University Press, 1975.

Weisman, A. D. *The Realization of Death: A Guide for The Psychological Autopsy.* New York: Jacob Aronson, 1974.

Williams, G. L. *The Sanctity of Life and The Criminal Law.* New York: Knopf, 1957.

Williams, R. H. "Our role in the generation, modification and termination of life." *Archives of Internal Medicine,* 1969, 124: 215-337.

Epilogue

The following newspaper account by a father mourning the loss of his young daughter demonstrates the fact that all the elements in a study of death and dying are interrelated —dying experience, loss and grief, meaning and decision. To reflect your own understanding of death and dying at this point, read the selection through twice; first for your personal reactions, and then to identify as many concepts and behaviors as you recognize from your study of the readings in this text.

THEN SUDDENLY,
IT WAS JENNIFER'S LAST DAY

Robert Becker

A nurse on the floor ushered us to a room and handed me a small, open-backed gown for Jen to wear.

"Leave my clothes on," the child insisted. "I want my shirt on. Don't take my shoes off." Jen was terrified. It was our seventh visit to Children's Hospital in three weeks, visits which invariably began in the outpatient clinic on the first floor with a technician pricking her finger for a blood sample, followed by a doctor's probings and palpations. The more recent trips, like this one, often turned into a two or three-day stay in the hospital, much to Jen's growing dismay.

Ten months earlier, when Jennifer was 20 months old, her mother and I noticed a lump on her side after lifting her from the tub one Sunday night. She had been lethargic for a couple of weeks before that, but the pediatrician said she was probably anemic and prescribed iron pills. After the swelling appeared, though, we took her to Alexandria Hospital where they operated and discovered neuroblastoma, the most common form of solid-tumor cancer that strikes infants and toddlers.

438

In the months that followed, we had taken her to a private oncologist for chemotherapy every other week, and to the radiologist every day for the first two months. We were lucky. The combination of drugs and radiation had worked and produced what the doctors said was "complete remission," which simply meant there was no trace of the disease. It was not to be confused with a "cure."

Still, we had begun to allow ourselves the luxury of believing she just might be cured anyway, when suddenly the lethargy, the failing appetite, the constant crying from the discomfort—and the tumor—all reappeared. A relapse.

Realizing there was little he could do, the oncologist, a rather large man with an air of determined detachment, arranged for Jen's admission to the fourth floor of Children's Hospital—the children's cancer ward.

But before Jen's first appointment at Children's, this bitter, abrupt change started me on the last stretch of a psychic marathon, a race known to countless families of the cancer-stricken—The Miracle Chase. I am talking now of hope and fear. Sunrise, sunset, the dread remains, the hope remains. I placed phone calls all around the country to leading hospitals and clinics. Was there any new treatment, any drug that looked hopeful? Desperate for help, I found none. Most likely, there was none then to be found. There still isn't.

The fourth floor at Children's brims with activity, at least during the day. Youngsters on short, spindly legs waddle along the length of the hallway like small penguins. Assorted toys, mostly the bulky wooden types found in pediatricians' waiting rooms, litter the hall at odd intervals, abandoned by youngsters whose interests have been diverted or who have been taken elsewhere for treatment.

At her insistence, I carried Jen up and down the long hallway pointing out other youngsters in their beds and trying to coax her with, "Look how that little boy is resting in his bed; wouldn't you like to take a little rest, too?"

"No, I want you to carry me," she shot back.

As a concession to get her to stay in bed, my wife Carolyn and I spent most of the day reading Jen's favorite books to her over and over. Periodically, someone would come in either to prick her finger, take her temperature or check the intravenous fluid tube that had been inserted once we got her settled down. By late afternoon, Jen finally fell asleep and a nurse offered to stay with her while we went downstairs to get something to eat. But we did so reluctantly, knowing Jen was never receptive to strangers in the first place and fearful of losing any time with her in the second.

When we returned about a half-hour later, there was Jen in the woman's arms, feebly smiling up at her. The whole scene went through us like a knife. Jen wanted so much to be near someone. She was so frightened at being alone that, surprisingly, she found comfort in this kindly stranger and actually asked the nurse to hold her. Happily, the nurse had the good sense and kindness of heart to pick her up, I.V. and all, and rock her—a gesture we would never forget.

That night Carolyn and I slept in shifts, watching over Jen when she woke to throw up bile. She didn't really have the strength to do anything more than simply turn her head. So we had to watch her carefully and occasionally slide a small stainless steel bowl beside her mouth to avoid soiling the bedsheets.

During the night, a thought kept recurring to me. It was something one of the doctors had said some nine or ten months ago, back in Alexandria Hospital. I had asked him why it was that Jen didn't seem to complain very much about her discomfort and pain. He said, "Children are often the easiest patients to treat simply because small youngsters in these circumstances, those with severe and sometimes painful illnesses like Jennifer's, don't know enough about life to complain. For them, this is what life is all about: they haven't yet experienced enough to know that life is not all pain. This is part of life and they just accept it."

The next morning, I sat on the edge of the bed and started to read a new book I had picked up, Gay Talese's "The Kingdom and the Power," while Carolyn slipped downstairs for a quick breakfast and Jen slept. I read only enough that morning to learn that *New York Times* reporter Tom Wicker's 106-paragraph on-the-spot report of the assassination of John F. Kennedy would be saved "by hundreds, perhaps thousands of readers" and that students and historians would be reading it again and again a half-century later. I wondered if 50 years from now anyone would give a damn that Jen died of cancer or even that she had lived at all.

But my thoughts were interrupted by our doctor who came into the room at that point to examine Jen. She was awake now and lay quietly as he breathed on his stethoscope and briskly rubbed it on his jacket to warm it before he touched her chest with it. For the first time, I thought I noticed some irregularity in her breathing as he bent over her; he stared at the wall as he listened.

"There's something in her lungs," he said. He wanted to put her in an oxygen tent. While the oxygen equipment was brought in, he wanted to have her X-rayed to see what that "something" was.

I wasn't prepared for all this. "Now wait a minute," I said. "She's really pretty uncomfortable. I don't see what an X-ray is going to accomplish."

The doctor tried to reassure me he only wanted to take a look to see if anything was obstructing her breathing.

This was all a little too sudden for me, but I reluctantly agreed.

Jen was difficult for them to handle in the X-ray department. They asked me to sit her up, turn her on her side and hold her head. Jen didn't want any part of this. "Daddy, my tummy hurts," she cried.

I was getting angry and impatient with the technicians. "Look, I'm sorry, but she can't sit up. You're not going to get her to sit up. Try something else. Let's get this over with."

I felt my eyes start to burn as I spoke now and I fought to hold back the tears. "She's dying," I said feebly. It was 10:30 a.m.

When we returned to the room, the oxygen tent was in place, draped over the top of the bed. An oxygen bottle was installed at the head of the bed.

To try to make Jen happy and comfortable, I read her a book, "Raggedy Ann and Fido." She paid close attention to the story, watching the pictures intently as I read. Midway through the story, she said, "Daddy, you hold me." That request has haunted me ever since she said it. I was terribly torn. There wasn't anything I wanted to do more than to pick her up. But I hesitated. I thought about the I.V. and the oxygen tent. It was supposedly doing her some good. So I didn't pick her up. Like a damn fool I went on with the story, trying to divert her attention.

She watched me read and looked at the pictures again as I held the book up for her. She even mumbled, "Uh-huh," or "Uh-uh," to questions I'd ask her about the story. Or I'd leave out key words in sentences and she'd fill them in.

I again noticed her starting to have trouble breathing. I reached under the tent and tried to elevate and arch her back and maybe turn her on her side to face Carolyn. I cranked the bed up a bit, hoping that by raising her head slightly, it might ease her breathing. Nothing helped.

"I'm going to get the doctor to make sure there's nothing wrong with her," I said to Carolyn on my way out.

I saw our doctor talking to nurses halfway down the hall, near the nurses' station. "Hey, Doc," I called. "Come here quick." He turned and started for me at a quick trot and followed me into the room. "Doc, she's not breathing right. What's going on?"

He examined her with his stethoscope but I couldn't detect any show of concern on his face. I don't remember exactly what he said, but I think he must have known what was happening.

Carolyn was standing right behind me and I began to talk to Jen. I held her right arm, the one with the I.V. still plugged into it, and stroked her forehead.

I kept telling her, "Daddy's going to make you feel better, baby. Everything's going to be all right." I thought perhaps she was getting upset or excited: her breathing became even more irregular. Then her attention turned away from me. She had been looking at me, but now she looked straight ahead. Her breaths began getting shorter and closer together, like gasping.

I still wasn't quite fully aware of how serious things were at this point. Somewhere along the line, the doctors had told us that we would be told when Jen entered the terminal phase.

I looked across the bed at the doctor. He wasn't doing anything. Just standing there looking at her. I looked back down at Jen and she was struggling for breath now.

Excited now, I shouted, "Hey! Hey, man! Doc!" I was waving my arms at him, directing him to the door. "Go get something. Go, man. Right now!"

He started for the door, then he stopped and started to say, "Well, Mr. Becker . . ." and then started to leave again.

Before he got past the foot of the bed, though, I motioned him back. I knew there was nothing he could do and I wanted him to stay there. I guess I was half hoping there might be some last-minute thing he could do. Maybe, too, I expected some help from him, for me.

There was a sound in Jen's throat. I felt Carolyn's fingers grasp my shoulders. Small flecks of saliva seeped through her teeth, and she gritted her teeth. Her gaze was still fixed ahead.

That tore me. "This is it," I thought. "Holy good God, man, this is it!" I could feel everything slipping away.

I began to plead, "No, no, Jen. Don't. No, no, Jen. . . ." I looked up at the doctor. "Doc, what's happening?" He had a deadpan look on his face. A nurse must have heard the commotion because I thought I heard the door shut.

Carolyn was vigorously patting my shoulders, trying to calm me down. She was saying something, but I didn't hear her.

I felt the sting in my eyes. "No, Jen. Don't. Don't go, Jen. Stay with me now. Don't go." And then her eyes rolled back. There was silence for a couple of seconds. Then a sudden tensing of her features, almost like shivering from a chill. then she relaxed. In that split second, I looked up and asked the doctor what time it was.

"Eleven twenty-five," he replied.

"I want to remember that."

For a few minutes, it was totally quiet in the room. None of us said a word. We all just looked at Jen.

Inside, a monologue was going on, telling all the other parts about what had just happened.

"Man, this really happened." the voice said. "She's gone.

443

That's the end of the line." Then it all began to cave in, all at once.

Carolyn was crying now, and I was coming unglued. I started talking to Jen again, quietly, almost whispering. "Jen, Jen. Come on, Jen. Jen . . ." Her lips were only slightly parted. Her eyes were half open. They were different, though. Not like the eyes of people who are alive. There was no contraction of the pupils. There was absolutely nothing.

"This is my child," I kept thinking. "How the hell does this happen? It's unbelievable something like this could really happen."

The thought of death had never completely registered in my mind; the finality of it, I mean. It's something the mind blocks out on its own. We had become accustomed to dealing with life on a minute-to-minute basis, almost totally without regard to what had passed or what lay ahead. But now, suddenly in the past few moments, all was very different and it all came rushing in on us, crushing us, that it has happened. This is it.

The doctor had left the room unnoticed by either of us until we finally stood up. Carolyn held my arm with both hands and helped me to stay calm long enough to say a prayer at the foot of the bed.

We left to call the family while the nurses unplugged the I.V. and tried to make Jen look comfortable. Everyone reacted predictably, crying at first, then trying to comfort us and finally saying they'd all come down together the next day.

After the calls we went back to the room. The nurses were still there.

"Say, look," I said to their somber faces. "I'm really sorry about coming unglued. I guess I really wasn't quite prepared.

"Oh, please don't apologize, Mr. Becker," said one nurse. "You have to do whatever you feel." She was right.

We stayed with Jen for the next three hours. Strangely, it seemed just like minutes. Neither of us was tense any longer. We were comfortable with Jen now. We no longer were anxious about the tumor spreading or causing her pain and discomfort. She didn't murmur or cry out or turn from side to side hoping to avoid the nagging pain. She just rested comfortably now.

Shortly after 3 p..m., we left the hospital. I looked up at the fourth floor window of Jen's room.

"I'm leaving her up there," I thought. "We're leaving her behind." And it was very strange for me, suddenly, going somewhere without Jen. I looked over at Carolyn and knew from the tears that she sensed the same loneliness. I imagined what Jen would feel being left like this. Even before she got sick, we rarely went out without her. She had a great fear of being separated from Carolyn.

When we got home, Carolyn went into our room to lie down while I went to Jen's room. I began to hear Carolyn crying softly, the sound muffled by the pillow. I hung my head over Jen's crib and let it all out, sobbing. Carolyn heard me and came in to comfort me. It was odd. Neither of us wanted the other to grieve. It hurt each of us to see the other cry.

Sun and moon. Time goes. Four years have passed since Jen died. The sorrow sears less. But an intense need to keep her memory alive remains. I dread that one day she might fade from memory and the incidents of her life and death drift into haziness. Recollections have already become clouded with the subsequent births of Krista, now three, and Kathleen, just turned three months. Krista, it seems, is an extension of Jen. The two are virtually indistinguishable in photographs. She delights in the same games we played with Jen so long ago, though Krista is a good deal more aggressive and certainly more bold about life than Jen.

And, as I watch Krista and her sister grow and pass through the stages of maturity Jen had before them I'm constantly reminded of a clipping someone handed me shortly after Jen died. I never found where it came from, but it was by a Richard J. Needham writing about relationships between parents and their children.

He said: "My favorite philosopher, George Santayana, had many distinguished friends, among them the Marchesa Iris Origo. When her little boy died, he wrote to her: 'We have no claim to any of our possessions. We have no claim to exist; and as we have to die in the end, so we must resign ourselves to die piecemeal, which really happens when we lose somebody or something that was closely intertwined with our existence.'

"This would seem a wise attitude to take toward children. They are not possessions, we have no claim on them, they owe us nothing. They are lent to us, you might say, and are taken away by death or, more commonly, by the natural process of growing up."

Appendices

Appendix A: Additional Materials for Structured Exercises
    i. Kidney Machine Exercise: Psychological Reports Sheet
    ii. A Proposal for Right to Die Legislation: Directive to Physicians

Appendix B: Physical Facts of Death
    i. Table:
    ii. Certificate of Death
    iii. Physician's Request for Post-mortem Examination
    iv. Permit for Disposition of Human Remains
    v. A Gift of Life: Uniform Donor Card
    vi. A Living Will

Appendix C: Additional Teaching Resources
    i. Disciplinary Schema
    ii. Topical Suggestions for Courses on Death and Dying
    iii. Multi-media References for Death and Dying

APPENDIX A:
ADDITIONAL MATERIALS FOR
STRUCTURED EXERCISES

KIDNEY MACHINE PSYCHOLOGICAL
REPORTS SHEET*

Re: Patients for Kidney Machine
From: Hospital Psychological Staff

In routine preadmission interviews the following patients were examined and evaluated as per the following data:

Re: Alfred—He is presently distraught about his physical condition and reports that it interferes with his work. Seems very committed to his work and appears to be legitimately on the verge of an important cancer discovery. It was hard for the staff to get him to talk about his work in terms that they could understand.

    Family relations seem strained and have been for some time because of his commitment to his work. The staff feels that he is a first-rate scientist and scholar who has contributed much and could contribute more to medical research. But they also believe him to be a mentally disturbed individual who, in time, will probably need psychiatric help.

---

*The Kidney Machine Psychological Reports Sheet is to be used in conjunction with the Structured Exercise number one in Chapter One.

Re: Bill—He is a well-oriented Negro, who does not appear to be swayed by the blandishments of black extremist groups. He is strongly devoted to his family and appears to be an excellent husband and father.

Bill's capacity for growth in his chosen occupation, however, seems limited. His high school record was poor, although he had no record of delinquency and was always regarded by his teachers as a student who tried hard. Therefore, he will probably not succeed with his business plans and will remain employed at a fixed rate permanently.

His wife is trained as a legal secretary. Her prognosis for employment is good, although Bill has discouraged her from seeking work because of mutual agreement to have her be a full-time mother. Bill seems unaware of the serious implications of his illness.

Re: Cora—One of the staff members evaluating Cora described her as a *professional Jew*. She is president of the local Hadassah organization and seems able to talk about nothing but her religion and her children. Although her recently found interest in interior decorating may be a sign of change, it was not clear to the staff whether this interest was real or only generated artificially when she heard of the interview requirement. ment.

She seems resigned to her illness and likely death. Her husband works long hours, is in good health, and enjoys the respect and love of his children. Cora's mother, who also lives with the family, handles most of the child care.

Re: David—Typical of young student activists, David is a bright—almost straight "A"—student who enjoys the respect of most of his teachers and friends. But he appears confused about his future and demonstrates a penchant for jeopardizing it by involving himself in various student "causes." Indeed, his college's dean of student affairs regards him as an individual who will "demonstrate for anything."

He is bitter, almost paranoid, about his illness. His father has invested a good deal of money, time, and emotion in him and has always hoped that David would become a lawyer.

449

His relations with his father are presently strained, however, and he seems only mildly concerned about his two sisters, although they still think highly of him. His future father-in-law, who is a highly successful businessman, expects him to enter the family enterprise upon college graduation.

Re: Edna—She is a self-contained, inner-directed woman and a model of the "career girl." It was clear to the staff that her natural aggressiveness and combative tendencies militated against any sort of marital attachment, and it is not impossible that she has lesbian tendencies.

Her employers regard her as indispensable. Her work record is superb, and her activities in church and charitable groups have been very effective. She is well regarded by all who know her, although she seems to have few, if any, close friends. She appears resigned to her death. In fact, she indicated that she would prefer to have someone other than herself go on the machine. Her offer did not seem in the least insincere.

The Directive to Physicians and list of definitions reprinted below appear in the "Natural Death Act" passed in California in September, 1976. The bill authorizes the withholding or withdrawal of life-sustaining procedures from adults who have a terminal condition and who have executed such a directive.

DIRECTIVE TO PHYSICIAN

Directive made this _____ day of _____ (month, year).

I _____, being of sound mind, willfully, and voluntarily make known my desire that my life shall not be artificially prolonged under the circumstances set forth below, do hereby declare:

1. If at any time I should have an incurable injury, disease, or illness certified to be a terminal condition by two physicians, and where the application of life-sustaining procedures would serve only to artificially prolong the moment of my death and where my physician determines that my death is imminent whether or not life-sustaining procedures are utilized, I direct that such procedures be withheld or withdrawn and that I be permitted to die naturally.

2. In the absence of my ability to give directions regarding the use of such life-sustaining procedures, it is my intention that this directive shall be honored by my family and physician(s) as the final expression of my legal right to refuse medical or surgical treatment and accept the consequences from such refusal.

3. If I have been diagnosed as pregnant and that diagnos-

is is known to my physician, this directive shall have no force or effect during the course of my pregnancy.

4. I have been diagnosed and notified at least 14 days ago as having a terminal condition by _____, M.D. whose address is _____, and whose telephone number is _____. I understand that if I have not filled in the physician's name and address, it shall be presumed that I did not have a terminal condition when I made out this directive.

5. This directive shall have no force or effect five years from the date filled in above.

6. I understand the full import of this directive and I am emotionally and mentally competent to make this directive.

Signed _____

City, County and State of Residence _____

The declarant has been personally known to me and I believe him or her to be of sound mind.

Witness _____

List of Definitions

(a) "Attending physician" means the physician selected by, or assigned to, the patient who has primary responsibility for the treatment and care of the patient.

(b) "Directive" means a written document voluntarily executed by the declarant in accordance with the requirements of Section 7188. The directive, or a copy of the directive, shall be made part of the patient's medical records.

(c) "Life-sustaining procedure" means any medical procedure or intervention which utilizes mechanical or other artificial means to sustain, restore, or supplant a vital function, which, when applied to a qualified patient, would serve only to artificially prolong the moment of death and where, in the judgment of the attending physician, death is imminent whether or not such procedures are utilized. "Life-sustaining procedure" shall not include the administration of medication or the performance of any medical procedure deemed necessary to alleviate pain.

(d) "Physician" means a physician and surgeon licensed by the Board of Medical Quality Assurance or the Board of Osteopathic Examiners.

(e) "Qualified patient" means a patient diagnosed and certified in writing to be afflicted with a terminal condition by two physicians, one of whom shall be the attending physician, who have personally examined the patient.

(f) "Terminal condition" means an incurable condition caused by injury, disease, or illness, which, regardless of the application of life-sustaining procedures, would, within reasonable medical judgment, produce death, and where the application of life-sustaining procedures serves only to postpone the moment of death of the patient.

APPENDIX B:
PHYSICAL FACTS OF DEATH

Once one begins the study of death, the question arises, "When I do die, what will be the cause?" The following table presents an introduction to current demographics of death in the United States.

DEATH RATES IN THE UNITED STATES FOR THE 25 LEADING CAUSES OF DEATH, BY COLOR AND SEX, 1969

Cause of death	Total population	White Male	White Female	Nonwhite Male	Nonwhite Female
All Causes	951.9	1,092.7	815.1	1,132.8	798.7
Diseases of heart	366.1	443.9	315.4	316.1	246.7
Malignant neoplasms	160.0	181.6	146.3	159.1	112.4
Cerebrovascular disease	102.6	94.4	109.5	105.2	106.9
Influenza and pneumonia	33.9	36.4	28.9	53.2	33.8
Accidents (other than motor vehicle)	30.0	38.7	19.0	58.7	22.8
Motor vehicle accidents	27.6	40.0	15.1	47.0	14.5
Certain causes in early infancy	21.4	22.2	14.5	51.5	36.3
Diabetes mellitus	19.1	15.7	21.0	17.3	29.5
Arteriosclerosis	16.4	15.2	19.3	9.7	9.6
Bronchitis, emphysema, and asthma	15.4	26.7	6.5	13.2	4.7
Cirrhosis of the liver	14.8	19.1	9.5	23.9	14.4
Symptoms and ill-defined conditions	13.0	12.4	7.4	41.8	29.0
Other diseases of arteries, arterioles, and capillaries	12.4	16.5	9.7	9.3	7.6
Suicide	11.1	17.2	6.8	8.1	2.8
Congenital anomalies	8.4	9.0	7.3	11.6	9.6
Homicide	7.7	6.0	2.0	58.1	11.7
Nephritis and nephrosis	4.7	4.5	3.6	10.3	8.6
Peptic ulcer	4.6	6.5	3.1	4.9	2.1
Infections of kidney	4.3	3.8	4.4	5.7	6.3
Hypertension	4.2	3.8	3.5	8.8	7.4
Hernia and intestinal obstructions	3.7	3.4	4.0	4.3	3.2
Tuberculosis	2.8	3.3	1.2	9.5	4.1
Benign and unspecified neoplasms	2.3	2.2	2.3	2.2	3.1
Cholelithiasis, cholecystitis, cholangitis	2.1	2.0	2.5	0.7	1.4
Other infective and parasitic diseases	2.0	2.0	1.8	3.4	3.3
All other causes	61.3	66.2	50.5	99.2	66.9

Source: Compiled from data in National Center for Health Statistics, "Final Mortality Statistics, 1969," *Monthly Vital Statistics Report,* Vol. 21, No. 4 (July 25, 1972), pp. 8-9, Table 5.

T. Lynn Smith and Paul E. Zopf, Jr., *Demography: Principles and Methods*, 2nd Ed. Port Washington, N.Y.: Alfred Publishing Co., Inc., 1976. pp. 433, 453.

SPECIFIC DEATH RATES FOR SELECTED CAUSES IN THE DEATH REGISTRATION STATES, 1900, 1920, 1940, 1960, and 1970

Cause of death	Number of deaths per 100,000 population				
	1900	1920	1940	1960	1970
Pneumonia and influenza	202.2	207.3	70.3	37.3	30.5
Tuberculosis of the respiratory system	174.5	99.8	42.2	5.6	2.1
Diarrhea, enteritis, and ulcertaion of the intestines	142.7	53.7	10.3	5.2	1.1
Diseases of the heart	137.4	159.6	292.5	369.0	360.3
Intracranial lesions of vascular origin	106.9	93.0	90.9	108.0	101.7
Nephritis	88.6	88.8	81.5	7.6	3.9
Congenital malformations, etc.	74.6	84.4	49.2	12.2	8.1
Other accidents	72.3	60.7	47.4	31.0	28.0
Cancer and other malignant tumors	64.0	83.4	120.3	149.2	162.0
Senility	50.2	14.2	7.7	11.4	14.1
Bronchitis	45.2	13.2	3.0	2.5	3.2
Diphtheria	40.3	15.3	1.1	0.0	0.0
Typhoid and paratyphoid fever	31.3	7.6	1.1	0.0	0.0
Puerperal causes (females only)	26.9	38.6	13.5	0.9	0.9
Tuberculosis (other forms)	19.9	13.4	3.7	0.5	0.6
Measles	13.3	8.8	0.5	0.2	0.0
Cirrhosis of the liver	12.5	7.1	8.6	11.3	15.8
Whooping cough	12.2	12.5	2.2	0.1	0.0
Dysentery	12.0	4.0	1.9	0.2	0.0
Syphilis	12.0	16.5	14.4	1.6	0.2
Hernia and intestinal obstruction	11.9	10.5	9.0	5.1	3.6
Diabetes mellitus	11.0	16.1	26.6	16.7	18.5
Suicide	10.2	10.2	14.4	10.6	11.1
Scarlet fever	9.6	4.6	0.5	0.0	0.0
Appendicitis	8.8	13.2	9.9	1.0	0.7
Malaria	6.2	3.4	1.1	0.0	0.0
Alcoholism	5.3	1.0	1.9	1.2	2.3
Diseases of the prostate (males only)	3.3	8.2	13.3	2.5	2.1
Ulcer of stomach or duodenum	2.7	3.6	6.8	6.4	4.1
Homicide	1.2	6.8	6.2	4.7	7.6
Pellagra	0.0	2.5	1.6	0.0	0.0
Cerebrospinal meningitis	. . . .	1.6	0.5	1.1	0.9
Motor vehicle accidents	. . . .	10.3	26.2	21.3	26.2

Source: Compiled from data in Forrest E. Linder and Robert D. Grove, *Vital Statistics Rates in the United States, 1900-1940* (1943), pp. 258-273; Robert D. Grove and Alice M. Hetzel, *Vital Statistics Rates in the United States, 1940-1960* (1968), pp. 595-603; National Center for Health Statistics, *Vital Statistics of the United States, 1966,* Vol. II, *Mortality,* Part A, Section 1 (1968), pp. 53-86, Table 22; and "Annual Summary for the United States, 1970," *Monthly Vital Statistics Report,* Vol. 19, No. 13 (September 21, 1971), p. 18, Table 7.

It is easy to lose sight of the physical facts of death, particularly in the interim between the moment of clinical death and final rites. Yet a complex bureaucracy exists to deal with the many stark details of closing out a civil existence; the following forms chart the passage from dying person to physical remains. Although they are official records from one state, they can be considered representative documents for other regions; the information reported tends to be standardized to facilitate nationwide collection of health statistics.

CERTIFICATE OF DEATH

STATE OF CALIFORNIA—DEPARTMENT OF PUBLIC HEALTH

REPORT OF AUTOPSY

Cause of Death as determined by Autopsy Surgeon: _____

Due To: _____

Due To: _____

Other Conditions: _____

SIGNATURE OF AUTOPSY SURGEON

NAME

P.F. #

WARD OR CLINIC _____

Duplicate of Official Death Certificate
TO BE RETAINED ON PATIENT'S HISTORY

562 - 76C136C - REV. 1/68

PHYSICIAN'S REQUEST FOR A POST MORTEM EXAMINATION

SOME OF THE REASONS YOUR PHYSICIAN EARNESTLY SEEKS YOUR PERMISSION TO EXAMINE THE BODY OF THE DECEASED:

1. If the cause of death is obscure there is no more final or definite method of determining this cause.

2. If the cause is presumably known, the knowledge gained from a post mortem examination will be of inestimable value in helping your physician in the treatment of those similarly afflicted.

3. The examination may reveal other unsuspected diseases, some of which could have been transmitted to a person or persons now living.

4. The post mortem examination will be performed by a pathologist very much as any operation is performed. The report of the examination can be of value in settling insurance claims.

5. Advancement of medical knowledge to the present high level has been made possible by the use of the post mortem examination.

CONSENT TO POST MORTEM EXAMINATION

For the purpose of determining the cause of death, and in the hope of furthering medical knowledge and progress, I, being the surviving spouse, child or parent, brother or sister, or other kin or person who has acquired the right to control the disposition of the remains of _____ ,

(NAME OF DECEASED)

hereby authorize the Department of Hospitals of the County of Los Angeles, to perform without charge to me a complete post mortem examination on the deceased, including removal, photographing, retention, and disposition of such specimens, organs and tissues including eyes as deemed proper for diagnostic, scientific or therapeutic purposes, including transplantation to a living person.

Witness _____   Signed _____

Date _____   Relationship _____

SPECIAL INSTRUCTIONS:

BODY RETURNED TO MORGUE IN GOOD CONDITION
AUTOPSY SURGEON _____
MORGUE ATTENDANT _____
DATE _____

Date _____   By _____

MORTUARY RECORDER

Autopsy No. _____

PRINT – Surname of Patient	First Name	Middle Name	P.F. Number	Ward Number

POST MORTEM REQUEST AND CONSENT
TO BE MADE IN DUPLICATE

PERMIT FOR DISPOSITION OF HUMAN REMAINS

STATE OF CALIFORNIA—DEPARTMENT OF PUBLIC HEALTH

DECEDENT DATA	NAME OF DECEDENT			DATE OF DEATH
	SEX	COLOR OR RACE	BIRTHPLACE (STATE OR FOREIGN COUNTRY)	DATE OF BIRTH
	PLACE OF DEATH—CITY OR TOWN		PLACE OF DEATH—COUNTY (OR STATE IF NOT IN CALIFORNIA)	

DISPOSITION	CHECK ONE ☐ BURIAL ☐ ENTOMBMENT ☐ CREMATION ☐ DISINTERMENT AND REINTERMENT	NAME AND ADDRESS OF CEMETERY OR COLUMBARIUM WHERE REMAINS ARE TO BE INTERRED
FUNERAL DIRECTOR AND INFORMANT	NAME OF FUNERAL DIRECTOR (OR PERSON ACTING AS SUCH)	NAME OF SPOUSE OR OTHER INFORMANT	ADDRESS OF SPOUSE OR OTHER INFORMANT

LOCAL REGISTRAR	In accordance with provisions of the California Health and Safety Code permission is hereby granted for disposition as specified in this permit.
	DATE PERMIT ISSUED	SIGNATURE OF LOCAL REGISTRAR ▶
CEMETERY OR COLUMBARIUM	DATE CREMATED OR INTERRED	SIGNATURE OF PERSON IN CHARGE OF CEMETERY OR COLUMBARIUM ▶

SEE INSTRUCTIONS ON REVERSE

(REV. 2-1-66) FORM VS-9

USE OF PERMIT

PERMIT FOR BURIAL, ENTOMBMENT OR CREMATION:

Upon presentation of a satisfactory and complete certificate of death, a permit is prepared in duplicate by the Local Registrar of the district in which the death occurred or the body was found. The original copy of the permit shall accompany the remains to the place of burial, entombment or cremation specified in the permit. The duplicate copy shall be retained by the Local Registrar of the district in which the death occurred or the body was found. This permit is the only authority required for the transportation of human remains. A permit issued in this State is valid and sufficient in any county it specifies as the place of interment, subject to the payment of any interment fees required by local law. The person in charge of the cemetery or columbarium shall complete and sign the permit in the spaces provided and forward the permit within 10 days to the Local Registrar of the district in which the cemetery is located.

PERMIT FOR DISINTERMENT AND REINTERMENT:

The permit is prepared in triplicate by the Local Registrar of the district where the remains are to be disinterred upon written application as provided by law and the payment of the fee of $0.50. The original copy of the permit shall be given to the person in charge of the cemetery or columbarium where the remains are to be disinterred. The duplicate copy of the permit shall accompany the remains to the place of reinterment specified in the permit. The triplicate copy shall be retained by the Local Registrar of the district where the remains are to be disinterred. This permit is the only authority required for the transportation of human remains. A permit issued in this State is valid and sufficient in any county it specifies as the place of reinterment, subject to the payment of any interment fees required by local law. The person in charge of the cemetery or columbarium where the remains are reinterred shall complete and sign the permit in the spaces provided and forward the permit within 10 days to the Local Registrar of the district in which the cemetery is located.

OSP

A GIFT OF LIFE

TO MY FAMILY AND PHYSICIAN —

It is my wish that upon my death, my body, or any part of it, be used for the benefit of mankind.

I, therefore, execute the following Deed of Gift, under the Anatomical Gift Act, and I request that in the making of any decision relating to my death, my intentions as expressed herein shall govern.

I am of sound mind and 18 years or more of age. I hereby make this anatomical gift to take effect upon my death. The marks in the appropriate places and words filled into the blanks below indicate my desires.

I give: my body _____ ; any needed organs or parts _____ ; the following organs or parts

_____

I give these to the following person or institution: the physician in attendance at my death _____ ;

the hospital in which I die _____ ; the following named physician, hospital, storage bank or other

medical institution _____ ;

the following individual for treatment _____ ;

for any purpose authorized by law _____ ; transplantation _____ ; therapy _____ ;

research _____ ; medical education _____ .

_____
signature of donor

Dated _____

_____
address of donor

Signed by Donor in presence of following who sign as witnesses

_____
witness

_____
witness

UNIFORM DONOR CARD

Name of Donor _____ Date of Birth _____

In the hope that I may help others, I hereby make this anatomical gift, if medically acceptable, to take effect upon my death. The words and marks below indicate my desires.

I give: (a) _____ any needed organs or parts

(b) _____ only the following organs or parts

Specify: _____

_____
Signature of Donor

Date & Place Signed _____

_____
Witness

_____
Witness

This is a legal document under the Uniform Anatomical Gift Act.

459

A LIVING WILL

TO MY FAMILY, MY PHYSICIAN, MY CLERGYMAN, MY LAWYER —

If the time comes when I can no longer take part in decisions for my own future, let this statement stand as the testament of my wishes:

If there is no reasonable expectation of my recovery from physical or mental disability,

I, _____

request that I be allowed to die and not be kept alive by artificial means or heroic measures. Death is as much a reality as birth, growth, maturity and old age—it is the one certainty. I do not fear death as much as I fear the indignity of deterioration, dependence and hopeless pain. I ask that drugs be mercifully administered to me for terminal suffering even if they hasten the moment of death.

This request is made after careful consideration. Although this document is not legally binding, you who care for me will, I hope, feel morally bound to follow its mandate. I recognize that it places a heavy burden of responsibility upon you, and it is with the intention of sharing that responsibility and of mitigating any feelings of guilt that this statement is made.

Signed _____

Date _____

Witnessed by:

_____

_____

Reprinted with permission of the Euthanasia Education Council, 250 West 57th Street, New York, N.Y., 10019.

460

APPENDIX C:
ADDITIONAL TEACHING RESOURCES

DISCIPLINARY SCHEMA

Papers in the text have been marked for their direct applicability (including thematic interest) to course work in different disciplines.

	Philosophy & Ethics	Psychology	Sociology	Gerontology	Medicine & Nursing	Anthropology	Literature	Law
Chapter One								
Phaedo: The Death Scene	•						•	
Death in American Society			•		•			
Do Not Go Gentle Into That Good Night				•			•	
To Waken An Old Lady				•			•	
The Struggle for Cultural Rebirth	•	•				•		
Frankenstein	•				•		•	•
Refinements in Criteria for the Determination of Death: An Appraisal				•	•		•	
Life and Death: Definitions			•		•		•	
Life and Death: Dividing the Indivisible	•	•	•		•	•		•
Chapter Two								
Help in the Dying Process		•		•	•			
What Is It Like To Be Dying?	•			•	•			
I Heard a Fly Buzz When I Died / Exultation Is the Going		•			•		•	•
Reaction to Extreme Stress: Impending Death by Execution	•		•					
Carpe Diem	•						•	
Death Be Not Proud	•						•	
Awareness of Dying		•	•	•	•			
The Foreshortened Life Perspective		•		•				

	Philosophy & Ethics	Psychology	Sociology	Gerontology	Medicine & Nursing	Anthropology	Literature	Law
Chapter Three								
Symptomatology and Management of Acute Grief		•		•	•			
Group Behavior at Funeral Gatherings		•	•			•		
Bereavement and Mental Health	•	•	•			•		
Thoughts for the Times on War and Death: Our Attitude Towards Death	•	•				•	•	
Survivors of Suicide		•			•		•	•
Daddy		•				•	•	
Religious Symbolism in Limbu Death-by-Violence	•		•			•		
Chapter Four								
The Child's Theories Concerning Death		•				•	•	
A Death in the Family		•			•		•	
Children and Death		•			•		•	
My Grandpa Died Today		•				•	•	
Childhood Leukemia: Emotional Impact on Patient and Family		•			•			
Children's Awareness of Fatal Illness			•					
Chapter Five								
Elective Death	•	•	•	•	•		•	
The Suicidal Patient: Adolescent Suicide		•	•		•			
Suicide Note	•	•					•	
The Enemy		•				•	•	
From Dakto to Detroit: Death of a Troubled Hero		•	•				•	
Bob Patrick		•	•		•		•	
Epilogue								
Then Suddenly It Was Jennifer's Last Day		•	•		•		•	

TOPICAL SUGGESTIONS FOR CURRICULAR PLANNING
ON DEATH AND DYING

The list below could be used in several ways:

1. *suggesting additional topics for adapting classroom presentations to audiences with specialized interests*

2. *assigning for brief research reports*

3. *compiling published sources or annotated bibliographies*

4. *suggesting topics for term papers*

abortion
accidental death
accident-proneness
aggression and violence
assassination
autopsies

———————————————

bullfighting
burial rites

———————————————

causes of aging
cemeteries
chemical and biological warfare
class and cultural differences
   in life expectancy
courage and death
cryonics

———————————————

death and mysticism
death customs
death fantasies
death of a culture
death of God
death of the soldier
different cultural approaches
donation of body parts
dynamics of prayer and
   supplication
embalming
epitaphs and eulogies
ethics and medical
   experimentation
euphemisms for death

———————————————

facing surgery
factors in life expectancy

fear of death

genocide
geriatric wards

holocaust experience
human sacrifice

images of death
infanticide
infant mortality
isolation and alienation

last words of the dying
legal rights of the dying and
  dead
life review
LSD therapy with dying

martyrdom
mass hysteria
myths of death, rebirth and
  resurrection

natural disasters

out-of-the-body experience
perception of time
personality factors in facing
  death

population and ecological
  control
post-mortem changes
poverty and death
psychopathologies of
  aging

racial segregation of the
  dying and dead
reincarnation
resistance to torture by war
  prisoners

samurai
science fiction/time
  machines
"sudden death" syndrome
survival in extreme
  environments
symbols for death

uncertainty of dying
use of sedatives

voodooism, magical rites,
  occultism

464

MULTI-MEDIA REFERENCES FOR DEATH AND DYING

Chapter One

Confrontations of Death - Film, color, 35 min. Oregon Division
of Continuing Education Film Library, P.O. Box 1491,
Portland, Oregon 97201 Seminar participants discover
their personal feelings about their own death through
listening to music, viewing slide on death and writing
their own eulogies.

Dead Man - Film, no sound, 3 minutes. Foundation of Thanatology, 67 Park Avenue. Room 11-B N.Y., New York
10016. Stark portrayal of the naked, dead body of an
old man.

Death and Life - Audiotape or audiocassette, 60 minutes.
The Center for Cassette Studies, 8110 Webb Avenue,
North Hollywood, California 91605. People from various
walks of life describe what death means to them, how they
visualize it, and what their fears are.

Joy of Love - Film, color, 9 minutes. University of Michigan,
Audio-Visual Education Center, 416 Fourth Street, Ann
Arbor, Michigan 48103. Silent film depicting courtship,
marriage, old age, and death.

The Life Cycle: Death - Audiotape or audiocassette, 30 minutes. The Center for Cassette Studies, 8110 Webb Avenue,
North Hollywood, CA 91605. Discussion of the meaning
of death in a time-bound culture, with reference to the
attitudes toward death held by other peoples.

Chapter Two

Death - Film, black and white, 43 minutes. Filmmakers Library, 290 West End Avenue, New York, New York 10001. Depicts the isolation of the dying in a hospital setting. Presents 52-year-old cancer patient portraying problems of meaningful communication with family, friends and hospital staff.

Dying - Film, black and white, 110 minutes, WGBH, 125 Western Avenue, Boston, Mass. 02134. Cinema verité portrayal of incidents in the dying of three cancer patients and the responses of their families. Contrasts different styles of dying in non-judgmental fashion.

Leinbach-Eisdorfer Series - Videotape, six programs. Health Sciences Learning Resources Center, T-252 Health Sciences Building, University of Washington, Seattle, Washington 98195. Interviews with the patient, his family and those who attended to his physical and spiritual needs. Interviews with the patient - 25 minutes. The role of the physician - 41 minutes, pain management - 37 minutes, religion and the clergy - 35 minutes, the grieving process, part 1 - 25 minutes, and the grieving process, part II—45 minutes.

How Could I Not Be Among You? - Film, color, 28 minutes. The Eccentric Circle, P.O. Box 4085, Greenwich, Connecticut 06830. Portrait of a poet confronted by premature death from leukemia.

Peege - Film, color, 28 minutes. Phoenix Films, 743 Alexander Road, Princeton, New Jersey 08540. Visit to a nursing home dramatizes the communication barriers between the aged and their families.

Ikiru - Film, black and white, 140 minutes. Macmillan Films, Inc., 34 MacQuesten, South, Mt. Vernon, New York

10550. Japanese with English subtitles. Depicts existential crisis of a widower in middle age whose terminal diagnosis results in personal growth.

Until I Die - Film, color, 30 minutes. Audio Visual Department, American Journal of Nursing Company, 10 Columbus Circle, New York, N.Y. 10019. Kubler-Ross explains her work with the terminally ill.

Chapter Three

Day of the Dead - Film, color, 15 minutes. Pyramid Films, 2801 Colorado Street, Santa Monica, California 90406. Mexico's Festival for the Day of the Dead.

Death - Family of Man Series, Film, color, 45 minutes. Time - Life Films, 100 Eisenhower Drive, Paramus, New Jersey 07652. Contrasting attitudes toward death in various cultures of the world.

Death, Grief, and Bereavement - Audiocassettes. Charles Press Publ. Inc., Bowie, Maryland 20715. Series of 18 programs by various authorities on death.

Journey's End - Film, color, 28 minutes. USC Division of Cinema, Film Distribution Section, University Park, Los Angeles, CA 90007. Portrays the difficulties in adjusting to widowhood. Dramatizes the value of making wills and funeral arrangements before the need occurs.

Last and Lasting Gift - Film, color, 28 minutes. Inland Empire Human Resources Center, 2 West Olive Avenue, Redlands, California 92373. Describes the alternatives to a funeral including the donation of body parts following death.

Those Who Mourn - Film, color, 5 minutes. Association Inst. Materials, 866 Third Avenue, New York, New York

10022. Explores the death of one man and its meaning to his wife.

Chapter Four

All The Way Home - Film, black and white, 103 minutes. Films Inc. 5625 Hollywood Boulevard, Hollywood, CA 90068. The effects of a man's death on a six-year old boy. The mother's initial withdrawal into grief and the family's inability to deal with the boy's need to understand.

The Dead Bird - Film, color, 13 minutes. Bureau of Audio-Visual Instruction, P. O. Box 2093, Madison, Wisconsin 53701. Four children discover a dead bird and prepare a burial for it.

Rabbit - Film, color, 15 minutes. The Eccentric Circle, P.O. Box 4085, Greenwhich, Connecticut 06830. A nine-year-old boy's first encounter with death.

You See, I've Had a Life - Film, black and white, 30 minutes. Eccentric Circle, Cinema, P.O. Box 4085, Greenwich, Connecticut, 06830. The family of a leukemic teenager attempts to share and face the experience with him.

Chapter Five

But Jack Was A Good Driver - Film, 12 minutes, color. C R M Educational Films, 1104 Camino del Mar, Del Mar, CA 92014. As the friends of a teenager killed in an automobile crash leave his funeral, they come to the realization that his death was probably a suicide.

Case of Suicide - Film, black and white, 30 minutes. Time-Life Films, 100 Eisenhower Drive, Paramus, New Jersey Case of a young woman who commits suicide and the guilt of those close to her.

Death of a Peasant - Film, color, 10 minutes. Mass Media, 1720 Chouteau Avenue, St. Louis, Missouri 63103. A Yugoslav peasant condemned to face a firing squad flees from the Germans, and then in the face of hopelessness decides to take his own life.

The Right to Die - Film, color, 56 minutes. Macmillan Films, Inc., 34 MacQuesten Parkway, South, Mount Vernon, conflicts as to whether one has the right to end his own life and whether technology should be withheld to enable a patient to die with dignity.

Whose Life is it Anyway? - Film, color, 60 minutes. The Eccentric Circle, P. O. Box 4085, Greenwich, Connecticut 06830. An artist paralyzed from the waist down and faced with the prospect of finishing out his life in a hospital bed requests that he be released from the hospital to die. His request is refused by doctors and his legal struggle follows.

INDEX